W9-BYI-129

PENROSE MEMORIAL LIBRARY
WHITMAN COLLEGE
WALLA WALLA. WASHINGTON 99362

Islamic Family Law in a Changing World : A Global Resource Book

edited by
Abdullahi A. An-Na'im

Zed Books Ltd
LONDON · NEW YORK

KMC
48·5
·F35
I 753
2002

Islamic Family Law in a Changing World: A Global Resource Book was first published by Zed Books Ltd, 7 Cynthia Street, London N1 9JF, UK and Room 400, 175 Fifth Avenue, New York, NY 10010, USA in 2002.

Distributed in the USA exclusively by Palgrave, a division of St Martin's Press, LLC, 175 Fifth Avenue, New York, NY 10010, USA

Editorial copyright © Law and Religious Program, Emory University, 2002

Cover designed by Andrew Corbett
Set in Monotype Baskerville and Univers Black by Ewan Smith, London
Printed and bound in Malaysia

The rights of the contributors to be identified as the authors of this work have been asserted by them in accordance with the Copyright, Designs and Patents Act, 1988.

A catalogue record for this book is available from the British Library
Library of Congress Cataloging-in-Publication Data: available

ISBN 1 84277 092 6 cased
ISBN 1 84277 093 4 limp

PENROSE MEMORIAL LIBRARY
WHITMAN COLLEGE
WALLA WALLA, WASHINGTON 99362

11.14 B

About this Series: General Editor,
Abdullahi A. An-Na'im

The present book comes out of two related research projects led by
Professor Abdullahi A. An-Na'im at the Faculty of Law, Emory University, and funded by the Ford Foundation. Both projects deploy the
notion of cultural transformation to promote human rights in African
and Islamic societies. The first explores this notion in theoretical terms
and then focuses on issues of women and land in Africa from customary, religious and statutory rights perspectives, with a view to linking
research to advocacy for securing the rights of women to own or
control land as a vital economic resource. The second project is a
global study of Islamic family law, including some country studies
and thematic studies, from a human rights perspective. Four volumes
are being published at this stage of these on-going projects:

VOLUME I *Cultural Transformation and Human Rights in Africa*, edited
by Abdullahi A. An-Na'im

VOLUME II *Islamic Family Law in a Changing World: A Global Resource
Book*, edited by Abdullahi A. An-Na'im

VOLUME III *Women and Land in Africa: Linking Research to Advocacy*,
edited by L. Muthoni Wanyeki

VOLUME IV *Islamic Family Law in Comparative Perspective*, edited by
Lynn Welchman

About the Editor

Abdullahi Ahmed An-Na'im is Charles Howard Candler Professor of
Law at Emory University, Georgia, USA. Prior to that he was Executive Director of Human Rights Watch/Africa in Washington, DC for
two years. He was born in the Sudan and educated at the Universities
of Khartoum, Cambridge and Edinburgh, and his distinguished scholarly career has spanned 25 years with appointments in various North
African, Canadian and US universities. He is the author of *Towards an
Islamic Reformation: Civil Liberties, Human Rights and International Law*
(Syracuse, NY: Syracuse University Press, 1990) and editor of numerous
volumes on human rights issues from a cross-cultural perspective.

PENROSE MEMORIAL LIBRARY
WHITMAN COLLEGE
WALLA WALLA, WASHINGTON 99362

Contents

Whitman College
Library

DEC 05 '02
0 304 5242
Acquisitions Dept.
MAR 3 1 2003

Abbreviations

CEDAW Convention on the Elimination of All Forms of Discrimination Against Women. On 18 December 1979, the Convention on the Elimination of All Forms of Discrimination Against Women was adopted by the United Nations General Assembly. It entered into force as an international treaty on 3 September 1981 after the twentieth country had ratified it. By the tenth anniversary of the Convention in 1989, almost one hundred nations had agreed to be bound by its provisions.

gopher://gopher.un.org/00/ga/cedaw/convention
http://www.un.org/womenwatch/daw/cedaw/cedaw.htm

CRC Convention on the Rights of the Child. Children's rights are most fully articulated in the Convention on the Rights of the Child. Created over a period of ten years with the input of representatives from different societies, religions and cultures; the Convention was adopted as an international human rights treaty on 20 November 1989.

http://www.unhchr.ch/html/menu3/b/k2crc.htm
http://www.unicef.org/crc/crc.htm

ICCPR International Covenant on Civil and Political Rights. Since the establishment of the UN, many steps have been taken towards a comprehensive international human rights system. The Universal Declaration of Human Rights, adopted by the UN General Assembly on 10 December 1948, represented the first step in the development of this system and contains a basic catalogue of human rights. In 1966, the 'international covenants' were adopted. These elaborate upon the content of the Universal Declaration. The International Covenant on Civil and Political Rights (ICCPR) and the International Covenant on Economic, Social and Cultural Rights (ICESCR) both came into force in 1976. As multilateral treaties, they are legally binding on all the states party to them. The Universal Declaration and the two Covenants, together with the First Optional Protocol to the ICCPR, have become known as the 'International Bill of Rights'.

http://www.unhchr.ch/html/menu3/b/a_ccpr.htm

ICESCR International Covenant on Economic, Social and Cultural Rights. For brief description see ICCPR description above.

http://www.unhchr.ch/html/menu3/b/a_cescr.htm

Preface

The material presented in this book was prepared under the auspices of a generous grant from the Ford Foundation for a major research project entitled 'Islamic Family Law: Possibilities of Reform through Internal Initiatives'. The project was implemented between September 1998 and April 2001, as explained below. In this Preface, I provide a brief overview of the concept, objectives and organization of the project as a whole, outline the role of various researchers in the preparation of the material included in this book, briefly explain how it can be used, and conclude with a note on transliteration.

About the Project

General principles of certain aspects of Shari'a, commonly known as Islamic Family Law (IFL), are supposed to govern such matters as marriage, divorce, maintenance, paternity and custody of children for more than a billion Muslims around the world. Identical principles do not apply everywhere or in the same manner because of significant theological, legal and other differences among and within Islamic societies, and because the practical application of Shari'a principles is often modified by customary practices or state policy. In this light, the first objective of this project is to verify and document the scope and manner of the application of IFL around the world.

Besides contributing to making this information more readily available, the purpose of this global survey is to lay the best possible factual foundation for any strategies that might be developed for the advocacy of significant reform of IFL in different Islamic societies today. But those reformist strategies must also be based on a clear appreciation of the political and sociological context of those societies. In particular, one must appreciate that IFL has become for most Muslims the symbol of their Islamic identity, the hard irreducible core of what it means to be a Muslim today. This is precisely because IFL is the main aspect of Shari'a that is believed to have successfully resisted displacement by European codes during the colonial period, and survived various degrees or forms of secularization of the state and its institutions in many Islamic countries.

Consequently, IFL has become the contested ground between conservative and fundamentalist forces, on the one hand, and modernist and liberal trends, on the other, in most Islamic countries. The question is therefore how to achieve significant and sustainable reform in the face of such rhetorical absolutist confrontations.

One premise of this project is that, to be effective in practice, reform proposals must not only be conceived and framed in realistic terms, but should also be advocated in ways that motivate and empower actual or potential supporters working within their own communities. Accordingly, the project seeks to develop and apply in specific and limited tentative 'pilot' format an integrated approach to reform – from research and analysis, to identification and articulation of reform proposals, to advocacy for change in partnership with those working within their own societies and communities. As a first step towards that long-term objective, the current phase of the project attempts to inform the formulation of reform proposals with a clear understanding of the status quo, and to facilitate debate and deliberation from different perspectives.

The other premise of this project is that IFL reform should be conditioned by a strong commitment to universal human rights norms, especially the human rights of women and children in the context of family and community. As discussed in the Introduction to this book, Shari'a, including those aspects that are presently known as IFL, has always been the product of human interpretation in specific historical contexts. In other words, the divine guidance of the Qur'an and Sunna (traditions of the Prophet) could be realized only through the efforts of scholars, policy-makers and opinion-leaders of each society in its own setting. This historically conditioned understanding of Shari'a does not deny its divine sources, but simply emphasizes that, since those sources must be understood and applied by human beings, that process should benefit from the experiences of all societies in the administration of justice. From this perspective, we believe that human rights now represent universally accepted standards of sound social policy for present-day Islamic societies. By approaching the issues from this perspective, the project seeks to provide opportunities for testing and promoting the practical consistency of IFL with international human rights.

Since it is unrealistic for this project to seek to achieve all its objectives at once, it is organized into different phases. During the initial phase, implemented from September 1998 to April 2001, we conducted a global 'mapping' survey of regional, social and cultural profiles as well as country-specific studies of legal, institutional and other aspects of the theory and practice of IFL. The outcome of this global survey is presented in this first book. Other more focused case studies will be published in a second book.

Contributors to the Preparation of this Book

This book has been produced through the collaboration of many researchers operating from the Law and Religion Program of Emory University, the primary location of the project, and the School of Oriental and African Studies (SOAS) of the University of London, England. I am listed as editor of this book by virtue of being the author of the original proposal and general director of the project as a whole. I also supervised the preparation of the social, cultural and historical profiles. All the country legal profiles were prepared under the supervision of Dr Lynn Welchman, lecturer and director of the Centre of Islamic and Middle Eastern Law at the School of Oriental and African Studies of the University of London. Ms Amy Wheeler was the administrative assistant for the project.

Svetlana Peshkova and Maria Fadlelmula prepared the initial drafts of the social, cultural and historical profiles at Emory University, Liazzat Bonate contributed a background paper on Central Asia, and Saira Zuberi was the main researcher on the legal profiles at SOAS. We would also like to thank following colleagues in SOAS who helped revise profiles in their areas of expertise: Ziba Mir-Hosseini, Fareda Banda, Martin Lau, Scott Newton and Werner Menski.

Deborah Scroggins, assisted by Susan Leisure, Marsha Ford and Maria Fadelmula, undertook a major revision and updating of the social, cultural and historical profiles. I also gratefully acknowledge the valuable assistance of Rohit Chopra in the preparation of the final manuscript of this book for publication.

The Content and Organization of this Book

I should first note that this book does not purport to present a comprehensive and completely up-to-date coverage of its subject matter. We have all attempted to find and organize the best available information, within the limitations of time and material resources available to us. All the information contained in this book was first presented on a web site (www.law.emory.edu/ifl) for nearly two years with emphatic invitation and appeal to all concerned to correct our factual assertions and/or challenge analysis. Unfortunately, we have not received a single response to this request. As this first phase of the project has concluded, we are obliged to present the best we were able to do, with the strong caveat that it should be seen as general background and basic information on the subject, rather than the basis of authoritative legal advice.

Some obvious omissions should be noted here. Some of the background chapters contain information on countries that are not individually profiled as separate 'legal profile' chapters. The sections on Southern Africa and Central Asia and the Caucasus do not contain any individual country legal profiles. In certain cases, such as Afghanistan, political realities preclude the possibility of obtaining information that is both current and credible. For certain countries, there is some information available for some of the topics covered under the legal profiles, but none available for the other topics. Here too, we have not included these country profiles.

Given unlimited time and resources, it might have been possible to trace and verify all the necessary information to produce accurate and comprehensive legal profiles for every country in the world where there are significant numbers of Muslims. But in addition to our time and resource limitations, we were also concerned that this could be an endless process, requiring fresh updating and revision, as the laws and practices of each country keep changing over time. Hence, in the interest of accuracy, contemporary relevance and consistency of format, we have provided only the best information we could collect and verify, at the cost of omitting a few country legal profiles, instead of offering incomplete profiles or unverified information. For those countries not profiled individually, material of a historical nature or offering socio-cultural information, which is more readily available, has been included in the 'background' chapters in each section.

The arrangement of the chapters in this book reflects its dual objective: one, to provide an overview of the influence of Islam on the socio-cultural and historical context in different regions of the world; and two, to provide information on specific legal rules and practices of IFL that apply in each country in each geographic region. The book is divided into nine sections, arranged in alphabetical order, each one dealing with a specific geographic region, namely, Central Asia and the Caucasus, East and Central Africa, Horn of Africa, Middle East, North Africa, Southern Africa, South Asia, Southeast Asia and West Africa. Each section begins with a chapter that provides an overview of the social, cultural and historical background of the region, with a focus on how Islamic law relates to this background. The history of the spread of Islam in the region, the relationship between customary, constitu tional and Islamic law, important political events, crucial legislative decisions – the relationship of such events to the socio-cultural realities of the region is explained and analysed in these chapters. Specifically, each such 'background' chapter deals with the following topics:

- The Region and its History
- Legal Practices and Institutions
- Seclusion of Women/Purdah
- Family in the Region
- Marriage
- Divorce
- Polygyny
- Children
- Custody of Children
- Inheritance and Land Rights

Within each section, there follow, in alphabetical order, legal profiles for each of the countries in that geographical area. This arrangement allows the reader to assess the information on the legal profiles in the light of the contextual information provided in the background chapter. It also allows for a comparative perspective, highlighting what is unique about the interpretation and implementation of IFL in a particular country, as well as what such practices two or more countries in a region may have in common. Each country chapter, that is, each country legal profile, covers the following topics:

- Legal history
- Schools of *fiqh*
- Constitutional status of Islam(ic law)
- Court system
- Relevant legislation
- Notable features
- Notable cases
- Law/case reporting system
- International conventions (with relevant reservations)

Also provided, immediately after the table of contents, is an alphabetical listing of country profiles, for those readers who may just want to refer to one or more particular country chapters. Finally, in addition to the following brief explanation of the simplified style of transliteration used in this book, a comprehensive glossary of the Arabic terms and other non-English terms used in the book is provided at the end of the book.

Note on Transliteration

We have simplified the system of transliterating Arabic terms in order make the book accessible to the widest possible range of readers, while also remaining faithful to the authentic pronunciation of Arabic terms. Many texts with Arabic terms use a simplified and modified system of transliteration, wherein they use just two diacritical marks: the single closing apostrophe ' to represent hamza and single opening apostrophe ' to represent 'ayn. Both hamza and 'ayn are Arabic letters that do not have any correspondence in the Latin alphabet. Hamza is a letter that is not even pronounced other than as a stop, while 'ayn denotes a guttural stop. In this text, we have chosen to simplify matters further by representing both hamza and 'ayn by a single neutral apostrophe mark '. The rationale for this pertains to the objectives of the text and the target audience for the book. It has been conceptualized as an information resource for academics in a range of disciplines and students at all levels of study, as well as laypersons.

Abdullahi Ahmed An-Na'im

Shari'a and Islamic Family Law: Transition and Transformation

Abdullahi Ahmed An-Na'im

The basic objective of the research project under which this volume has been prepared is to explore the possibilities of reform in Islamic Family Law (IFL) from a human rights perspective. In order to found that effort on the most factual and least controversial information, we have attempted to collect and organize in this volume a global overview of Islamic societies and aspects of the legal systems of their countries that are most relevant to family law. To provide some context for understanding this material in relation to the underlying objective of the project as a whole, I will present in this Introduction an overview of the nature and development of Shari'a in general, and its transition into being limited to family law matters in particular, as is the case today in most Islamic countries. By Islamic countries I mean those countries with majority Muslim populations, regardless of the nature of the state and its ideology or legal system. Against the background of this review of well-known and widely accepted developments, I will argue for the transformation of family law into a normative system that is guided by modern notions of social policy as well as Islamic precepts, but not bound by Shari'a, or represented as such. An understanding and justification of this transformation is critical for the realization of the reform objectives of this project as a whole. But first, a brief clarification of the terms 'Shari'a' and 'Islamic Law' as used in this book.

The term Shari'a refers to the general normative system of Islam as historically understood and developed by Muslim jurists, especially during the first three centuries of Islam – the eight to tenth centuries CE. In this commonly used sense, Shari'a includes a much broader set of principles and norms than legal subject matter as such. While the term Islamic Law is generally used to refer to the legal aspects of Shari'a, it should also be noted that Muslims tend to believe that the legal quality of those principles and norms derives from their assumed religious authority. Yet, whenever enforced or applied by the state, Shari'a principles are legally binding by virtue of state action, through either enactment as law by the legislative organs of the state or enforcement by its courts. This critical point is clear from the fact that a particular view of Shari'a, whether of one school of Islamic jurisprudence (*madhhab*) or of a certain jurist within a given school, is applied by state officials, to the exclusion of the views of other schools or jurists. Accordingly, Islamic Family Law is that part of Shari'a that applies to family relations (such as marriage, divorce and custody of children), also called Muslim Personal Status Law, *Shari'at al-ahwal al-shakhsiyah* in Arabic, through the political will of the state.

But since this limited sense of Shari'a is a very recent phenomenon, generally emerging during the colonial period of the late nineteenth and early twentieth centuries, a broader understanding of the nature and development of Shari'a in general is necessary for addressing issues of IFL in particular. However, in view of the continued confinement of Shari'a to family law matters after independence in the vast majority of Islamic countries, the relationship between these limited principles and the broader framework of Shari'a becomes conceptually and legally problematic. There are serious risks of distortion and stagnation in maintaining the normative authority of IFL on the basis of a pre-modern system that is becoming increasingly unfamiliar to legal professionals, policy-makers and the public at large, and applying it within the radically different constitutional and legal framework of the modern nation-state. For example, a particular Shari'a view of maintenance (*nafaqa*) for a divorced woman, or which parent is entitled to custody of children, is part of a wider network of legal and social relations as perceived by the jurists who articulated that view in the first place. The application of such views out of that broader context, and without the possibility of its revision and reformulation in the light of significant changes in those legal and social relationships, can be seriously counterproductive, even from the perspective of the founding jurists of Shari'a, let alone today's societies. Yet there is no possibility of legitimate and coherent revision and reformulation of such IFL principles in isolation from the broader understanding of Shari'a according to the jurist(s) who framed those principles in a totally different historical context.

As I will argue later in this chapter, these problems can be addressed only through a transformation of the nature and content of family law in Islamic countries. In my view, this transformation is already happening because family law in the vast majority of these countries today is enacted in statutory form by the state, rather than being derived from traditional sources of Shari'a as such. Moreover, whether a judgment is based on a statute or a selection by a judge, it is legally binding and enforceable only by the authority of the state. This is of course quite different from voluntary compliance out of religious commitment, which is the realm of moral sanction, not the administration of justice by the state. Instead of purporting to base the legal authority of family law on a Shari'a jurisprudence that has ceased to exist as a living and evolving system, I argue, it is better to recognize openly that this field, like all other law, derives its authority from the political will of the state. A clear acknowledgement of this reality will open the door for more innovative approaches to family law reform that may still be guided by Islamic principles, without being confined to outdated understandings of Shari'a. This will enable Islamic countries to make family law more consistent with other aspects of their legal systems, including their constitutional and international law obligations to protect the human rights of women.

It may appear that such recognition and opening of possibilities for more innovative approaches will by themselves resolve the most critical family law issues, such as equality between spouses during marriage and at its termination. In particular, it may be argued that to accept the unavoidability of the foundational role of human choice and interpretation in the formulation of any aspect of the normative system of Islam does not address the question of what to do about categorical and explicit texts of the Qur'an and Sunna of the Prophet on marriage, divorce, inheritance, and so forth. In my view, however, these ideas will in fact make it possible to found family law on sound social policy for present-day Islamic societies, even if that means the non-application of apparently categorical and explicit texts of the Qur'an and Sunna. The role of human agency therefore means, I suggest, reflection on the policy rationale and meaning of those texts in the context of seventh-century Arabia, rather than their acceptance as immediately and literally applicable in all social settings for eternity. In other words, human agency today should decide how to realize the underlying rationale of those texts as sound social policy in that historical context, and seek to articulate an equivalent purpose in the modern context.

I have attempted to make a more detailed and substantiated argument for these admittedly controversial propositions elsewhere, drawing on the work of the late Sudanese Islamic reformer Ustadh Mahmoud Mohamed Taha (An-Na'im 1990: Chapters 2 and 3).

In this Introduction, I will try to highlight some aspects of that argument in terms of the nature and development of Shari'a in relation to family law in particular. From this perspective, it seems to me that much of the confusion about the role of Shari'a in the modern context is caused by two factors. First, there is a lack of appreciation of the critical role of human agency in the conception and development of any normative system of Islam. Moreover, there is also a grossly exaggerated sense of the practical application of Shari'a as a comprehensive, self-contained and immutable normative system in the pre-colonial period. The critical role of human agency in the interpretation of the Qur'an and Sunna (traditions of the Prophet) is evident from the fact that these divine sources were revealed in a human language (Arabic) and can be understood and applied only in the specific context of the time and place. That obvious reality is clearly reflected in the extreme diversity of opinion among and within various schools of Islamic jurisprudence (*madhahib*), thereby forcing rulers and subjects alike to select from competing views that are deemed to be equally valid from a Shari'a point of view. This point can also be demonstrated from a review of the actual history of Shari'a and its application throughout Islamic history.

Historical Overview of Shari'a and its Application

To begin with, I do accept the general conclusion of earlier Western scholars of Islam that there was little systematic development of the methodology and general principles of Shari'a during the Medina state of the first four *Khulafa* (632–61 CE), and the Umayyad state (661–750) (Schacht 1959; Coulson 1964). I also appreciate more recent scholarship that is improving our knowledge of that early period and refining and qualifying some of the conclusions of earlier scholars (Al-Azmeh 1988; Burton 1990, 1994; Calder 1993; Hallaq 1997; Melchert 1997). However, these insights do not repudiate the main thrust of earlier conclusions about the timing of the systematic development of Shari'a, as explained below. It is true, as one would expect, that some general principles began to emerge during the first century of Islam through the practice of community leaders and provincial governors and judges, as well as the views of leading scholars of that period. But it is equally clear to me that the more systemic development of Shari'a, as it came to be known and accepted by Muslims today, began with the early Abbasid era (after 750 CE).

This view of the relatively late evolution of Shari'a as a coherent and systematic normative order in Islamic history is clear from the time-frame for the emergence of the major schools of thought (*madhabib*, singular *madhhab*), the authoritative collection of Sunna as the second and more detailed source of Shari'a, and the development of its essential methodology (*usul al-fiqh*). All these developments took place about 150 to 250 years after the Prophet's death.

In other words, the first several generations of Muslims could not have known and applied Shari'a as it came to be accepted by the majority of Muslims for the last one thousand years. Since those early generations are also generally accepted by the majority of Muslims to be more devout than subsequent generations, it follows that the application of Shari'a in that historical sense is not essential for the piety or religious fidelity of an Islamic community.

The early Abbasid era witnessed the emergence of the main surviving schools of Islamic jurisprudence, especially the Sunni schools of Abu Hanifah (d. 767), Malik (d. 795), al-Shafi'i (d. 820), Ibn Hanbal (d. 855), and Ja'far al-Sadiq (d. 765 – the founder of the main school of Shi'a jurisprudence). However, the subsequent development and spread of these schools has been influenced by a variety of political, social and demographic factors. These factors sometimes lead to shifting the influence of some schools from one region to another, confining them to certain parts, as is the case with Shi'a schools at present, or even to the total extinction of some schools, such as those of al-Thawri and al-Tabari in the Sunni tradition. The initial geographical spread and present-day status of the main surviving Sunni schools can be briefly outlined as follows.

The Hanafi and Maliki schools, in addition to being the first to develop, also became the most geographically widespread. Having originated in Iraq, the centre of power of the Abbasid dynasty, the Hanafi school enjoyed the important advantage of the official support of the state, and was subsequently brought to Afghanistan and later to the Indian subcontinent, while emigrants from India brought it to East Africa. This connection with the ruling authority was to remain a characteristic of the Hanafi school down to the period of the Ottoman Empire (Weiss and Green 1987: 155; Melchert 1999: 318–47). Thus Hanafi law is currently followed in Turkey, Iraq (together with the Shi'a Ja'fari School), Syria, the Balkan states, Cyprus, Jordan, Sudan (via Egypt), Israel and Palestine (together with the Shafi'i school), Egypt and the Indian sub-continent. The Maliki school grew out of the city of Medina, and spread to Sudan, Eritrea, Libya, Tunisia, Algeria, Morocco, Gambia, Ghana, Nigeria and Senegal and to the eastern coastal territories of Arabia on the Gulf, such as Kuwait. The Shafi'i school started in Cairo, where its founder lived for the last five years of his life, spread to Yemen (together with the Ja'fari school) and the Indian coastline, and then via the Arab trade routes to East Africa and Southeast Asia. Currently, Shafi'i views predominate in Malaysia, Indonesia, Singapore, the Philippines, Sri Lanka and the Maldives. The Hanbali school was always the least popular of the Sunni schools, and was on the verge of extinction when it was revived by the puritanical movement of Ibn Abdel

Wahab in Arabia in the late eighteenth century. It remains limited to that region to the present day.

Two points should be emphasized here about the preceding review of the current followings of these schools that are relevant to the argument of this Introduction. First is the difference between the popular followings of the school in specific societies, on the one hand, and the application of Shari'a by the state, on the other. Due to the confinement of the latter to family law matters, the popular following of a school relates to religious 'rituals' or rites such as prayer and fasting. This raises the question of the meaning and legitimacy of Shari'a itself in the modern context, when the religious belief of the community of believers in the unity and inviolability of so-called religious and legal matters in Shari'a is impossible to maintain in the actual practice of those communities or the law and administration of justice by their government. Second, as explained below, not only is the application of Shari'a principles by the state in family law matters done through statutory enactment, but also the content of those states has become strongly and openly eclectic, combining views within a school (*madhhab*), and from different schools (*madhahib*), mixing Sunni and Shi'a views, so that the end result would not be acceptable to any of the scholars, schools or traditions whose 'authority' is invoked in support of the application of a given principle or rule. In other words, legislators and judges first decide what the rule ought to be, and then go into an increasingly arbitrary 'fishing' expedition for nominal support among any of the schools or scholars of Shari'a they can find for their personal preferences or official judgment and political expediency. I am not concerned here with the correctness or validity of the outcome of such processes. My point is simply that this cannot legitimately be called an application of Shari'a, as historically understood. Before returning to this analysis later, let us continue with describing the history and background of these current social and official practices.

The timing of the emergence and the early dynamics of each school also seem to have influenced the content and orientation of their views on Shari'a. For instance, the Hanafi and Maliki schools drew more on pre-existing practice than did the Shafi'i and Hanbali schools, which elaborated their views from the theory of Shari'a. These differences reflect the influence of the timing and intellectual context in which each school emerged and developed. This may also explain the similarities in the views of the latter two schools, in comparison to the earlier two, and the stronger influence of reasoning and social and economic experience on the Hanafi and Maliki schools in contrast to the other Sunni schools. However, the principle of consensus (*ijma*) apparently acted as a unifying force that tended to draw the substantive content of all these four Sunni schools together through the use of independent juristic reasoning (*ijtihad*). Moreover, the consensus of all the main schools has always been that, if there are two or more variant opinions on an issue, they should all be accepted as equally legitimate attempts to express the particular rule (*hukm*) (Weiss 1998: 122–7; Kamali 1991: 168–72.)

But a negative subsequent consequence of the strong emphasis on consensus is the notion that all possibilities of *ijtihad* had ended by the tenth century because Shari'a had been fully and exhaustively elaborated by that time. This rigidity was probably necessary for maintaining the stability of the system during the decline, even breakdown, of the social and political institutions of Islamic societies. As with the issue of the timing of the systematic development of Shari'a mentioned above, more recent scholarship is questioning this commonly held view about the diminishing possibilities of *ijtihad* (Hallaq 1994; Gerber 1999: 'Introduction'). But the point is of course relative. It is true that there have been subsequent developments and adaptations of Shari'a through legal opinions (*fatwa*) and judicial developments, as outlined below. But it is also clear that these took place firmly within the framework of already established broader principles and methodology, rather than by radical innovation in either regard. It is simply untenable to claim that there has been any change in the basic structure and methodology of Shari'a as determined through the process outlined above. Specialists will probably continue to contest the precise extent or scope of belief in the immutability of Shari'a over the last thousand years or so, and to refine our knowledge of how the system worked in practice at different stages of its history (Al-Azmeh 1988a, 1988b; Hallaq 1997). But the fact remains that the core content of Shari'a has continued to reflect the social, political and economic conditions of the eighth to tenth centuries, thereby growing more and more out of touch with subsequent developments and realities of society and state, especially in the modern context (Schacht 1974: 394–5).

The Abbasid rulers inherited the legacy of Umayyad legal developments mainly in the areas of government administration and judicial decisions that were founded on judges' personal opinions of the relevance and meaning of principles of the Qur'an and Arab or local customary practice (Esposito 1984: 72). But since they were keen to enhance their Islamic legitimacy, as the basis of their successful challenge to the Amway dynasty, the Abbasid rulers also actively encouraged the application of Shari'a by state-appointed judges. To that end, they created the position of chief judge (*qadi al-quda*), who had the responsibility of appointing and dismissing other judges, subject to the overriding authority of the Khalifa, of course. A notable occupant of that office was Abu Yufus (d. 798), the leading Hanafi jurist of the time (Weiss and Green 1987: 85). In that way, the Abbasid state sought to transform Shari'a into positive law through the judiciary. But as agents of the state, Shari'a judges did not have complete monopoly over the judicial process. A variety of other openly 'secular' (*mazalim*) courts also had jurisdiction in a wide variety of fields of the administration, while the Khalifa retained ultimate judicial authority, even over matters formally assigned to judges (Weiss and Green 1987: 152). The religious nature of Shari'a, and its focus on regulating the relationship between God and human beings, was probably one of the main reasons for the persistence and growth of secular courts to regulate a wide range of practical matters in the administration of justice and process of government in general (Al-Mawardi 1996/2000). As Noel Coulson has observed, the distinction between the jurisdiction of the *mazalim* and Shari'a courts at that time came very close to the philosophy of a division between secular and religious courts (Coulson 1964: 122). That early acceptance of a 'division of labour' between different kinds of courts has probably contributed, among other factors, to the eventual confinement of Shari'a jurisdiction to family law matters in the modern era, as discussed below.

Another aspect of the legal history of Islamic societies that is associated with the religious nature of Shari'a is the development of private legal consultation (*ifta*). Scholars who were independent of the state were issuing legal opinions at the request of provincial governors and state judges, in addition to providing advice for individual persons from the very beginning of Islam (Masud et al. 1996: 8–9). These activities expanded in scope and geographical reach as the jurisprudence of the various schools evolved and the sources and techniques of Shari'a developed during the early Abbasid era. This type of private advice persisted through subsequent stages of Islamic history, and became institutionalized in the mid-Ottoman period, as indicated below. Such private advice will probably continue into the future to satisfy the religious needs of Islamic communities. But there is a significant difference between this sort of moral and social influence of private actors, and the enforcement of Shari'a by the state, which is the main concern of this Introduction.

The balance between the practical needs of state and society, on the one hand, and the moral imperatives of Shari'a as historically understood, on the other hand, was not easy to maintain in practice. The traditional approach here has always been a delicate division of juristic labour between official judges and independent scholars providing moral guidance to their communities on private voluntary basis. On the one hand, matters of legal procedure and evidence in

the adjudication of adversarial cases through binding and enforceable judgments fell within the jurisdiction of state judges and courts. On the other hand,
non-binding advisory *fatwa* continued to be pronounced by learned scholars of
Shari'a to individuals seeking advice (see Masud et al. 1996: 3). As the corpus
of substantive law and jurisprudence grew, the accumulation of *fatwa* issued by
scholars of Shari'a (*muftis*) in different settings served to stimulate the development of Shari'a 'from below', in response to the specific needs of Islamic
communities, albeit within the confines of the established framework (Masud
et al. 1996: 4). Still, that degree of practical adaptability did not succeed in
preventing the encroachment of European codes from the mid-nineteenth
century. As openly secular state courts applying those colonial codes began to
take over civil and criminal matters, the domain of Shari'a was progressively
limited to the family law field. Whatever the reasons may have been, family law
remained the primary aspect of Shari'a that successfully resisted displacement
by European codes during the colonial period, and survived and outlasted
various degrees or forms of secularization of the state and its institutions in a
number of Islamic countries. As such, IFL has become for most Muslims the
symbol of their Islamic identity, the hard irreducible core of what it means to
be a Muslim today.

The critical factor in this transition that is particularly relevant to our
purposes here is the role of the state in mediating the relevance of Shari'a as
part of broader legal and political systems of government and social organization, because that is the role the state is playing today. But the need to
transform IFL as part of the legal system of modern Islamic states can be
better appreciated in the light of an understanding of the nature and process
of transition into this modern context. While the case for the transformation
of the basis of family law I am proposing draws on those earlier experiences,
it is probably more urgent today than it was in the recent past.

Transition into the Modern Era

The main changes in the above-mentioned approach to division of labour
between state judges and advice by independent scholars (*ifta*) in the modern
era have been the progressive expansion of the secular jurisdiction of the
courts and institutionalization of *ifta*. I will first review the latter phenomenon
before turning to the expansion of secular jurisdiction of state courts, which
is the main focus of the rest of this section. However, I will deal with these
developments with special reference to the Ottoman experience because of its
strong influence on similar developments in many Islamic countries today.

During the Mamluk period (1250–1516) in Egypt and Syria, *ifta* was largely still a private activity that was independent of state control or regulation. In other words, the authority of those independent scholars was derived from their standing among their peers and the confidence of the general public in their competence and piety. This was the same process through which the main Sunni schools evolved in the first place, except that the content and methodology of the legal and religious opinion being issued was confined to the established schools of Shari'a from the tenth century, as indicated above. It was not uncommon for *muftis* to attend Shari'a courts where judges might consult with them before issuing their judgments, especially in difficult cases. The Mamluks did not appoint *muftis* as judges in Shari'a courts, although they did appoint a relatively small number to serve in the secular (*mazalim*) courts that were established by the Sultan and his governors. The Mamluk Sultans also apparently employed a small number of *muftis* to advise them on matters of policy, thereby reinforcing their own political legitimacy among their Muslim subjects (Masud et al. 1996: 10).

The independence of *muftis* continued into the early Ottoman period, but as the state expanded and developed into an empire, they were gradually incorporated into an increasingly centralized judicial administration. Beginning with the reign of Murad II (1421–51), a single *mufti*, designated as *Shaykh al-Islam* (the wise and learned scholar of Islam) came to be recognized as the ultimate source of authority in matters relating to Shari'a. By the time of Selim I (1512–20), the *Shaykh al-Islam* exercised considerable moral influence in the capital city of Istanbul. These developments culminated in the reign of Sulayman (1520–66), when the *Shaykh al-Islam* became responsible for a complex hierarchy of jurists scattered throughout the empire. As the demand for *fatwa* increased, the Sultan established an official department for issuing *fatwas*, with a professional staff headed by the *fatwa* supervisor, thereby beginning the process of institutionalization and bureaucratization of this function (Masud et al. 1996: 11–12).

A related significant development during that period was the patronage of the Hanafi school by the Ottoman dynasty. From the earliest days of their rule, the Ottoman Sultans appear to have given official status to this school, presumably because it was already established in the cities of pre-Ottoman Anatolia that provided the first judges and jurists in the Ottoman realms. By the mid-sixteenth century, the Hanafi school had spread with the Ottoman conquest to the Balkan peninsula and Hungary, and had become the predominant school in the Middle East to the west of Iran, both in the practice of the courts and in the curriculum of the colleges. However, there was a

tension between that reality and the need to maintain the traditional independence of Shari'a – since rulers are supposed only to foster the development of
Shari'a, without claiming or appearing to create or control it (Imber 1997: 25).
Like all members of higher ranks of the religious–legal profession, the *Shaykh
al-Islam* reached his position through direct royal patronage, and relied for his
promotion on the support of a family or faction. He was never, in reality, out
of and above everyday politics.

Ebu's-Su'ud, who served as *Shaykh al-Islam* from nearly thirty years (1545–
74) is credited with having attempted to reconcile the supremacy of Shari'a
with the sovereignty of the Sultan. But that must have been more a matter of
personality and the relative standing of the Shari'a scholar in relation to the
particular Sultan – while both claims are essentially political in any social
setting, the religious authority of Shari'a is fundamentally different from the
temporal authority of the Sultan. The point can clearly be illustrated from
pre-Reformation Europe to post-Khomeini Iran.

The need for systematic reasoning and citation of sources and precedents
in the expanding field of *ifta* gave rise to a form of legal literature that consisted
almost entirely of quotations arranged in ways that lent authority to the
author's arguments. The majority of *fatwas* survive in the collections devoted
to the opinions of either a single or several *Shaykh al-Islam*. The compilers of
these volumes organized the *fatwas* under legal headings and subheadings such
as marriage, lease, trust or lawsuits, i.e., procedure – thereby making them a
practical source of reference for students, judges, *muftis* and others with an
interest in the law. But the basic legal concepts and methodology, as they had
been established by the eleventh century, remained unchanged, as jurists
continued to follow the doctrine and techniques of their *madhhab*, although
some adaptation must have taken place for the *fatwas* to be relevant and useful.
On the question of land, for example, a number of Hanafi jurists from the
time of the Transoxanian jurist Qadikhan (d. 1196) onwards adapted the
classical theory of land ownership and taxation to describe the forms of tax
and tenure that were prevalent in their own day. Ebu's-Su'ud came to draw on
this tradition in the sixteenth century for his own formulation of Ottoman
land law (Imber 1997: 37; Hallaq 1994: 31).

Similar developments can also be observed in Safavid Iran from 1501 to
1722, where Twelver Shi'ism (Ja'fari school) became the state religion, and
Shari'a scholars occupied a range of positions, some of which may have
included public *fatwa*-issuing functions. In Timurid Central Asia and the Indian
subcontinent an official bearing the title *Shaykh al-Islam* or its equivalent was
in charge of all religious matters, including the issuing of *fatwas* (Masud et al.

1996: 13–15). Throughout these areas, earlier efforts to reconcile and negotiate the relationship between Shari'a and secular administration of justice continued, subject to regional context and theological variations between Sunni and Shi'a approaches.

In the Ottoman Empire, as elsewhere, Shari'a was the law of religious community, while *qanun* was the law of the state. The two systems had grown independently of one another, Shari'a as the outcome of juristic speculation that reached its maturation two centuries before the emergence of the Ottoman imperial state, while *qanun* was a systematization of specifically Ottoman feudal practice that in many essential areas, such as land tenure and taxation, ran counter to the doctrines of Shari'a jurists. As noted above, Ebu's-Su'ud is credited with having redefined the basic laws of land tenure and taxation in terms that he borrowed from the Hanafi tradition, in an effort to reconcile the two. The synthesis he developed remained in force until the promulgation of a new Ottoman code of land law in 1858 (Imber 1997: 51). Thus, despite the purported intellectual and ideological hegemony of Shari'a throughout the Islamic world, secular law that derived its authority from either custom or the will of a human political actor had to be devised and applied. This was simply unavoidable then, and would be even more compelling in today's complex world, because Shari'a did not provide all the tools and material required for a comprehensive and sustainable practical legal system (Gerber 1999: 29; Imber 1997: Chapter 2).

Moreover, with the rise of European imperial powers since the sixteenth century, a new dimension was added to the dynamics of transition. In the Ottoman Empire, this took the form of granting the consular courts of European powers jurisdiction over cases involving their nationals and also Ottoman nationals belonging to the religious communities taken under the protection of these foreign states. This system developed into a powerful political structure that, combined with military and economic pressure from European imperial powers, including loss of territory, became the motivating force behind the *Tanzimat* reforms of the Ottoman law and the legal system in the second half of the nineteenth century. Initially this consisted of formally removing from Shari'a jurisdiction whole areas of law where its ultimate authority used to be at least nominally acknowledged, even where its principles had been mixed with customary and *qanun* law for centuries. This process began after the Egyptian occupation of Palestine and Syria between 1831 and 1840, when criminal and administrative matters began to be transferred to local councils set up in districts, leaving Shari'a courts to deal with personal status/family law and property matters.

In addition to justifying these changes in the name of strengthening the state and preserving Islam, *Hatt-i Humayun* (an imperial edict) also emphasized the need to ensure equality among Ottoman subjects, thereby laying the foundation for a major reconstruction of the legal system regarding the rights of non-Muslims. This edict provided for secular or *nizamiyah* mixed courts composed of Muslim and non-Muslim judges to hear commercial and criminal cases between people of all religions. It also stipulated that non-Muslims of recognized communities could take inheritance issues to their own religious court, rather than to Shari'a courts as had been the practice. This was more than a mere reaffirmation of the *Millet* policy of communal religious jurisdiction in matters of personal status/family law, under which Shari'a courts had exercised a far wider jurisdiction, including residual jurisdiction, and heard all mixed cases. The competence of non-Muslims to testify in judicial proceedings was validated, another significant departure from traditional Shari'a doctrine, and *nizamiyah* courts applied European (mostly French) codes, thereby excluding Shari'a jurisdiction (Welchman 2000: 34–6). These *Tanzimat* reforms, inspired largely by political motives, introduced into Ottoman law a Commercial Code of 1850, a Penal Code of 1858, a Commercial Procedure of 1879, a Code of Civil Procedure of 1880, and a Code of Maritime Commerce. In form, all Ottoman codes followed the European civil law model of attempting a comprehensive enactment of all relevant rules. Although Shari'a jurisdiction was significantly displaced in these ways, an attempt was still made to retain some elements of it, such as the right of the victim's family to blood money (*diya*) in cases of homicide by virtue of Article 1 of the Penal Code.

The *Majallah*, which came to be known as the Civil Code of 1876, although it was not devised as such, was promulgated over a ten-year period (1867–77) to codify the rules of contract and tort according to the Hanafi school, combining European form with Shari'a content. It did not cover non-contractual obligations, family law or real property, but did include some procedural rules applicable to those subjects. This major codification of Shari'a simplified a huge part of Islamic law (legal aspects of Shari'a), and made it more easily accessible to litigants and jurists/lawyers alike, especially as the latter group became increasingly less familiar with Shari'a principles and methodology.

Although it was not originally seen as exclusive, the *Majallah* acquired a position of supreme authority soon after its enactment. The reasons for that may include the fact that it represented the earliest and politically authoritative example of an official promulgation of large parts of Shari'a by the authority of a modern state, thereby transforming Shari'a into law (Messick 1993: 57). Moreover, that legislation was immediately applied in a wide range of Islamic societies throughout the Ottoman Empire, and continued to apply in some parts into the second half of the twentieth century.

Second, it included some provisions drawn from other sources than the consensus of Hanafi law, thereby expanding possibilities of 'acceptable' selectivity from within the Islamic tradition. This selectivity (*takhayyur*) among equally legitimate doctrines of Shari'a was already acceptable in principle, but not done in practice. By applying the principle to include minority views within the Hanafi school, the *Majallah* opened the door for more wide-reaching subsequent reforms, despite their initially limited purpose (Pearl and Menski 1998: 19–20; Welchman 2000: 36–7). Subsequent reforms began to incorporate views from other schools, and even individual views of early jurists not adopted by any of the Sunni school, and all of this was justified by reference to the Sultan's (the state's) established power to select some juristic views over others for practical enforcement.

Important reforms of family law matters in particular began with an imperial edict in 1915 that granted wives a limited right to petition for divorce (*faskh*), contrary to the doctrine of the Hanafi school. These reforms were extended and consolidated for application as law in Shari'a courts, as promulgated in the Ottoman Law of Family Rights of 1917, and included rules of procedure that did not exist in the Hanafi school. The significance of that process lay not only in its impact for the law applicable throughout the domains of the Ottoman Empire in the Middle East and North Africa, but in its establishment of a reform methodology beyond the confines of any particular school (*madhhab*).

This trend towards increased eclecticism in the selection of sources and the synthesis of Islamic and Western legal concepts and institutions not only became irreversible, but was carried further, especially through the work of the Egyptian jurist Abd al-Razzaq al-Sanhuri (d. 1971). The pragmatic premise of al-Sanhuri's work was that the Shari'a could not be reintroduced in its totality, and could not be applied in any way, especially in matters relating to land law and commercial law, without strong adaptation to the needs of modern Islamic societies. He applied these ideas in drafting of the Egyptian Civil Code of 1948, the Iraqi Code of 1951, the Libyan Code of 1953, and the Kuwait Code and Commercial Law of 1960/1.

One significant consequence of these developments has been making the entire corpus of Shari principles available and accessible to judges, other state officials and opinion leaders of Islamic societies everywhere. Paradoxically, that same openness and accessibility of Shari'a emphasizes the impossibility of its consistent and legitimate application in the modern context, by exposing major theoretical problems and differences within and between different schools and traditions of Islamic societies. Besides obvious difficulties of agreement between Sunni and Shi'a communities that sometimes coexist within the same country, as in Iraq, Lebanon, Saudi Arabia, Syria and Pakistan, different *madhahib* and opinions may be followed by the Muslim community within the same country, though not formally applied by the courts. In addition, judicial practice may not necessarily be in accordance with the *madhhab* followed by the majority of the Muslim population in the country, as in North African countries that inherited official Ottoman preference for the Hanafi *madhhab*, while popular religious practice (as opposed to state family law enforcement) is according to the Maliki *madhhab*. Given the imperatives of certainty and general application of law, the immediate and compelling questions raised by the realities of profound difference among and within Shari'a schools include the question of how selection from conflicting opinions can be made, by whom, and according to which criteria.

Another consequence of the exposure of the true nature of Shari'a is the challenge of keeping it intellectually and normatively alive in a radically transformed world (Masud et al. 1996: 26–7). In particular, the most significant impact of European colonialism and global Western influence is the fundamental transformation in the essential character of knowledge and its means of transmission. Curricular changes in educational institutions meant that Shari'a, formerly the centrepiece of advanced instruction in Islamic knowledge, was displaced by a spectrum of secular subjects, many derived from Western models. The study of Islamic jurisprudence (*fiqh*) was removed to pure Islamic institutions or to specialized law schools, where it competes with offerings in secular/Western law. In contrast to the extremely limited degree of literacy and the privileged position of scholars of Shari'a (*ulama*) in the past, modern Islamic societies are well on their way to achieving mass basic literacy and reliance on a variety of new expertise. Consequently, the scholars of Shari'a have not only lost their monopoly on knowledge of the 'sacred' sources of Shari'a, but a large part of those sources was no longer viewed as sacred or unquestionable by an increasing number of ordinary 'lay' Muslims.

But the most significant transformation of Islamic societies for our purposes here relates to the nature of the state itself in its local and global context. Although there are serious objections to the manner in which it happened under colonial auspices, the establishment of European model nation-states for all Islamic societies, as part of a global system based on the same model, has radically transformed political, economic and social relations throughout the region (Piscatori 1986). By retaining this specific form of political and social organization after independence from colonial rule, Islamic societies have freely chosen to be bound by a minimum set of national and international obligations of membership in a world community of nation-states. While there are clear differences in the level of their social development and political stability, all Islamic societies today live under national constitutional regimes (even where there is no written constitution) and legal systems that require respect for certain minimum rights of equality and non-discrimination for all their citizens. Even where national constitutions and legal systems fail to acknowledge and effectively provide for these obligations, a minimum degree of practical compliance is ensured by the political, economic, security, legal and other unavoidable realities of international relations. I am not suggesting here that the majority of Islamic countries are already living up to these obligations. Rather, the point is that these countries openly acknowledged these principles as being applicable to them. Moreover, if these countries were to live in accordance with Shari'a, they would have to transform themselves totally, from their political boundaries to the nature of government, and live in almost total economic and political isolation from the rest of the world.

Towards Transformation of the Basis of Family Law

Against the background of these conclusions I will now focus on the need to transform the basis of family law in Islamic countries. This argument is based on the following propositions, which, I believe, are substantiated by the preceding review and analysis. First, the notion of an immutable body of principles of Shari'a as universally binding on all Muslims for eternity is simply not supported by the actual practice of Muslim societies and their states throughout history. Second, Shari'a has not had exclusive jurisdiction in the administration of justice throughout Islamic history, as the state always exercised secular jurisdiction, nor was Shari'a free from state supervision wherever the state permitted it to be enforced. Third, the ability of individual Muslims to seek and act upon independent *fatwa* has always been a valuable resource for addressing the personal religious needs of believers, even regarding what might technically be 'legal subject matter'. The institutionalization of this function does not exhaust the possibilities of independent legal advice, which believers can observe voluntarily without state enforcement or control. Fourth, recent Islamic law reforms and social developments that made the entire corpus of Shari'a available and accessible to all concerned also exposed the moral and political problems of selective enactment and enforcement of some of these norms over others.

The question I wish to discuss in this final section is whether family law can continue to be presumably governed by Shari'a when all other aspects of the legal system are subject to secular state law. I will address this broad question through an examination of the following issues. Why has family law remained within the domain of Shari'a, and how can that situation be justified? Does this really mean that this field is governed by 'divine law', or is it really a matter of human opinion that is represented by its authors, as the sole expression of divine will? What might be a better alternative to the current situation that would achieve equality and fairness for Muslim women within an Islamic perspective, without compromising the religious identity of Islamic societies and personal piety of individual believers?

As explained above, all aspects of the legal systems of most Islamic countries are now governed by secular legislation, except what has come to be known as personal status/family law, inheritance (*mirath*) and religious endowment (*waqf*), where Shari'a jurisdiction has been retained. Reasons often cited for this situation include the following (Mir-Hosseini 1993: 10–11). First, these have traditionally been the most developed areas of Shari'a, over which the *ulama* had the highest monopoly. In particular, it is claimed that since the Qur'an and Sunna regulate matters of family law and inheritance in more explicit detail than that devoted to subjects such as commercial and land law, it was therefore possible and more practical to introduce radical changes and reforms in other areas where no major rival jurisdiction existed. Second, the governments of Islamic countries apparently deployed, whether consciously or unconsciously, the Western liberal distinction between public and private domains. Family law could then be left in the hands of the *ulama*, as it was deemed to be a private matter of religion and therefore politically less significant. In other words, national governments followed the lead of colonial powers in taking away from Shari'a jurisdiction matters of state interest in the fields of public law, economy and administration, and avoided any confrontation on family law that was deemed to be politically insignificant.

In addition to scholarly refutations of these arguments (Messick 1993), each of these reasons raises more questions than it answers. Thus, generally speaking, the extent to which any government succeeded in reforming the pre-existing legal system was conditioned by a variety of factors, including the balance of power between conservative and modernist groups that continues to fluctuate to the present time. In such political calculation, governments have so far opted against bidding for control over family law to appease conservative and fundamentalist forces. But why should these forces accept that, and not demand the same for commercial and criminal law? In other words, such policies of appeasement are only likely to encourage those forces to settle for nothing less than total control over the state and its institutions.

However, as indicated above, because of the diversity and fluidity of its doctrines and principles Shari'a cannot be captured within the framework of formal enactment and enforced by the state as part of a unified legal system. As a moral code for the individual's relationship with God, it does not maintain a clear distinction between moral and legal aspects of human behaviour. As an ideal moral order extrapolated from a premise in legal science (*usul al-fiqh*), rather than pragmatic human experience, Shari'a defies containment in clearly defined legal principles of general application. As Schacht puts it, the development of Shari'a was a 'unique phenomenon of legal science not the state playing the part of legislator' (Schacht 1964: 210). Its provisions were open-ended and flexible, with built-in variations on the consequences of its principles on the basis of individual moral choices that cannot be evaluated by an impersonal institution such as a court of law in the modern sense of the term. In short, Shari'a ceases to be what it is supposed to be by the very act of enacting it as the positive law of the state (An-Na'im 1998–99: 29–42).

The sad irony is that, by failing to face the real issue here, the so-called modernizing elite in control of the state in Islamic societies chose to sacrifice the basic human dignity and rights of women for the sake of political expediency. By conceding family law to the control of the *ulama*, that elite made IFL the 'last bastion of religion' in the administration of justice. That is, the secularization of all other aspects of the law has had the effect of reinforcing the religious tone of family law as the only remaining field left for the domain of Shari'a. Paradoxically, it is precisely because there was little opposition to the abrupt abandonment of Shari'a in other areas of the law that family law became a sensitive and disputed issue. As a result, the debate over family law is a sore spot in the Muslim psyche, and a highly symbolic location of the struggle between the forces of traditionalism and modernism in the Muslim world.

There are two important dimensions to this debate. First, it is conducted almost entirely within the Islamic framework, whereby the possibility of state enactment and enforcement of Shari'a is taken for granted. Second, the debate has acquired a sharp political edge, and in some instances family law reforms had to be withdrawn for fear of a 'religious backlash' against governments desperate for political legitimacy and support at any cost. The debate is thus the product of its time, bearing traces of the underlying tensions between differing world-views. At the root of the debate is the shift in the balance of power between religion and state, brought about by a host of factors, such as the failure of nationalist leaders to deliver on the promise of political independence and development after independence.

There is nothing new about this political manipulation of religious legitimacy since the beginning of Islamic history. What is novel is the ways in which gender relations have now become an integral part of this politics, a reflection of the changed position of women in the Muslim world (Kandiyoti 1991: 'Introduction'). In the earlier parts of the twentieth century the modernists had the upper hand and aimed to change the gender relations in favour of greater autonomy and equality for women. But by the end of the century, fundamentalists had a stronger political platform, and chose to make stopping and reversing any advances towards equality for women the symbol of their political power. The issue at both ends of the century was the same question of women's liberation and emancipation. Whereas fundamentalists construe the abandonment of Shari'a in the family law field as the final blow to an Islamic order that is distinctly patriarchal, modernists see such abandonment as a necessary step towards a more egalitarian society. The basic fallacy of casting the issues in these terms is equating family law, as applied in Islamic societies today, with historical understandings of Shari'a, let alone Islam as a religion.

It may appear that in the vast majority of Islamic countries, as shown in the material contained in this volume, family law is at least nominally derived from Shari'a. But in fact the substance and mode of application of this law has little to do with the essential nature of Shari'a, as envisioned by its founding jurists. The very premise of the debate is flawed, and it is bound to remain polemical unless it addresses more pertinent questions that have hitherto been overlooked, if not deliberately suppressed. To what extent is IFL relevant to the life of today's Muslims, and if it is, how far and through what processes is it translated into social reality (Mir-Hosseini 1993: 12–13)? We know little of the ways in which Shari'a-based family law, this so-called last bastion of the Islamic ideal and identity of social relations, operates in today's world. That is why this project seeks to provide a detailed description of the current situation in as many Islamic societies as possible.

The perspective presented in this Introduction is intended to offer a framework through which the issues discussed can be clarified in the specific contexts of countries and regions where Shari'a-based family law operates. Thus, in the information provided, the reader can appreciate the relationships (or sets of relationships) between statutory law, Shari'a-based family law, the history of Islam in a region, customary social practices, the impact of colonialism, and other, more recent, political events. But the perspective in which this information is presented can also, it is to be hoped, highlight the tensions between the legacies of historical events, political and administrative systems, and concrete practices, as well as the mode and nature of possible mediations of these tensions. By seeking to facilitate comparison of the legal profiles of two or more nation-states within the same region, the structure and content of this book emphasizes the point I have made earlier, namely, that *human agency* plays a critical role in the conception and development of any normative system of Islam. For example, while both Tunisia and Egypt are North African countries, sharing much in common by way of a regional history, IFL in Tunisia is conceived and operates in markedly different ways from those of Egypt. As the information in this book makes clear, this is a result of *human actions and decisions*, whether informed by the project of post-colonial nation-building or by subsequent events in the country's political history. Since the emphasis on context is as much geographical as historical – indeed, the two are inseparable – the focus here is on showing how both the historical and geographical dimensions, in addition to the political, need to be taken into account in understanding IFL in each country of the region.

To summarize, the content of each chapter and schematic of the book as a whole provide a point of departure and context for assessing the information on each country and region. This arrangement and presentation of the material, and the perspective that guides it, demonstrate the futility of adopting a reductive approach to the study of Shari'a-based family law. The detailed description of IFL in the world today is intended not only to serve as a 'resource book', but also to encourage a more candid and thorough examination of the underlying issues.

For my part, I am hereby calling for a clear and categorical acknowledge-ment of the fact that family law in Islamic countries today is not, and indeed cannot and should not be, founded on Shari'a. Like all aspects of the legal system of each country, family law is really based on the political will of the state, and not on the will of God. After all, there is no way of discovering and attempting to live by the will of God except through the agency of human beings. Since that is the case, those responsible for the enactment and applica-tion of family law must be politically and legally accountable for their actions, instead of being allowed to hide behind claims of divine command.

In conclusion, I wish to emphasize that I am proposing these admittedly controversial views under my personal responsibility, without detracting from the factual nature of the material presented in this book, or implying that these are necessarily the views of any of the researchers who contributed to its preparation. Instead of holding back on expressing these views at this stage,

I am putting them forward in the hope that readers will reflect on them as they examine the contents of this book.

Bibliography

Al-Azmeh, A. (ed.) (1988a) *Islamic Law: Social and Historical Contexts*, London: Routledge.

— (1988b) 'Islamic legal theory and the appropriation of reality', in A. Al-Azmeh (ed.), I*slamic Law: Social and Historical Contexts*, London: Routledge, pp. 250–61.

al-Mawardi, (1996/2000) *Al-Ahkam al-Sultaniyya w'al-Wilayat al-Diniyya (The Ordinances of Government)* trans. Wafaa Hassan Wahba, Reading: Garnet (Centre for Muslim Contributions to Civilization).

Anderson, J. N. D. (1959) *Islamic Law in the Modern World*, New York: New York University Press.

Anderson, N. (1976) *Law Reform in the Muslim World*, London: Athlone Press.

An-Na'im, A. A. (1990) *Toward an Islamic Reformation: Civil Liberties, Human Rights and International Law*, Syracuse, NY: Syracuse University Press.

— (1998–99) 'Shari'a and positive legislation: is an Islamic state possible or viable?', in E. Cotran and C. Mallat (general editors), *Yearbook of Islamic and Middle Eastern Law*, Vol. 5, London, Boston and The Hague: CIMEL SOAS and Kluwer Law International, pp. 29–41.

Burton, J. (1990) *The Sources of Islamic Law*, Edinburgh: Edinburgh University Press.

— (1994) *An Introduction to the Hadith*, Edinburgh: Edinburgh University Press.

Calder, N. (1993) *Studies in Early Muslim Jurisprudence*, Oxford: Clarendon Press.

Charnay, J. P. (1971) *Islamic Culture and Socio-Economic Change*, Leiden: E.J. Brill.

Coulson, N. J. (1964) *A History of Islamic Law*, Edinburgh: Edinburgh University Press.

— (1969) *Conflicts and Tensions in Islamic Jurisprudence*, Chicago, IL: University of Chicago Press.

Engineer, A. A. (1999) *The Qur'an, Women and Modern Society*, New Delhi: Sterling Publishers.

Esposito, J. L. (1982) *Women in Muslim Family Law*, New York: Syracuse University Press.

— (1984) 'Law in Islam', in Y. Haddad, B. Haines and E. Findly (eds), *The Islamic Impact*, New York: Syracuse University Press, pp. 69–86.

Gerber, H. (1999) *Islamic Law and Culture 1600–1840*, Leiden: E.J. Brill.

Hallaq, W. B. (1994) 'Was the gate of *ijtihad* closed?' in W. B. Hallaq (ed.), *Law and Legal Theory in Classical and Medieval Islam*, Hampshire: Variorum Ashgate Publishing, pp. 3–34.

— (1996) '*Ifta* and *ijtihad* in Sunni legal theory: a development account', in M. K. Masud, B. Messick and D. S. Powers (eds), *Islamic Legal Interpretation: Muftis and their Fatwas*, Cambridge, MA: Harvard University Press, pp. 33–43.

— (1997) A *History of Islamic Legal Theory: An Introduction to Sunni Usul al-Fiqh*, Cambridge: Cambridge University Press.

Hillal Dessouki, A. E. (1982) 'Official Islam and political legitimation in the Arab countries', in B. F. Stowasser (ed.), *The Islamic Impulse*, London: Croom Helm.

Hodgson, M.G. S. (1974) *The Venture of Islam*, Vols 1–3, Chicago, IL: University of Chicago Press.

Hourani, A. (1962) *Arabic Thought in the Liberal Age 1798–1939*, London: Oxford University Press.

Imber, C. (1997) *Ebu's-Su'ud: The Islamic Legal Tradition*, Stanford, CA: Stanford University Press.

Kamali, M. H. (1991) *Principles of Islamic Jurisprudence*, Cambridge: Islamic Texts Society.

Kandiyoti, D. (1991) 'Introduction', in D. Kandiyoti (ed.), W*omen, Islam and the State*, London: Macmillan.

Masud, M. K., B. Messick and D. S. Powers (1996) '*Muftis, fatwas*, and Islamic legal interpretation', in M. K. Masud, B. Messick and D. S. Powers (eds), *Islamic Legal Interpretation: Muftis and their Fatwas*, Cambridge, MA: Harvard University Press, pp. 3–32.

Mayer, A. E. (1984) 'Islamic law', in M. Kelly (ed.), *Islam: The Religious and Political Life of a World Community*, New York: Praeger, pp. 226–42.

— (1990) 'The Shari'ah: methodology or a body of substantive rules', in N. Heer (ed.), *Islamic Law and Jurisprudence*, Seattle: University of Washington Press, pp. 177–98.

Melchert, C. (1997) *The Formation of the Sunni Schools of Law, 9th–10th Centuries*, Leiden: Brill.

— (1999) 'How Hanfaism came to originate in Kufa and traditionalism in Medina', *Islamic Law and Society*, 6, 3: 318–47.

Messick, B. (1993) *The Calligraphic State*, Berkeley: California University Press.

Mir-Hosseini, Z. (1993) *Marriage on Trial: A Study of Islamic Family Law – Iran and Morocco Compared*, London: I.B.Tauris.

Pearl, D. and W. Menski (1998) *Muslim Family Law*, 3rd edn, London: Sweet and Maxwell.

Piscatori, J. (1986) *Islam in a World of Nation States*, Cambridge: Cambridge University Press.

Rosen, L. (2000) *The Justice of Islam: Comparative Perspectives on Islamic Law and Society*, Oxford: Oxford University Press.

Schacht, J. (1959) *Origins of Muhammadan Jurisprudence*, Oxford: Clarendon Press.

— (1964) *An Introduction to Islamic Law*, Oxford: Oxford University Press.

— (1971) 'On the title of the *fatawa* Alamgiriyya', in C. E. Bosworth (ed.), *Iran and Islam: In Memory of the Late Vladimir Minorsky*, Edinburgh: Edinburgh University Press, pp. 475–8.

— (1974) 'Law and the state', in J. Schacht and C. E. Bosworth (eds), *The Legacy of Islam*, Oxford: Oxford University Press, pp. 392–423.

Sharabi, H. (1988) *Neopatriarchy: A Theory of Distorted Change in Arab Society*, Oxford: Oxford University Press.

Tibi, B. (1988) *The Crisis of Modern Islam: A Preindustrial Culture in the Scientific-Technological Age*, trans. J. Von Sivers, Salt Lake City: University of Utah Press.

Weeramantry, C. G. (1988) *Islamic Jurisprudence: An International Perspective*, New York: St Martin's Press.

Weiss, B. (1998) *The Spirit of Islamic Law*, Athens: University of Georgia Press.

Weiss, B. G. and Green, A. H. (1987) *A Survey of Arab History*, revised edn, Cairo: American University in Cairo Press.

Welchman, L. (2000) *Beyond the Code: Muslim Family Law and the Shari'a Judiciary in the Palestinian West Bank*, The Hague: Kluwer Law International.

Part I

Central Asia and
the Caucasus

1 Social, Cultural and Historical Background

The Region and its History

Islam reached Central Asia only 20 years after the death of the Prophet Mohammed, and the region has played a pivotal role in Islamic history and politics. During the Middle Ages, Islamic art and philosophy flourished in the kingdoms of Khorasan, Bukhara, Herat and Samakarand. Meanwhile a Turkish Central Asian dynasty, the Ottomans, slowly conquered the Christian Byzantine Empire. In 1453, the Ottomans took possession of Constantinople. They became the leaders of the Muslim world, ruling for four centuries an Empire that swept from the Balkans to the borders of Iran. When the Ottoman empire finally collapsed after World War I, the Turkish republic that took its place became the first and only Muslim government to replace Shari'a law with a secular legal code that encompassed family law. During the same period, the heart of the Central Asia fell under Russian domination. Towards the end of the twentieth century, however, Islamic rebels in Afghanistan expelled the Soviet Union from their country, helping to destroy the Soviet empire and bring about an Islamic revival in Central Asia.

The history of Central Asia is the history of nomadic tribes who have periodically invaded and conquered the area, and the sedentary, farming peoples who have resisted and absorbed them. Central Asia's nomadic culture was established by around 1700 BCE. Since the dawn of recorded history, Persians, Huns, Chinese, Mongols and Arabs of the Umayyad dynasty in Damascus (Rashid 1994) have overrun the region. The Arab conquest was part of Islam's early expansion. By 651 CE, Arab forces had taken control of the city of Merv. The Arabs began an extensive conversion and settlement process; over 50,000 Arab families relocated to Merv in the years following the conquest. By 713, Arabs ruled most of Central Asia from the kingdom of Khorasan, which included what is today western Afghanistan,[1] northern Iran and Turkmenistan. One of the most important Muslim dynasties was the Persian Samanid dynasty, whose capital was at Bukhara. Islamic art, culture

---

1. All references to Afghanistan in this chapter are to the situation there as of mid 2001.

and science thrived under the Samanids until the invasion of Mongol warlord Ghengis Khan in 1220. The Mongols captured Bukhara, burned it to the ground and killed over 30,000 Muslims. The region survived a handful of subsequent invasions and changes of control until the end of World War I, when a communist Russia eventually conquered Central Asia and the Caucasus and divided the region into Soviet republics (Lapidus 1990: 303–33).

As a result of constant invasions and conquerors, Islam in Central Asia has developed a distinct presentation. The majority of Muslims in Central Asia belong to the Sunni Hanafi sect, the most liberal of the four Sunni schools of thought. In fact, Hanafi Muslims constitute approximately 90 per cent of the population in Afghanistan, a country now in the midst of fundamental Islamic control (Rashid 2000). The Hanafi are not only liberal in terms of Islam; they are traditionally tolerant of other religions. Throughout history, Christians, Hindus, Sikhs and Jews have played important roles in the culture and politics of the region (Rashid 2000).

Today Muslims represent a majority in the region, although a very small majority in some countries. Afghanistan contains the largest percentage of Muslims, with 99 per cent of its 27 million professing Islam. Turkey, with only a slightly lower percentage of Muslims, has a much larger population of some 65 million. Uzbekistan's 25 million people, Tajikistan's six million, Turkmenistan's five million and Kyrgyzstan's five million are all over 75 per cent Muslim, with significant Russian and Eastern Orthodox populations of between 10 and 20 per cent. Kazakhstan has the most religiously diverse population, with its fifteen million people almost evenly divided between Muslims and Christians. Muslims make up about 12 per cent of the Republic of Georgia's population. They also form a majority in the Caucausian republics of Azerbaijan, Dagestan and Chechnya. (All population figures are based on mid-2000 estimates from the Population Reference Bureau.)

Legal Practices and Institutions

Over the last two hundred years, Turkey has introduced a series of legal reforms unique in the Muslim world. As early as 1839, the Ottoman Sultan Abdulmecid instituted a reform charter known as *Tanzimat* or 'Reorganization'. Under his reforms, women's education was seen as crucial to the development of Turkish society, and women were encouraged to continue their education (Arat 1998). In 1870, the Ottoman government issued a new civil code administered in state rather than Shari'a courts. Ottoman women had the right to testify in court. They could also enter contracts independently and pursue defaulters in court.

Kemal Ataturk, the founder of modern Turkey, made a far more radical break with traditional Islamic law in 1917. His government adopted a new European system of personal law. Among other changes, the new law abolished polygyny and gave women the same rights to divorce and inheritance as men. In 1926, the Ataturk regime formally abolished the Shari'a. As a result, Turkey has a fully secular legal framework, taken directly from Swiss civil and Italian penal codes (Arin 1997). Turkish women were given the right to vote and the practice of veiling was banned. Women were also given the same judicial rights as men, such as that of witnessing (Arat 1998). In 1930, Turkish women gained the right to vote and to run for election in municipal elections. The right was extended to national elections in 1934 (Arat 1998). More recently, the government scrapped laws naming husbands the heads of their families.

Decades later, the Turkish public remains divided over the role of Islam in public life. In the 1990s, the Turkish Welfare Party won several election victories by promising a greater role for Islamic law. In 1997, over 8,000 women protested in Ankara to oppose Prime Minister Erbakan's support for reintroducing some parts of Shari'a to Turkey's legal code (Women's International Network 1997).

The twentieth century was a period of intense secularization for the rest of Central Asia, too. Once the Soviet Union had gained control of the region in the 1920s, it embarked on a series of anti-religious drives. Here, as in other parts of the Islamic world, colonizers used the alleged degradation of women under Islamic law as a justification for their assault on the local culture. Shari'a law was abolished; polygyny and the brideprice were made illegal. In 1923, in Azerbaijan, Shari'a was denounced as a legal code for family law, and new state family courts were set up to rule over divorces and custody of children (Heyat 2000). During Soviet rule, all but a handful of Central Asia's 24,000 mosques were modified into clùbs and community centres, the pilgrimage to Mecca was banned, and the printing and distributing of the Qur'an was prohibited. However, a significant number of unofficial mosques continued to function. In northern Tajikistan, for example, over 200 'unofficial' mosques were in operation during the Soviet period (Poliakov 1992).

Since the former Soviet Central Asian republics gained independence in 1991, mosques have been reopening at the rate of ten per day. Nevertheless, none of the countries has taken any serious steps to restore Islamic law. Their governments speak the language of secular democracy, but most practise some form of authoritarianism. Islam is encouraged, but Islamic parties are not. For example, in Uzbekistan, President Islam Karimov went on a pilgrimage to Mecca in the early 1990s, but now views devout Muslims as a threat to Uzbekistan's unity. In fact, he closed the main mosque in eastern Uzbekistan in 1995 (Bird 1997). The country of Kyrgyzstan was originally hailed as the 'Switzerland of Central Asia', although it has not been able to maintain a peaceful and democractic system.

Afghanistan is the only country in the region today whose legal framework is based on Islamic law. Prior to 1925, the country, like its Central Asian neighbours, was governed by Shari'a (Rashid 2000). In 1925, Afghanistan enacted its first civil legal code. Afghanistan's practice of Islam historically was a tolerant one. Ninety per cent of Afghanis belong to the Hanafi Sunni sect (Rashid 2000). The country also contains a large Shi'ia minority, the Hazaras. However, the Soviet Union's traumatic invasion of the country in 1979, and the devastating civil war that followed its ejection in 1989, radically altered the historical Afghan interpretation of Shari'a. The ruling Taliban ('students of Islam') who emerged in 1994 mostly belong to the Pashtun people, who have historically dominated Afghanistan. The Pashtuns account for about 40 per cent of Afghanistan's population. They follow a tribal code known as Pashtun-wali; there is a blurry line between Islamic law and Pashtunwali in Afghanistan. The Taliban's leaders were educated in the *madrassas*, or Islamic schools, of Pakistan. In every region they have seized power, their first act has been to ban women from public places, jobs and institutions. The most important court in the country is now the Kandahar Islamic Supreme Court, because of its proximity to the Taliban leader, Mullah Omar. The court appoints Islamic judges, *qadis* and assistant *qadis* in the provices. A parallel system exists in the Afghan capital of Kabul where the Justice Ministry and the Supreme Court of Afghanistan are based. According to Attorney-General Maulvi Jalilullah Maulvizada, Afghanistan's legal revolution is not yet completed. 'All the laws are being Islamicized. The laws repugnant to Islam are being removed. It will take us several years to get through all of them' (Rashid 2000: 103).

All of the countries of Central Asia and the Caucasus that formerly belonged to the Soviet Union have signed and ratified the UN Convention on the Elimination of All Forms of Discrimination Against Women (CEDAW) (UNICEF 1999). Afghanistan signed the CEDAW in 1980, but has never ratified it. Turkey was the first country in the region to become a party to the Convention, ratifying it in 1985.

Seclusion of Women / Purdah

Practices of purdah vary greatly among Central Asia's many ethnic groups. The pre-Soviet Kazakhs had no tradition of veiling or seclusion. On the other hand, in the Islamic city of Bukhara, women were routinely secluded or completely veiled in public. Traditionally, Tajik women were also characterized by almost total seclusion, due to both cultural and Islamic norms (Harris 2000). However, this trend changed throughout Central Asia with Soviet control. The Marxist-Leninist government encouraged the 'liberation' of women from the home and into the productive sphere, particularly in the urban areas. In fact, in the 1930s, the leadership in Moscow ordered all women to burn their veils. Women were given legal equal access to employment, family law and social support provisions under Soviet rule. Girls were required to attend school. By the end of the Soviet period, 96 per cent of Central Asian girls were literate, while 90 per cent of adult women worked outside the home.

In the last ten years, Islamist movements have sought to revive seclusion as an ideal for women. In direct response to the Soviet pressure to bring women out of the home, many Central Asian Muslims have come to regard veiling as the statement of anti-Russian nationalism. For example, in Uzbekistan, veiling has recently become common. Women who follow the opposition Wahabi movement have recently discarded the traditional and colourful Uzbek dress for full-body white veils as statements of recapturing religious/national identity (Rashid 1994). In Tajikistan, women are encouraged to abandon Western-style clothes, which are associated with the Soviet Union. Islamist groups are also promoting partial or full veiling and voluntary seclusion (although no serious move has been made to make seclusion mandatory in Tajikistan). Public opinion among the Tajiks is not strongly opposed to veiling, although men in particular have voiced opposition to seclusion. In an already fragile economy, few families can afford to support themselves solely on the economic contributions of men (Harris 2000). Seclusion of new brides is still common in Central Asia, although this practice is not a result of Islamic prescriptions, but rather an enforcement of a woman's fragile status within her new husband's family (Bastug and Hortacsu 2000).

The Taliban in Afghanistan has legally institutionalized the most rigid seclusion of women known to the region. Upon taking control, the Taliban closed all girls' schools, effected complete segregation of the sexes in the medical field, outlawed makeup, and mandated wearing of the *burga* for all women in public, even non-Afghan women (Rashid 2000). Men are not exempt from these strict laws; most forms of entertainment have been banned and men are now required to maintain long beards or risk imprisonment (Rashid 2000). Although Islamic law requires four witnesses to convict a person of adultery, the government does not prosecute families who execute women suspected of having sex outside marriage in 'honour killings'.

There are some signs that local opposition has led the Taliban to moderate some of its strictures. After UN protests, the Taliban retracted a ban on local women working for international NGOs (Kim 2000). Further, the degree to which the Taliban has been able to enforce restrictions on women's education seems to depend on local custom. In the resisting northeast, a large Tajik population continues to support education for girls. The Swedish Committee for Afghanistan estimates that 16,000 girls have access to primary education in the country's six northern provinces (Kim 2000). Outside the rebelling areas, the UN estimates that 10,000 girls are also attending some form of classroom education in Kabul. A few classes are even being held in mosques. When Pashtun tribal elders demanded education for girls, Taliban governors did not and could not object (Rashid 2000).

In response to the Taliban's restrictions on females working outside the home, northern women have founded the Afghanistan Women's Association, which now has over 3,000 members and is organizing home-based crafts projects for women to gain economic self-sufficiency (Kim 2000). The Taliban's strict seclusion laws are unfamiliar to some of Afghanistan's peoples. For example, prior to the Taliban, Hazara women in central Afghanistan con-stituted twelve of the 80-member Central Council of the main regional political party. However, Taliban officials have told reporters that if they compromised on their rules affecting women, they would lose the support of their followers, who consider the strict seclusion of women a matter of Islamic principle (Rashid 2000).

Seclusion and veiling in Turkey is discouraged, and even illegal in some contexts. Turkey historically had loose rules regarding women's seclusion. In Ottoman times, women had access to public markets (although their husbands had the right to appropriate any income they earned). The Ataturk regime pro-hibited the use of headscarves or veils in state buildings and institutions, as well as in Turkish universities (Holland 1999). With the rise of Islamist movements in the 1980s, women's participation in the workforce has fallen. In the 1970s, 38 per cent of Turkish women were in the workforce; by 1995, this number had declined to 31 per cent (Zeytinoglu 1998). Voluntary veiling based on principles of Islamic dress has also been on the increase in the last 20 years. University students have been among the most fervent suporters (Ilyasoglu 1998).

Honour killings are punishable by death in Turkey, but they continue to happen in poor regions such as the country's Kurdish-dominated eastern and southeastern provinces. Judges in cases involving honour killings come under huge social pressure to reduce the sentences in the light of what is regarded as 'provocation' (Zaman 2000).

Family in the Region

Traditional Turkish families in Central Asia are patrilineal and patrilocal. Families are part of lineages with established authority and responsibilities. Lineages are also clan-based, with clear understanding of clan allegiances for mutual aid and defence (Hortascu and Bastug 2000). Family patterns in both historical and modern Turkmenistan are also patrilineal and patrilocal (Bastug and Hortascu 2000). In fact, claims to Turkmen ethnicity are exclusively traced through fathers.

In Turkey, the early twentieth-century push towards Westernization weakened clan identities and the extended family. The Family Names Act of 1935 required the adoption of a family surname. Lineage or clan surnames were banned, and families were forced to adopt a family name. In general, the Western-style nuclear family was held up as an idealized model.

Scholars generally agree that in theory and tradition, the region of Central Asia and the Caucasus is patrilineal and patriarchal. However, the effects of economic and political instability, with the accompanying processes of urbanization and increased poverty, have made it difficult for families to remain true to tradition. In environments where sons often have more social and economic status than fathers, and economic pressures require women to supplement family incomes, traditional patriarchy is hard to maintain. The family nevertheless remains the most important institution in the region – the group most people turn to for security and help.

Marriage

Under Soviet rule, the central marriage code was designed to establish equality between spouses, secularize marriage and make divorce simple and accessible to both partners. Social benefits were connected with a woman's employment status, not her marital status. Most of the countries in Central Asia and the Caucasus have maintained the majority of these legal provisions (UNICEF 1999). Nevertheless, many Central Asian families still expect to arrange their daughters' marriages. A 1992 study of rural and urban residents revealed that 30 per cent of brides did not know their grooms before marriage (Barbieri et al. 1996).

In traditional Turkish culture, marriages are almost always arranged, with the purpose of forming alliances between clans. Women, upon marriage, become part of the husband's clan; their status within the family depends on the number of male children they bear and their skills in performing expected duties as wife, mother and daughter-in-law (Hortacsu and Bastug 2000). Although many marriages today are based on mutual consent of spouses, paternal consent is still a requirement, maintaining a semblance of the tradition of arranged marriages (Bastug and Hortascu 2000).

One component of Turkey's civil family code requires that valid marriages require a civil ceremony, and that both bride and groom enter marriage consensually (Imamoglu 2000). As the German scholar Wiebke Walther has written, Turkey's experience shows that 'a body of law cannot simply be transplanted to a country where it is not part of the tradition'. Although the law theoretically does not recognize marriage ceremonies performed by imams, since 1933, the Turkish government has had to pass at least eight 'amnesty laws' recognizing the legitimacy of such unions (Walther 1993: 232). Approximately half of the marriges in Turkey are still arranged, despite the longstanding legal code (Imamoglu 2000). A study in Turkey in the early 1990s estimated that 56 per cent of marriages in Turkey were still arranged by families (Hortacsu and Oral 1994). Under Turkish law, a man who abducts a woman from her family receives a lesser sentence if he agrees to marry her. In the case of rape, men face more severe penalties if the woman is a virgin (Y. Arat 1998). The Turkish state supports the traditional role of women in the home. If a woman leaves her job within a year of marrying, she is entitled to severance pay (Zeytinoglu 1998).

Under the Turkish Criminal Code, husbands do not have a right to beat their wives, but domestic violence is a crime only if the beaten partner complains. The maximum punishment for domestic violence is 30 months, but most convicted abusers are sentenced to seven days or fewer. A 1988 study found that 45 per cent of Turkish men think a husband has a right to beat his wife if she disobeys him. A similar 1991 study in Istanbul showed that 49 per cent of women thought that cases exist where a woman deserves to be beaten by her husband. Some 40 per cent of the women in the same study reported being beaten by their husbands (Y. Arat 1998).

Marriage ages in the region vary, although in some areas of the former Soviet Union there seems to be a move towards younger marriage age in urban areas, a phenomenon opposite to that of many other Islamic communities. The Soviet Union set the marriage age for girls at 18. In the capital of Dushanbe, many girls are now married at 15 or younger, whereas girls in rural areas are often not married until ages 20–22 (Harris 2000). In Kazakhstan, the legal age for girls is set at 17, although, as in Tajikistan, early marriages are on the increase. The marriage age was set in Azerbaijan in 1923 at 16 for girls and 18 for boys (Heyat 2000). In her discussion of Tajikistan in particular, Harris explains this pattern as a result of either economic necessity or concern for virginity, or a combination of both. Studies in Central Asia and the Caucasus suggest that domestic violence has increased in the post-Soviet era. In 1997, 25 per cent of women in Azerbaijan reported regular beatings and prohibitions against leaving the house alone. In Tajikistan, 23 per cent of women reported physical domestic abuse. Hospital admission records in Kyrgyzstan indicate that domestic violence injuries requiring medical attention are also increasing (UNICEF 1999).

Dowry and Brideprice

Brideprice is customary in Central Asia, particularly for those living in rural areas. In Turkmenistan, the brideprice usually consists of animals, money and goods, and is delivered by the groom's father to the bride's father before the wedding. Turkmen marriages also require both indirect dowry paid by the women in the groom's family to the bride and traditional dowry paid by the bride's family to the bride (Bastug and Hortacsu 2000).

The Soviets prohibited brideprice and dowry, but enforcement of the prohibition was rare, and the practice remained strong. In Kazakhstan, brideprice, known as *kalym*, has come out into the open in the post-Soviet era. According to Kazakh custom, the groom makes the bride's family a gift of livestock. Kazakh women sometimes bring some of their family's livestock into the marriage. Only the children of the marriage, not the husband and his family, may inherit this bridewealth. In Tajikistan, the average *kalym* price grew by 300 per cent in the 1980s (Poliakov 1992: 55). Similarly, in Turkey, the *baslik* (paid by the father of the groom to the father of the bride) has been repeatedly declared illegal. However, the practice remains common among rural families. Depending on their looks or wealth, some girls can fetch as much as $50,000 (Zaman 2000).

Divorce

The Turkish civil code makes no distinction between men and women in applications for divorce (Arin 1997). Divorce by repudiation, even among devout Muslims, is rare in Turkey, and is used only as a last resort (Vergin 1985). As early as 1916, Turkish women were granted legal rights to ask for divorce. In the case of polygyny, the first wife may ask for her marriage to be dissolved. In this case, the husband is legally required to pay the *mahr* for the first wife (Vergin 1985).

Soviet civil codes required equal ownership and distribution of marital assets upon divorce. Most states in Central Asia and the Caucasus have maintained these legal codes upon independence from the USSR (UNICEF 1999). Kazakhstan, in any case, had a long tradition of giving equal rights to men and women in the case of divorce. In the Soviet era, Uzbekistan's civil code did not discriminate between men and women with regard to divorce. But in recent years, Uzbek legislators have been making divorce more difficult for women to obtain. Uzbek courts have refused to grant divorce petitions from women who have not received permission from their local authorities. Additionally, courts have barred women whose husbands do not agree to the divorce from any claims to marital property (Human Rights Watch 2000).

Afghanistan follows strict Islamic divorce procedures. Interestingly, both the marriage rate and the divorce rate have dropped in the region since 1989. In the Caucasus, the marriage rate has dropped by 49 per cent and the divorce rate has dropped by 57 per cent. In Central Asia, the numbers are not as dramatic, although there has still been a decrease: the marriage rate has dropped by 31 per cent and the divorce rate by a much smaller 7 per cent (UNICEF 1999). Researchers explain these declines as a result of economic hardship. Families are finding it much more difficult to finance dowries in the current economic conditions, a factor that inevitably delays or cancels marriages (UNICEF 1999).

Polygyny

Polygyny was officially banned in Kazakhstan in 1920, but the practice continued and has increased in recent years. Polygyny in Kazakhstan particularly takes the form of taking a woman over the age of 25 as a second wife.

Turkey first restricted polgyny in 1917, by requiring the consent of the first wife to any subsequent marriage of the husband. The practice was banned completely with the adoption of the Turkish Civil Code in 1926 (Arat 1998). It still happens on rare occasions, but generally only among the urban rich (Vergin 1985) and in rural areas (Zaman 2000). The second wife is called the *kuma*, and is married in a religious ceremony conducted by the imam. The *kuma* has no legal rights under Turkish civil law.

Custody of Children

In most former Soviet states, women are provided maternity leave by the state, ranging from 126 to 180 days of 100 per cent salary leave, and extended parental leave for two to three years that can be taken by any relative acting as the primary caretaker and funded by a state stipend (UNICEF 1999). Due to state economic hardships, the Republic of Georgia has abandoned extended parental leave. In addition, the state pays women a family allowance for each child under 16, whether or not the woman is married. This allowance is transferable to another person if the mother is not the primary caretaker (Saktanber and Ozatas-Baykal 2000; Moghadam 2000). Regardless of length of maternity and parental leave, maternal custody of children is codified, recognized and funded by the state.

In Turkey, in the case of divorce or a spouse's death, women are generally awarded custody, both by custom and when courts decide (Arin 1997).

Inheritance / Land Rights

In 1876, constitutional reform in Turkey gave women equal inheritance with male siblings (Arat 1998). Under the Turkish Civil Code, women are legally guaranteed rights of inheritance in cases of the death of a parent or the death of a spouse (Arin 1997).

References

Arat, Y. (1988) 'Feminist institutions and democratic aspirations: the case of the Purple Roof Women's Shelter Foundation', in Z. F. Arat (ed.), *Deconstructing Images of 'The Turkish Woman'*, New York: St Martin's Press, pp. 295–309.

Arat, Z. F. (ed.) (1998) *Deconstructing Images of 'The Turkish Woman'*, New York: St Martin's Press.

Arin, C. (1997) 'The legal status of women in Turkey', *Women's International Network News*, 23: 62.

Barbieri, M., A. Blum, E. Dolkigh and A. Ergashev (1996) 'Nuptiality, fertility, use of contraception, and family policies in Uzbekistan', *Population Studies*, 50: 69–88.

Bastug, S. and N. Hortacsu (2000) 'The price of value: kinship, marriage and metanarratives of gender in Turkmenistan', in F. Acar and A. Gunes-Ayata (eds), *Gender and Identity Construction: Women of Central Asia, the Caucasus and Turkey*, Leiden: E.J. Brill, pp. 117–40.

Bird, C. (1997) 'Uzbek leader fears strong Islam in desert nation', Reuters News Service, 6 November.

Harris, C. (2000) 'The changing identity of women in Tajikistan in the post-Soviet period', in F. Acar and A. Gunes-Ayata (eds), *Gender and Identity Construction: Women of Central Asia, the Caucasus and Turkey*, Leiden: E.J. Brill, pp. 205–28.

Heyat, F. (2000) 'Azeri professional women's life strategies in the Soviet context', in F. Acar and A. Gunes-Ayata (eds), *Gender and Identity Construction: Women of Central Asia, the Caucasus and Turkey*, Leiden: E.J. Brill, pp. 177–201.

Holland, B. (1999) 'In a knot over head scarves in Turkey', *Christian Science Monitor*, 91: 1.

Hortacsu, N. and A. Oral (1994) 'Comparison of couple- and family-initiated marriages in Turkey', *Journal of Social Psychology*, 134: 229–40.

Hortacsu, N. and S. Bastug (2000) 'Women in marriage in Ashkabad, Baku and Ankara', in F. Acar and A. Gunes-Ayata (eds), *Gender and Identity Construction: Women of Central Asia, the Caucasus and Turkey*, Leiden: E.J. Brill, pp. 75–100.

Human Rights Watch (2000) *World Report 2000*, http://www.hrw.org/wr2k/

— (2001) *World Report 2001*, <http://www.hrw.org/hrw/wr2k1/>

Illyasoglu, A. (1998) 'Islamist women in Turkey: their identity and self-image', in Z. F. Arat (ed.), *Deconstructing Images of 'The Turkish Woman'*, New York: St Martin's Press, pp. 241–62.

Imamoglu, O. (2000) 'Changing gender roles and marital satisfaction in Turkey', in F. Acar and A. Gunes-Ayata (eds), *Gender and Identity Construction: Women of Central Asia, the Caucasus and Turkey*, Leiden: E.J. Brill, pp. 101–16.

Kim, L. (2000) 'Tenacity under Afghan *burqas*', *Christian Science Monitor*, 92: 6.

Lapidus, I. M. (1990) *A History of Islamic Societies*, Cambridge: Cambridge University Press.

Moghadam, V. (2000) 'Gender and economic reforms: a framework for analysis and evidence from Central Asia, the Causasus and Turkey', in F. Acar and A. Gunes-Ayata (eds), *Gender and Identity Construction: Women of Central Asia, the Caucasus and Turkey*, Leiden: E.J. Brill, pp. 23–43.

Poliakov, S. P. (1992) *Everyday Islam: Religion and Tradition in Rural Central Asia*, Armonk, NY: M.E. Sharpe.

Rashid, A. (1994) *The Resurgence of Central Asia: Islam or Nationalism?*, Karachi: Oxford University Press and London: Zed Books.

— (2000) *Taliban: Militant Islam, Oil and Fundamentalism in Central Asia*, New Haven, CT: Yale University Press.

Saktanber, A. and A. Ozatas-Baykal (2000) 'Homeland within homeland: women and the formation of Uzbek national identity', in F. Acar and A. Gunes-Ayata (eds), *Gender and Identity Construction: Women of Central Asia, the Caucasus and Turkey*, Leiden: E.J. Brill, pp. 229–48.

Tekeli, S. (ed.) (1995) *Women in Modern Turkish Society: A Reader*, London: Zed Books.

UNICEF (1999) *Women in Transition*, Florence: International Child Development Centre.

Vergin, N. (1985) 'Social change and the family in Turkey', *Current Anthropology*, 26: 571–4.

Walther, W. (1993) *Women in Islam*, Princeton, NJ and New York: Markus Wiener Publishing.

Women's International Network (1997) 'Turkey: 8000 women protest premier's support for Islamic law', *Women's International Network News*, 23: 74.

— (2000) 'Afghanistan: the struggle to educate girls', *Women's International Network News*, 26: 70.

Zaman, A. (2000) 'In Modern Turkey, women continue to pay the price for honor rights', *Los Angeles Times*, 10 September, p. A3.

Zeytinoglu, I. U. (1998) 'Constructed images as employment restrictions: determinates of female labor in Turkey', in Z. F. Arat (ed.), *Deconstructing Images of 'The Turkish Woman'*, New York: St Martin's Press, pp. 183–97.

Part II
East and Central Africa

1 Social, Cultural and Historical Background

The Region and its History

Islam was an integral part of the East African coastal culture by as early as 1000 CE. Islam arrived on the coast through contact with religious teachers, merchants and slave traders (Martin 1986; Oded 2000). Along the eastern coast and the islands of Kenya and Tanzania, Islam had become an important force by the seventeenth century, and remains the dominant religion today. The arrival of the Islamic religion and the concurrent Indian Ocean trade network helped to develop the coastal region into the distinct cultural and political entity known as the Swahili coast. In the seventeenth century, this 2,000-mile coast came under the domination of the Sultan of Oman, who moved his capital to the island of Zanzibar in the nineteenth century. In Zanzibar, many Omani families maintained their Arabian identity. As the historian John Middleton argues, they were 'true colonial rulers' who exploited the local people (Middleton 1992: 13). Islamic law and customs flourished in this period and many Arabs and Indians immigrated to the island and the coast.

Islam spread to the rest of Eastern and Central Africa during the nineteenth century, first through teachers and religious leaders from Hadramaut in Yemen and from the Comoro Islands, and then later through the expansion of the slave trade inland from the coast. Today, in Kenya Muslims represent approximately 20 per cent of the total population of 30 million and in Uganda, 10 per cent of the population of 23 million (Population Reference Bureau 2000). The Muslim population in Tanzania is significantly higher, constituting 35–40 per cent of the population of 35 million (Oded 2000; Population Reference Bureau 2000). The higher population percentage in Tanzania is a result of the concentration of trade centres in Tanzania and the importance of Zanzibar in African–Arab trading. Similarly, the Muslim population in Kenya is also concentrated on the coast and in the important trading centres of Mombasa, Malind and Lamu. The Muslim minority in Uganda is concentrated in the southern part of the country and in Kampala, the capital; the majority are Swahili or African Muslims (Ofcansky 1996). In Rwanda and Burundi, the practice of Islam is relatively new, introduced only in the 1900s, and Muslims in both countries count for less than 5 per cent of the total populations of six million in Burundi and seven million in Rwanda (Population Reference Bureau 2000). Most Muslims in these two countries either converted to Islam themselves, or are the children or grandchildren of converts (Kagabo 1988).

Other than along the Swahili coast, Islam in Eastern and Central Africa is largely an urban religion, with sections of major cities identified as Muslim neighbourhoods. Although there are considerable Muslim populations in this region, the individual communities are fragmented, generally either integrated into the larger population or living as separate communities.

Most indigenous African Muslims in the region are Sunnis. There is also a large Asian population, principally Shi'ite (Thobani 1984). Most of the Asians are the descendants of some 32,000 Indians who came to East Africa from 1896 to 1901 as indentured labourers working on the British construction of the Uganda Railway (Ofcansky 1996). Another group of Asians descend from the Indian traders who have been active along the coast since the fifteenth century, although it was not until the late nineteenth century that a significant number of Indians settled in East Africa. The earliest Indian settlers lived and prospered on the island of Zanzibar under the Sultan. When the Sultan first arrived in Zanzibar, there were only 300 to 400 Indians on the island. By 1866, this number had grown to 6,000 (Ofcansky 1996).

Legal Practices and Institutions

Legal codes within East Africa vary, although all give some form of recognition to Islam. These legal recognitions often date back to the colonial era. For example, in 1895 the British colonial government and the Sultan of Zanzibar reached an agreement to recognize and 'preserve the Islamic way of life' (Oded 2000).

In Kenya, the British implemented the familiar triple court system: common law courts, customary or traditional courts and Islamic Shari'a courts. The Kenyan government abolished formal local customary courts in 1967, although anecdotal evidence shows that many people still employ traditional judicial mechanisms at the local level. If both parties to a case are Muslim, then the dispute is adjudicated in Islamic courts and governed by Islamic law. Women have traditionally been excluded from Islamic offices such as judge or prayer leader (Strobel 1979). If one party is non-Muslim, then the case falls under the jurisdiction of the common law courts. This system was codified in the 1963 Constitution, although debates continue around consolidating the three courts into one common system.

In Tanzania, the mostly non-Islamic mainland and the Muslim-dominated island of Zanzibar have separate legislative, executive and judicial institutions. Except for the issue of marriage, both the mainland and Zanzibar have dual legal systems, consisting of statutory/civil laws and religious/customary laws. In 1971, the Marriage Act consolidated family law under a uniform code, which still recognizes Islamic unions and the right to polygamy. However, Zanzibar is exempt from this uniform code and still maintains separate judicial administration for Muslims. In addition, Tanzania enforces affirmative action for women (applying to both Muslim and non-Muslim women), which calls for 25 per cent female representation at the local levels and 15 per cent female representation in parliament (Mukangara and Koda 1997).

Seclusion of Women / Purdah

Practices of purdah vary greatly from group to group, ranging from little more than a nod to modesty in some areas to nearly complete seclusion among the coastal upper classes. On the Swahili coast, from Kenya south through Tanzania, and including Zanzibar and other islands off the coast, women's seclusion and modesty have traditionally been extremely important, particularly among the upper classes (Sims 1984).

In Mombasa, Kenya, an Islamic city, class is closely linked with the level of purdah, which in turn is closely linked with women's participation in making decisions in the society. A movement in the early twentieth century illustrates this connection (Strobel 1976). Before the 1920s, upper-class Muslim women maintained very strict seclusion. Poorer women, particularly those of slave status, did not. Their position in society required that they work. At the same time, it allowed them certain liberties that their wealthier counterparts did not enjoy. Among the activities engaged in by these women were certain dance performances at ceremonial gatherings. These dancers were not covered up and they were watched by everyone, including men. In the 1920s, young women of the upper classes began forming dance groups, performing only in sheltered settings where men were not present. But, partially due to a fierce competition between these groups, they gradually moved into more and more public settings, eventually performing publicly and without their traditional coverings. When the dance craze died out, the two primary dance groups became women's organizations, struggling for certain changes in women's position in society. Through this process, a generation of women grew accustomed to being out in public, deciding what they wanted and expressing their own perspectives.

On the whole, the required level of seclusion depends on a variety of factors, including class, ethnicity and local community practices. However, a concern for women's modesty remains. On the Swahili coast, even women who are not secluded generally wear a full black robe that covers their other clothes when they go out in public. Again, the level of seclusion is dependent on local context. The anthropologist Peter C. Forster points out that Muslim women on Mafia Island are allowed greater social participation, even attending the main mosque with men. However, among the nearby coastal Zaramo, women's public participation – religious, political and economic – is very limited (Forster 1995). The importance of preserving women's modesty is also legally recognized is some areas. For example, in Kenya, married women are exempted from being photographed for national identity cards, and schoolgirls in state schools are allowed to remain veiled (Freeman 1993).

Regardless of what women must wear, there is some evidence of women's participation in public life. In Kenya, there are two active Muslim women's associations that seek better education and training for women, but within a model of seclusion of women (Strobel 1976). Also, in 1992, a Muslim woman ran for parliament for the Mombasa district, backing her claim to a right to run for office on Islam, and challenging her critics to 'read the holy book afresh' (Tripp 1996: 303). In Tanzania, the leaders of the Tanzanian Media Women's Association are mostly Muslim, although it is not a specifically Islamic organization (Tripp 1996). This organization has spoken out on questions of inheritance laws, domestic violence and teen pregnancy, and has done educational work on starting non-governmental organizations. Nevertheless, it appears that some Muslim Tanzanian women are still cut off from the public sector as a result of religious concerns.

Theoretically, a Ugandan woman married under Shari'a law is required to keep even her face covered in public (Tamale and Okumu-Wengi 1995). Similarly, she is not to speak in public without being asked to, nor is she to challenge her husband's opinions. The existence and success of the Uganda Muslim Women's Association suggests that these prescriptions are not universally enforced. The wives of wealthy men, however, are usually nearly completely secluded. They do not go out in public except to go to the mosque on Fridays, and no men outside their families see them at any other time.

Female circumcision (excision of the clitoris and, in some places, infibulation) is widespread in Kenya, Tanzania and parts of Uganda. Although Tanzania has prohibited the practice, there is little enforcement (M2 Presswire 2000; Hosken 1982).

Overall, women in East Africa, both Muslim and non-Muslim, are disadvantaged and face multiple obstacles compared to men. The overwhelming obstacle is poverty. All of the countries except Kenya rank in the low human development category in the 1999 *Human Development Report* published by the United Nations Development Programme. When taking gender empowerment (a UNDP measure that accounts for women's social options, status and power) into consideration, all – again except Kenya – rank in the bottom 20 countries in the world (UNDP 1999). The difficulty in obtaining quality education is also a major obstacle for East African women. For example, in Tanzania, women accounted for only 37 per cent of all students registered in public secondary schools from 1982 to 1990 (Rwebangira 1996).

Family in the Region

The lineage patterns in this region differ widely, even among culturally and ethnically similar groups. The most consistent are the Asians, who are almost exclusively patrilineal (Thobani 1984). The vast majority of Swahili are also patrilineal (Middleton 1992). The Bantu groups in central Tanzania, about half of whom are Muslims, tend to be matrilineal (Brain 1984). In recent years, it appears that in some areas this pattern has been changing towards an emphasis on paternal ties. The northern Bantu population, about one-third of whom profess Islam, is mostly patrilineal (Brain 1984). However, in one cluster of northern Bantu groups, where Muslims make up about half the population, descent follows maternal lines (Kikopa 1981). For example, the Luguru, an ethnic group in northeastern Tanzania that is approximately 85 per cent Muslim, are matrilineal (Olson 1996). However, government regulations concerning land, property and personal status within the family are increasingly shifting family organization towards patrilineal patterns.

Marriage

Both the Asians and the Swahili in East and Central Africa practise some form of paternal first-cousin marriage, although it appears to be more common among the Swahili (Thobani 1984; Middleton 1992). The upper-class Swahili of the region traditionally encouraged first-cousin marriage, whereas among the Swahili slave population, it was standard to marry either a slave of the same slave-owner, or a slave of a family tied to that slave-owner by marriage (Romero 1988).

In Tanzania, a 1971 law incorporated customary and religious marriage into a uniform marriage code, giving both customary and Islamic marriages state sanction, but also subjecting them to state regulations, which include protections for women (Freeman 1993). The law stipulates that:

- marriages must be registered as monogamous or polygynous and cannot be changed; however, marriages are not considered invalid if they are not registered;
- marriage must be voluntary by both the man and woman, theoretically prohibiting forced or arranged marriages;
- women who cohabit with a man for two years have the legal rights of wives;
- bridewealth is no longer a requirement for a marriage to be legal; and
- corporal punishment by either spouse is outlawed (Bryceson 1995).

The Tanzanian government recognizes four types of marriages: 1) monogamous Christian marriage; 2) polygynous Muslim marriages; 3) civil marriages (which are understood to be potentially polygynous); and 4) traditional/customary marriages (which are also understood to be potentially polygynous) (Mukangara and Koda 1997). However, the Marriage Act explicitly states that it takes precedence over both Islamic and customary law in regulation of all four types of marriage (Rwebangira 1996). The Marriage Act guarantees women's rights to property acquired on her own, as well as rights to matrimonial assets. Furthermore, the law requires judges to take domestic activities into account as contributions to marital assets (Mukangara and Koda 1997). Despite these legal protections, Felician Tungaraza argues that the law has not produced consistent or effective results. Most people fail to register marriage, and few women are financially or socially able to pursue court remedies. When women do go to court, judges with traditional attitudes towards women seldom uphold or enforce the women's rights outlined in the law (Tungaraza 1995).

Among the matrilineal Luguru in Tanzania, cross-cousin marriages are traditionally the ideal. It is unclear whether this is due to religious considerations or to the desire to keep land firmly within a given lineage (Kikopa 1981). Many groups in Uganda, both Islamic and non-Islamic, practise the levirate, by which the brothers of a deceased husband inherit his widows as their wives (US Department of State 1998b). Among Muslims in Rwanda and Burundi, the only preference among marriage partners seems to be for another Muslim, as might be expected, given how small the communities are (Kagabo 1988).

Throughout the region, the average age for a woman's first marriage is between 19 and 22. Each of the countries has laws concerning the minimum age for marriage, generally around 15 for girls. In practice, these age minimums vary by custom and religion, with Muslim girls often marrying younger than their contemporaries. For example, in Uganda, the minimum marriage ages for those entering customary unions are 16 for girls and 18 for boys. However, in Islamic unions in Uganda, girls can be married after entering puberty, which is usually around 13 or 14 (Fiedler 1998). Similarly, on the coastal islands, particularly among the poor, girls are marriageable shortly after reaching puberty (Romero 1988). In Tanzania, the minimum marriage age for girls is 15, although the average age of marriage in 1994 was 23 for women and 25 for men (Mukangara and Koda 1997).

The conflict between education and early marriage has become a public debate in Tanzania (Mnzavas 1997). In 1997, an arranged marriage under Islamic law between a member of parliament and a girl still in school was highly publicized. Human rights advocates and lawyers began calling for a law banning marriages of schoolgirls as well as for increased enforcement of the 1978 Education Act, which requires parents and the government to provide seven years of compulsory education up to the age of 13. Robert Makaramba, a law faculty member at the University of Dar es Salaam, argues that even if Islamic marriage laws allow for marriages of young girls, the Education Act prohibits such marriages. Early marriage is one of the factors contributing to Tanzanian women's low literacy rates; the enrolment ratio of girls to boys declines with each year in school, with a primary school drop-out rate of 30–40 per cent for girls (US Department of State 1998a).

In Kenya, girls who are the children of Islamic or customary marriages can be legally married off by their guardian before puberty (Mucai-Kattambo et al. 1995). The girl then has the right to repudiate the marriage upon reaching puberty. The practice of child marriages is diminishing and there is a general sense that early marriage is not good for girls. Some of the girls who leave their first marriage at puberty have started returning to school to finish their education.

Dowry and Brideprice

Traditional Shari'a law requires that the dower (*mahr*) be paid if a marriage contract is to be considered valid. Further, once paid, the dower is considered the sole property of the woman to use any way she sees fit. Among Asians in East Africa, dowry is considered a necessary requirement for marriage (Thobani 1984). They also often pre-arrange alimony at the same time, in case of divorce.

Among the coastal Swahili and the matrilineal Luguru of mainland Tanzania, it is customary for the groom to provide two payments. The first payment is representative of the Islamic *mahr* and is given to the bride. In the case of the Luguru, this payment is often given by the bride to her maternal grandmother (Kikopa 1981). The second payment is more of a customary African practice of providing a brideprice for the bride's family (Romero 1988). The bride's family, in turn, is expected to provide furniture and other household necessities for the newly married couple. The brideprice is sometimes forgone if the bride is marrying into a prestigious family in the religious community (Romero 1988). As is typical of many Islamic and non-Islamic East African groups, if the couple divorces, the brideprice is not returned to the groom.

In Rwanda and Burundi, the future husband must pay brideprice to the bride's male guardian; again, this is representative of traditional African marriage patterns (Kagabo 1988). The same practice is found among the Christians, which is not surprising given that many families include both Muslims and Christians.

Divorce

Divorce practices seem to be determined largely by the customs of each country. However, frequently the law has different requirements for Muslims or people married under customary law and for those married under civil law. Islamic family law in the region recognizes three methods of divorce or marriage dissolution: 1) *talaq* or repudiation by the husband; 2) *khula* or *mubaraat*, separation by mutual agreement; and 3) *tafriq*, a judicial order of separation. In addition, Islamic courts require maintenance for women during their *'idda* (waiting period) after divorce (Nasir 1990).

In Kenya, if a couple is married under Shari'a law, the husband can divorce his wife by *talaq* (Mucai-Kattambo et al. 1995). After a divorce, the woman has a right to maintenance for a three-month period. In order to divorce his wife, a man does not have to give any reason; in contrast, a woman may only initiate a divorce for three reasons: her husband's inability to consummate the marriage; his failure to provide for her; and, if the woman was married as a child, she can repudiate her husband when she reaches puberty (Mucai-Kattambo et al. 1995). In the 1970s, legislation was introduced into parliament that would have allowed a woman to seek a divorce in the case of irreparable breakdown in a marriage. This bill, which was supported by male Muslim leaders but opposed by the Muslim Women's Association, was not passed (Strobel 1976).

In Tanzania, *talaq* is the most common way for a man to announce that he wants a divorce (Kikopa 1981). A divorce is not finalized, however, until the couple has met with the state-run Marriage Conciliatory Board and there has been a court decree of divorce. It appears that divorced women do not face social pressure to remarry. The 1971 Marriage Act requires that all divorces be made final in civil court. The goal of this requirement was to decrease the rate of divorce. However, the legal requirements for obtaining divorce have not had this effect. As Tungaraza points out, 1.43 per cent of the population aged ten and above was divorced in 1978; by 1988, this had grown close to 4 per cent (1995). The marriage law provides no clear-cut provision for the division of matrimonial assets, and many unemployed women end up with nothing (M2 Presswire 1998). Further, because many marriages are not initially registered and subsequently not officially dissolved, women have little basis for legal demands of marital property or legal remarriage (Freeman 1993).

For the Luguru, until the 1970s, divorce was a simple and common matter, initiated by both men and women (Kikopa 1981). It appears that changes in Tanzanian law, rather than adherence to Islam, have made divorce more difficult for Luguru women to obtain. In Uganda divorce by repudiation is allowed and is quite common (Tamale and Okumu-Wengi 1995). Muslim women basically have no statutory right in Uganda to maintenance after the divorce, although on occasion they can get orders from the court requiring it. Even when an order is obtained, the sums are insignificant and rarely collected. Ugandan civil law allows men to divorce their wives on the grounds of adultery, while women must prove that their husbands are guilty of at least two marriage offences to be granted a divorce (Freeman 1993).

The informality of Muslim weddings in Rwanda and Burundi is matched by a lack of ceremony for divorce. Frequently couples just separate and remain married but do not see each other for years or even decades (Kagabo 1988). Sometimes even close family members do not know whether a couple is actually divorced or not. Women are not subjected to strong societal pressures to remarry.

Polygyny

Throughout the region, laws provide for a variety of marriage regimes, usually civil, customary and Islamic, but the way in which individuals negotiate through these systems differs from country to country. Most African societies are traditionally polygynous, although the practice declined as a result of colonization and conversion to Christianity (Tungaraza 1995).

The two largest Muslim majority groups in the region, Asians and Swahili, have two very distinct patterns of marriage. The Asian populations allow for polygyny, but rarely actually practise it (Thobani 1984). In Swahili culture, polygyny is common, although it is unusual for a man to have four wives (Sims 1984). Among men who do have more than one wife, there is little uniformity of living arrangements. Each wife may live separately from the others and from her husband, who circulates between his wives' households, or they may all live together, with the first wife being treated as an elder.

In Tanzania, if the groom is Muslim, the couple may choose either the civil or the Islamic marriage regime (Kikopa 1981). If they choose the Islamic model, it is assumed that the marriage is either polygynous or potentially so. The Luguru, the matrilineal Muslim group discussed above, also practise polygyny (Kikopa 1981). Traditionally, if a Luguru man married more than one woman, each wife lived on the land of her own lineage, and the husband visited each in turn. Government policies in the 1970s encouraged both men and women to be more involved in the economic life of a specific village, resulting in a change to the tradition of polygynous men moving between their wives. Thus polygynous men and their wives began residing in the same household and women therefore had to leave their own lineage's land. It is unclear how government changes since that time have affected the residence choices of the Luguru.

Kenyan laws regulate Islamic and customary marriages together, treating them in largely the same way. In both systems polygyny is legal. Nevertheless, there are certain differences in the way the state relates to first wives and subsequent wives, often discriminating against the latter (Mucai-Kattambo et al. 1995). For example, payments for national health insurance are ordinarily taken out of a man's salary for both himself and his wife. If, however, a man has two wives, the second wife's insurance premiums are not automatically deducted from her husband's salary, leaving her uncovered by the health service. Although it is possible to ask for her payments to be deducted as well, this rarely happens, a problem attributed to limited knowledge of the insurance system (Mucai-Kattambo et al. 1995). It is not clear which of the spouses has the ability or the responsibility to ensure that the wives are all covered by health insurance.

Ugandan law assumes that all marriages entered into by Muslims are governed by Shari'a and allows for polygyny, whatever the couple's individual preferences may be (Tamale and Okumu-Wengi 1995). Approximately 40–50 per cent of all unions in Uganda are polygynous (Women's Watch 1998). Further, a wife has no legal status to prevent her husband from taking another wife (US Department of State 1998b). Recently, in response to the AIDS epidemic, the Ugandan parliament proposed limiting polygyny to two wives and then only if the first wife was barren and consented to the second marriage. The loudest outcry against the proposed law came from the Muslim population (All Africa News Service 1998). They argued that polygyny was part of their religion and that even if they did not actually practise it, they should be allowed to do so if they chose. They also announced that they would ignore the provision if it passed into law.

Rwandans, who are predominantly Christian (only about 1 or 2 per cent of the population is Muslim), generally frown on polygyny. However, among the Muslims, polygyny is almost universally practised by those men who can afford to have multiple wives (Kagabo 1988). Marriages in the Muslim community have traditionally not been registered with the state and are sometimes carried out without an imam. It appears that Muslims have begun marrying more in accordance with Rwandan law since the 1970s (Kagabo 1988). It should be noted, however, that because there are so few Muslim Rwandans, information about them is necessarily anecdotal.

Custody of Children

Custody practice is clearest in Uganda, where the father has custody rights for any child no longer breast-feeding (Tamale and Okumu-Wengi 1995). When women do retain custody, Ugandan civil law entitles women to 2,000 Ugandan shillings per month per child in maintenance, but women are rarely able to collect this fee (Fiedler 1998).

In Tanzania, custody is governed by civil law, regardless of the type of marriage. The 1963 Law of Persons Act declared that children born inside marriage belonged to the father (Rwebangira 1996). However, the 1971 Marriage Act requires custody to be decided in the best interest of the child, but routinely defers to custom in individual cases (Freeman 1993). Prior to 1971, custody of Muslim children was administered under Islamic law; however, the uniform codification of the Marriage Act included child custody regulations. Practically, if a woman files for custody, the father will not contest the motions. However, in the absence of contestation, the father generally gets custody. Further, the Marriage Act provides that a father is responsible for the maintenance of children until 18 years of age, regardless of custody (Rwebangira 1996).

Custody patterns also vary depending on local lineage patterns. Among the matrilineal Muslims, the child belongs to his or her mother and her lineage, and remains with the mother in case of divorce. If the mother dies, the child still remains with the members of the matriline and is usually maintained by a maternal uncle (Kikopa 1981).

While most family laws addressing children assume a married context, the predominantly Muslim island of Zanzibar also regulates the conception of illegitimate children. Although not directly related to child custody, a law enacted in the 1960s makes it a criminal offence to conceive a child outside marriage (Mbogora 1999). The maximum penalty for this crime is two years' imprisonment for women and up to five years' imprisonment for men. Further, all methods of family planning, including condoms, are prohibited in Zanzibar and also subject to criminal prosecution. These laws do not apply to the mainland of Tanzania.

Inheritance / Land Rights

Throughout Eastern and Central Africa, customary practices frequently override laws, both statutory and Islamic, that in theory protect women's right to inherit.

In Kenya, Muslims are exempt from the national Law of Succession Act, which provides for equal inheritance between men and women (Mucai-Kattambo et al. 1995). Instead, Muslims inherit according to Qur'anic prescriptions. In terms of property rights more generally, a married couple does officially have equal ownership of most kinds of property, whatever marriage regime they have chosen. However, ownership rights may not be equal in practice, as fewer women have access to legal protection of those rights due to financial hardships or lack of education about their rights (Mucai-Kattambo et al. 1995). Further, married women are required to have the authorization of their husbands when buying land (FEMNET 1992). Muslim women protested against a proposed civil rights bill in 2000 that would have given equal inheritance rights to sons and daughters, arguing that the bill would contravene Shari'a (Astill 2000).

In Tanzania, inheritance is governed by three different legal frameworks: customary, Islamic and statutory. Customary laws are applied in most inheritance cases involving Africans. Custom differs between ethnic groups, but the widow is generally excluded (Rwebangira and Mukogoye 1995). While daughters in non-Muslim patrilineal groups almost never inherit land, or inherit only use rights, those in Muslim communities may fare better (Kikopa 1981). In fact, as Mukangara and Koda argue, Muslim women have greater rights to inheritance claims if the estate is administered under Islamic law than if it is administered under customary law. Under Islamic inheritance law, wives are entitled to one-fourth of the assets if the couple has no children, and one-eighth if children are present. If a man had more than one wife, these shares are divided equally among the wives (Nasir 1990). Although Tanzanian law assumes that all Muslims are married under Shari'a law, it makes the opposite assumption about inheritance. For Shari'a inheritance law to apply, it must be shown that the deceased was a Muslim, that he or she had left oral or written instructions that Islamic law should govern the distribution of the estate, and that the person lived in a way that demonstrated an intent that the estate be divided according to Islamic prescriptions (Kikopa 1981). If any of these conditions is judged to be missing, customary law applies. Although the Tanzanian constitution prohibits discrimination based on sex or religion, these protections are not enforced in cases of customary inheritance. Moreover, the 1971 Marriage Act provides for inheritance and property rights for women. However, as stated earlier, application of these provisions depends on the status and wishes of the head of the household. As a result, women's legal inheritance rights are commonly ignored, particularly in rural areas (US Department of State 1998a).

The Luguru provide one clear example of customary inheritance law in a Muslim community. Clearly, as the Luguru have a matrilineal society, their law should be viewed not as representative of customary law of inheritance throughout the country, but merely as one example. In the past, land belonged to the lineage, and each member of the lineage had the right to live on and cultivate the land (Kikopa 1981). In the case of divorce or death, the land reverted to the lineage. If there were no children, the house, as the property of the couple, would be demolished and the materials divided up between the two families. Houses are no longer destroyed; rather, whichever spouse remains in the house compensates the other (or his or her lineage) for building materials. Although the practice is illegal, it appears that when a woman's husband dies, frequently the deceased husband's relatives will force the widow out of the house without any compensation at all. If a man acquires property other than the land of his or his wife's lineages, on his death it is inherited by his sister or, if he has no sister, his wife. On the death of this woman (the sister or the wife), the inheritance passes to her sons, and on their deaths to her daughters (Rwebangira and Mukogoye 1995). There is a trend in recent years, however, for inheritance to be more patrilineal, with a man's children inheriting from him directly, often with a bias towards the sons.

Ugandan law allows women married under Shari'a law to inherit according to Islamic prescriptions (Tamale and Okumu-Wengi 1995). However, in Uganda customary practices usually take precedence over either civil or religious laws, and women are, for the most part, excluded from inheriting or owning property generally.

Bibliography

All Africa News Service (1998) 'Polygamy contributing to AIDS deaths in Uganda', *Africa News*, 6 April.

Astill, J. (2000) 'Kenyan leaders to block "divisive" Equal Rights Bill', *Guardian*, 21 November.

Brain, J. (1984) 'Bantu, Central Tanzanian', in R. V. Weekes (ed.), *Muslim Peoples: A World Ethnographic Survey*, 2nd edn, Vol. 1, Westport, CT: Greenwood Press, pp. 101–3.

Bryceson, D. F. (1995) 'Gender relations in rural Tanzania: power politics or cultural consensus?', in C. Creighton and C. K. Omari (eds), *Gender, Family and Household in Tanzania*, Aldershot, UK: Ashgate Publishing, pp. 37–9.

FEMNET (1992) *Country Summaries*, Harare: African Women's Development and Communication Network (FEMNET).

Fiedler, A. A. (1998) 'Women–Uganda: Uganda debates marital rights … and wrongs', *Interpress News Service*, 8 December.

Forster, P. G. (1995) 'Anthropological studies of kinship in Tanzania', in C. Creighton and C. K. Omari (eds), *Gender, Family and Household in Tanzania*, Aldershot, UK: Ashgate Publishing, pp. 70–117.

Freeman, M. (1993) *Human Rights in the Family*, Minneapolis: International Women's Rights Action Watch, Humphrey Institute.

Hosken, F. P. (1982) *The Hosken Report*, 3rd edn, Lexington, MA: Women's International Network News.

Kagabo, J. H. (1988) *L'Islam et les Swahili au Rwanda*, Paris: Ecole des Hautes Etudes en Sciences Sociales.

Kikopa, J. R. (1981) *Law and the Status of Women in Tanzania*, Addis Ababa: African Training and Research Centre for Women.

M2 Presswire (1998) 'UN: Tanzanian Report before Women's Anti-Discrimination Committee', *M2 Presswire*, 2 July, M2 Communications.

Martin, B. G. (1986) 'The spread of Islam', in P. M. Martin and P. O'Meara (eds), *Africa*, 2nd edn, Bloomington, IN: Indiana University Press, pp. 87–102.

Mbogora, A. (1999) 'Rights in Tanzania: jail terms for pregnancy out of wedlock', *Interpress Service*, 20 January.

Middleton, J. (1992) *The World of the Swahili: An African Mercantile Civilization*, New Haven, CT: Yale University Press.

Mnzavas, A. (1997) 'Tanzania: call for a ban on child marriages', *Interpress Service*, 17 September.

Mucai-Kattambo, V., J. W. Kabeberi-Macharia and Patricia Kameri-Mbote (1995) 'Law and the status of women in Kenya', in J. W. Kabeberi-Macharia (ed.), *Women, Laws, Customs and Practices in East Africa: Laying the Foundation*, Nairobi: Women and Law in East Africa, pp. 80–109.

Mukangara, F. and B. Koda (1997) *Beyond Inequalities: Women in Tanzania*, Dar es Salaam: Tanzania Gender Networking Programme and Southern African Research and Documentation Centre.

Nasir, J. J. (1990) *The Islamic Law of Personal Status*, 2nd edn, London: Graham and Trotman.

Oded, A. (1984) 'Ganda', in R. V. Weekes (ed.), *Muslim Peoples: A World Ethnographic Survey*, 2nd edn, Vol. 1, Westport, CT: Greenwood Press, pp. 271–7.

— (2000) *Islam and Politics in Kenya*, Boulder, CO: Lynne Rienner Publishers.

Ofcansky, T. P. (1996) *Uganda: Tarnished Pearl of Africa*, Boulder CO: Westview Press.

Olson, J. S. (1996) *The Peoples of Africa: An Ethnohistorical Dictionary*, Westport, CT: Greenwood Press.

Population Reference Bureau, *2000*, <http://www.prb.org/>

Romero, P. (1988) 'Mama Khadija: a life history as an example of family history', in P. Romero, *Life Histories of African Women*, Atlantic Highlands, NJ: Ashfield Press, pp. 140–58.

Rwebangira, M. K. (1996) *The Legal Status of Women and Poverty in Tanzania*, Uppsala, Sweden: Nordiska Afrikainstitutet.

Rwebangira, M. and M. C. Mukogoye (1995) *The Law of Inheritance in Tanzania*, Nairobi: Women and Law in East Africa.

Sims, M. (1984) 'Swahili', in R. V. Weekes (ed.), *Muslim Peoples: A World Ethnographic Survey*, 2nd edn, Vol. 2, Westport, CT: Greenwood Press, pp. 732–8.

Strobel, M. (1976) 'From Lelemama to lobbying: women's associations in Mombasa, Kenya', in N. J. Hafkin and E. G. Bay (eds), *Women in Africa: Studies in Social and Economic Change*, Stanford, CA: Stanford University Press, pp. 183–211.

— (1979) *Muslim Women in Mombassa, 1890–1975*, New Haven, CT: Yale University Press.

Tamale, S. and J. Okumu-Wengi (1995) 'The legal status of women in Uganda', in J. W. Kabeberi-Macharia (ed.), *Women, Laws, Customs and Practices in East Africa: Laying the Foundation*, Nairobi: Women and Law in East Africa, pp. 24–45.

Thobani, A. H. (1984) 'Asians of East Africa', in R. V. Weekes (ed.), *Muslim Peoples: A World Ethnographic Survey*, 2nd edn, Vol. 1, Westport, CT: Greenwood Press, pp. 54–8.

Tripp, A. M. (1996) 'Urban women's movements and political liberalization in East Africa', in K. Sheldon (ed.), *Courtyards, Markets, City Streets: Urban Women in Africa*, Boulder, CO: Westview Press, pp. 285–308.

Tungaraza, F. S. K. (1995) 'The family and social policy in Tanzania', in C. Creighton and C. K. Omari (eds), *Gender, Family and Household in Tanzania*, Aldershot, UK: Ashgate Publishing, pp. 299–316.

United Nations Development Programme (1999) *1999 Human Development Report*, New York: United Nations Development Programme.

US Department of State (1998a) *Tanzania Country Report for Human Rights Practices for 1998*, Washington, DC: United States Government.

— (1998b) *Uganda Country Report for Human Rights Practices for 1998*, Washington, DC: United States Government.

2 Legal Profiles

KENYA, Republic of

Legal history European colonial interest in Kenya began with Portuguese efforts to establish safe ports in the area of Mombasa from 1498. The Omanis captured Mombasa in 1696. British interests in the East African region in the mid- to late nineteenth century led to the formation of the British East Africa Company. In 1895, within a decade of the founding of the East Africa Company, the area from the coast to the Rift Valley was declared the British East Africa Protectorate. Kenya gained independence in June 1963. Under the British protectorate, Kenya had parallel legal systems with African courts applying customary law, and appeals lying with the African Appeal Court, then with the District Officer and then a Court of Review. Muslim personal law was applied by Courts of *Liwalis*, *Mudirs* and *Qadis'*, with appeals lying with the Supreme Court (renamed the High Court after independence). The process of integrating the judicial system began in 1962, when powers of administrative officers to review African Courts' proceedings were transferred to magistrates. The process was completed by the passage of two acts in 1967. The Magistrates' Courts Act 1967 abolished African Courts and the Court of Review and established District and Resident Magistrates' Courts and a High Court. The *Qadis'* Courts Act 1967 established six *Qadis'* Courts for the application of Muslim personal status law.

In 1967, two presidentially appointed commissions began looking into marriage and divorce law and inheritance law. The commissions produced drafts of uniform family and inheritance codes to replace the existing customary, statutory, Islamic and Hindu laws then in force. The commission dealing with inheritance laws recommended a uniform code applicable with certain exceptions for customary laws. The bill based on its recommendations led to much heated debate. Criticisms included that the proposed law was too foreign, anti-Muslim, and afforded too many rights to women and illegitimate children. The bill was eventually passed in 1972. The marriage and divorce laws commission produced a draft code that was as uniform as the commission deemed feasible, but since the 1970s efforts to enact a uniform marriage law have been unsuccessful. Marriage law continues to be governed by several regimes: civil, Christian, Hindu and Muslim marriages are governed by separate legislation and communal laws, and customary law marriages are also afforded official recognition.

The protectorate-era legislation relating to the application of Muslim personal law has been retained. The acts in force basically afford recognition to marriages solemnized under Islamic law, provide for the registration of Muslim marriages and divorces, delineate the jurisdiction and procedure of *Qadis'* Courts and instruct the application of the principles of personal law applicable to the parties involved, without substantive codification of that law.

Schools of *fiqh* Kenya has a very diverse Muslim population due to Arab and South Asian settlement, local conversion and intermarriage, and thus various schools are represented. The majority are Shafi'i, and there are also sizeable Hanafi communities as well as Ja'fari, Isma'ili, Zaydi and Ahmadi minority communities.

Constitutional status of Islam(ic law) The Constitution was adopted on 12 December 1963, and has been amended several times, most notably in 1964, when Kenya became a republic, and in 1991, when a multiparty system was restored. The Constitution does not provide for any official state religion. Article 66(1) to (5) provides for the establishment of *Qadis'* Courts.

Court system Local courts applying customary law were abolished in 1967, when reform and unification of the judiciary was completed. There are four levels of courts: Resident and District Magistrates' Courts (1st, 2nd and 3rd classes), Senior Resident and Chief Magistrates' Courts; a High Court, and the Court of Appeal. Islamic law is applied by *Qadis'* Courts, where 'all the parties profess the Muslim religion' in suits relating to 'questions of Muslim law relating to personal status, marriage, divorce or inheritance'. There are eight *Qadis'* Courts in Kenya, presided over by a Chief *Qadi* or a *qadi* appointed by the Judicial Services Commission. Appeals lie to the High Court, sitting with the Chief *Qadi* or two other *qadis* as assessor(s).

Notable features The minimum marriage age is governed by the Marriage Act for statutory marriages (requiring parties to be 16 years of age) and by the relevant personal laws applicable; for Muslims, neither the Mohammedan Marriage, Divorce and Succession Act nor the Mohammedan Marriage

Registration Act provides a specified minimum age. The applicable legislation refers only to Muslim law and does not specify any particular school. Although there are provisions for marriage registration, registration does not define validity and marriages conducted under statutory (includes the Marriage Act as well as the African Christian Marriage Act), customary, Muslim and Hindu law are all recognized. Polygyny is governed by classical law. Although it is a criminal offence to marry under statutory law and contract a subsequent marriage under Islamic or customary law, there are no legislative restrictions on polygyny outside the statutory regime.

Talaq and judicial divorce are governed by classical law, as are post-divorce maintenance provisions. In matters of child custody and guardianship, *Qadis'* Courts generally grant custody to the mother until the age of seven years for boys and 14 for girls, at which point custody reverts to the father. The statutory legislation applicable (the Guardianship of Infants Act) directs that courts must adjudicate with the interests of the ward as the primary consideration, and an increasing number of women are applying to the regular court system, where custody over boys and girls under 16 is generally awarded to the mother.

Under the Law of Succession Act 1981, uniform legislation on intestate succession was made applicable to all Kenyans, with specific exemptions for the application of customary laws; a Muslim testator could provide in his/her will that the estate should devolve according to Islamic law. In 1990, an amendment was passed inserting an exemption for Muslims.

Law/case reporting system   Case reporting is through the *Kenya Law Reports*, *Kenya Appeal Reports* and *Kenya Court of Appeal Decisions*.

International conventions (with relevant reservations)   Kenya acceded to the ICCPR and ICESCR in 1972, with a reservation to Article 10(2) of the ICESCR. Kenya acceded to the CEDAW in 1984, without reservations. Kenya signed and ratified the CRC in 1990, without reservations.

Background and sources
Anderson, J. N. D. (1954) *Islamic Law in Africa*, London: HMSO.

Butegwa, F. (1989) 'Kenyan women's awareness of their rights: report of a field study', in A. M. Mbeo and O. Ooko-Ombaka (eds), *Women and Law in Kenya: Perspectives and Emerging Issues*, Nairobi: Public Law Institute, pp. 53–70.

Center for Reproductive Law and Policy and International Federation of Women Lawyers (1997) 'Kenya', in *Women of the World: Laws and Policies Affecting their Reproductive Lives – Anglophone Africa*, New York: Center for Reproductive Law and Policy and International Federation of Women Lawyers (Kenya Chapter).

Hirsch, S. (1998) *Pronouncing and Persevering: Gender and the Discourses of Disputing in an African Islamic Court*, Chicago, IL: University of Chicago Press.

Mwangi, K. (1995) 'The application and development of Shari'a in Kenya: 1895–1990', in M. Bakari and S. S. Yahya (eds), *Islam in Kenya: Proceedings of the National Seminar on Contemporary Islam in Kenya* (1994, Mombasa, Kenya), Nairobi: Mewa Publications, pp. 252–9.

Redden, K. R. (1990) 'Kenya', in K. R. Redden (ed.), *Modern Legal Systems Cyclopedia*, Vol. 6, Buffalo, NY: Hein.

Rubin, N. N. and E. Cotran (eds) (1967–1970) *Annual Survey of African Law*, Vols 1–4, London: Frank Cass.

TANZANIA, United Republic of

Legal history The Bantu ancestors of the majority of the present-day Tanzanian population settled in the region in approximately 500 CE. Arab settlers in the coastal regions introduced Islam to the region in the ninth and tenth centuries. European interest in the region began to increase with Portuguese explorers arriving in the region in the late fifteenth century, although the Portuguese never established settlements in Tanzania. In the late nineteenth century, Germany gained increasing control over the area from the coast inland to Ruanda and Urundi, establishing the Protectorate of German East Africa. Soon after, in 1890, the islands of Zanzibar and Pemba were declared a British Protectorate. Following World War I, the League of Nations extended the British mandate to Tanganyika, while other parts of German East Africa (Rwanda and Burundi) were placed under a Belgian protectorate. A legislative council was established in 1926 and Tanganyika became a UN trust territory in 1946. The legislative council was expanded over the next decade in order to provide equal representation to Africans, Asians and Europeans. The Tanganyikan African National Union (TANU), established by Julius Nyerere in 1954, began calling for increasing African representation and by the late 1950s for full independence. TANU's appeal was clear from elections held in 1958 and 1960, and Tanganyika achieved its independence in December 1961, becoming a republic one year later. Zanzibar achieved independence in 1963, and the Sultan was overthrown the following year. The two states unified in April 1964 to form the United Republic of Tanzania. Both independent states had a single-party system and the two parties eventually merged to form the Chama Cha Mapinduzi (CCM). Under increasing internal and international pressure, the Tanzanian government introduced constitutional reforms permitting the establishment of opposition parties in 1992.

Under the federal agreement unifying Tanganyika and Zanzibar, the two units have separate legislative, executive and judicial institutions. Union matters are defined in the first addendum to the Constitution; personal status comes under those areas defined as 'non-union matters', thus the Marriage Act that applies in mainland Tanzania is not applicable in Zanzibar. Prior to 1971, Muslim, Christian, Hindu and customary laws governed marriage and divorce, in addition to a civil marriage regime. The proposal of a new marriage law in 1967 aroused intense debate, especially relating to the role of the Shari'a in matters relating to Muslim personal status. One of the proposals drawing most criticism related to the requirement of the first wife's permission for contracting a polygynous marriage. Despite much criticism and opposition, the Uniform Marriage Act passed into law in Tanganyika in 1971. The new act integrated existing marriage laws while preserving the right to religious solemnization and the option of polygyny. Elements that are uniformly applicable relate to the basic requirement of free consent, a common definition of permanent impediments to marriage, a minimum marriage age (although there is some leeway provided by grounds for judicial discretion and by the terms of the Penal Code), a common definition of void or voidable marriages, and certain preliminaries such as a notice period before marriage.

More recently, the Law Reform Commission of Tanzania has conducted several long-term studies, through its Family Law, Child Law and Succession Law Committees, on the reform of those applicable laws. The committees have recommended such changes as raising the minimum marriage age to 18 for both parties, raising the 'tender age' presumption stating that women are the more appropriate custodians for children under seven years to 14 years, harmonizing succession laws, and gradually eliminating the category of 'illegitimacy'.

Schools of *fiqh* The majority of Tanzanian Muslims are Shafi'i, with significant Hanafi, Ja'fari and Isma'ili communities and small Ibadi, Maliki, Hanbali and Ahmadi communities. The majority of Zanzibar's population is Muslim, with Christianity and indigenous religions predominant in Tanganyika.

Constitutional status of Islam(ic law) The Constitution was adopted on 25 April 1977, with major revisions in 1984 and the insertion of a Bill of Rights in 1988. It adopts no official state religion.

Court system The judiciary is organized under the Magistrates' Courts Act 1963. There are primary courts in each of 25 administrative regions; the jurisdiction of primary courts includes all civil suits related to customary and

Islamic law and all civil and Christian matrimonial suits. The next level of courts are District Courts, then Resident Magistrates' Courts, then two High Courts in Zanzibar and Tanganyika. The Court of Appeal serves as the highest court in the judiciary.

Notable features The minimum marriage age under the Marriage Act 1971 is 18 for males and 15 for females. Courts may permit under-age marriage of parties who have reached 14 years of age if specific circumstances make the marriage appear desirable. The Penal Code provides that persons of 'African or Asiatic descent' may marry or permit marriage of a girl under twelve years of age in accordance with their custom or religion so long as the marriage is not intended to be consummated before she attains twelve years. The Marriage Act only specifies the free consent of marrying parties for validity, and dispenses with the need for the guardian's consent if they have attained 18 years of age. Marriage registration is obligatory and non-compliance is punishable by a fine, but will not render the marriage void. The Marriage Act provides for the licensing of religious functionaries as Marriage Registrars.

Polygyny is permitted with the consent of the first wife; the marrying parties must state in the notice of intention to marry whether the marriage is intended to be monogamous, polygynous or potentially polygynous. There is a re-buttable presumption that customary and Muslim marriages are potentially polygynous and others monogamous. It is also possible to 'convert' a marriage to polygynous or monogamous by the spouses' joint declaration. This facility exists in the registration of civil marriages as well, although Christians married in church cannot do so as long as both parties remain Christian. Maintenance of the wife or wives is specified as the husband's duty, and becomes the wife's duty in cases where her husband is incapacitated and unable to earn a living. The court may order the payment of maintenance in limited circumstances where the husband refuses or neglects to support his wife.

The Marriage Act provides that, except in extreme cases, no petition of divorce is to be heard before a marriage has subsisted for two years. Either spouse may apply for divorce on grounds of breakdown, but no decree of divorce can be granted unless the court is convinced of irreparable breakdown. The party seeking the divorce must first apply to the Marriage Conciliatory Board. The board must certify failure to reconcile parties before the divorce suit can be initiated. Evidence of irreparable breakdown of marriage for the court's purposes must indicate one of the following grounds: mental or physical cruelty; wilful neglect; desertion; voluntary separation; or change of religion that dissolves the marriage under the religious law the parties were subject to at the time of their marriage. *Talaq* is not recognized as an automatic dissolution of marriage – a concession provides that any act dissolving a marriage under Islamic law is a compelling ground for divorce, but the act must have occurred after the Marriage Conciliatory Board has certified its failure to reconcile the couple. In dividing marital property and passing decisions on maintenance, courts must consider the customs of the parties' community, the contribution made by each party towards acquisition of the property in money, property or work, the debts owed by either party for acquiring property for their joint benefit, and the needs of infant children. Beyond that, the court may order maintenance for former wives in very limited circumstances, such as enforcing the Muslim wife's right to maintenance during *'idda*. In determining matters of child custody and guardianship, the courts are directed to consider paramount the welfare of the ward. There is a rebuttable presumption that children should remain with the mother until the age of seven. Courts are also directed to consider the customs of the community to which the parents belong, the economic circumstances of both parents, the housing that both parents can provide, and the behaviour of the mother and whether or not she is considered to have contributed to the marital breakdown.

Succession is governed by statutory, customary, Islamic and Hindu law in Tanganyika. The Non-Christian Asiatic (Succession) Ordinance directs the application of the personal law of the deceased according to the individual's religion. Islamic law is applicable to African Muslims under the Judicature and Applications of Laws Ordinance, empowering courts to apply Islamic law to matters of succession in communities that generally follow Islamic law in matters of personal status and inheritance. The courts, in determining the appropriate legal regime to apply to cases where there is a conflict of laws (i.e., when there is a dispute over the division of the estate of an African Muslim who also came under a system of customary law), employ two tests: the 'mode of life' and the 'intention of the deceased' tests. In deciding between the application of customary or statutory law, the 'mode of life' test considers whether the deceased was part of a community where the customary law is widely accepted and applied. The 'intention of the deceased' test considers statements and deeds of the deceased that could have indicated his/her preference.

Law/case reporting system Law reporting is through the *Gazette of the United Republic of Tanzania*, and there are loose-leaf editions of the *Laws of Mainland Tanzania* issued periodically. Reports of High Court and Court of

Appeals decisions are published in the *Tanzania Law Reports*, which replaced the *High Court Digest* in 1975.

International conventions (with relevant reservations) Tanzania acceded to the ICCPR and ICESCR in 1976, without reservations. Tanzania signed the CEDAW in 1980 and ratified it in 1985, without reservations. Tanzania signed the CRC in 1990 and ratified it in 1991, without reservations.

Background and sources

Center for Reproductive Law and Policy and International Federation of Women Lawyers (1997) 'Tanzania', in *Women of the World: Laws and Policies Affecting their Reproductive Lives – Anglophone Africa*, New York: Center for Reproductive Law and Policy and International Federation of Women Lawyers (Kenya Chapter).

Redden, K. R. (1990) 'Tanzania', in K. R. Redden (ed.), *Modern Legal Systems Cyclopedia*, Vol. 6, Buffalo, NY: Hein.

Rubin, N. N. and E. Cotran (eds) (1967–1970) 'Tanzania', in *Annual Survey of African Law*, Vols 1–4, London: Frank Cass.

Rwebangira, M. K. (1996) *The Legal Status of Women and Poverty in Tanzania*, Uppsala: Scandinavian Institute of African Studies.

Rwezaura, B. A. (1991) 'Tanzania: family law and the new bill of rights', *Journal of Family Law*, University of Louisville, 29, 2: 453–61.

— (1997) 'Tanzania: gender justice and children's rights: a banner for family law reform in Tanzania', in A. Bainham (ed.), *The International Survey of Family Law*, The Hague: Martinus Nijhoff, pp. 413–43.

Part III

Horn of Africa

1 Social, Cultural and Historical Background

The Region and its History

Muslim Arab traders and settlers began pushing south from Egypt into northern Sudan in the seventh century. They settled in the area and began intermarrying with the local population. The Muslim traders who came to the region were generally wealthy, and marrying into their families carried a great deal of prestige. Over time Islam and the Arabic language also became firmly established in the north. However, Islam spread quite slowly to the interior of the Sudan, only reaching the western and central regions around the fifteenth century. In the nineteenth century, Sudan fell under the colonial domination of Egypt and Britain. It gained independence in 1954. Today about two-thirds of Sudan's population of 29 million are Muslim. Another 30 per cent, most of them southerners, practise indigenous religions or Christianity.

Islam reached the rest of the Horn of Africa from across the Red Sea. The Prophet Mohammed himself encouraged a band of persecuted Muslims to flee Arabia to Ethiopia and to seek protection from Ethiopia's Christian king. By the middle of the ninth century, Arab traders and artisans had settled in trading centres along the coast of what are now Eritrea, Djibouti and Somalia. In the eleventh, twelfth and thirteenth centuries, two Arabian sheiks speeded the conversion of Somalia when they married into local families, giving rise to two of the largest clan-families in Somalia today, the Darood and the Isaaq.

From the south of the Horn, Islam spread north and west from the Somali coast, reaching what is now southern Ethiopia in the ninth century. Muslim holy men and the Sufi brotherhoods helped set the mystical tone of Islam in the region. Within a few centuries, there were numerous Islam-dominated states in the region, principally governed by Hadiya-Sidama-speaking ethnic groups. These states lost power in the sixteenth century with the rise to power of the Oromo, an ethnic group that practised the indigenous religions of the area. Muslims were faced with the choice of leaving the region or submitting to the Oromo regimes, including their religious practices. For the next two centuries, the Muslim populations, unable to practise Islam openly, were cut off from each other. An eighteenth-century wave of Islamicization from Somalia and Harar, a Muslim city in Ethiopia, reconnected these lowland communities. Muslims live throughout Ethiopia, but large concentrations can be found in Bale, Harerge and Welo. Meanwhile the highland Amhara and Tigrayan peoples have remained Christian (Lapidus 1990).

Ethiopia was the only African state not to be colonized in the nineteenth century, and until its monarchy was overthrown in 1974, very few non-Christians held high positions in government or the military. However, Italy ruled Eritrea from 1889 until it surrendered the province to Britain in 1941. In 1952, an Eritrean government federated with Ethiopia replaced the British military administration. Eritrea rebelled against Ethiopia a few years later, finally gaining independence in 1993.

Somalia's seven million people are almost entirely Muslim today. The overwhelming majority are ethnic Somalis who speak the Somali language and trace their ancestry to the same ancestor, Samaale. They are divided into six large clan-families, four of them pastoral and two agricultural. Each clan-family is divided into primary lineages, which are in turn divided into secondary and sometimes tertiary lineages. Related lineages within a clan form alliances to pay and receive blood compensation for each other in the case of homicide.

Somalia was divided between Britain and Italy during the colonial period. The two parts were reunited with independence in 1960, but in the early 1990s Somalia collapsed into civil war. The northern part of Somalia formerly controlled by the British has once again established itself as an autonomous territory, while the rest of Somalia remains without a formal government. With the disintegration of the central state, the lineage system has become the country's main form of social and economic organization.

Muslims make up an estimated 40 per cent of Ethiopia's population of about 64 million (Ofcansky 1991). Neighbouring Eritrea, with a population of four million, is about evenly divided between Christians and Muslims. Tiny Djibouti, with only 638,000 people, is mostly Muslim.

Nearly all the Muslims in the Horn are Sunni, but they belong to hundreds of different ethnic groups and they speak many different languages. As they adopted Islam, they did not necessarily shed their attachment to the traditions and beliefs of their earlier religion. In much of the region, indigenous customs remain an important part of religious and cultural practice. Ethiopia, in particular, saw no Arab immigration. Its Muslim peoples do not speak Arabic and never adopted any Arab traditions related to marriage, inheritance and other customs (Abbink 1999).

Legal Practices and Institutions

The disconnected nature of the Muslim communities in the Horn is evident in their application of Shari'a. The practice of Shari'a varies throughout the region: some groups apply classical Islamic law across the board while others use a blend of Islamic and customary codes. Some, such as the Beja in Sudan and Djibouti, have abandoned many of their local customs in order to adhere to Islamic family law. Others accept Shari'a in the abstract but continue to practise their own customs. This is particularly noticeable in decisions about marriage partners and inheritance. Finally, certain groups known to be very devout Muslims, such as the Harari, a group of about 30,000 who live in the Ethiopian city of Harar, continue to practise traditions that are contrary to Islamic law, not even accepting Shari'a when it conflicts with their own customs.

Under Emperor Haile Selassie, Ethiopian Muslims could bring matters of personal and family law before Islamic courts. Many did and probably continue to do so. However, others deal with such matters in terms of customary law. Ethiopia's 1995 Constitution allows for decisions regarding marital and family issues to be decided according to prevailing local religious or customary laws, so long as all parties involved consent. Additionally, Ethiopia's court system includes Shari'a courts operating at all levels of jurisprudence in cases that involve marriages that occurred under Islamic law or where all involved parties are Muslim. These courts also address concerns involving inheritance disputes (Ofcansky 1991: 123).

Sudan's imposition of Shari'a as state law in 1983 is a major factor in the current civil war between the north and south. Shari'a was always the basis for personal status law in the north; the post-1983 reforms extended its reach to civil courts. When President Mar Haas Ahmad al-Bashir came to power in 1989, the Sudanese government embarked on a wholesale project of Islamicizing the entire legal code (Fleuhr-Lobban 1993).

At independence, Somalia had four distinct legal traditions: English common law, Italian law, Shari'a and Somali customary law. In 1973, President Siad Barre introduced a unified civil code that sharply curtailed both Shari'a and Somali customary law. However, both legal codes have made a comeback since the central government disintegrated. Clan or lineage councils administer Somali customary law in the areas they control. The councils consist of all the adult males in the group (Metz 1992a). Since 1997, religious leaders have also set up local courts in the capital and a few other cities that pass judgments according to Shari'a. Wealthy contributors from the Gulf fund the Shari'a courts. The militiamen who enforce their rulings are devout Muslims who do not smoke, drink or chew the local stimulant, a narcotic leaf called *qat* (Murray 2000).

Seclusion of Women / Purdah

Women in the Islamic societies of the Horn abide by a strict code of modesty aimed at protecting the honour and dignity of their families. Although there is no formal purdah, there is a high level of *de facto* segregation by sex, as work and social roles of men and women keep them apart much of the time. With the exception of a small number of educated women from elite families, women remain in the household, eating after men and sitting separately at all festivities (Ofcansky 1991). Men and women have separate eating and sleeping quarters. For example, Somali women are not strictly secluded or covered, but men do not enter the women's part of the home, except that of their wives or other female relatives.

Sudanese and Somali women do not attend mosques, where in addition to religious worship, most discussion of public matters takes place. Sudan's Islamic government has taken several measures to reduce the public employment of women in recent years. The governor of Sudan's capital, Khartoum, in 2000 decreed that women should not work in the public service sector where they might come in contact with men (Dow Jones International News 2000).

Most of the Muslim peoples of the Horn practise infibulation, a severe form of female circumcision in which a young girl's labia majora, labia minora and often clitoris are removed. The remaining tissue is stitched back together, leaving only a small hole for the passage of urine. A midwife may enlarge the opening when a girl is married or when she gives birth to a child. Despite international conferences, legislation and government efforts since the 1920s to eradicate infibulation, the practice seems to be spreading. Infibulation is believed to protect virginity and control women's sexuality. Islamic leaders of the Shafi'ite school of law predominant in Sudan, and Egypt, consider female circumcision a religious duty (Walther 1993).

The question of dress depends on the community. Traditional dress for most northern Sudanese, Somali and Ethiopian women includes a single long piece of cloth that can be wrapped around the body and head. In recent years, some urban women in Sudan and Somalia have adopted the new forms of veiling promoted by Islamists in the Middle East and elsewhere (Murray 2000). Among the Bilin of Eritrea, non-Muslim and Muslim women seem to have about the same level of freedom to move about and speak in public. In Sudan's Nuba mountains, women are more free and independent than are most women in the Sudan, again with no great distinction made between Muslim and non-Muslim women. For the Taqali, a solidly Muslim group of about 180,000 in the Nuba mountains, there is a distinction between women who live in the mountains themselves and women who live on the lower plains, the latter enjoying less independence than their highland counterparts. In general, a woman's worth is measured in terms of her role as a wife and mother. The only economic activities open to all but a few urban women are midwifery, the manufacture of small craft items and the care of small domestic animals.

Family in the Region

People in the Horn give primary allegiance to their extended families. Central governments tend to be weak or non-existent in the Horn. Instead families do much of the work of protecting their members, educating the young, caring for the sick and elderly and settling disputes.

Most of the ethnic groups in the Horn are patrilineal, although many, such as the Nuba, appear to have been matrilineal before they converted to Islam. One group, the Beg, 1.5 million camel- and sheep-herders living in eastern Sudan, southern Egypt and Eritrea, appear to have changed their way of tracing descent, perhaps as a result of converting to Islam. They are strongly patrilineal; however, written descriptions of them from the Middle Ages suggest that at that time there were matrilineal. Additionally, there are still significant traces of matrilineality, such as an important relationship between a man and his maternal uncles.

The Hararis in Ethiopia trace their families bilaterally. The Sinyar, a group of approximately 26,000 people on the Chad/Sudan border, almost all of whom are Muslim, have traditionally been matrilineal, although it appears that this tradition is fading. In the Nuba mountains of the Sudan, people living in the southern part of the mountains tend to be matrilineal, in the north and east they are patrilineal, and in the southeast families are traced bilaterally.

Somalis trace their family relationships through the father. Men's place in their patrilineage greatly influences their standing, and to some degree dictates their association and relation with other clans. Women remain part of their patrilineal kinship group after marriage; the bloodwealth for a murdered married woman is shared between her own family and the family of her husband. If matrilineal relationships lack the intense obligation of patrilineal ones, Somalis nevertheless recognize maternal kin, who may also be important sources of support (Barnes and Boddy 1994).

Marriage

There is little uniformity between the traditions of different ethnic groups in the Horn regarding choices of marriage partners.

In Sudan, a valid marriage is contracted by two agents representing the bride and the groom. Usually the fathers of the marriage partners, the agents agree on a dower and on a payment schedule. They also sign the marriage contract before a registrar of marriages and divorces. The legal rights and responsibilities of the husband and wife begin after the signing of the contract, even though actual cohabitation and the consummation of the marriage may not begin for months (Fluehr-Lobban 1993: 111).

In Eritrea and Sudan, the Beja encourage marriage to a person's paternal parallel cousin (father's brother's child). It appears that, as with the Beja's descent pattern, their marriage preferences are a result of their conversion to Islam. Before converting, the Beja only allowed marriage outside of their clans. The Berti also encourage close cousin marriage, again with the ideal being marriage to a man's father's brother's daughter. Other first cousins, on either the father's or mother's side, are also good marriage partners, as are other members of the same patrilineage (Weekes 1984).

Often, even when a community accepts Shari'a precepts in determining marriage preferences, first-cousin marriage is adopted in theory but not in practice. The Beri are slowly accepting first-cousin marriage in principle, but rarely actually practise it. Among the Jabarti, too, first-cousin marriage is acceptable but seldom practised.

The Fur, a group of 720,000 Muslims in western Sudan, have two very distinct preferred marriage patterns. Those who live in the mountains view marriage to a person's maternal parallel cousin (mother's sister's child) as the ideal marriage, although marriage to other cousins is desirable as well. The Fur of the lowlands forbid marriage of maternal parallel cousins, as both spouses might have been nursed by both women, and a marriage between two people who were nursed by the same woman is viewed as potentially violating Shari'a.

Besides the question of whom a person may marry within a community, there is also the issue of who, outside of the community, is an acceptable marriage partner. As a rule, northern Sudanese Muslims do not marry their daughters to non-Muslims. But Muslim men sometimes marry or cohabit with Christian or pagan women. The children of such unions are raised as Muslims and have the same rights as children born to Muslim mothers (Metz 1992b).

In Ethiopia and Eritrea, inter-religious marriage is common, to the extent that Muslim women sometimes marry Christian men without being ostracized by their families. However, as the anthropologist Jan Abbink has noted, Islamic revivalist movements have recently targeted such practices as violations of Shari'a (Abbink 1999). Meanwhile some Ethiopian and Eritrean groups, such as the Harari, do not even recognize the Shari'a law allowing Muslim men to marry Christian or Jewish women. The Harari seldom marry outside of their ethnic group. When they do, they marry Muslims from other groups. The Jabarti also never marry outside Islam. Inter-religious marriage is common in Eritrea.

The Argobba, a very small and entirely Muslim group in Ethiopia (numbering only about 9,000 in 1984), have rules of exogamy that parallel Shari'a prescriptions but are not necessarily about religion. Argobba men can marry Oromo women (about 60 per cent of Oromo are Muslims), but Argobba women may not marry Oromo men. Descriptions of this rule do not mention whether Argobba men may marry non-Muslim Oromo women. As there are so few Argobba and they are patrilineal, this pattern of bringing new women into the community through marriage is critical for the preservation of the group. While it is unclear at what age marriages take place among Ethiopian Muslim populations, the civil code establishes the legal ages as 15 for females and 18 for males. Additionally, the code also requires that all parties freely consent to the marriage for it to be legal.

Somali girls often marry for the first time when they are between the ages of 15 and 20, while boys' first marriages often occur when they are between 18 and 25. Parents or other senior relations usually control the choice of the first marriage partner.

The Beja and many other groups in the Horn practise the levirate, in which a man's brothers inherit his wives after his death. Among most of the peoples of the Horn, brideprice is given by the groom's family to the bride's family, rarely to the bride herself. The specifics of the gifts, what they are, and who exactly receives them vary from group to group.

Among the Berti in northern Darfur Province and the Bilin, a group of about 50,000, approximately two-thirds of whom are Muslim, the first time a man marries, his father is responsible for the brideprice, which is given to the bride's family. Among the Beja of eastern Sudan, the woman's father, mother and maternal uncle all receive gifts of livestock and other goods.

The Fur have a system of brideprice in which the groom gives a set number of cows and rolls of cotton cloth to his bride, her mother and her father, her maternal aunt and uncle, and her paternal aunt (in recent years, however, cash has often been substituted). The groom's father usually helps raise the money for the brideprice for his son's first marriage, though not for subsequent marriages. The groom does brideservice, which sometimes leads to permanent residence with the bride's family.

The Masalit also have a system of giving cows, goats and money to the bride, her mother and other members of her family. Again, the groom must move on to the land of the bride's mother and work for her; in this case until the couple's first baby is born. This is true as well for subsequent marriages, although the period of the husband's labour for his new wife's mother may be somewhat shorter (Weekes 1984: 501). Some Beja also practise brideservice, although their period of service is longer, three years, and it is for the benefit of the bride's father, rather than her mother.

Among Somalis, brideprice is given to the bride herself and, if the marriage ends, she is ordinarily entitled to keep it. The brideprice primarily consists of livestock provided by the husband's father and relatives, unless he can provide it himself. After marriage, the wife is responsible for managing and controlling the flocks of goats and sheep that provide subsistence for her and her children (Lewis 1973).

Divorce

Divorce is common in the Horn of Africa. In Djibouti in the 1960s, for example, there were nearly half as many divorces each year as weddings. In Djibouti and the Sudan, Shari'a, as interpreted by the states, is the only law governing marriage and divorce. Sudanese courts have traditionally granted divorces to women more readily than in some Islamic countries. Divorce on the grounds of harm to the wife is a widely accepted principle. Harm, as interpreted by Sudanese jurists, can include insulting behaviour and attempting to marry a second wife, as well as physical abuse and desertion. Prior to every divorce, judges ask the couple to submit to arbitration, appointing neutral parties from both families to seek the cause of the discord and see if the problems can be resolved (Fluehr-Lobban 1993: 113).

After a divorce, a Masalit woman generally keeps the house, the field she cultivates and her stock of grain, and she is entitled to support from her ex-husband for their children. Divorced women often do not remarry.

Among the groups where each spouse has their own estate, such as the Fur, each spouse keeps their own home. For the Sinyar, the wife owns the family compound, and on divorce it is the husband who leaves.

Somali men can divorce their wives very easily. Women, on the other hand, cannot initiate divorce. They can, through a Shari'a court, have their marriages annulled only in certain limited circumstances. Women who have their marriages annulled against the wishes of their husbands are labelled *nabuusha* and shunned in their communities (Barnes and Boddy 1994). A woman can also try to persuade her husband to grant a divorce, but in doing so, she will forfeit her brideprice. Even women whose husbands divorce them often end up losing their brideprice as well as the huts they live in.

Among the Nuba of Sudan, while the gold jewellery given to a woman upon her engagement is usually hers to keep upon divorce, there are times when she may be required to return it. Specifically, if she divorces her husband and they have no children, the husband reclaims all the jewellery he has bought for his wife, as well as any household goods or furniture. It is generally reasoned that the woman will remarry (and therefore receive these items from her new husband), while the ex-husband is expected to need the items to give to a new wife. However, if there are children, the wife will generally retain ownership of the furniture, household goods and jewellery.

Polygyny

All the Muslim peoples of the Horn accept that a man may have more than one wife, but few men actually do, as taking an additional wife costs more than most men can afford. Nevertheless, there are differences between the ethnic groups. Among the Berti, a group of about 80,000 Muslims in western Sudan, only wealthy men take second wives. At any time, about one-fifth of Berti men are in polygynous unions. Men with more than one wife do not have a single household. Rather, each wife has a compound and the husband moves from one compound to another (Weekes 1984).

Masalit men frequently have two wives. The man must live with his wife at her family's home for at least one year and until a child is born. After the birth of the first child, the couple may live near either family. As a result of the possibility of choosing between the families, a polygynous man may have wives in different villages.

The Daju also commonly have two wives. Like some Masalit co-wives, Daju women in polygynous unions not only have separate compounds, they are usually in different villages. Beri men are also polygynists if they can afford it. While it appears that few men actually have multiple wives, men who enjoy a position of power in a community, particularly clan chiefs, sometimes exceed the Qur'anically prescribed limit of four wives.

At the other extreme are the Harari of Ethiopia. There is almost no polygyny in this group. In the 1980s, a researcher found that Hararis knew of only two men in their city who had married more than one woman.

Children

Somalis attach a great deal of importance to a girl's modesty from an early age. By the age of about seven, boys begin to tend the camels, away from the camps, thus creating a natural separation of boys and girls. Among the Nuba, male and female children also undergo a *de facto* separation at an early age, where by the age of two, male and female children may begin learning their respective roles by performing simple tasks for their male and female relatives (Lewis 1973).

Between the ages of eight and 14, northern Sudanese boys leave the women's quarters and begin to sleep and eat in the men's quarters. Girls of eight and over, meanwhile, must play in the women's quarters and help in the house when not at school (Cloudsley 1984).

Custody of Children

Among the Somali, as the husband is considered to hold all rights over children born within the marriage, it is his decision as to with whom the children would reside. Usually, young children remain with the ex-wife until they are old enough to go to the father's household, while older children remain with the father immediately upon divorce. In Sudan, male children generally remain with their mother until the age of seven, while female children remain until approximately the age of nine (Fluehr-Lobban 1993).

A Masalit woman also keeps custody of her children until they reach the age of ten, and she is entitled to support from her ex-husband for their children. After the age of ten, it appears that children of divorced parents stay with their fathers (Weekes 1984).

Inheritance / Land Rights

There are two general patterns of inheritance in the Horn. Some groups follow the inheritance rules set out in the Qur'an, with women inheriting half the share of men of the same relation to the deceased. For example, the Argobba and Daju organize inheritance according to the Qur'anic prescriptions. The Beri adopted this system of inheritance as they adopted Islam and acknowledge that it is not the way they distributed a deceased person's property in the past. Other groups, though Muslim, follow local customs rather than the Shari'a prescriptions for inheritance, often cutting women out of inheritance altogether.

Among the Jabarti, land goes from father to son, and the Taqali also transfer land according to paternal ties. The Berti seek out advice from local Muslim religious leaders, but, either because of or despite the advice, they do not pass property along to women. Among the Beja, women are allowed to own livestock (the principal form of property), but they cannot inherit it. Similarly, Somali women rarely inherit livestock (again, the primary capital good in the society), though they may be entitled to do so according to the Qur'an.

Bibliography

Abbink, J. (1999) 'Ethiopian Islam and the challenge of diversity', *ISIM Newsletter*, 4, December, p. 24.

Barnes, V. L. and J. Boddy (1994) *Aman: The Story of a Somali Girl, as Told to Virginia Lee Barnes and Janice Boddy*, New York: Pantheon Books.

Cloudsley, A. (1984) *Women of Ombdurman: Life, Love and the Cult of Virginity*, London: Ethnographia.

Dow Jones International News (2000) 'Rights group condemns Sudan decision to ban women working', 8 September.

El-Dareer, A. (1982) *Woman, Why Do You Weep?*, London: Zed Books.

Fluehr-Lobban, C. (1993) 'Personal status law in Sudan', in D. L. Bowen and E. Early (eds), *Everyday Life in the Middle East*, Bloomington: Indiana University Press, pp. 109–18.

Lapidus, I. M. (1990) *A History of Islamic Societies*, Cambridge: Cambridge University Press.

Lewis, I. (1973) 'The Somali of Somalia and North-Eastern Kenya', in A. Molnos (ed.), *Cultural Source Materials for Population Planning in East Africa: Beliefs and Practices*, Vol. 3, Nairobi: East African Publishing House, pp. 428–35.

Metz, H. C. (ed.) (1992a) *Somalia: A Country Study*, Washington, DC: Federal Research Division, Library of Congress.

— (ed.) (1992b) *Sudan: A Country Study*, Washington, DC: Federal Research Division, Library of Congress.

Murray, K. (2000) 'Shari'a is the only rule of law in Somalia', *Reuters News Service*, 13 October.

Ofcansky, T. P. (ed.) (1991) *Ethiopia: A Country Study*, Washington, DC: Federal Research Division, Library of Congress.

Walther, W. (1993) *Women in Islam*, Princeton, NJ: Princeton University Press.

Weekes, R. (ed.) (1984) *Muslim Peoples: A World Ethnographic Survey*, Westport, CT: Greenwood Press.

2 Legal Profiles

ETHIOPIA, Federal Democratic Republic of

Legal history Ethiopia was occupied by Italy from 1936 to 1941, although Eritrea came under Italian rule from 1886 to 1941. During World War II, the British defeated the Italians and established a protectorate over Eritrea. The 1950 UN resolution to unify Eritrea and Ethiopia was implemented in 1952. The movement for Eritrean independence developed into an armed struggle in 1961. A Civil Code passed in 1960 governs civil, religious and customary law marriages. Emperor Haile Selassie I (reigned 1930–74) attempted to modernize the state, but the nation was struck by famine and a long-standing conflict with Eritrea; both factors are considered to have contributed to the 1974 military coup ending Selassie's rule.

Lieutenant-Colonel Mengistu Haile Mariam became the head of state and the government was oriented towards Marxism. All religions, including Ethiopian Orthodox Christianity, were officially placed on equal footing under the new regime. The Eritrean People's Liberation Front won several strategic successes against Ethiopia in the late 1980s and early 1990s, declaring the Provisional Government of Eritrea in May 1991. At the same time, 17 years of military rule under a junta ('Derg') ended in 1991 amid growing pressure from democratic opposition forces. From 1991 to 1995 a transitional government, a coalition of 27 political parties, ruled Ethiopia. A 1993 referendum in Eritrea resulted in a massive vote for independence.

A new Ethiopian constitution was adopted in 1994, and elections were held in 1995 leading to the election of Meles Zenawi as prime minister and Negasso Gidada as president. The Federal Democratic Republic of Ethiopia was established in August 1995.

Schools of *fiqh* The majority of Muslims are Shafi'i. The other major religion is Ethiopian Orthodox (or Monophysite) Christianity. There are also small Jewish and animist minority communities.

Constitutional status of Islam(ic law) The current Constitution was adopted in 1995. Article 34 (on Marital, Personal and Family Rights), section 5 states: 'This Constitution shall not preclude the adjudication of disputes relating to personal and family laws in accordance with religious or customary laws, with the consent of the parties to the dispute.' Article 78(5) also provides for the establishment or recognition of religious or customary courts, pursuant to Article 34(5).

Court system Regular courts are organized at four levels. The Supreme Court has appellate jurisdiction and sits in Addis Ababa. The High Courts sit in the 14 provincial capitals and have original and appellate jurisdiction. The *Awraja* courts are convened in each of the 102 administrative subdivisions. *Woreda* courts are established in each of the 556 districts.

Under the 1944 legislation, Shari'a courts are organized into three levels: *Naiba* Councils serve as courts of first instance, *Qadis'* Councils as intermediate courts and the Court of Shari'a as the highest court.

Shari'a courts have jurisdiction in two kinds of cases. The first are: marriage, divorce, maintenance, guardianship of minors, and family relationships, provided that the marriage to which the case pertains was concluded under Islamic law or the parties are all Muslims. The second are: cases concerning *awqaf*, gifts, succession, or wills, provided that the donor is a Muslim or the deceased was a Muslim at the time of his/her death.

Shari'a courts have unclear legal status, as the Mohammedan Courts Act 1944 establishing them was never actually repealed, and yet the 1960 Civil Code makes no exceptions for Muslims or Muslim personal law. The Court of Shari'a continues to sit as a division of the Supreme Court.

Notable features The Civil Code sets the minimum marriage age at 18 years for males and 15 for females, regardless of whether the marriage is contracted under civil, religious or customary law, although the new Family Law may have changed the minimum age to 18 for both males and females. Both the Constitution and the Civil Code state that consent to marriage obtained by violence renders marriage invalid, but the Civil Code provides that consent granted due to 'reverential fear' of an ascendant or other person is not equivalent to consent obtained by violence.

Polygyny is abolished, backed by sanctions provided in the Penal Code. The Civil Code states that spouses owe each other 'respect, support and assistance' and provides that the husband is the head of the family and determines the place of the marital home, that the wife must obey him in all lawful things that he orders and that he owes his wife protection. A marriage contract may be drawn up settling the financial aspects of marriage, as well as other reciprocal rights and duties, but it cannot change any mandatory legal provisions and has no effect unless approved by family arbitrators or by courts.

Talaq is abolished. Under the Civil Code, all divorce law is uniform regardless of whether the marriage was contracted under civil, religious or customary law. Judicial divorce may be sought by either spouse for 'serious causes' or 'other causes'. Serious causes are: adultery; desertion of the marital home without knowledge of that party's whereabouts for two years; a spouse's confinement to a lunatic asylum for a minimum of two years; and judicial declaration of the absence of a spouse. Couples seeking divorce for either 'serious' or 'other' cause must first appoint family arbitrators who will attempt to effect a reconciliation, and if efforts fail, arbitrators can grant a divorce, preferably on mutually agreed terms. If 'serious cause' for divorce can be established for which one spouse bears the burden of fault, family arbitrators may divide common property unevenly. If no 'serious cause' is established, property is divided unevenly to the disadvantage of the spouse who petitioned for divorce. Arbitrators' decisions can be appealed to the court.

The Civil Code does not refer to support payments to former spouses. The Penal Code does make it an offence to refuse maintenance for either an existing or a former spouse. Support payments are often granted to the wife during the course of divorce litigation and deducted from her share of communal property once it is divided.

The Civil Code provides that child custody and maintenance arrangements are to be made only with consideration for the interests of the ward. In the absence of any 'serious reason', wards are to remain with the mother until the age of five.

Law/case reporting system Law reporting is through the *Federal Negarit Gazeta.*

International conventions (with relevant reservations) Ethiopia acceded to the ICCPR and ICESCR in 1993, without reservations. Ethiopia signed the CEDAW in 1980 and ratified it in 1981, with a reservation to Article 29(1). Ethiopia acceded to the CRC in 1991, without reservations.

Background and sources

CEDAW (1996) *Concluding Observations on Ethiopia's Combined Initial, Second and Third Periodic Report,* January, New York: United Nations.
Center for Reproductive Law and Policy and International Federation of Women Lawyers

(1997) 'Ethiopia', in *Women of the World: Laws and Policies Affecting their Reproductive Lives – Anglophone Africa*, New York: Center for Reproductive Law and Policy and International Federation of Women Lawyers (Kenya Chapter).

Ethiopia (1993) *Combined Initial, Second and Third Periodic Report to CEDAW*, 21 May, New York: United Nations.

Redden, K. R. (1990) 'Ethiopia', in K. R. Redden (ed.), *Modern Legal Systems Cyclopedia*, Vol. 6, Buffalo, NY: Hein.

SOMALIA

Legal history The Somali Republic was formed on 1 July 1960, upon the union of British Somaliland, which gained independence on 26 June, and Italian Somaliland, which gained independence from Italian-administered UN trusteeship on 1 July. Early legislation in British Somaliland was based on the importation of British–Indian legislation in the late nineteenth and early twentieth centuries. The British later promulgated the Natives' Betrothal and Marriage Ordinance 1928 and *Qadis'* Courts Ordinance 1937 specific to Somaliland. The Subordinate Courts Ordinance 1944 repealed the 1937 Ordinance, limiting the jurisdiction of *Qadis'* Courts to matters of personal status. Under Italian rule in the south, there was a well-developed system of *Qadis'* Courts, which retained jurisdiction over civil and minor criminal matters.

Upon independence, the republic was faced with the task of unifying legislation and judicial structures drawn from Italian, British, customary and Islamic legal traditions. After a military coup in 1969, the new regime embarked on a programme of legal reform based on scientific socialism. In the early to mid-1970s, debate regarding family law reform led to the appointment of a commission to prepare a draft code. The draft produced by the commission was enacted in 1975, with significant modifications made by President Siad Barre and Secretary of State for Justice and Religious Affairs Abdisalem Shaykh Hussain. The code aimed to abolish customary laws, and abrogated previous British- and Italian-era legislation relating to family law. Article 1 of the Family Code 1975 provides that the leading doctrines of the Shafi'i school, and general principles of Islamic law and social justice, are to serve as residuary sources of law.

Civil war ensued after the ousting of Barre in January of 1991, with competition for power between various factions. The collapse of the UN peacekeeping mission led to a final pullout of international troops in spring 1995. In August 2000, a majority of Somali leaders signed a transitional charter, to be in force for three years, and elected a parliament for the transition period. Fighting continues in the south, with some orderly government established in the north.

Schools of *fiqh* The majority of Muslims are Shafi'i. There is a small Christian minority.

Constitutional status of Islam(ic law) The current Constitution was adopted in August 1979. Article 3 (Section 1, Chapter 1) declares Islam the state religion.

Court system After independence, the Shari'a and customary courts were formally recognized as courts of *Qadis'*. Their judicial role is very small and jurisdiction is limited to civil matters such as marriage and divorce.

The regular court system is constituted at four levels: Supreme Court, Courts of Appeal, Regional Courts and District Courts. District Courts have two sections, civil and criminal. The civil section has jurisdiction over all cases arising from Shari'a or customary law or civil cases where the matter in dispute does not exceed 3,000 Somali shillings. Judges are directed to consider Shari'a or customary law in rendering decisions. Regional Courts are divided into three sections, civil and criminal (first instance), assize, and labour. Courts of Appeal are divided into two sections: general appeals and assize appeals.

Notable features The minimum marriage age is 18 years for both parties. The female party may marry at 16 years with her guardian's consent, and the court may grant an exemption from the minimum age requirements in case of necessity. A girl who has reached 16 years but is under 18 years may be represented in the contract of marriage by her father (in the absence of the father, the guardians in order are: mother, grandfather, elder brother, uncle, a court-appointed guardian or judge). The court is also empowered to overrule the objection of a guardian to the marriage of a female ward between 16 and 18 years.

Marriage is to be registered at the nearest District Court or authorized office within 15 days (40 days for residents of rural areas); failure to register is punishable by a fine. The essential elements of marriage as outlined in Article 6 are as follows. Proposal and acceptance by the contracting parties before two witnesses. A marriage contracted under compulsion is invalid. A man may not contract a second marriage without the written permission of the District Court. The court's authorization requires ascertainment of one of the following conditions: sterility of the wife of which the husband was not aware at the time of marriage, attested by a panel of doctors; incurable chronic or contagious illness of the wife, certified by a doctor; the wife's sentencing to more than two years in prison; the wife's unjustified absence from the matrimonial home for more than one year; or the existence of social necessity (grounds for which are not defined).

The Family Code provides that marriage is based on equal rights and duties; the husband is declared the head of the family, the parties are obliged to cohabit, and the wife is obliged to follow her husband. Both parties are obliged to share the expenses of the matrimonial home in proportion to their incomes if they are able to do so. If either party fails in his/her duty to maintain and is not destitute, the other party may obtain a court order for maintenance (the sums and time period for arrears of maintenance are not specified). The court is empowered to award interim maintenance and authorize the claimant to contract debts against the defaulting partner if s/he finds it impossible to obtain maintenance from the defaulter.

The Family Code provides that the right of *talaq* belongs to the husband 'subject to the authorization by the competent court'. The court may authorize divorce only after reconciliation efforts (of up to 60 days) have failed, and the court may not authorize more than one *talaq* at a time. Divorce by a minor or insane person, or pronounced under compulsion, is declared invalid. Either party may seek a judicial dissolution on the following grounds: incurable disease of the other spouse making cohabitation dangerous or impossible; disappearance of the other party for a period of over four years; habitual failure to maintain by the responsible party; serious disagreement between spouses making conjugal life impossible (after reconciliation efforts of up to 60 days); perpetual impotence or sterility of the other party; and the other spouse's sentencing to over four years imprisonment. The wife is entitled to seek a dissolution if the husband has been granted permission to marry polygynously by the District Court, on condition that there are no children from the marriage. Where the reason for a *talaq* or *faskh* is deemed to be the husband's fault, the court shall order him to maintain his former wife for three months to one year; if the wife is deemed to be at fault, the court shall order her to pay her husband a sum not less than her dower in compensation. The mother is entitled to custody of male children until the age of ten and female children until the age of 15, with the court empowered to extend custody until age 18 for the male or female ward if s/he is not able to look after him/herself. If the mother remarries and the husband is within the prohibited degrees to the ward(s), or in case she is widowed and remarries, she may retain custody. Maintenance of children is the duty of both parents until the age of majority for sons and until marriage or until she is able to support herself through gainful employment for the daughter.

The power of the testator to make a bequest is limited to one-third of the estate, unless the consent of the heirs is obtained. A bequest in favour of an heir is similarly limited by requiring the consent of the other heirs. Article 158 states that 'In conformity with the principles of the 1st and 2nd Charter of the Revolution females and males shall have equal rights of inheritance'. Heirs are identified as: spouses, children, grandchildren, parents, grandparents, full siblings, paternal and maternal aunts and uncles. The widow or widower is entitled to half of the estate if there are no children or grandchildren, or one-fourth if there are. Sons and daughters are entitled to equal shares, and the same applies to grandchildren. The shares of other heirs are also specified in the Code, as are grounds for inclusion or exclusion of heirs and reduction of shares.

Law/case reporting system   Laws are published through the *Official Gazette.*

International conventions (with relevant reservations) Somalia acceded to the ICCPR and ICESCR in 1990, without reservations.

Background and sources

Gavlak, D. (2000) 'Somalia's new president works to build peace', *Christian Science Monitor*. 14 September.

Mahmood, T. (1995) 'Somalia', in *Statutes of Personal Law in Islamic Countries: History, Texts and Analysis*, 2nd edn, New Delhi: India and Islam Research Council, pp. 78–81, 208–13.

Nelson, H. D. (ed.) (1983) *Somalia: A Country Study*, 3rd edn, Washington, DC: Library of Congress, Federal Research Division.

Pearl, D. (1987) *A Textbook on Muslim Law*, 2nd edn, London: Croom Helm.

Redden, K. R. (1990) 'Somalia', in K. R. Redden (ed.), *Modern Legal Systems Cyclopedia*, Vol. 6, Buffalo, NY: Hein.

SUDAN, Republic of the

Legal history   The legal system is based on English common law and Islamic law. Sudan came under Egyptian-Ottoman rule from the time of the Egyptian defeat of the Funj Kingdom in 1822. After the opening of the Suez Canal in 1869, European interest in the region increased; British General Charles Gordon was appointed a governor of Egyptian Sudan in 1873. The Mahdist revolt led by Muhammad Ahmad al-Mahdi in 1880 led to the capture of Khartoum from the Egyptians in 1885. The British re-established control over the region in 1898 under General Horatio Kitchener. The British and Egyptians shared sovereignty during the Condominium period from 1899. An agreement to allow for a three-year transition period to independence in 1953 led to self-rule in 1956.

Civil war between the north and south continues to plague Sudan. Three extended periods of military rule have been punctuated by briefer periods of multiparty parliamentary rule. The last elected government was suspended after a military coup on 30 June 1989. Sadiq al-Mahdi was overthrown by the military and an Islamist coalition led by Lieutenant-General Umar al-Bashir and Dr Hasan al-Turabi and martial law was imposed. From 20 January 1991, the Revolutionary Command Council imposed Islamic law on all residents of northern states regardless of religion.

On 1 July 1998, a new Constitution came into force following a referendum the previous month. Lieutenant-General al-Bashir became president and Dr al-Turabi became speaker of the parliament. On 12 December 1999, president al-Bashir dissolved parliament and declared a state of emergency. In April 2000, the state of emergency was extended through the end of 2000.

Sources of law are Islamic law, constitutional law, legislation, judicial precedent, and custom. In family law, judicial circulars (*manshurat*) issued by the Qadi al-Quda (first issued in 1916) serve to institute reforms or instruct the application of particular interpretations. The Family Code, passed in 1991, codified Shari'a principles and interpretations of some of the *manshurat* and abolished others. Section 5 of the Code indicates Hanafi *fiqh* as a residual source of law; the Supreme Court (Shari'a Circuit) is vested with power to issue interpretations of the Code.

Schools of *fiqh*   The Maliki school was the predominant *madhhab* in Sudan, although the dominant school is now the Hanafi, due to Egyptian and Ottoman influence.

Constitutional status of Islam(ic law)   The Constitution came into force on 1 July 1998, after being approved in a referendum the previous month. Article 1 states that Islam is the religion of the majority of the population, but does not proclaim it to be the state religion; Article 65 identifies the sources of law as Shari'a, the consensus of the people, the Constitution, and custom. Prior to the enactment of the Constitution, Sudan had largely been governed through a series of 'constitutional decrees'. Article 137 repealed all of the constitutional decrees except Constitutional Decree No. 14, which provides for implementation of the 21 April 1997 Peace Accord.

Court system The court system consists of a Constitutional Court, a High Court, Court of Appeals and courts of first instance. During the Islamization campaign of 1983, the government reunified civil and Shari'a courts, which had been divided during the colonial period. There is nothing in the new Constitution to suggest that there has been a change in the treatment of Shari'a in the courts.

Notable features The Muslim Personal Law Act 1991 requires that both parties to a marriage be past the age of puberty and willingly consent to the marriage. The male guardian marries adult women with their consent, although the *qadi* is empowered to act in this capacity if her guardian refuses his consent without justification. The guardian retains entitlement to seek dissolution on the grounds of lack of *kifa'a* of the husband, defined as *kifa'a* in religion and morals.

Classical rules apply to regulate polygyny. Provision is made for stipulations to be inserted in the marriage contract. The wife is entitled to maintenance, assessed according to the circumstances of the husband; arrears can be claimed for up to three years preceding the date of submission of the claim at court. The wife loses the right to maintenance if she refuses to move to the marital home or leaves it without a Shari'a justification, including if she works outside the house without her husband's consent, provided he is not being arbitrary in his prohibition on her working. The wife is required to obey the husband in accordance with the classical rules, but a ruling for obedience cannot be forcibly executed.

Reforms standard to the region to the rules on *talaq* have been introduced, affecting the validity of *talaq* accompanied by a number in word or sign, *talaq* in the form of an oath, and *talaq* intended to induce someone to do something. In a further reform to classical law, the wife must be informed of the husband's revocation of a revocable *talaq* during her *'idda* period in order for the revocation to be valid.

The wife may seek judicial divorce on the grounds of the husband's incurable physical or mental illness rendering it impossible for the wife to continue to live with him without harm; the husband's impotence not curable within one year; the husband's cruelty, or discord between the spouses; the husband's inability to pay maintenance; and divorce by 'ransom' where a wife held to be disobedient by the court may waive her rights in return for a divorce and if the husband refuses to agree, arbitrators must be appointed. If the wife establishes that she suffers from remaining with him, a *talaq* will be ordered by the court.

After divorce the wife is entitled to maintenance for the *'idda* period and to *mut'a*, to be assessed according to the means of her ex-husband to a maximum of six months' maintenance. This is unless the divorce was a judicial divorce by reason of the man's poverty and inability to pay maintenance or for some physical reason arising in the wife, or unless the divorce was by *khul'*.

A divorced mother is entitled to custody of her male children till they are seven years old and females till they are nine; the court may extend these periods if it is proven to be in the interests of the wards, until the sons reach puberty and the daughters consummate marriage. The father or other male guardian is to maintain scrutiny of all matters related to the raising of the children in the custody of their mother. The court has certain discretion to allow a woman who marries a man who is not a *mahram* to retain custody if the interests of the ward so require. The custody of a woman of a different religion from the father ends when the child is five, or earlier if there are fears for their faith being affected. Child support is the responsibility of the father until the daughter is married and the son is of an age when he is able to earn his own living. In a reform to the law of succession, the *radd* has been extended to include the spouse relict after the fractional heirs and the succession of cognate relatives.

Law/case reporting system Case reports are published in the *Sudan Law Journal and Reports*. Laws are published in the *Sudan Gazette*.

International conventions (with relevant reservations) Sudan acceded to the ICCPR and the ICESCR in 1986, without reservations. Sudan signed and ratified the CRC in 1990, without reservations.

Background and sources

Amin, S. H. (1985) *Middle East Legal Systems*, Glasgow: Royston.

Fluehr-Lobban, C. (1986) *Islamic Law and Society in the Sudan*, London: Frank Cass.

Hale, S. (1996) *Gender Politics in Sudan: Islamism, Socialism and the State*, Boulder, CO: Westview.

Mahmood, T. (1995) 'Sudan', in *Statutes of Personal Law in Islamic Countries: History, Texts and Analysis*, 2nd edn, New Delhi: India and Islam Research Council, pp. 35–8, 163–7.

O'Fahey, R. S. (1997) 'Defining the community: the national front, its opponents and the Shari'a issue', *Islam et sociétés au sud du Sahara*, 11: 55–65.

Pearl, D. (1987) *A Textbook on Muslim Law*, 2nd edn, London: Croom Helm.

Redden, K. R. (1990) 'Sudan', in K. R. Redden (ed.), *Modern Legal Systems Cyclopedia*, Vol. 6, Buffalo, NY: Hein.

Rubin, N. N. and E. Cotran (eds) (1967–1972) *Annual Survey of African Law*, Vols 1–6.

Safwat, S. (1988) 'Islamic laws in the Sudan', in A. al-Azmeh (ed.), *Islamic Law: Social and Historical Contexts*, London: Routledge, p. 231–49.

— (1994) 'Sudan', *Yearbook of Islamic and Middle Eastern Law*, 1: 237–53.

'Women and the law in Sudan: first and second reports' (1997, 1999), *Women Living Under Muslim Laws*, Vols 1–3 (1997) and Vols 1–3 (1999).

Part IV
Middle East

1 Social, Cultural and Historical Background

The Region and its History

The Middle East lies at the junction of Africa, Asia and Europe. The world's oldest civilizations were born there, as were three of the world's great religions: Judaism, Christianity and Islam. From the point of view of most Muslims, the rise of Islam is the most significant event in the region's long and complex history. Muslims make up the majority of the population in every Middle Eastern country except Israel, and Islamic values and institutions and values permeate every aspect of Middle Eastern society.

The Prophet Mohammed first heard what Muslims believe to be the word of God around 610, outside Mecca in what is today Saudi Arabia. After an interval without visions, he communicated a steady stream of divine commands to his followers until his death in 632. These revelations were collected into the Qur'an. The sayings of the Prophet, or the *hadith*, form a second source of knowledge about the Prophet's life and teaching.

The religion the Prophet Mohammed founded contained the design for a political as well as a social system. In pre-Islamic Arabia, tribal affiliation was the major social bond. However, as the Middle Eastern scholar John L. Esposito argues, 'Islam replaced this with a community whose membership was based upon a common faith rather than male blood ties; religious rather than tribal affiliation become the basis of Islamic society' (Esposito 1998: 5). For the community of new Muslims, Mohammed was a leader with multiple roles. He was a religious authority as well as the head of state. He was a judge as well as commander of the military. He was the head of a family as well as a people. The way he handled his responsibilities in all these realms remains a social ideal for Muslims to this day: the *Sunna*, or 'fine example' of the Prophet.

At the crux of the new Islamic way of life were the Prophet's teachings on family law. The basic social and political unit in pre-Islamic Arabian society was the kin-based patriarchal clan. However, in Mohammed's youth, the Arabs agreed upon no single form of marriage, much less on rules for the guardian-ship of children, the protection of women, or the distribution of property. In such conditions of confusion, the effect of the Qur'an's guidelines was to strengthen the patriarchal clan. Women could no longer marry more than one man at a time. Rules such as those laying down the *'idda* period in which a woman may not remarry were provided to assure knowledge of paternity. At the same time, the Qur'an set a new moral tone for family life. Women and children were no longer considered chattels, but were seen as individuals with rights and needs of their own (Lapidus 1990: 29–31).

As Mohammed's followers went on to conquer all of the Middle East as well as much of Asia, Africa and Europe, the idea of the Islamic family as the basic building-block of Islamic society remained at the heart of the Muslim concept of the *umma*, the community of believers. The four great schools of Islamic law that grew up in the Middle Ages each interpreted the Qur'anic regulations in slightly different ways, and in every place and time, local custom subtly or not so subtly altered the weight given to different parts of Muslim family law. Nevertheless, the basic rules laid out in the Qur'an regarding the rights and obligations of family members to each other remained basically unchallenged until the advent of European colonialism in the nineteenth century. As the Egyptian writer Leila Ahmed has noted, 'For the first time since the establishment of Islam, the treatment of women in Islamic custom and law – the license of polygamy, easy male access to divorce, and segregation – were openly discussed in Middle Eastern societies' (Ahmed 1992: 128).

Family law became a topic for discussion because the colonial officials used the treatment of Muslim women both as an explanation for the 'backwardness' of Middle Eastern societies and as a justification for European domination of those societies. In the early twentieth century, Middle Eastern intellectuals concerned with the need for the Islamic world to 'catch up' with Europe took up the issue of women as part of a broader nationalist programme of political, social and cultural reform. The nationalists wanted to secularize Muslim societies, separate state and religion, reduce the domain of Islamic law and repudiate the authority of the Ottoman Empire. As countries such as Iraq, Syria, Iran, Jordan and Lebanon gained independence, the nationalists were able to put many parts of their programme into action. But attempts to change family law remained politically sensitive. In the second half of the twentieth century, public disappointment with the results of the nationalist project fostered the growth of Islamist movements who have sought to set up govern-ments based on their understanding of Shari'a. Since oil was discovered in the Middle East, Saudi Arabia and several other Gulf states have used their oil revenues to help finance schools, charities and political associations that promote their conservative interpretation of Islam and Shari'a. In 1979, Islamic revolutionaries overthrew the Shah of Iran and instituted an Islamic theocracy. Islamist intellectuals and organizations with roots in the Middle East have continued to gain influence throughout the region and beyond.

For the Islamists, as for their secular antagonists, women and family law are a key battleground. As Yvonne Haddad and Jane I. Smith have put it, 'Absolutely basic to the Islamist discourse is the rejection of the West and the conviction that "freedoms" enjoyed by the Western women are among the key factors in the moral and ethical disintegration of the West' (Haddad and Smith 1996: 138). The Islamists tend to see the role of women as divinely prescribed in Islamic family law, and they have resisted reforms based on non-religious arguments. On the other hand, the Islamic revival they have helped provoke has sparked debate over whether a deeper understanding of Islam might lend itself to changes in the way family law historically has been understood in the Middle East. Iran, in particular, has been the scene of paradox. The enforcement of Islamic dress and other measures that initially seemed likely to push women back into the home have instead had the effect of legitimizing women's public presence. Meanwhile, the incorporation of Shari'a into the apparatus of a modern nation-state has forced Iran's clerics to re-examine the law to deal with new social realities (Mir-Hosseini 1999: 7).

The kingdom of Saudi Arabia exercises a greater influence over the Islamic world than its population of about 22 million might suggest. Each year, millions of Muslims make the pilgrimage to the holy city of Mecca. The Saudi monarchy came to power in the eighteenth century by championing the cause of the Islamic reformer, Ibn Abd al-Wahhab, who wanted to return to what he considered the fundamental principles of the Qur'an. In recent decades, the Saudis have also spent their vast oil wealth to promote the strict interpretation of Islamic law favoured by their Wahhabi sect. The Saudi monarchy is committed to upholding Shari'a. The country has a relatively high birth rate, and about 40 per cent of the population is under 15 years of age. More than 75 per cent of the total population is urban; large sections of the country are empty deserts. The Saudi population is almost entirely Sunni. Shi'ites, who are adherents of Shi'ism, the second major branch of Islam, make up about 4 per cent of the population and are found mostly in the oases of Al-Hasa and Al-Qatif. The only Christians are foreign industrial employees and businessmen. Public worship and display of non-Muslim faiths is prohibited.

The kingdom of Kuwait has been an important Gulf state for centuries. In the eighteenth and nineteenth centuries, Kuwait flourished economically as one of the most important trading ports in the Middle East (al-Mughni 1993). For many years, the ports of Zubara and Kuwait City operated as intermediaries between the Persian Empire and the British East India Company (al-Mughni 1993). With the discovery of oil in Kuwait, the small kingdom became even more crucial in the Gulf trade. Three other small oil-rich Gulf states are Bahrain, Qatar and the United Arab Emirates.

Like its neighbours, the wealthy country of Oman has become increasingly urban. About 50 per cent of Oman's some 2 million people live in Muscat and the Batinah coastal plain northwest of the capital. Muscat and Oman were converted to Islam in the seventh century CE, during the lifetime of Mohammed. The Sultan of Muscat and Oman played a major role in extending Islam to East Africa by conquering the island of Zanzibar. Sultan Qaboos bin Sa'id assumed power on 24 July 1970, in a palace coup directed against his father, Sa'id bin Taymur. His first measures were to abolish many of his father's harsh restrictions, which had caused thousands of Omanis to leave the country, and to offer amnesty to opponents of the previous regime, many of whom returned to Oman. He also established a modern government structure, and launched a major development programme to upgrade educational and health facilities, build a modern infrastructure and develop the country's resources.

Yemen has a generally homogeneous, ethnically Arab population of about 17 million. The northern parts of Yemen are primarily Sunni, while the southern Yemeni are predominantly Shi'ia. Yemen is one of the oldest centres of civilization in the Near East. In the seventh century, Islamic caliphs began to exert control over the area. After this caliphate broke up, the former north Yemen came under control of imams of various dynasties, usually of the Zaidi sect, who established a theocratic political structure that survived until modern times.

Syria's 16 million inhabitants are almost all Muslim. Most are Sunni, although a large minority belong to sects such as the Alawis, the Druse, the Ismaili, the Yezdis or the Shi'ites. Syria is ruled by a military regime under the control of the Ba'ath party. Islam is not mentioned in the Constitution. However, it is acknowledged that the head of the state must be a Muslim and the Shari'a is embodied in the 1953 Syrian law of personal status (Lapidus 1988). The Muslim Brotherhood opposed the Syrian government in the 1960s and 1970s, but its revolts were crushed.

Jordan's conservative monarchy bases its rule over a Jordanian–Palestinian population of about 6 million on upholding a relatively relaxed interpretation of Shari'a. Lebanon emerged from years of civil war only in the 1990s. The fragile division of power between its Muslim majority and Christian minority is still unstable. In the West Bank and Gaza, Muslims form a majority of Palestinians. Although secular nationalists have historically dominated the Palestinian movement, Hamas and other Islamist groups have gained influence in recent years.

Iraq's population of 23 million, which is overwhelmingly Muslim, consists of three main groups: Arab Shi'ites, Arab Sunnites and Kurdish Sunnites. The Arab Shi'ites make up about three-fifths of the total population and live mainly in the south and southeastern parts of the country. Arab Sunnites account for about one-third of the population and are concentrated in the central area of eastern Iraq, around Baghdad. The Kurds, who are Sunnite Muslims and speak a language related to Farsi or Persian, live in the north and northeast and make up almost one-fifth of the population. Iraq is the only Arab country in the Middle East with a Shi'ite majority, but Arab Sunnites dominate its government. Iraq's Ba'athist government is officially secular, although Shari'a is recognized as one source of Iraqi law.

Iran is a multilingual and diverse cultural society, but most of its 67 million people are Shi'a Muslims. Nearly one-half of the people speak Farsi, and another quarter speak some other Indo-European language or dialect. The Kurds are also a small but significant percentage of Iran's population. They have resisted the Iranian government's efforts, both before and after the revolution of 1979, to assimilate them into the mainstream of national life. Iran's *ulama* of religious teachers, students and politicians dominated its revolution and have maintained authority over its Islamic republic. Shortly after the revolution, the Islamic republic sought to overturn a number of the Pahlavi monarchy's reforms, particularly in the area of family law. As time has passed, Iran has reintroduced many of these reforms, as well as passing new laws revising interpretation of Shari'a in cases of divorce, family planning and segregation of the sexes.

Legal Practices and Institutions

The central institution of Saudi Arabian government is the monarchy. No formal constitution exists. A system of Islamic courts administers justice according to the Shari'a. The king appoints the judges on the recommendation of the Supreme Judicial Council. The independence of the judiciary is protected by law. The king acts as the highest court of appeal and has the power to pardon. All Saudi political and religious positions are reserved for men; laws maintaining the segregation of men and women make it impossible for women to exercise overt political power over men. Two women are equal to one man in the country's legal proceedings. In court, a Saudi woman may witness a legal document if another woman agrees to witness it with her. In a trial, it takes the testimony of two women to match that of one man. However, women have the right of access to a Shari'a court in civil matters concerning their own property.

Oman's sultanate has no constitution, Western-style legislature or legal political parties. Oman's judicial system traditionally has been based on Islamic law. The Shari'a courts fall under the jurisdiction of the Ministry of Justice, *Awqaf*, and Islamic Affairs. Oman's first criminal code was not enacted until 1974. The current structure of the criminal court system was established in 1984 and consists of a Magistrates' Court in the capital and four additional Magistrates' Courts. In the less-populated rural areas among the nomadic Bedouin, tribal custom is often the law.

The two parts of the new state of Yemen had markedly contrasting legal traditions. In the north, both Islamic law and tribal law were in operation. In the south, family and personal status laws were based on Shari'a, but there was a long history of applying British commercial law, and common law in many civil and criminal disputes. The unified state of Yemen has attempted to integrate all three systems into its legal and judicial systems. In 1974, several family law reforms liberalized the codes. Polygyny was restricted, but not banned. Further, the reforms required consent for marriage, limited the *mahr*, gave women equal rights to initiate divorce and explicitly stated favour for mothers in custody disputes (Moghadam 1993).

Qatar is ruled by a hereditary emir who presides over a fairly homogeneous native Qatari population. The ruling family, the Al Thani, make up as much as 40 per cent of the native Qatari population. Qatar introduced civil and criminal codes in 1971, and all civil and criminal cases fall within the purview of a system of secular courts. Islamic law is now essentially confined to personal and family matters. It follows very closely the lead of Saudi Arabia on most issues, in part because, like Qatar, Saudi Arabia adheres to the conservative Hanbali school of Islamic jurisprudence.

Before the 1979 revolution, Iran was one of the most liberal Muslim states, with a legal system comparable to those of Tunisia and Turkey. In 1962, Iranian women were given the right to vote. Further, the 1967 Family Protection Act protected women on many issues: women were given the right to initiate divorce, child custody rights were increased, and polygamy was limited. After the revolution, the Islamic Republic suspended the Family Protection law as un-Islamic. It later reintroduced many parts of the law, such as the use of special courts for family law. Iran opened the first theological college for female

Shi'i scholars in 1986. Among the all-male seminaries and colleges that produce Iran's clerical leaders, women's issues are taken more seriously than before the revolution. Women, who lost the right to practise law after the revolution, can now serve as lawyers and assistant or 'research' judges (Poya 1999: 102). In the 1990s, all major political parties included women in their slates for election. In 1997, eight women nominated themselves for president, although the Council of Guardians did not approve any of them. The women's vote played a critical role in the 1997 elections and the 13 female deputies serving in Iran's parliament have become extremely vocal on women's issues (Mir-Hosseini 1999).

Over the last 20 years, Syrian women have held a number of high government and private offices. However, the Syrian writer Bouthaina Sha'aban complains that women are still not adequately represented in Syria's legal and justice systems. 'Although women graduating from law colleges constitute one-eighth of the graduates, and women graduating from Shari'a college constitute one-quarter of the graduates, female representation in both the legal and the justice systems in Syria is very low indeed. This reflects badly on the legislation and implementation of laws concerning marriage, child custody, divorce, benefits, etc.' (Sha'aban 1996: 56).

Kuwait operates under a constitutional monarchy. Its legal system draws heavily on Egypt's French-inspired system. Most of Kuwait's commercial laws are based on Western secular codes, but in personal status and family laws, Kuwait's laws are based on the Maliki version of Shari'a (Longva 1997). Women do not have the right to vote.

Women have voted in Jordan since 1974. In 1989 they constituted about half of voters. However, they have seldom won political office. Islamist groups have campaigned against women running for office.

Women occupy many high offices in Iraq, but the Iraqi legal code is subject to the will of President Saddam Hussein of Iraq, who once told his nation on television that 'a law is a piece of paper on which we write one or two lines, and then sign it underneath: Saddam Hussein, President of the Republic of Iraq'.

Several years ago Yemen appointed a woman to its 15-member Supreme Court, despite the opposition of conservative Shari'a scholars (Carapico 1996).

Seclusion of Women / Purdah

Traditionally, Middle Eastern societies made a relatively sharp division between the roles of men and women. The public sphere was almost always reserved for men; women had domain over the family and the household.

Face-veiling has been recorded in the Middle East as far back as 1500 BCE. Long before Islam, the movements of Middle Eastern women were more circumscribed than those of men. Most of the social restrictions on women appear to originate in cultural notions of patriarchy and honour. The idea that a man's honour depends on the sexual behaviour of his daughters and his sisters, the women for whom he has responsibility, is particularly widespread. Until the early twentieth century, families who could afford it kept their women isolated from the marketplace, politics and social life with men (Lapidus 1988). In many countries, virginity until marriage is not just a cultural expectation, but also a legal one. Most countries in the Middle East have criminal sanctions against sexual intercourse outside of marriage (al-Mughni 1993).

Veiling and conservative Islamic dress had been declining in such countries as Iraq, Jordan, Syria and Lebanon, but recent decades have seen a resurgence. In many cases, it is not seclusion that prompts women to wear Islamic dress, but their emergence in the public sphere. As record numbers of Muslim women have entered schools, universities and the labour force, they have used Islamic dress to signify their adherence to the Islamic moral code and to protect themselves from male harassment. As Leila Ahmed writes, 'The adoption of the dress does not declare women's place to be in the home, but, on the contrary, legitimizes their presence outside it' (Ahmed 1992: 224).

To veil or not is not an option in Saudi Arabia or Iran. The governments of both countries enforce a dress code for women as part of the legal segregation of the sexes. Religious police may stop a Saudi woman who leaves her house without being fully veiled. All Saudi public facilities are segregated. Women may work only in occupations where they will not come in contact with unrelated men. They are barred from praying in mosques. They need the permission of a male guardian to obtain a passport or travel outside the kingdom (Altorki 1986). Women are not allowed to drive, further confining them to the private domain (Altorki and Cole 1997).

After the 1979 revolution in Iran, the Islamist regime began to enforce women's seclusion. In 1980, veiling or *hijab* was made compulsory by law. The Ministry of Education banned sex-integrated schools. Further, childcare centres were closed down, effectively eliminating women's public employment. The new government also made a woman's right to work conditional on gaining the permission of her husband. Finally, many tourist beaches were segregated by sex (Moghadam 1993). However, over the past 20 years, these restrictions have been increasingly loosened. Although married women must have their husbands' permission to work outside the home, more women do so today in Iran than before the revolution (Esfandiari 1997) and more women than men are enrolled in institutions of higher learning (Poya 1999). The government has expanded employment opportunities, so that most families have come to depend at least partly on the earnings of their female members. Although almost all women still veil, styles of cloth and wear vary greatly (Moghadam 1993). Adultery is strictly outlawed and men have the legal right to kill their wives if they are unfaithful.

Iraq and Syria have facilitated the movement of women into the workplace by subsidizing childcare. On the other hand, Iraq issued a regulation in 1982 that married women were not allowed to travel without their husbands. Further, unmarried women must have written permission from their fathers or guardians (Moghadam 1993). At the same time, the Iraqi government instructed women to fill the vacant jobs of men in the army, sending out contradictory messages on women's place in Iraqi society (Moghadam 1993).

Islamist movements in the region have had significant effects on women's access to public space. In Gaza in the 1980s, an Islamist group called Mujama proposed a return to stricter Islamic social codes among Palestinians. Women were pressured to veil. In May 1988, Mujama youths broke into classrooms and demanded that schoolgirls wear *hijab* (Moghadam 1993).

Historically, women from wealthy families in Kuwait have been strictly secluded, although women in the middle and lower classes were not under such strict seclusion, as most of these families could not afford servants to perform duties outside the household (al-Mughni 1993). However, women who left the household were still required to follow strict dress codes: women dressed in a long black cloak called an *abbaya* and veiled with a similar black cloth called a *boshiya* (al-Mughni 1993). Longva argues that veiling in Kuwait intensified in the mid-1980s with the increase in immigration. Veiling has been used as a way to distinguish Kuwaiti women from non-Kuwaiti women (Longva 1997). Women in Kuwait have also been excluded from political activities. Although the question of suffrage has been debated in Kuwait, women still do not have the right to vote. In 1982, a bill was introduced into the National Assembly to allow women to vote but not to hold office. The bill was debated for only a few hours, and lost by a vote of 27 to 7 with 16 abstentions. Many members of the Assembly who had been in favour of granting women the vote abstained in fear of a backlash by Islamists in Kuwait (al-Mughni 1993). After the war with Iraq, many Kuwaiti women argued that denying women the right to vote and participate in the political process was a violation of the country's 1961 Constitution, which prohibits discrimination on the basis of gender (Prusher 2000). The Emir of Kuwait, Sheikh Jaber al-Sabah, issued a royal decree in June 1999 to allow women to vote and run for public office. However, a bill to put his decree into effect was defeated in the National Assembly by a vote of 32 to 30 in November 1999 (Prusher 2000). Between 1986 and 1988, 42 women in Kuwait were arrested for giving birth outside marriage. Of these, eleven were jailed for more than two years, 17 were forced to marry the father of the child and 14 were put under the guardianship of male family members (al-Mughni 1993).

Female circumcision, usually in the form of excision of the clitoris, is common in many Arab states such as Yemen, Bahrain, Oman and the United Arab Emirates (Hosken 1982).

Family in the Region

In the Middle East, kinship remains the principal unit of social and economic organization. The family into which an individual is born is the most important social group to which he or she will ever belong, providing protection, food, shelter, income, reputation and honour. Patrilineal family units continue to live in close proximity and marry endogenously; cross-cousin marriage is predominant. Young people are taught to respect and defer to their older kin, who in turn take responsibility for younger relatives. Females are taught to respect and defer to their fathers, brothers, grandfathers, uncles and cousins, who are taught to protect and care for them. A married man is often called not by his own name, but as a reference as a father to his first-born son. Women are almost exclusively identified as the daughter, wife or mother of a man. Unmarried women are pitied and considered social and familial failures in many communities (Joseph 1996).

Marriage

Courtship, engagement and marriage customs vary widely according to location, education and social class. The women of the two families involved usually play a large role in arranging the match, while the older males of families determine the bridewealth or *mahr*, as well as the clothes, jewellery and other gifts to be given by both sides. Among Muslims, there are three different forms of payment given at marriage: 1) *jahaz* (gifts to the bride by her father) or *mahr* (gifts from her in-laws); 2) *shirbaha* (cash provided by the groom to the bride's father to purchase the *jahaz*), a practice common in Iran; and 3) traditional Islamic *mahr* (Moghadam 1993). This amount is stipulated in the marriage contract, and consists of a direct *mahr*, given at the time of the marriage, and often a deferred *mahr*, given in some situations of divorce (Moors 1995). Women are entitled to claim the deferred *mahr* in cases where the husband repudiates the wife or where the wife has a valid reason to ask the court to dissolve the marriage (Moors 1995).

Economic and political crises in the Middle East have caused changes in the *mahr*. For example, in 1988, the first year of the Intifada, the average price of the *mahr* among Palestinians decreased by 10–25 per cent (Moors 1995). Further, the effects of the Intifada have also been linked to decreased marriage ages for both boys and girls, as well as decreased registration of marriages, making women's potential claims to maintenance vulnerable (Moors 1995). The country of Oman has placed limits of the amount of the *mahr*, although these limitations are routinely ignored (Eickleman 1997).

When the family arranges a marriage, it usually accepts some responsibility for the outcome. In Syria, Sha'aban writes that the parents of a woman whose marriage is failing will see to it that she and her children are provided for if she went into the marriage on their recommendation (Sha'aban 1996: 55).

Most Middle Eastern countries have introduced a minimum age for marriage. Jordan's 1951 Law of Family Rights raised the minimum age for marriage to 15 for both boys and girls (Moors 1995). In Syria, the legal marriage age for girls is 17, although parents may petition the court to marry off a girl who is 15 or 16; while in Iraq girls must be 18 to marry (Moghadam 1993)

The age at which girls can marry has shifted back and forth in Iran. The Pahlavi regime had raised the marriage age for girls to 18 (Hoodfar 1995). The post-1979 regime under Khomeini lowered this to nine years of age. However, as of August 2000, the reformist parliament in Iran was considering a new bill to raise the minimum marriage age for girls to either 15 or 16 (however, the Guardian Council subsequently rejected the Majlis decision to raise the marriage age) (*Iranian Times* 2000). Iran's Islamic Republic is also unique in sanctioning temporary marriages, or *muta*, as a legal form of union (Hoodfar 1995).

In several Arab countries, women who marry men from another country lose some of their civil rights. A Syrian woman married to a foreigner cannot pass on her nationality to her children (Sha'aban 1996). In Kuwait, non-Kuwaiti men who marry Kuwaiti women are not given residence based on marriage; instead they are required to leave the country if they cannot find employment and secure a residence permit. Even when such a permit is granted, the couple may still be forced apart. Permits are issued for only one year at a time, and upon renewal are reviewed by the Interior Minister, who has unequivocal power to renew or terminate permits. Likewise, children of such unions are also required to obtain residence permits to remain in Kuwait and are not entitled to the free health care available to all Kuwaiti citizens (al-Mughni 1993).

Divorce

Divorce is fairly common in the Middle East. Several Arab countries have modified their family codes to require men who divorce their wives to give them maintenance beyond the three-month *'idda* period. Article 17 of the 1953 Syrian Law of Personal Status provided that if the *qadi* judges that a husband has repudiated his wife without reasonable cause, the *qadi* can require the husband to pay compensation up to the equivalent of one year's maintenance (Pearl and Menski 1998). In Iraq, the Personal Status Act of 1959 required either a declaration from the court for a divorce or registration of repudiation during the wife's *'idda* for the divorce to be valid. The 1976 Jordanian Law of Personal Status stipulates that in cases where the husband has arbitrarily repudiated his wife, she is entitled to ask for a maximum of one year's maintenance (Moors 1995).

Although Syrian women are entitled to register a right to divorce in their marriage contracts, few women know it and it is considered socially unacceptable for brides to ask to preserve their right to divorce their husbands. Meanwhile Syrian men in some cases have the right to divorce their wives without the women attending court. Courts rarely enforce the payment of compensation to divorced women. In most cases, the husband owns the house and can force a divorced wife to leave (Sha'aban: 1996).

In Iran, the government has made a model marriage contract available to marrying couples that gives the divorced wife a right to half the property acquired during the marriage, provided she does not seek the divorce herself and is not at fault. Another article of the contract consists of a power of attorney from the husband to the wife, permitting her to divorce herself on twelve different grounds (Esfandiari 1997: 43). Regardless of the marriage contract, an Iranian man must secure the court's permission to divorce his wife. In 1994, the Iranian parliament enacted a law giving a divorced woman the right to monetary compensation for the years she worked in her husband's home as a mother and housewife. In 1997, a law was passed requiring courts to calculate the *mahr* payments husbands must pay divorced wives according to an index updated for inflation (Poya 1999: 101–2).

Polygyny

Polygyny has declined throughout the Middle East (Soffan 1980: 42). Several states officially have restricted the practice. In Syria, as early as 1953, the Law of Personal Status attempted to limit polygyny. Article 17 of the Law gave the *qadi* power to refuse permission to marry a second wife if a man cannot prove he is financially capable of supporting both women (Pearl and Menski 1998). The 1959 Iraqi Law of Personal Status restricted polygyny even further. Not only did a man have to convince a judge that he could financially support two wives, he also had to show 'lawful interest' in the second marriage and convincing evidence that both women will be treated equally (Pearl and Menski 1998: 243). Second marriages without approval were declared invalid, although in 1963, this invalidity was amended.

In Iran, second marriages still require the consent of the first wife, who has the right to initiate divorce if she does not consent (Hoodfar 1995). However, this right is not often used, as women are often better off economically in a polygynous marriage than as a divorced woman.

Children

Children of both sexes are valued in the Middle East, but a woman traditionally gains more status when she gives birth to a male child. The mother–son tie is often the closest relationship a woman has with a male; while daughters leave the home, boys stay and take care of their parents in old age. The ties between brothers and sisters are also close. Ideally a brother defends his sister, while a sister serves as a kind of second mother to her brother (Bowen and Early 1993). Although Middle Eastern countries have established compulsory education for girls and boys, girls still lag behind men in literacy (Lapidus 1990).

As in any social system, children represent a variety of social and religious values. In one context, children are seen as a solidifying factor in a marriage; childless couples are not viewed as being as stable as those with children (Shami and Taminian 1997). Perhaps partly for this reason, the Middle East has maintained one of the highest regional birth rates in the world.

Bearing children is sometimes viewed as a national duty. For example, in the Iraq–Iran war, the Iraqi government instructed women that their national duty required them to bear five or more children to narrow the gap between the vastly disparate populations (at the time, Iraq's population was approximately 15 million and Iran's was 47 million). In 1986, all forms of birth control disappeared from Iraqi pharmacies (Moghadam 1993). The population of

Oman is growing the fastest, at an estimated 3.8 per cent per year (Eickleman 1997). Based on regional growth rates, demographers estimate that the population of the Arabian peninsula will double from the early 1990s to the early years of the new century (Eickleman 1997).

After Iran's birth rates jumped in the post-revolutionary period, the Islamic Republic launched a full-fledged birth control programme promoting the benefits of small families. Iran has also adopted the International Labour Organization's Convention No. 3, which applies to all employed women and provides for twelve weeks of maternity leave including a required leave after childbirth (Moghadam 1993).

Family planning is also under discussion in the Middle East. A recent study in Jordan found that 80 per cent of men, 86 per cent of women, 82 per cent of male religious leaders and 98 per cent of female religious leaders believe that family planning and contraceptive use is consistent with Islamic tenets on family and sexuality (Underwood 2000). Fewer than one per cent of those interviewed considered family planning to be prohibited by Islamic law.

Custody of Children

In case of divorce, Saudi boys remain with their mothers until the age of seven or nine and girls until the time of marriage (unless the mother remarries, in which case she forfeits custody of her children.) Usually a divorced Saudi woman will bring her children with her to her father's house (Altorki 1986: 81).

If a divorced Syrian woman has a home and does not remarry, she will be allowed to retain of her boys until the age of nine and her girls until the age of eleven. But since husbands usually own the marriage home, they often persuade courts to give them custody on the grounds that the woman has no proper home for them (Sha'aban 1996).

Iran's Islamic republic at first gave guardianship of girls over the age of seven and boys over the age of two to fathers, and in the case of their death, to their male kin. During the Iran–Iraq war, however, war widows were granted the right to raise their children and to keep their husband's salary, pension or other living expenses without the interference of his male kin. Subsequently, other widows gained the same rights (Poya 1999: 101).

Inheritance / Land Rights

In pre-Islamic Arabia, inheritance was the exclusive right of male relatives, primarily sons, fathers and brothers. Women were excluded from inheritance rights based on their lack of participation in tribal disputes. One of the major Islamic reforms to inheritance in the area was the Qur'anic requirement of inheritance for both widows and daughters (Esposito 1998). Although women's inheritance under Islamic law is generally half that of men, it represents a radical change from previous systems, which completely excluded women (Fluehr-Lobban 1993). However, despite these protective sanctions, Joseph argues that women often forgo their inheritance for their brothers' sake; this practice is seen as a form of insurance or security for the protection provided by the brother for the woman and her children (Joseph 1997).

In areas under the Ottoman Empire, two forms of inheritance were common. Property held in full ownership – buildings, orchards, vineyards and moveable property – was inherited under Islamic codes of succession. This type of property is called *mulk*. Agricultural land, known as *miri*, was often land for which individuals could obtain user rights, but ownership rested with the state. This type of land was usually inherited under the secular law of succession under the Ottoman Empire (Moors 1995).

In Kuwait, inheritance oftens follows tradition over Islamic decrees, particularly for women who married young. Often fathers leave their property, both mobile and immobile assets, exclusively to sons (al-Mughni 1993). Among Palestinians, women in situations with no or few contending heirs fare much better than other women. Daughters without brothers and widows without sons often stand the best chance of inheriting their due shares (Moors 1995).

Saudi women inherit exactly according to Qur'anic rules, but only a few women actually manage their own property (Altorki 1986).

References

al-Mughni, H. (1993) *Women in Kuwait: The Politics of Gender*, London: Saqi Books.

Ahmed, L. (1992) *Women and Gender in Islam*, New Haven, CT: Yale University Press.

Altorki, S. (1986) *Women in Saudi Arabia: Ideology and Behavior Among the Elite*, New York: Columbia University Press.

Altorki, S. and D. P. Cole (1997) 'Change in Saudi Arabia: a view from "Paris of Najd"', in N. S. Hopkins and S. E. Ibrahim (eds), *Arab Society: Class, Gender, Power, and Development*, Cairo: The American University in Cairo Press, pp. 29–52.

Bowen, D. L. and E. A. Early (1993) *Everyday Life in the Middle East*, Bloomington: Indiana University Press.

Carapico, S. (1996) 'Women and public participation in Yemen', in S. Sabbagh (ed.), *Arab Women: Between Defiance and Restraint*, New York: Olive Branch Press, pp. 62–4.

Eickleman, C. (1997) 'Fertility and social change in Oman: women's perspectives', in N. S. Hopkins and S. E. Ibrahim (eds), *Arab Society: Class, Gender, Power, and Development*, Cairo: The American University in Cairo Press, pp. 85–104.

Esfandiari, H. (1997) *Reconstructed Lives: Women and Iran's Islamic Revolution*, Washington, DC: Woodrow Wilson Center Press.

Esposito, J. (1998) *Islam and Politics*, 4th edn, Syracuse, NY: Syracuse University Press.

Fluehr-Lobban, C. (1993) 'Toward a theory of Arab-Muslim women as activists and scholars in secular and religious movements', *Arab Studies Quarterly*, 15: 87–107.

Goldberg, E., R. Kasaba and J. Migdal (eds) (1993) *Rules and Rights in the Middle East: Democracy, Law and Society*, Seattle: University of Washington Press.

Haddad, Y. Y. and J. I. Smith (1996) 'Women in Islam: the mother of all battles', in S. Sabbagh, *Arab Women: Between Defiance and Restraint*, New York: Olive Branch Press, pp. 137–50.

Harik, I. (1997) 'Pluralism in the Arab world', in N. S. Hopkins and S. E. Ibrahim (eds), *Arab Society: Class, Gender, Power, and Development*, Cairo: The American University in Cairo Press, pp. 345–58.

Hoodfar, H. (1995) 'Population policy and gender equity in Post-Revolutionary Iran', in C. M. Obermeyer (ed.), *Family, Gender and Population in the Middle East*, Cairo: The American University in Cairo Press, pp. 105–35.

Hosken, F. P. (1982) *The Hosken Report: Genital and Sexual Mutilation of Females*, 3rd rev. edn, Lexington, MA: Women's International Network News.

'Iran assembly pushes on women's rights' (2000), *The New York Times*, 10 August, p. A8.

Iranian Times (2000) 'Minimum marriage age, uncertainty continues', BBC report, 15 November. http://www.iranian.com/Times/2000/November/Salehabad/1107front.html

Joseph, S. (1997) 'Brother–sister relationships: connectivity, love, and power in the reproduction of patriarchy in Lebanon', in N. S. Hopkins and S. E. Ibrahim (eds), *Arab Society: Class, Gender, Power, and Development*, Cairo: The American University in Cairo Press, pp. 227–62.

— (1996) 'Gender and family in the Arab world', in S. Sabbagh (ed.), *Arab Women: Between Defiance and Restraint*, New York: Olive Branch Press, pp. 194–202.

Lapidus, I. (1990) *A History of Islamic Societies*, Cambridge: Cambridge University Press.

Longva, A. N. (1997) 'Kuwaiti women at a crossroads: privileged development and the constraints of ethnic stratification', in N. S. Hopkins and S. E. Ibrahim (eds), *Arab Society: Class, Gender, Power, and Development*, Cairo: The American University in Cairo Press, pp. 407–22.

Mir-Hosseini, Z. (1999) *Islam and Gender: The Religious Debate in Contemporary Iran*, Princeton, NJ: Princeton University Press.

Moghadam, V. M. (1993) *Modernizing Women: Gender and Social Change in the Middle East*, Boulder, CO: Lynne Rienner Publishers.

Moors, A. (1995) *Women, Property and Islam: Palestinian Experiences, 1920–1990*, Cambridge: Cambridge University Press.

Pearl, D. and W. Menski (1998) *Muslim Family Law*, 3rd edn, London: Sweet and Maxwell.

Poya, M. (1999) *Women, Work and Islamism*, London: Zed Books.

Prusher, I. (2000) 'Kuwaiti women seek right to vote', *Christian Science Monitor*, 92: 180.

Sha'aban, B. (1996) 'The status of women in Syria', in S. Sabbagh (ed.), *Arab Women: Between Defiance and Restraint*, New York: Olive Branch Press, pp. 54–61.

Shami, S. and L. Taminian (1997) 'Children of Amman: childhood and child care in squatter areas of Amman, Jordan', in N. S. Hopkins and S. E. Ibrahim (eds), *Arab Society: Class, Gender, Power, and Development*, Cairo: The American University in Cairo Press, pp. 183–92.

Soffan, L. U. (1980) *The Women of the United Arab Emirates*, London: Croom Helm and Totowa, NJ: Barnes & Noble Books.

Underwood, C. (2000) 'Islamic precepts and family planning: the perceptions of Jordanian religious leaders and their constituents', *International Family Planning Perspectives*, 26: 110.

'United Arab Emirates: raped woman sentenced to death by stoning' (2000), *Off Our Backs*, 30: 4.

Walther, W. (1993) *Women in Islam: From Medieval to Modern Times*, Princeton, NJ: Markus Wiener Publishing.

2 Legal Profiles

BAHRAIN, State of

Legal history Bahrain has had a long exposure to the British legal system and has a mixed legal system drawing from both English common law and codified systems and from Islamic law. The Ottoman Empire lost control over Bahrain in 1861; the territory became a British protectorate in 1880. Bahrain gained full independence from its protectorate status in August 1971. Upon independence, a Legislative Committee was appointed to establish an independent legal system. Since that time, Bahraini law has followed a similar pattern to other Arab states' legislation, particularly Egyptian codes.

Personal law remains uncodified, and is administered by Shari'a courts regulated by the Bahrain Courts Law 1971. The Judicature Law also indicates the residuary sources of law in the absence of applicable provisions of law: judgments are to be derived from principals of the Shari'a; in the absence of applicable *shar'i* provisions, on custom (with particular customs having precedence over general customs); and final resort is to natural law or the principles of equity and good conscience. The National Assembly was dissolved in 1975, and the Amir has ruled by decree since that time.

Schools of *fiqh* The Ja'fari school is the predominant *madhhab* in Bahrain, and there are significant Sunni minorities following either the Shafi'i or Maliki school.

Constitutional status of Islam(ic law) The Constitution of the State of Bahrain was adopted on 26 May 1973. Article 1(a) affirms that 'Bahrain is an Arab Islamic State'. Article 2 affirms Islam as the religion of the state and identifies the Shari'a as a main source of legislation.

Court system The judiciary is divided into regular and Shari'a courts. The Shari'a courts are divided into Shi'i and Sunni departments applying Ja'fari and Shafi'i or Maliki *fiqh*, respectively. These courts have jurisdiction over all disputes relating to Muslim personal status, except disputes over estates. Disputes over estates fall under the jurisdiction of the competent civil courts, although those courts are obliged to divide estates in accordance with Islamic law. The Junior Shari'a Courts (Ja'fari and Sunni Departments) hear personal status cases in the first instance. The High Shari'a Court of Appeal (Ja'fari and Sunni Courts) has appellate jurisdiction over Senior Shari'a Court decisions. Each High Shari'a Court consists of a president and a number of judges; sittings are validly held in the presence of two judges, one of whom must be the president of the court or his deputy. A Decree Law (no. 8) 1989 establishing the Court of Cassation also directs that this court has exclusive jurisdiction to decide cases filed simultaneously in the civil and Shari'a courts or before two Shari'a courts or to settle any dispute arising from conflicting judgments between such courts, as well as jurisdiction over civil and commercial matters and personal status suits involving non-Muslim non-Bahrainis.

Notable features Personal status law remains unlegislated. The Shari'a courts apply classical Islamic personal status law to Muslims without reference to state law.

Law/case reporting system Laws are published in the *Official Gazette*. Case reporting is restricted to the judgments of the Court of Cassation, the highest court in Bahrain. There are no official publications of Shari'a Court decisions.

International conventions (with relevant reservations) Bahrain acceded to the CRC in 1992, without submitting any reservations.

Background and sources

Amin, S. H. (1985) *Middle East Legal Systems*, Glasgow: Royston.

Ballantyne, W. M. (1986) *Commercial Law in the Arab Middle East: The Gulf States*, London and New York: Lloyd's of London Press.

El Alami, D. S. and D. Hinchcliffe (1996) *Islamic Marriage and Divorce Laws of the Arab World*, London and Boston: Kluwer Law International.

Mahmood, T. (1995) 'Gulf', in *Statutes of Personal Law in Islamic Countries: History, Texts and Analysis*, 2nd edn, New Delhi: India and Islam Research Council, p. 85.

Redden, K. R. (1990) 'Bahrain', in K. R. Redden (ed.), *Modern Legal Systems Cyclopedia*, Vol. 5, Buffalo, NY: Hein.

IRAN, Islamic Republic of

Legal history Iran was ruled by a series of dynasties for 2,500 years. Shi'ism became the official religion under Safavid rule (1501–1722). The increasing influence of foreign powers in the region under the Qajars (1795–1925) began with a series of capitulations to Europeans, beginning with the Russians, in the nineteenth century. In 1906 the first constitution was promulgated. A series of laws were enacted thereafter, relating to criminal, civil, commercial and family law. By 1936, legislation made secular education a prerequisite for serving judges. Major changes were introduced in the area of family law under Reza Shah with the passage of the Family Protection Law 1967 (significantly amended in 1975) abolishing extra-judicial divorce, requiring judicial permission for polygyny and only for limited circumstances, and establishing special Family Courts for the application of the new personal status legislation. The 1979 revolution brought an end to the Pahlavi dynasty (1925–79). The Supreme Judicial Council issued a proclamation directing courts that all un-Islamic legislation was suspended. The Council was given remit to revise all existing laws to Islamize the legal system, with Ayatollah Khomeini's *fatawa* serving as 'transitional laws'. The sources of law are Islamic law, constitutional law, legislation, informed sources such as custom, revolutionary principles, and so on.

Schools of *fiqh* The Ja'fari school is the predominant *madhhab* in Iran. There are also Hanafi Muslim minorities, as well as Zoroastrian, Baha'i, Christian and Jewish minorities. The officially recognized religions are Sunni Islam, Zoroastrianism, Judaism, and various Christian denominations. Under a 1933 law relating to the rights of non-Shi'i Iranians, courts are to apply the personal status laws applicable to the litigants belonging to officially recognized religions.

Constitutional status of Islam(ic law) The current Constitution was adopted on 2–3 December 1979, with significant revisions expanding presidential powers and eliminating the prime ministership in 1989. Article 4 provides that all civil, penal, financial, economic, administrative, cultural, military, political and any other laws must be based on Islamic criteria. Article 12 provides that the official state religion is Islam and the Twelver Ja'far schools; other schools of law are to be accorded full respect and freedom of religious practice, including matters of personal status.

Court system Special courts established by the Family Protection Act 1967 were dissolved after the revolution. The 1979 Constitution provides that the chief of the Supreme Court and the Prosecutor-General must be *mujtahids*. The Special Civil Courts were established in 1979 to adjudicate over matters relating to family law, succession and *awqaf*.

The court structure since the Revolution is as follows (numbers as of 1984): Revolutionary Courts: (70 branches); Public Courts: Civil Courts (205), Special Civil Courts (99), 1st Class Criminal Courts (86), 2nd Class Criminal Courts (156); Courts of Peace: Ordinary Courts of Peace (124), Independent Courts of Peace (125); Supreme Court of Cassation (22).

Notable features The Civil Code provides that marriage before puberty is invalid unless authorized by the natural guardian. When it is authorized before puberty, the minimum age of marriage is nine. The marriage of a virgin girl (even after puberty) requires permission of the father or paternal grandfather; a Special Civil Court may grant permission if the guardian refuses without valid reason. The Identity Office must be notified of all temporary or permanent marriages and their dissolution. Temporary marriage is permitted, and must be for a fixed time period. Polygyny is permitted. Marital obedience and maintenance are governed subject to classical conditions.

A twelve-article law on marriage and divorce passed in 1986 allows the wife the right to obtain a divorce if the husband marries without her permission or does not treat co-wives equitably in the court's assessment. A wife who is not *nashiza* may take the matter to court if her husband refuses to pay maintenance, and the court will fix a sum and issue a maintenance order. Arrears of maintenance to the wife have precedence over all other liabilities against the husband. (In temporary marriage, the wife is entitled to maintenance only if the contract contains such a stipulation.) The husband may deny his wife the right to work in any profession 'incompatible with the family interests or with the dignity of himself or of the wife'. The wife's refusing of conjugal relations where the husband has contracted venereal disease is not seen as disobedience.

Talaq is governed by classical Shi'i law, requiring a specific formula and two male witnesses. A conditional formula of divorce is invalid. Amendments of 1992 provide that registration of divorce without a court certificate is illegal. The wife may obtain a *khul'* in return for consideration of more or less than nuptial gift (*mahr*). Judicial divorce is available on the following grounds: proven insanity of either spouse; husband's castration or inability to consummate marriage (husband's lunacy or impotence are grounds whether they occurred before or after the contract); defect of the wife interfering with conjugal relations or her total blindness, contracting leprosy or becoming seriously crippled if they existed at time of contract; husband's non-maintenance, after failure to comply with maintenance order (whether he is unable or unwilling); and where continuation of marriage constitutes proven difficulty or hardship for the wife, if the husband refuses to divorce her. A 1992 amendment law extended the wife's access to divorce by the addition of the following grounds: husband's non-maintenance for up to six months for any reason; husband's bad behaviour, keeping bad company, etc., making the continuation of married life impossible for the wife; husband's incurable disease constituting a danger to the wife; husband's madness in cases where annulment of marriage would not be possible according to the Shari'a; husband's non-compliance with a court order to avoid demeaning or dishonourable employment; husband's conviction of five or more years; husband's addiction constituting a danger to his family and marriage; husband's desertion or leaving the marital home for six months without legitimate cause (legitimate cause being determined by the court); husband's conviction for a crime bringing dishonour to family (definition of a dishonourable crime to be determined by the court); husband's infertility for five years of marriage or his contracting a sexually transmitted disease; husband's disappearance for six months; and husband's polygynous marriage without his first wife's consent, if the court considers the co-wives are not being treated equally. A woman is entitled to half of her husband's assets if the court finds the divorce was initiated by the husband and was not caused by any failure on the wife's part. A reform introduced in 1992 extended the divorced wife's financial rights from maintenance during *'idda* and her deferred dower to the right to sue for payment for household services rendered to their husbands during marriage, although the measure is difficult to apply in practice, partly because of the difficulty in assessing wages for housework.

The mother's custody ends at two years for boys and seven for girls; custody reverts to the father if the mother remarries. The mother may be granted custody in certain cases if the father is proved unfit to care for the child.

Succession is governed by classical law; descendants of predeceased children of the deceased inherit in place of their parents. Children of Baha'i marriages are not recognized as legitimate and, therefore, are denied inheritance rights.

International conventions (with relevant reservations) Iran signed the ICCPR and ICESCR in 1968 and ratified both covenants in 1975 without reservations. Iran signed the CRC in 1991 and ratified it in 1994 with a general declaration and reservation to the effect that the Islamic Republic makes reservation to the articles and provisions that might be contradictory to the

Islamic Shari'a, reserving the right not to apply any provisions incompatible with Islamic Laws and the international legislation in effect.

Background and sources

Amin, S. H. (1985) *Middle East Legal Systems*, Glasgow: Royston.

Haeri, S. (1990) 'Divorce in contemporary Iran: a male prerogative in self-will', in C. Mallat and J. Connors (eds), *Islamic Family Law*, London: Graham and Trotman, pp. 55–70.

Lawyers' Committee for Human Rights (1993) *The Justice System of the Islamic Republic of Iran: a Report of the Lawyer's Committee for Human Rights*, New York: Lawyers' Committee for Human Rights.

Mahmood, T. (1995) 'Iran', in *Statutes of Personal Law in Islamic Countries: History, Texts and Analysis*, 2nd edn, New Delhi: India and Islam Research Council, pp. 65–9, 193–4.

Mir-Hosseini, Z. (1993) *Marriage on Trial: A Study of Islamic Family Law, Iran and Morocco Compared*, London: I.B.Tauris.

— (1998) 'Mariage et divorce: une marge de négociation pour les femmes', in N. Yavari-d'Hellencourt (ed.), *Les femmes en Iran: pressions sociales et stratégies identitaires*, Paris: L'Harmattan.

Pakzad, S. (1994) 'The legal status of women in the family in Iran', in M. Afkhami and E. Friedl (eds), *In the Eye of the Storm: Women in Post-Revolutionary Iran*, London: I.B.Tauris, pp. 169–79.

Ramazani, N. (1993) 'Women in Iran: the revolutionary ebb and flow', *Middle East Journal*, 47, 3: 409–28.

Redden, K. R. (1990) 'Iran', in K. R. Redden (ed.), *Modern Legal Systems Cyclopedia*, Vol. 5, Buffalo, NY: Hein.

Taleghani, M. A. R. (ed. and trans.) (1995) *Civil Code of Iran*, Littleton, CO: F.B. Rothman.

IRAQ, Republic of

Legal history Iraq has a mixed legal system that draws on both Sunni and Shi'i *fiqh* for the law applied in Shari'a courts. The legal system as a whole also includes constitutional law, legislation and statutory provisions, usage and custom, judicial precedent and authoritative juridical opinions. Iraq, the birthplace of the Hanafi school of *fiqh*, came under Ottoman rule in the seventeenth century. From 1850, a number of new civil, penal and commercial codes were adopted by the Ottomans, based on European (mainly French) models, but the OLFR 1917 was never implemented in Iraq as the Turks lost control over the region by the end of World War I, when a British Mandate was established. The British administrators did not adopt the OLFR as it was not part of local law and because of the fact that Iraq had an almost equal proportion of Sunni and Shi'i inhabitants. A monarchy was established under King Faisal in 1921 following the Arab revolt; Iraq gained full independence from its Mandate status in 1932. A military coup in 1958 brought an end to the monarchy and Iraq became a republic.

The Iraqi Law of Personal Status 1959 was based on the report of a commission appointed the previous year to draft a code of personal status and applies, according to Article 2, to all Iraqis except those specifically exempted by law, mainly relating to Christian and Jewish minorities. The ILPS provides that, in the absence of any textual provision, judgments should be passed on the basis of the principles of the Islamic Shari'a in closest keeping with the text of the ILPS. Article 1 of the Civil Code also identifies Islamic law as a formal source of law.

Schools of _fiqh_ The Ja'fari and Hanafi are the predominant schools in Iraq. There are also Christian and small Jewish and Yezidi minorities.

Constitutional status of Islam(ic law) The provisional constitution was adopted on 22 September 1968 and came into effect from 16 July 1970. Article 4 of the current provisional constitution declares Islam the state religion. (A new constitution was drafted in 1990 but was not adopted.)

Court system Courts of Personal Status hear all cases involving Muslims, whether Iraqi or not. These courts have jurisdiction over marriage, divorce, legitimacy, succession, _awqaf_, and so on. Shari'a courts operate independently from the regular courts. The Code of Personal Status 1959 is a unified code applicable to Shi'a and Sunni Iraqis.

Notable features The minimum marriage age is 18 for men and women; judicial permission for under-age marriages may be granted at 15 years if fitness, physical capacity and guardian's consent (unless the guardian's objection is considered unreasonable) are established. No relative or third party has the power of compulsion; a marriage contract concluded by coercion is void if it has not been consummated. Likewise, no relative or third party may prevent a person having legal capacity from marrying. Court registration without charge is obligatory and requires documentation of age, identity, stipulation of the amount of dower, medical reports, and so on; unregistered marriages may be proven by the affirmation of both parties.

Polygyny is permitted only by judicial permission, obtainable on the condition that the husband must show some lawful benefit and financial ability to support more than one wife. Permission is not to be granted if the judge fears unequal treatment of co-wives. The ILPS provides penalties of imprisonment and/or fines for non-compliance with its provisions relating to marriage, guardianship, registration and polygamy.

Upon marriage, the husband is obliged to maintain his wife (in accordance with the circumstances of both spouses) subject to classical conditions. Maintenance for a wife who is not *nashiza* is deemed to be a debt from the time that the husband ceases to pay maintenance; the wife is not entitled to maintenance if she leaves the marital home without her husband's permission or lawful cause, or if she is imprisoned or refuses to travel with her husband without lawful cause. The wife's right to work is not expressly mentioned, although the implication is that she would require her husband's permission to do so.

Talaq must be confirmed by the Shari'a Court's judgment or registered with the court during the *'idda* period. *Talaq* by a man who is intoxicated, insane, feeble-minded, under coercion, enraged (*madhush*), or seriously ill or in near death is ineffective, as is *talaq* that is not immediate or is conditional or in the form of an oath. All *talaqs* are deemed single and revocable except the third of the three *talaqs* pronounced.

The wife is entitled to request a dissolution if the husband does not fulfil any lawful condition stipulated in the marriage contract. Either party may request dissolution upon the following grounds: such harm as makes continuation of marriage impossible; marital infidelity; if the marriage was contracted without judicial permission before either party attained 18 years of age; if the marriage was concluded outside of court by means of coercion and was not consummated; if the husband marries polygynously without judicial permission; and if any of the above grounds are not proved, then on grounds of discord (in which case the court must initiate reconciliation procedures; if reconciliation efforts fail and the husband refuses to pronounce *talaq*, courts may grant judicial divorce; if the wife is found to be at fault, her financial rights are then forfeit). The wife may request a judicial divorce upon the following grounds: if the husband is imprisoned for three years; if her husband abandons her for two years without lawful reason; if her husband does not consummate the marriage within two years of the contract; husband's impotence or affliction (if this occurs after consummation, it must be confirmed by a medical report); husband's infertility if the wife has no living son by him; husband's serious illness that would cause the wife harm; non-maintenance after a grace period of up to 60 days; husband's failure to maintain due to his absence, disappearance, concealing his whereabouts,.or imprisonment for more than one year; and if the husband refuses to pay maintenance arrears after a 60-day grace period.

The wife may also request judicial separation before consummation in return for any dower and proven expenditure on the part of the husband for the purposes of the marriage. All judicial divorces are considered less irrevocable. The wife may also obtain a *khul'* from her husband in return for a consideration that may be more or less than her dower. The option of puberty is not specifically regulated, but is mentioned in the provision defining the waiting period. The former husband is obliged to maintain the divorced wife (even if she was deemed *nashiza*) during her *'idda* period. According to legislation passed in 1983, the repudiated wife also has a right to live in the marital home without her former husband for three years provided that she was not disobedient, did not request or agree to the divorce, and does not own her own house or flat. The divorcée is entitled to custody of boys or girls until the age of ten, extendable to 15 years if it appears to be in the minor's best interests. Upon attaining 15 years, the ward may choose which parent to live with, or choose any other relative if such a choice appears reasonable to the court.

The original 1959 legislation on succession was based on Ottoman law regulating the inheritance to the right to *miri* (government) property. The Ottoman law, in turn based mainly on German law, equalized male and female inheritance rights. The 1959 legislation also introduced obligatory bequests to grandchildren by predeceased sons or daughters, as well as complete freedom of the testator to make a will within the limits of the bequeathable one-third of the estate. Amendments made in 1963 allowed female descendants of the deceased to exclude collateral male agnates. The provisions relating to intestate succession were also amended in 1963, repealing the Ottoman-inspired reforms and adopting the Shi'i system of classifying heirs; within the Shi'i system of classification, Sunni principles are applied to the division of estates among the heirs.

Law/case reporting system Law reporting is through the Iraqi official journal, *al-Waqa'i al-'Iraqiyya*.

International conventions (with relevant reservations) Iraq signed the ICCPR and the ICESCR in 1969 and ratified both conventions in 1971. The general declarations submitted by Iraq related to its entry not signifying recognition of the state of Israel, and to its entry not constituting entry to the Optional Protocol to the ICCPR.

Iraq acceded to the CEDAW in 1986, with a reservation relating to Iraq not considering itself bound by Article 2(f) and (g), Article 9(1) and (2) and Article 16. The reservation to Article 16 states concerns the provisions of the Islamic Shari'a according women rights equivalent to the rights of their husbands thereby ensuring a just balance between spouses. Iraq acceded to the CRC in 1994, with a reservation to Article 14(1) relating to the child's freedom of religion, stating that 'allowing a child to change his or her religion runs counter to the provisions of the Islamic Shari'a'.

Background and sources

Amin, S. H. (1985) *Middle East Legal Systems*, Glasgow: Royston.

Anderson, N. (1976) *Law Reform in the Muslim World*, London: University of London.

El Alami, D. S. and D. Hinchcliffe (1996) *Islamic Marriage and Divorce Laws of the Arab World*, London and Boston: Kluwer Law International.

el-Mukhtar, S. (1995) 'Iraq', *Yearbook of Islamic and Middle Eastern Law*, Vol. 1, London: Centre of Islamic and Middle Eastern Law, School of Oriental and African Studies, University of London, pp. 157–77.

Iraq (1983) *Official Gazette*, English edn, no. 11, 16 March, pp. 4–5.

Mahmood, T. (1995) 'Algeria', in *Statutes of Personal Law in Islamic Countries: History, Texts and Analysis*, 2nd edn, New Delhi: India and Islam Research Council, pp. 15–10, 116–29.

Mallat, C. (1990) 'Shi'ism and Sunnism in Iraq: revisiting the codes', in C. Mallat and J. Connors (eds), *Islamic Family Law*, London: Graham and Trotman, pp. 71–91.

Nasir, J. J. (1990) *The Islamic Law of Personal Status*, 2nd edn, London: Graham and Trotman.

Pearl, D. (1987) *A Textbook on Muslim Personal Law*, 2nd edn, London: Croom Helm.

Redden, K. R. (1990) 'Iraq', in K. R. Redden (ed.), *Modern Legal Systems Cyclopedia*, Vol. 5, Buffalo, NY: Hein.

ISRAEL, State of

Legal history   Palestine remained under Ottoman rule from 1517 until 1917. The state of Israel was established in 1948 after the period of British Mandate rule from 1922 ended, followed by war with the Arab states. A majority of the Palestinian population became refugees in neighbouring Arab countries. Israel also has a significant Palestinian minority, a majority of whom are Muslim.

The Israeli legal system is a mixture of English common law, British Mandate regulations, and, in personal status law, Jewish, Christian and Muslim law. In matters of personal status, the system of shared jurisdiction in particular areas has allowed for legislation to intervene in the application of Muslim law (still based on the OLFR [Ottoman Law of Family Rights] 1917 implemented by the British Mandatory administration) by way of penal sanctions and procedural devices used indirectly to effect changes in the law. However, the core of personal status relating to marriage and divorce is still based on religious laws.

Schools of *fiqh* The Hanafi school is officially the main school of law, although this is a legacy of Palestine's Ottoman history. Much of the Muslim population, particularly in rural areas, is Shafi'i. Israel also has Christian and Druze minorities.

Constitutional status of Islam(ic law) The Basic Law on the Judicature regulates the creation of religious courts (*beit din*), which includes the Muslim religious courts. There is no formal constitution; some of the functions of a constitution are served by the Declaration of Establishment (1948), the basic laws of the parliament (Knesset), and the Israeli citizenship law, as well as other documents of constitutional significance.

Court system Muslim, Druze, Christian and rabbinical religious courts are separate. Muslim religious courts have exclusive jurisdiction over all matters concerning Muslim personal status. The courts apply the Ottoman Law of Family Rights 1917 (as amended after being adopted in Palestine by ordinance in 1919) and have jurisdiction, with the consent of the parties involved, over adoption and inheritance.

Notable features The minimum marriage age is 17 for females under the Marriage Age Law 1950 and as determined by the personal status law applicable to the prospective grooms (18 years under the OLFR). There is scope for judicial discretion (granted to civil courts) if the wife in an underage marriage is pregnant or a child has been born (without a minimum age) or for 'special circumstances' (specified by case law) from the age of 16 years for females. There are penal sanctions of imprisonment and/or fines for non-compliance for the husband, the person arranging the marriage, and the person officiating, although the law does not invalidate under-age marriages. The *wali*'s permission is required for the marriage of a female below the minimum marriage age of 17 years.

Marriage registration is obligatory, but non-registration does not invalidate the marriage according to religious law. The wife may insert a stipulation in the marriage contract that the husband may not take an additional wife; if he does so, she or the co-wife will be divorced. There is no forcible execution of an obedience judgment; maintenance claims between spouses or involving minor children are governed by the personal law applicable to the defendant, whether the case comes before the secular or religious courts. Claims for maintenance are not to be heard after the completion of the *'idda* period after a divorce, and arrears of maintenance cannot be claimed.

The OLFR invalidates *talaq* uttered under coercion or intoxication and also introduces the requirement of notification of divorce to the Shari'a court, but notification is procedural and does not affect the validity of a repudiation. The Women's Equal Rights Law 1951 provides penal sanction of imprisonment for a husband's unilateral decision to divorce against his wife's will and in the absence of a court judgment permitting such repudiation, but the repudiation remains valid. Under the OLFR, judicial dissolution is available to the wife on the following grounds: defect or illness of the husband (failure to consummate marriage, impotence, infectious disease and mental illness); non-payment of maintenance by an absent husband; discord and strife (after the appointment of arbitrators to form a family council, with such council empowered to determine fault should reconciliation efforts fail); and irregular/void marriage. The Age of Marriage Law also provides contracting of marriage of a girl under 17 years as grounds for requesting a dissolution before the wife attains 19 years of age (or at the request of the wife's guardian or a welfare officer before she attains 18 years). A divorcée who is not disobedient (*nashiza*) is entitled to deferred dower and maintenance during her *'idda* unless she re-nounced such rights.

Compensation paid to the wife became a regular feature in divorce after the passage of the Women's Equal Rights Law, which established penal sanc-tions for the unilateral repudiation of the wife against her will and without a court judgment. The Women's Equal Rights Law extended adjudication of the division of property to the regular civil courts. The Spouses (Property Relations) Law 1973 directs the application of the 'community property rule' with the presumption that parties have an equal share in marital property if the parties opt for adjudication under state law. Under the Capacity and Guardianship Law 1962, in the absence of a specific agreement between spouses, the wife has preference in matters of custody over minor children until six years. Courts are to base judgments on the wards' best interests. Upon the death of one party, guardianship is to revert to the surviving parent. Courts are empowered to appoint guardians for minors, with the ward's interests being the sole criteria for exercise of judicial discretion.

The Succession Law 1965 permits co-wives to share in the estate of the deceased husband. Muslims over 18 may opt for the application of *shar'i* inheritance law, or the Ottoman Law of Succession 1913 (initially equalizing rights of male and female heirs to *miri* property, i.e., state-owned property granted to individuals) as amended by the Women's Equal Rights Law (extend-ing Ottoman legislation to *mulk* and movable property).

Law/case reporting system Law reporting is through the *Israeli Official Gazette*. Case reports of Shari'a court decisions are published in bulletins of the Muslim and Druze Divisions of the Ministry of Religious Affairs (*Majallat al-Akhbar al-Darziyya* and *Majallat al-Akhbar al-Islamiyya*).

International conventions (with relevant reservations) Israel signed the ICCPR and ICESCR in 1966 and ratified them in 1991. Israel submitted a reservation to Article 23 of ICCPR relating to the establishment of gender equality in the area of family law. The declaration states that 'matters of personal status are governed in Israel by the religious law of the parties concerned. To the extent that such law is inconsistent with its obligations under the Covenant, Israel reserves the right to apply that law.' Israel signed the CEDAW in 1980 and ratified it in 1991. Israel submitted a reservation to Article 7(b) relating to gender equality in the formulation and implementation of policy, including holding public office and performing public functions at all levels of government. The Israeli reservation states that, other than in the area of religious courts, the article has been fully implemented in Israel, and that the reservation concerns the inadmissibility of appointing women judges in religious courts where this is prohibited by the communal laws applicable to a particular community. Israel also expresses its reservation to Article 16 on gender equality in family law 'to the extent that the laws on personal status which are binding on the various religious communities in Israel do not conform with the provisions of that article'. Israel signed the CRC in 1990 and ratified the convention in 1991, without reservations.

Israel signed the Convention to Consent to Marriage, Minimum Age for Marriage and Registration of Marriages in 1962.

Background and sources

Ibrahim, I. (1998) 'The status of Arab women in Israel', *Critique: Journal of Critical Studies of the Middle East*, 12: 107–20.

Israel (1997) *Initial and Second Periodic Report to CEDAW*, 8 April, CEDAW 17th Session, 7–25 July 1997, New York: United Nations.

Layish, A. (1975) *Women and Islamic Law in a Non-Muslim State: A Study Based on Decisions of the Shari'a Courts in Israel*, New York: Halstead Press.

— (1994) 'Reforms in the law of personal status of the Muslims in Israel: legislation and application', *Recht van de Islam*, 12: 45–57.

Redden, K. R. (1990) 'Israel', in K. R. Redden (ed.), *Modern Legal Systems Cyclopedia*, Vol. 5, Buffalo, NY: Hein.

Reiter, Y. (1997) 'Qadis and the implementation of Islamic law in present day Israel', in R. Gleave and E. Kermelli (eds), *Islamic Law: Theory and Practice*, London: I.B.Tauris, pp. 205–31.

Welchman, L. (1990) 'Family law under occupation: Islamic law and the Shari'a Courts of the West Bank', in C. Mallat and J. Connors (eds), *Islamic Family Law*, London: Graham and Trotman, pp. 93–115.

JORDAN, Hashemite Kingdom of

Legal history Jordan remained a part of the Ottoman Empire until World War I and was then placed under an indirect form of British Mandate rule. The Ottoman legal system was retained; in 1927 many Ottoman laws (including the Ottoman Law of Family Rights 1917) were re-enacted with some alterations. The Hashemite Kingdom of Jordan was established as a fully independent state in 1947, with Islam as the state religion. The first constitution was adopted the following year, and the state embarked on the process of developing a national legal system to replace the vestiges of Ottoman rule.

In 1947, a provisional Law of Family Rights was enacted. It remained in force until it was replaced in 1951 by the new Law of Family Rights, largely following the form of the OLFR (Ottoman Law of Family Rights). The JLFR 1951 was the first in a series of codifications of Islamic family law issued in the 1950s by the national legislatures of newly independent Arab states. A new Constitution was adopted in 1952, retaining the religious and communal basis of jurisdiction in personal status matters. By this time, the Palestinian territory of the West Bank, including East Jerusalem, had come under Jordanian rule, and until 1994, even during the Israeli occupation from 1967, the Shari'a courts of the West Bank were under the authority of the Jordanian Qadi al-Quda and applied Jordanian law.

A Civil Code and Civil Procedure Code were enacted in 1952 and 1953, the former replacing the Ottoman Majalla of 1876. The 1952 Civil Code was replaced in 1976, the new code drawing from Syrian legislation (which in turn was modelled on the Egyptian Civil Code of 1948). The same year, the Jordanian Law of Personal Status replaced the 1951 JLFR. The JLPS revises the JLFR in a number of significant ways, providing for a more comprehensive code, while retaining reference to the classical Hanafi rules in the absence of a specific reference in the text. Discussions continue on the draft text of a new personal status law.

Court system The Jordanian legal system draws from the Ottoman heritage in the communal jurisdiction of the religious courts of different communities over matters of personal status. In its civil court system it follows the French model. The Shari'a courts are established in the Constitution along with the religious tribunals of other recognized communities and include First Instance Courts with a single *qadi* and the Shari'a Court of Appeal. The other two categories of courts established in the Constitution are the civil or regular courts (*nizamiyya*) and 'special tribunals'. The Constitution grants the Shari'a courts exclusive jurisdiction in matters of Muslim personal status. Precise jurisdiction of and procedure in the Shari'a courts is defined in the Law of *Shar'i* Procedure 1959; the rules governing qualification and functions of *shar'i qadis* and lawyers are to be found in the Law of Organization of Shari'a Courts 1972 and the Law of *Shar'i* Advocates 1952 respectively, both of which have been amended a number of times.

Schools of *fiqh* The Hanafi *madhhab* is the dominant school in Jordanian law.

Constitutional status of Islam(ic law) The 1952 Constitution declares Islam to be the state religion. It does not specify the sources of legislation as a whole, although in regard to the Shari'a courts it states that 'the Shari'a courts in the exercise of their jurisdiction shall apply the rulings of the Shari'a law'.

Notable features The minimum marriage age is 16 for men and 15 for women (all ages in the personal status law are calculated by the lunar calendar) and the Penal Code provides penalties for all those involved in carrying out under-age marriages. An under-age marriage can nevertheless be recognized as valid if the wife has fallen pregnant or given birth by the time of a suit to dissolve their marriage coming to court, or if both spouses have by that time reached the minimum age. In the event of a contract between a woman aged under 18 and a man 20 years or more her senior, the *qadi* is required to ascertain that the bride has freely given her consent to the marriage and that it is in her interest. The consent of the guardian is required for a female aged under 18 to marry, but not for a divorcée or widow aged over eighteen; the law thus implicitly requires the consent of the guardian to the first marriage of a woman of any age, although the *qadi* can override the *wali*'s refusal if it has no justification in law. Criminal sanctions are provided for those violating the mandatory registration requirements for marriage and divorce.

There are no constraints on polygyny beyond the classical injunctions that a man must treat co-wives equitably and provide them with separate dwellings. The registration fee for a polygynous contract of marriage is higher than that for a monogamous union. The marriage contract requires a man to disclose his social status to the woman he is marrying, but there is no requirement that an existing wife be notified of a subsequent polygynous marriage by her husband.

The institution of the 'house of obedience' is maintained but without forcible execution of an 'obedience' ruling made against the wife beyond disqualifying her from maintenance rights against her husband.

As elsewhere in the region, *talaq* uttered by a man who is drunk, asleep, in a faint, coerced, or 'overwhelmed' (*madhush*) has no effect, while oaths on *talaq* and conditional *talaq* do not give rise to *talaq* if the intention was to get someone to do or not do something. A 'triple *talaq*' as in *talaq* accompanied by a number in word or sign or – significantly – repeated in a single session has the effect of a single revocable *talaq* only. To give rise to the greater finality of irrevocable *talaq*, three *talaqs* must be pronounced not only separately but in three separate sessions.

Grounds for which the wife may petition for divorce are similar to those introduced elsewhere in the region from the time of the OLFR. They include failure to maintain, physical desertion or the absence of the husband for a year or more, a prison sentence of three years or more, 'discord and strife', breach of a binding stipulation in the marriage contract, and various grounds associated with the mental and physical health of the husband (the latter also being entitled to petition for divorce on similar health grounds). The law allows either party to insert stipulations into the contract and to sue for dissolution if they are broken. Either spouse may also petition for divorce on the grounds of discord and strife.

The law provides for compensation for arbitrary *talaq* up to a maximum of the equivalent of a year's maintenance for the wife divorced 'without legitimate cause' and retains the classical rules requiring the ex-husband to pay for his divorced wife breast-feeding and undertaking custody of their children. A divorced mother is entitled to custody of her children until they reach puberty, subject to the classical conditions. During marriage, the wife has no financial obligations for her own upkeep and her medical expenses are included in the maintenance she is due from her husband. In the area of succession, changes to classical Hanafi law have been made in allowing the spouse relict to share in the *radd* or proportional return of the remainder of the estate to those holding fixed shares, should circumstances so permit; and in providing for the 'obligatory bequest' (*al-wasiya al-wajiba*) to orphaned grandchildren, although restricting this to the grandchildren through predeceased sons, not daughters.

Notable cases   In 1989, an apostasy case against Toujan al-Faisal, a journalist and parliamentary candidate, was heard in the First Instance Shari'a Court of south Amman. Jordan has no apostasy law but the petitioners sought that she should be declared an apostate, and divorced from her husband. Al-Faisal was standing in the elections at the time; the court eventually ruled no jurisdiction and on appeal in 1990 the Shari'a Court of Appeal, which had agreed to hear the section of the petition relating to divorce on the grounds of alleged apostasy, found that there was no evidence of apostasy and dismissed the case.

Law reporting *The Official Gazette*. Practitioners' collections of principles of Shari'a appeal court decisions.

International conventions (with relevant reservations) Jordan is a party to both international covenants. It signed the CEDAW in 1980 and ratified it in 1992 with the following reservations: Article 9(2) regarding equal nationality rights for men and women, particularly in marriage; Article 15(4) on equal rights regarding freedom of movement and choice of domicile (because 'a wife's residence is with her husband'); and Article 16(1) on equal rights in marriage and family relations. Jordan signed the CRC in 1990 and ratified it in 1991, with reservations to Articles 14, 20 and 22 concerning adoption and children's rights to freedom of choice of religion. Accession to Convention to Consent to Marriage, Minimum Age for Marriage and Registration of Marriage in July 1992.

Background and sources

Amin, S. H. (1985) 'Jordan' in S. H. Amin, *Middle East Legal Systems*, Glasgow: Royston.

El Alami, D. S. and D. Hinchcliffe (1996), 'Jordan', in *Islamic Marriage and Divorce Laws of the Arab World*, London and Boston: Kluwer Law International, pp. 79–114.

Gallagher, N. (1995) 'Women's human rights on trial in Jordan: the triumph of Toujan al-Faisal', in M. Afkhami (ed.), *Faith and Freedom*, London: I.B.Tauris, pp. 209–31.

— (1995), appended translation of article by T. al-Faisal, 'They insult us … and we elect', in M. Afkhami (ed.), *Faith and Freedom*, London: I.B.Tauris, pp. 232–7.

Mahmood, T. (1995) 'Jordan', in *Statutes of Personal Law in Islamic Countries: History, Texts and Analysis*, 2nd edn, New Delhi: India and Islam Research Council, pp. 20–4, 129–36.

Redden, K. R. (1990) 'Jordan', in K. R. Redden (ed.), *Modern Legal Systems Cyclopedia*, Vol. 5, Buffalo, New York: Hein.

Welchman, L. (1988) 'The development of Islamic family law in the legal system of Jordan', *ICLQ*, 37: 868–86.

KUWAIT, State of

Legal history The Ottoman Empire ruled present-day Kuwait as part of Basra province from the late seventeenth century, and the Ottoman legal and judicial system functioning in Iraq was applied to Kuwaiti territory. However, the local rulers adhered to the Maliki school. In the late nineteenth century, a Treaty of Protection placed Kuwait under British extra-territorial control, and Kuwait became an administrative subdivision of 'British India'. While the British did establish a Western-style judicial administration, it served only the non-Arab inhabitants of Kuwait.

The British protectorate in Kuwait ended in 1961, by which time Shaykh 'Abdullah al-Salim al-Sabah had begun the process of legal and judicial reform; the process of codification was initiated by the country's leaders during the early 1960s. In 1959, Sheikh 'Abdullah enlisted the services of the re-nowned Arab jurist 'Abd al-Razzaq al-Sanhuri, leading to the enactment of a number of codes inspired by Egyptian and French models. While matters relating to civil and commercial law and procedure were codified in the 1960s, it was not until the 1980s that the Civil Code 1980 and the Kuwaiti Code of Personal Status 1984 were enacted.

Schools of *fiqh* The Maliki school is the official *madhhab* in Kuwait. There is also a significant Ja'fari Shi'a minority.

Constitutional status of Islam(ic law) The Constitution was adopted on 11 November 1962. Article 2 states that '[t]he religion of the State is Islam, and the Islamic Shari'a shall be a main source of legislation'. Article 1(2) of the Civil Code also directs that, in the absence of a specific legislative provision, judges are to adjudicate according to custom (*'urf*), and in the absence of an applicable principle of custom, be guided by the principles of Islamic jurisprudence (*fiqh*) most appropriate under the general and particular circumstances. Following the Iranian Revolution, Kuwait's rulers stated that they would begin Islamizing the law and enacting laws which were fully in agreement with the Shari'a.

Court system Under the 1959 Law Regulating the Judiciary, Kuwaiti courts are competent to hear all disputes concerning personal status, and civil, criminal and commercial matters. There are three levels of courts: Courts of First Instance (having several divisions, including personal status) in every judicial district; High Court (with five divisions, including personal status); and the Supreme Court (divided into the Division of High Appeal and the Cassation

Division). For the application of personal status laws, there are three separate sections: Sunni, Shi'i and non-Muslim (for the application of family laws of religious minorities). After judgments by the Courts of First Instance, appeals lie with the High Court, and then with the Cassation Division of the Supreme Court.

Notable features No substantive minimum marriage age is specified, rather, capacity to marry requires a party to have reached puberty and be of sound mind. The contract may not be registered where the female has not reached 15 years or the male 17 years. No claim arising from marriage shall be heard if either party is under-age at the time of the claim or if the claim is not established by official documentation of marriage. A woman who has been married previously or has attained 25 years has 'freedom of choice' in marriage; however, she cannot conclude the contract herself and still requires her *wali* to do so, in accordance with classical Maliki rules. Polygyny is governed by classical law.

Maintenance is considered a debt against the husband from the date he fails to provide maintenance, up to a maximum period of two years' arrears from the date of the claim. Judgments for obedience cannot be forcibly executed. A wife's going out to work is not deemed a violation of her marital obligations if her working is not contrary to her family's interests.

Talaq uttered by a man who is insane, feeble, under coercion, intoxicated, mistaken, disoriented or enraged is not effective, nor are forms of *talaq* that are not immediate effective. *Talaq* to which a number is attached shall be effective as a single revocable *talaq*, except for the third of three. The wife may obtain a *khul'* from her husband in return for appropriate recompense. The rules on *khul'* include explicit prohibition of coercion in reaching a *khul'* agreement and invalidate any condition of the settlement by the father stipulating his custody over children from the marriage.

The wife may seek a judicial divorce on the following grounds: the husband's non-maintenance; *ila'*, should the wife request a divorce; the husband's absence of one year or more without proper justification (on the basis of *darar*/injury); and the husband's imprisonment for three years or more. Either spouse may apply for a judicial divorce on grounds of *darar*/injury caused by such word or action as makes continued matrimony impossible or for any breach of a valid stipulation recorded in the marriage contract; *darar*/injury is established by the testimony of two male or one male and two female witnesses and divorce on such grounds follows reconciliation efforts, with the possibility of an award being made as compensation for the aggrieved party. Annulment is available on following grounds: defect of either spouse that makes cohabitation harmful or interferes with conjugal relations; and difference of religion arising from conversion or apostasy after marriage. The divorcée is entitled to compensation equal to not more than one year's maintenance in addition to maintenance during *'idda*, except for cases of divorce for non-maintenance due to the husband's poverty, divorce for *darar*/injury caused by the *khul'*, or annulment at the wife's request. The divorced mother's right to custody ceases at puberty for boys and majority or age of marriage for daughters.

The 1971 Law on Obligatory Bequest introduced obligatory bequests to favour orphaned grandchildren; this applies to descendants through sons and through daughters, the first generation only.

Law/case reporting system Laws and summaries of important Court of Cassation decisions are published in the Kuwaiti *Official Gazette*.

International conventions (with relevant reservations) Kuwait signed the CRC in 1990 and ratified it in 1991, with a general reservation upon signature to all provisions of the Convention 'incompatible with the laws of Islamic Shari'a and the local statutes in effect'; and declarations upon ratification relating to Article 7 and its relation to Kuwaiti Nationality Law as applicable to orphans born in Kuwait and Article 21 on adoption as a system not recognized by the Islamic Shari'a, 'the main source of legislation'.

Kuwait acceded to the CEDAW in 1994, with reservations to Article 7(a) relating to gender equality in suffrage and eligibility for election ('inasmuch as the provision … conflicts with the Kuwaiti Electoral Act under which the right to vote and run in elections is reserved for men'); Article 9(2) on gender equality in nationality rights ('inasmuch as it runs counter to the Kuwaiti Nationality Act, which stipulates that a child's nationality shall be determined by that of his father'); and Article 16(f) on equal rights of guardianship, wardship, trusteeship and adoption ('inasmuch as it conflicts with the provisions of the Islamic Shari'a, Islam being the official religion of the state').

Kuwait acceded to the ICCPR and ICESCR in 1996. Kuwait submitted a number of interpretative declarations relating to the following Articles of the ICCPR: Articles 2(1) and 3, relating to the provisions of the Kuwaiti Constitution (especially Article 20 thereof), and the exercise of rights within the limits set by Kuwaiti law; and Article 23, relating to the supremacy of Kuwaiti national law ('which is based on Islamic law') in areas where there is conflict between national personal status laws and the provisions of the Convention. The reservation to Article 25(b) states that Kuwaiti electoral law restricts to males the right to stand and vote in elections. Kuwait also submitted two interpretative declarations and a reservation to the ICESCR. The interpretative declaration to Articles 2(2) and 3 is almost the same as Kuwait's first declaration to the ICCPR.

Background and sources

Amin, S. H. (1985) *Middle East Legal Systems*, Glasgow: Royston.

— (1991) *Legal System of Kuwait*, Glasgow: Royston.

Ballantyne, W. M. (1986) *Commercial Law in the Arab Middle East: The Gulf States*, London: Lloyd's of London Press.

El Alami, D. S. and D. Hinchcliffe (1996) *Islamic Marriage and Divorce Laws of the Arab World*, London and Boston: Kluwer Law International.

Mahmood, T. (1995) 'Kuwait', in *Statutes of Personal Law in Islamic Countries: History, Texts and Analysis*, 2nd edn, New Delhi: India and Islam Research Council, pp. 24–6, 127–31.

Nasir, J. J. (1990) *The Islamic Law of Personal Status*, 2nd edn, London: Graham and Trotman.

Pearl, D. (1987) *A Textbook on Muslim Law*, 2nd edn, London: Croom Helm.

Redden, K. R. (1990) 'Kuwait', in K. R. Redden (ed.), M*odern Legal Systems Cyclopedia*, Vol. 5, Buffalo, NY: Hein.

LEBANON (Lebanese Republic)

Legal history   The legal system draws *inter alia* on elements of Ottoman law, canon law, and codes based on French models. Lebanon became a part of the Ottoman Empire in 1516 and remained under Ottoman rule, with relative autonomy, for three centuries. It was under a French mandate from 1918 to 1943 and although French civil law had a great influence on the development of the Lebanese legal system and judiciary, the French authorities did not affect any substantive changes to the Ottoman Law of Family Rights 1917 or to uncodified aspects of personal law. During the 1920s, the borders of Lebanon were redefined and the Republic was established. Lebanon has a very heterogeneous population, leading to the development of a highly complex system of power-sharing for the major religious communities. However, the proportion of Maronite Christians and Sunni and Shi'a Muslims in the population changed significantly over the span of half a century, and updating the census data providing the bases for the system of power-sharing is an issue that has proved difficult for the modern state of Lebanon to address.

The inequalities inherent in the power-sharing agreement that failed to adapt to changing circumstances, as well as the effects of the Palestinian struggle for self-determination, led to a descent into civil war in 1975. Lebanon, which has a large Palestinian refugee population, accepted an Arab-brokered peace accord in the early 1990s. During the late 1990s, there was considerable popular pressure for reform of laws regulating women's rights.

Schools of *fiqh* The Ja'fari and Hanafi schools are the predominant *madhahib* in Lebanon. There are also Druze, Ismai'li and 'Alawi/Nusayri minorities. Several Christian denominations are represented, including Orthodox and Catholic denominations and one Protestant church, and there is a small Jewish minority. There are over fifteen different officially recognized religious sects in Lebanon.

Constitutional status of Islam(ic law) The Constitution was adopted on 23 May 1926 and has been amended numerous times. The Constitution guarantees that the personal status and religious interests of the various recognized religious communities of Lebanon are to be respected.

Court system Communal jurisdiction over personal status is recognized for Muslims, Druze, Christians, and Jews. There are two levels of Shari'a courts (with Sunni and Ja'fari judges presiding over cases involving Sunni and Ja'fari litigants, respectively): Shari'a Courts of First Instance and a Supreme Shari'a Court in Beirut sitting with three *qadis* and a civil judge acting as attorney-general. There are also two levels of Druze courts, the Courts of First Instance and a Supreme Court of Appeal.

Notable features The age of capacity is 18 years for males and 17 for females among Sunnis; scope for judicial discretion on the basis of physical maturity and the *wali*'s permission is from 17 years for males and nine for females. For Shi'as, the marriage age is real puberty for both, or 15 for males and nine for females with judicial permission. For the Druze, the marriage age is 18 for males and 17 for females, or 16 and 15 with judicial permission. A mature female of 17 years may apply to the court to marry and the requirement of guardian's permission may be waived if his objection appears unfounded. The *wali*'s right of *ijbar* is retained for Lebanese Ja'faris.

Marriage registration is a requirement governed by the Family Rights Law and Sunni and Ja'fari Shari'a Judiciary Act. The Shari'a Court having jurisdiction over the domicile of either spouse has exclusive authority to solemnize marriage contracts, and the personal status officer is only to record contracts solemnized according to the terms of legislation; a copy of the marriage contract must be sent to the Personal Status Administration for official registration. Failure to register does not invalidate Muslim marriages, but such marriages will not be recognized without a Shari'a court ruling.

Maintenance and disobedience are governed by classical law. There are no restrictions on polygyny other than classical injunctions to treat co-wives equally; there is express legal recognition of the validity of stipulations inserted into the marriage contract restricting the husband's right to marry polygynously (e.g., effecting the divorce of one or the other co-wife in case of breach of the stipulation).

Talaq uttered while intoxicated or under coercion is invalid, while *talaq* upon condition (for Sunnis) or deferred until a future time is valid. A husband who repudiates his wife is obligated to inform the judge of his exercise of *talaq* within 15 days and then the Department of Personal Status. Failure to register with the Department of Personal Status does not invalidate the divorce, but the husband will be subject to criminal penalties. For the Shi'a, classical rules regarding a specific formula under particular conditions apply.

The wife may request a judicial divorce on the following grounds: husband's failure to consummate the marriage; husband's affliction making cohabitation without harm impossible; husband's insanity; husband's failure to maintain and his concealment of his whereabouts, or his absence, disappearance or intermittent cohabitation with his wife; and either spouse may apply for divorce on grounds of marital discord (after reconciliation efforts) where a judicial decision determines fault and appropriate recompense for the aggrieved party. All judicial divorces for such grounds are irrevocable. For the Shi'a, judicial divorce is not recognized, though some Shi'i interpreters do accept judicial intervention. For the Druze, divorce is possible only by decision of a *madhhab* judge. If the *madhhab* judge finds no legal justification for the divorce, the husband will be obliged to pay damages to the wife. Druze may also annul marriage by mutual consent, before a judge and two witnesses, and this creates a permanent and indissoluble bar between the former spouses. Maintenance during the *'idda* is obligatory except for a woman judged to be disobedient.

Among Sunnis, the divorced mother's right to custody ends at seven years for boys and nine for girls; at two years for boys and seven for girls for the Shi'a (unless the mother remarries) subject to the wards' best interests; and at seven years for males and nine for females for the Druze.

Legislation relating to inheritance law directs the application of classical provisions relating to the division of *mulk* property for Sunni, Shi'a and Druze communities. Druze succession law is similar to the Sunni except that Druze do not exclude descendants of predeceased heirs. *Miri* property continues to be governed by the Ottoman Inheritance Law 1913, which gives equal portions to males and females.

Law/case reporting system Law reporting is through the *Journal Officiel*.

International conventions (with relevant reservations) Lebanon acceded to the ICCPR and ICESCR in 1972, without reservations. Lebanon signed the CRC in 1990 and ratified it in 1991, without reservations. Lebanon acceded to the CEDAW in 1997, with a number of general reservations to Articles 9(2), 16(1)(c), (d), (f) and (g), and 29(1).

Background and sources

Bilani, N., Najjar I. and A. E. El-Gemayel (1985) 'Personal status', in A. E. El-Gemayel (ed.), *The Lebanese Legal System*, Vol. 1, Washington, DC: International Law Institute in cooperation with Georgetown University, pp. 267–390.

El Alami, D. S. and D. Hinchcliffe (1996) *Islamic Marriage and Divorce Laws of the Arab World*, London and Boston: Kluwer Law International.

Mahmood, T. (1995) 'Algeria', in *Statutes of Personal Law in Islamic Countries: History, Texts and Analysis*, 2nd edn, New Delhi: India and Islam Research Council, pp. 27–9, 141–9.

Nasir, J. J. (1990) *The Islamic Law of Personal Status*, 2nd edn, London: Graham and Trotman.

Redden, K. R. (1990) 'Lebanon', in K. R. Redden (ed.), *Modern Legal Systems Cyclopedia*, Vol. 5, Buffalo, NY: Hein.

OMAN, Sultanate of

Legal history Omani tribes adopted the tenets of Ibadi Islam in the seventh to eighth centuries. European incursions into the area of present-day Oman began with the Portuguese in the early sixteenth century. The expulsion of the Portuguese in 1650 was followed by a period of ascendancy of Omani power in the Gulf and Indian Ocean region; by the end of the 1600s, the Omani empire included Bahrain and Zanzibar. The decline of the empire began in the following century. Omani leaders signed treaties of protection with the British in 1798 and 1800 as French interest in the Indian Ocean increased and a series of treaties and agreements concluded with the British in the nineteenth century brought Oman under increasing British influence, with an 1891 treaty bringing Oman under British protection. The sovereignty of the Sultanate of Oman and Muscat was formally recognized in 1951 under Sultan Sa'id ibn Taimur.

Efforts at judicial reform began with the overthrow of the previous Sultan

(Said bin Taimur, reigned 1932–70) by his son Qaboos in a bloodless coup supported by the British. Since that time, Oman has adopted a number of codes relating to commercial, criminal, labour, and tax laws, among other areas. Personal status remains unlegislated. Efforts at regulating the Shari'a courts were unsuccessful, leading to the establishment of separate courts and judicial tribunals to enforce state law beginning in the 1970s. There are both Shari'a and state courts now, with the former applying Ibadi law within an increasingly limited area of jurisdiction, and the latter applying those laws promulgated by royal decree. Ultimate appeal lies with the Sultan. There have been tentative efforts at establishing a more representative form of government. Sultan Qaboos introduced a *Majlis al-Istishari* (consultative council) in 1981, an informal advisory body comprised entirely of appointed members. This was replaced by a *Majlis al-Shura* in 1990 with members chosen by the Sultan from slates of three citizens put forward by notables of each district. The new *Majlis* is empowered to review legislation and state development plans and adopt and recommend amendments by a two-thirds majority.

Schools of *fiqh* Oman is the only state in which the Ibadi school is the predominant *madhhab*. There are also Sunni and Shi'i minorities, as well as Hindu and Christian (mainly expatriate) communities.

Constitutional status of Islam(ic law) In November 1996 a Basic Law, in effect a constitution, was decreed by Sultan Qaboos to regulate several important areas of governance. Chapter 1 of the Basic Law is entitled 'The State and the System of Government'. Article 2 declares Islam the official state religion, and provides that the Shari'a is 'the basis for legislation'.

Court system The judiciary is comprised of Shari'a courts, magistrates' courts, and several specialized courts and tribunals. Shari'a courts hear civil and minor criminal cases, and judgments are made according to Ibadi doctrine. The Court of Appeal in Muscat, staffed by three *qadis*, hears appeals from the first instance Shari'a courts. The highest level of judiciary is the Complaints Committee.

Since the 1970s, the jurisdiction of Shari'a courts has been reduced. Magistrates' Courts hear misdemeanour cases. The Criminal Court in Muscat hears cases involving felonies and serves as an appellate court. Other specialized courts and quasi-judicial tribunals in various areas of land, commercial, labour and tax law apply state-issued legislation.

The Sultan issued several royal decrees to establish a law on judicial authority and to affirm the independence of the judiciary as called for in the 1996 Basic Charter. The decrees formally establish the judiciary as an independent, hierarchical system composed of a Supreme Court, an Appeals Court, Primary Courts (one located in each region), and, within the primary courts, Divisional Courts. Within each of the courts there are to be divisions to handle commercial, civil, penal, labour, taxation, general and personal cases (the latter under Shari'a). The general prosecutor, which currently falls under the Royal Omani Police Chief Inspector, is to become an independent legal entity. Implementation of these decrees is expected to take place during 2000.

Notable features   Classical Ibadi *fiqh* is applied to personal status matters.

Law/case reporting system   Law reports of Royal Decrees and Ministerial Decisions are published in the *Official Gazette*.

International conventions (with relevant reservations)   Oman acceded to the CRC in 1996, with a number of reservations. The reservation to Article 21 states that a general reservation is submitted to provisions that do not accord with Islamic law or the Sultanate's state legislation, particularly those provisions relating to adoption. The reservation to Articles 14 and 30 states that Oman does not consider itself bound by those provisions that grant children the freedom of religion or that 'allow a child belonging to a religious minority to profess his or her own religion'.

Background and sources

Amin, S. H. (1985) *Middle East Legal Systems*, Glasgow: Royston.

Ballantyne, W. M. (1986) *Commercial Law in the Arab Middle East: The Gulf States*, London: Lloyd's of London Press.

El Alami, D. S. and D. Hinchcliffe (1996) 'The uncodified law', in D. S. El Alami and D. Hinchcliffe (eds), *Islamic Marriage and Divorce Laws of the Arab World*, London and Boston: Kluwer Law International, pp. 1–32.

Mahmood, T. (1995) 'Gulf', in *Statutes of Personal Law in Islamic Countries: History, Texts and Analysis*, 2nd edn, New Delhi: India and Islam Research Council, p. 85.

Redden, K. R. (1990) 'Oman', in K. R. Redden (ed.), *Modern Legal Systems Cyclopedia*, Vol. 5, Buffalo, NY: Hein.

Riphenburg, C. J. (1998) *Oman: Political Development in a Changing World*, Westport, CT: Praeger.

PALESTINE/Palestinian Territories of West Bank
and Gaza Strip

Legal history The Palestinian territories of the West Bank, including East Jerusalem, and the Gaza Strip are that part of Palestine not included in the territory on which the state of Israel was established in 1948. Legally the territories share a history of Ottoman law and custom, and British Mandate legislation along with Shari'a and customary rules. From 1948 to 1967 the West Bank, including East Jerusalem, was ruled by Jordan while the Gaza Strip was administered by Egypt.

After 1967 Israeli military orders regulated large areas of life for Palestinians in both the West Bank and Gaza Strip while Israel illegally annexed the territory of East Jerusalem. Since the bilateral PLO–Israeli 'Oslo Accords' set the framework of a peace process, the unification of laws in the two areas became part of the agenda of the Palestine national Authority established under the terms of the agreements. Currently Jordanian law governs personal status for Muslims in the West Bank; East Jerusalem Muslims have recourse either to that law or to the law applied in the Israeli Shari'a system, which comprises the Ottoman Law of Family Rights as amended by Israeli legislation since 1948; and Gazan Muslims are governed by personal status law issued during the Egyptian administration of the Strip.

Some regulations have been issued since the 1994 Oslo Accords by the Palestinian Qadi al-Quda, which are applied in both areas. The most appropriate opinion of the Hanafi school is the residual law in Muslim personal status matters in both areas. Recognized Christian communities apply their own personal status laws in their own tribunals. Work is reported to be proceeding on the text of a Palestinian personal status law, a matter of substantial interest in different sectors of Palestinian civil society.

Schools of *fiqh* The Hanafi school is the predominant *madhhab* in Palestine, as well as in Jordan and Egypt, the states whose legislation continues to govern personal status in the West Bank and Gaza, respectively.

Constitutional status of Islam(ic law) The draft Basic Law for the transitional period (which has not yet been ratified by Yasser Arafat, the President of the PNA) provides that 'the principles of the Islamic Shari'a are a principal source of legislation' (Article 4/2) and that 'matters of personal status are to be dealt with by Shari'a and religious courts' (Article 92/1).

Court system Regular courts include Magistrates' Courts and First Instance Courts with High Courts with appellate jurisdiction for civil and criminal
matters. Complexities in unifying courts and laws in the two areas of the West
Bank and Gaza Strip are one of the challenges facing the Palestinian Authority.
The Shari'a courts in both areas apply personal status law, using the execution
offices in the regular court system. A Shari'a Court of Appeal for the West
Bank has been established under the PA which sits for the moment in Nablus,
with Jordan maintaining direction of the Shari'a first instance and appeal
courts in East Jerusalem. The Shari'a Court of Appeal in the Gaza Strip is
also now under PA jurisdiction.

Notable features [*For the rules of Muslim personal status currently applicable in
the West Bank see under Jordan. For Muslim Palestinians marrying under Israeli law in
East Jerusalem see under Israel.*] In the Gaza Strip, the Egyptian-issued Law of
Family Rights sets puberty as the minimum age of marriage with no marriage
allowed of a female aged under nine or a male aged under twelve. The
Palestinian Qadi al-Quda issued an administrative decision in 1995 raising
these ages to a minimum of 15 for the female and 16 for the male, as in the
Jordanian law. All ages are calculated according to the lunar calendar.

The LFR assumes that there is a guardian and that where there is not, the
qadi acts as guardian for the woman in marriage. Marriage registration is
mandatory but failure to register does not invalidate the marriage.

Polygyny is governed by classical law, but the woman is allowed to stipulate
in the contract that the husband shall not take another wife while married
to her, and may seek divorce if he subsequently breaks the terms of that
stipulation.

The rules of maintenance and obedience are maintained in their classical
form.

On *talaq*, standard reforms to the classical Hanafi rules, as implemented in
Egypt in the 1920s, have been included in the LFR; extra-judicial *talaq* is valid
but registration is obligatory. The same rules on judicial divorce apply as in
the West Bank, except that a wife is entitled to petition for divorce on the
grounds of injury, and a husband is not entitled to apply on grounds of
'discord and strife'.

There has been no amendment in the LFR to the classical Hanafi rules on
post-divorce maintenance, or on arrears pre-dating submission of the maintenance claim.

Law/case reporting system *Palestinian Official Gazette.*

International conventions (with relevant reservations) Not applicable (until statehood is formally recognized and implemented, Palestine cannot become a state party to international instruments).

Background and sources

El Alami, D. S. and D. Hinchcliffe (1996) *Islamic Marriage and Divorce Laws of the Arab World*, London and Boston: Kluwer Law International.

Welchman, L. (1990) 'Family law under occupation: Islamic law and the Shari'a courts of the West Bank', in C. Mallat and J. Connors (eds), *Islamic Family Law*, London: Graham and Trotman, pp. 93–115.

— (1999) *Islamic Family Law: Text and Practice in Palestine*, Jerusalem: WCLAC.

QATAR, State of

Legal history From its early history, the region now known as Qatar has come under Persian, Portuguese, Ottoman and British influence. Qatar was considered a part of Bahrain by the British until the 1860s, although the ruling al-Khalifah family of Bahrain exercised only limited control over Qatar. In 1868, a treaty of cooperation was signed between Britain and the al-Thani tribe settled around Doha; the treaty outlawed warfare at sea and directed that any conflicts be referred to the British Resident in the Gulf. Wahhabism became influential in the region due to an alliance forged between the al-Thani tribe and Wahhabis and their allies in the late eighteenth century; the al-Thani tribe became the ruling family of the region by the 1893 after Shaykh Jasim al-Thani, appointed governor by the Ottomans in 1879, asserted his own rule.

The Ottoman Turkish garrison was expelled from Doha and relations with Britain were further strengthened by the 1916 Treaty of Protection making Qatar a British protectorate. The Treaty of Protection continued in force until 1971 when Qatar declared its independence. Since that time, a Penal Code, Civil and Criminal Procedure Codes, and Laws on Judicial Organization have been adopted. Personal law remains uncodified, administered by the Shari'a courts.

Schools of *fiqh* The Hanbali school is the predominant *madhhab* in Qatar.

Constitutional status of Islam(ic law) The amended provisional basic regulation was passed on 19 April 1972, replacing the Provisional Constitution adopted in 1970. Article 1 declares Islam the state religion and provides that 'the Islamic Shari'a Law shall be a fundamental source of its legislation'. Article 9 guarantees equal public rights and requires equal public duties without distinction for race, sex or religion.

Court system Qatar maintains a dual system of civil and Shari'a courts. The first civil courts were established in 1962. The Shari'a courts' jurisdiction has increasingly been limited to family law matters (marriage, divorce, wills, succession), although they retain some criminal jurisdiction. Shari'a courts are staffed by *qadis*, who administer uncodified (mainly Hanbali-Wahhabi) personal status law and are organized into two levels: Shari'a Courts of First Instance and the Shari'a Court of Appeal.

Notable features Classical Hanbali *fiqh* is applied to personal status matters.

Law/case reporting system Law reporting is through the *Official Gazette*.

International conventions (with relevant reservations) Qatar signed the CRC in 1992 and ratified it in 1995, submitting a general reservation to any 'provisions incompatible with Islamic Law' upon signature and confirming it upon ratification.

Background and sources
Amin, S. H. (1985) *Middle East Legal Systems*, Glasgow: Royston.

Ballantyne, W. M. (1986) *Commercial Law in the Arab Middle East: The Gulf States*, London: Lloyd's of London Press.

El Alami, D. S. and D. Hinchcliffe (1996) 'The uncodified law', in D. S. El Alami and D. Hinchcliffe, *Islamic Marriage and Divorce Laws of the Arab World*, London and Boston: Kluwer Law International, pp. 1–32.

El Mallakh, R. (1979), *Qatar: The Development of an Oil Economy*, New York: St Martin's Press.

Mahmood, T. (1995) 'Gulf', in *Statutes of Personal Law in Islamic Countries: History, Texts and Analysis*, 2nd edn, New Delhi: India and Islam Research Council, p. 85.

Redden, K. R. (1990) 'Qatar', in K. R. Redden (ed.), *Modern Legal Systems Cyclopedia*, Vol. 5, Buffalo, NY: Hein.

SAUDI ARABIA, Kingdom of

Legal history Saudi Arabia was never directly colonized, although parts of the present-day state had come under nominal or intermittent Ottoman control since the sixteenth century. Turkish garrisons were at times stationed in Mecca, Medina, Jeddah and other centres, but the Ottomans exercised only limited powers and local rulers had a high degree of autonomy in internal affairs. The Ottomans' final efforts at occupying eastern Arabia in 1871 to forestall the growing British influence at their borders in the Arabian Gulf eventually failed. The basis of the Wahhabi state of Saudi Arabia was established in 1902, when 'Abd al-Aziz al-Sa'ud and his followers gained control of Riyadh, signalling the beginning of the third period of Saudi-Wahhabi dominance in the region. 'Abd al-Aziz consolidated his territorial gains over the next decade, expanding out of the surroundings of Riyadh and the eastern part of the region into the areas where the Ottomans were expelled. The Kingdom of Saudi Arabia was declared on 22 September 1933 over those lands that had come under 'Abd al-Aziz's control by conquest and by forging numerous alliances.

Following the 1979 seizure of the Grand Mosque in Mecca, the decline in oil prices in the 1980s, and the effects of the second Gulf War, tentative efforts have been made to establish a more representative form of governance. A *Majlis al-Shura* (Consultative Council) was introduced by King Fahd in 1993. The *Majlis* had 61 appointed members; in 1996 this was increased to 90 members. Although the *Majlis* has no legislative powers, it may examine government policies and propose laws or amendments to existing laws. Decisions or suggestions from the *Majlis* are first sent to the Council of Ministers for review, and then to the king for his approval.

The main sources of Saudi law are Hanbali *fiqh* as set out in a number of specified classical scholarly treatises by authoritative jurists, other Hanbali sources, other schools of law, state regulations and royal decrees (where these are relevant), and custom and practice. Royal decrees have been used to direct courts to base judgments on several authoritative classical treatises by Hanbali jurists (such as the *al-Mughni* of ibn Qudamah). A resolution of the Supreme Judicial Council passed in 1928 also directed the courts to rely on particular Hanbali sources in civil matters, ranked as follows: *Sharh Mutaha al-Iradat* of al-Bahuti, *Kashshaf al-Kina an Matn al-Ikna* of al-Bahuti, commentaries of al-Zad, commentaries of al-Dalil, and if no suitable provision is found, then secondary sources in Hanbali legal manuals, and lastly, reference to authorities of other *madhahib*. If no answer is found in officially sanctioned sources, recourse may be had to *ijtihad*. 'Traditional' areas of law continue to be governed by Shari'a law while certain spheres of law relating to corporate, tax, oil and gas, immigration law, and so on, have been regulated by royal decrees and codes.

Schools of *fiqh* The Hanbali school is the official *madhhab* in Saudi Arabia. There is also a Shi'i minority adhering to the Ja'fari school.

Constitutional status of Islam(ic law) Saudi Arabia has no formal constitution. The functions of a constitution are served by the Basic Law articulating the government's rights and responsibilities issued by King Fahd in March 1992. Article 1 of the Basic Law declares Islam the official state religion and the Qur'an and Sunna the Constitution. The Basic Law also provides that '[t]he state protects the rights of the people in line with the Islamic Shari'a', affirms the independence of the judiciary and states that administration of justice is based on 'Shari'a rules according to the teachings of the holy Qur'an, the Sunna, and the regulations set by the ruler provided that they do not contradict the holy Qur'an and Sunna'. Article 9 of the Basic Law states that 'the family is the kernel of Saudi society, and its members shall be brought up on the basis of the Islamic faith'. Article 26 provides that the state protects human rights 'in accordance with the Islamic Shari'a'.

Court system Shari'a Courts have general and residual jurisdiction, i.e., jurisdiction over any case or matter the jurisdiction over which has not been expressly assigned to another tribunal. There are four levels of Shari'a courts: Minor Courts, General Courts, Cassation Court, and the Supreme Judicial Council. Civil claims may also go to the *Amarah*, in which case the Amir attempts to guide the parties in a dispute to a compromise; the matter is ultimately referred to the courts if a settlement is not reached. There are also a number of specialized tribunals for settling disputes in specific areas, such as commercial or labour law; these specialized tribunals are formed under various ministries outside of the Ministry of Justice. The highest appellate tribunal in all matters, the Board of Grievances, is also independent of the Ministry of Justice, and since its reorganization in 1982 has been made directly responsible to the king.

Notable features Standard Hanbali *fiqh* is applied to personal status cases.

Law/case reporting system Law reporting is through the *Official Gazette*.

International conventions (with relevant reservations) Saudi Arabia acceded to the CRC in 1996, with a general reservation to 'all such articles as are in conflict with the provisions of Islamic law'.

Background and sources

Aba-Namay, R. (1998) 'The new Saudi representative assembly', *Islamic Law and Society*, 5, 2: 235–65.

Amin, S. H. (1985) *Middle East Legal Systems*, Glasgow: Royston.

Anscombe, F. F. (1997) *The Ottoman Gulf: The Creation of Kuwait, Saudi Arabia, and Qatar*, New York: Columbia University Press.

Ballantyne, W. M. (1986) *Commercial Law in the Arab Middle East: The Gulf States*, London: Lloyd's of London Press.

El Alami, D. S. and D. Hinchcliffe (1996) 'The uncodified law', in D. S. El Alami and D. Hinchcliffe, *Islamic Marriage and Divorce Laws of the Arab World*, London and Boston: Kluwer Law International, pp. 1–32.

Fandy, M. (1999) *Saudi Arabia and the Politics of Dissent*, New York: St Martin's Press.

Mahmood, T. (1995) 'Gulf', in *Statutes of Personal Law in Islamic Countries: History, Texts and Analysis*, 2nd edn, New Delhi: India and Islam Research Council, p. 85.

Redden, K. R. (1990) 'Saudi Arabia', in K. R. Redden (ed.), *Modern Legal Systems Cyclopedia*, Vol. 5, Buffalo, NY: Hein.

Vassiliev, A. (1997), *The History of Saudi Arabia*, London: Saqi Books.

SYRIA (Syrian Arab Republic)

Legal history Syria served as the centre of the Umayyad caliphate until the Abbasid Revolution of 756. After a succession of Arab, Crusader, Kurdish, and Mamluke rulers, Syria came under Ottoman control in 1516. Following the expulsion of the Ottomans after World War I, the League of Nations declared a French mandate over the region in 1922, from which Syria gained independence in 1946.

The Ottoman Law of Family Rights continued to govern matters of personal status until 1953. The *Qadi* of Damascus, Shaykh 'Ali al-Tantawi, drafted a comprehensive treatise on personal law, based on *takhayyur* according to principles most suitable to changing social conditions. After the publication of al-Tantawi's treatise, the government established a Commission to prepare a draft code of personal law. The Commission based its draft on principles from al-Tantawi's code, the OLFR, various Egyptian laws enacted from 1920 to 1946, and the unofficial code prepared by Egyptian jurist Qudri Pasha. The Syrian Law of Personal Status (*Qanun al-Ahwal al-Shakhsiyya*) 1953 produced by the Commission covers matters of personal status, family relations and intestate and testamentary succession and was the most comprehensive code issued in the Arab world to that date. Article 305 of the SLPS directs that, for matters not specified in the text, resort shall be had to the most authoritative doctrine of the Hanafi school. Major amendments were made to the SLPS in 1975, particularly relating to the areas of polygyny, dower, maintenance, *mut'a*, cost of nursing, custody of children, and guardianship.

Schools of *fiqh* The Hanafi school is the predominant *madhhab* in Syria, and there are Ja'fari, Druze, Isma'ili and 'Alawi minorities. There are also several Christian denominations and very small Jewish communities based in Damascus, Al-Qamishli and Aleppo.

Constitutional status of Islam(ic law) The Constitution was adopted on 13 March 1973. Article 3(1) declares that the religion of the President of the Republic shall be Islam. Article 3(2) declares Islamic jurisprudence a main source of legislation.

Court system Courts having jurisdiction over personal status matters are Shari'a courts for Sunni and Shi'i Muslims, *madhhabi* courts for the Druze, and *ruhi* courts for Christians and Jews. There is one single-*qadi* Shari'a court of first instance per district (except Damascus and Aleppo, where there are three each). Each of the three types of courts has its own appellate courts. Final appeal for all the religious courts lies with the Family Section of the Court of Cassation in Damascus, the highest court of the regular system.

Shari'a courts have both general jurisdiction (relating to all Syrians without respect to religion and to non-Syrians originating from countries where Islamic personal status laws are applied, i.e., over matters of guardianship, succession, ascertaining capacity, missing persons, filiation, matrimonial issues, and maintenance of relatives) and special jurisdiction (relating to Muslim Syrians in matters of personal status including marriage, dissolution, *mahr*, custody and maintenance, and *awqaf*). The Code of Personal Status applied to Muslims by the Shari'a courts has specific exemptions for Druze, Christians and Jews.

Notable features The minimum marriage age is 18 years for males and 17 for females, with scope for judicial discretion for males of 15 years and females of 13 years if either the father or grandfather serving as *wali* consents and the parties appear physically able. If the court finds incompatibility in age between betrothed parties, the judge may withhold permission for marriage. Both parties require their *walis'* permission for marrying under the age of full capacity, though a judge may overrule a *wali*'s unreasonable objection to the marriage of his female ward (conditional upon equality of status or *kafa'a* between the betrothed parties).

Marriage registration is obligatory and applications for marriage must be submitted to the judge, requiring documentation attesting to identity, age, residence, guardian's identity, medical certificate, civil status, and so on, of the betrothed parties. Marriages contracted out of court are not to be certified without such procedures with the exception of cases where the wife is pregnant or a child has been born, although extenuating circumstances do not prevent the application of legal sanctions for non-compliance with registration requirements.

The judge may refuse permission for a polygynous marriage unless the husband is able to establish lawful cause and financial capacity. The wife's financial rights are forfeit if she works outside the home without her husband's consent or if she is deemed disobedient due to leaving the matrimonial home without lawful justification or refusing to cohabit with her husband. Arrears of maintenance shall be awarded the wife from the date her husband fails to maintain her, up to four months prior to the date of the claim.

Talaq uttered while intoxicated, disoriented/enraged, under coercion, during death sickness or grave illness, or in order to coerce, is ineffective. *Talaq* to which a number is attached shall be considered a single irrevocable repudiation (except the third of three).

The wife may seek a judicial divorce on the following grounds: a defect in the husband preventing consummation (although such right is forfeit if the wife accepted the defect except in the case of the husband's impotence); husband's insanity; husband's absence without justification for one year; husband's sentencing to three years' imprisonment, after he has served one year of the sentence; and the husband's failure to maintain – if non-maintenance is due to the husband's inability to provide maintenance, the judge shall grant a grace period of up to three months. Either spouse may apply for a judicial divorce on grounds of discord causing such harm as makes cohabitation impossible (after reconciliation efforts). The divorced wife may be awarded compensation of up to three years' maintenance (in addition to the maintenance owed her during her *'idda*) if the judge finds the husband's exercise of *talaq* to have been arbitrary. The divorced mother has the right to custody over boys until the age of nine and girls until the age of eleven. The *qadi* may extend the mother's custody over girls until marriage, or over boys or girls until they attain *rushd*, if the guardian is not the father, or if the court finds that the father is not to be trusted with the children.

The law relating to succession is based mainly on Hanafi *fiqh*, as embodied in the Code of Personal Status, although it is influenced by Egyptian reform legislation from the 1940s. The doctrine of *radd* (return) was extended to permit surviving spouses to share in the division of the residue of their deceased partners' estates. Obligatory bequests have also been introduced to benefit orphaned grandchildren through predeceased sons.

Law/case reporting system   Law reporting is through the *Official Gazette.*

International conventions (with relevant reservations)   Syria acceded to the ICCPR and ICESCR in 1969, submitting the following reservations: the first reservation relates to non-recognition of the state of Israel; the second reservation – relating to Articles 48(1) and 26(1) of the ICCPR and ICESCR, respectively – states that these provisions are incompatible with the aims of the Covenants, as they do not allow all states 'without distinction or discrimination' to become parties to the Covenants.

Syria signed the CRC in 1990 and ratified it in 1993, with a general reservation to any provisions that are not in conformity with Syrian legislation or the principles of the Islamic Shari'a, with particular reference to Article 14 on children's freedom of religion, and Articles 2 and 21 concerning adoption.

Background and sources

Amin, S. H. (1985) *Middle East Legal Systems*, Glasgow: Royston.

Anderson, J. N. D. (1955) 'The Syrian law of personal status', *Bulletin of the School of Oriental and African Studies*, University College London, 17: 34–49.

Berger, (1997) 'The legal system of family law in Syria', *Bulletin d'Etudes Orientales*, XLIX: 115–27.

El Alami, D. S. and D. Hinchcliffe (1996) *Islamic Marriage and Divorce Laws of the Arab World*, London and Boston: Kluwer Law International.

el-Hakim, J. (1994) 'Syria', *Yearbook of Islamic and Middle Eastern Law*, Vol. 1, London and Boston: Kluwer International, pp. 142–55.

Mahmood, T. (1995) 'Syria', in *Statutes of Personal Law in Islamic Countries: History, Texts and Analysis*, 2nd edn, New Delhi: India and Islam Research Council, pp. 39–41, 167–73.

Nasir, J. J. (1990) *The Islamic Law of Personal Status*, 2nd edn, London: Graham and Trotman.

Pearl, D. (1987) *A Textbook on Muslim Law*, 2nd edn, London: Croom Helm.

Redden, K. R. (1990) 'Syria', in K. R. Redden (ed.), *Modern Legal Systems Cyclopedia*, Vol. 5, Buffalo, NY: Hein.

UNITED ARAB EMIRATES

Legal history The UAE is a federation of seven Emirates: Abu Dhabi, Sharjah, Ajman, Fujayrah, Umm al-Qawain, Dubai and Ra's al-Khaymah. Sources of law are Islamic law, constitutional law, and legislation.

The area now known as the United Arab Emirates was known as the 'pirate coast' by the early nineteenth century. From the 1820s, the British entered into a number of treaties with local rulers in order to protect their shipping interests. A perpetual maritime truce signed in 1853 gave the British remit over handling of foreign relations for the region. Full independence was attained in December 1971, with Ra's al-Khaymah, the last Emirate to join the federation, becoming a part of the Union the following year.

Schools of *fiqh* The majority of Emiriti nationals are Sunni Muslim; there is a significant Shi'a minority, as well as small Christian and Hindu minorities. The federation has a very high proportion of expatriates.

Constitutional status of Islam(ic law) Article 7 of the Provisional Constitution, adopted on 2 December 1971 and made permanent in 1996, declares Islam the official state religion of the Union, and affirms that Islamic Shari'a shall be a principal source of legislation.

Court system The Abu Dhabi Courts Law 1968 regulates the jurisdiction of Shari'a courts, although personal status law remains uncodified. The other six Emirates do not have similar legislation or organized judiciaries, so Shari'a courts are not regulated. Important civil and criminal cases are brought before the ruler in person.

The Sharjah Courts Law 1971 created civil courts competent to hear commercial and labour disputes, with limited criminal jurisdiction. The Law Establishing the Union Supreme Court 1973 and the Union Law 1978 established the Union Courts of First Instance and Appeal and transferred jurisdiction from tribunals in Abu Dhabi, Sharjah, Ajman and Fujayrah to these courts. Union Courts of First Instance deal with civil, commercial and administrative disputes, including personal status cases, arising in the permanent capital.

Notable features Personal status law remains unlegislated. The Ministry of Labour and Social Affairs has been made responsible for welfare payments to those who require such assistance. Under the 1977 Social Security Law, eligibility extends to widows, orphans, divorced women or women separated from their husbands, unmarried women, families of prisoners, women married to foreign nationals, and so on. The ministry also disburses funds to local women's organizations, including the main national umbrella group, the UAE Women's Federation.

Notable cases Judgment no. 8/97: in 1997 the Dubai Court of Cassation ruled that a divorced mother who had remarried retained custody rights over children due to a written agreement between the parents whereby the father agreed not to claim custody even if his former wife remarried.

Judgment no. 16/15: in 1984 the Abu Dhabi Court of Cassation ruled that a Muslim wife has the right to a divorce where the husband has physically abused her and the dispute between them has not been resolved.

Law/case reporting system Law reporting is through the *UAE Gazette*, with some of the Emirates having their own official gazettes (e.g., *Ra's al-Khaymah Gazette*, *Dubai Gazette*).

International conventions (with relevant reservations) The United Arab Emirates acceded to the CRC in 1997 with the following reservations: the reservation to Article 7 states that 'nationality is an internal matter … whose terms and conditions are established by national legislation'; the UAE will be bound by Article 14 (relating to children's rights and freedoms) only to the extent that the provision 'does not conflict with the principles and provisions of Islamic law'; Article 17 (on access to information and the functions of mass media) is to be applied in light of the requirements of domestic statutes; and the UAE does not consider itself bound by the provisions of Article 21 'given its commitment to the principles of Islamic law' in accordance with which 'the UAE does not permit the system of adoption'.

Background and sources

Amin, S. H. (1985) *Middle East Legal Systems*, Glasgow: Royston.

Ballantyne, W. M. (1986) *Commercial Law in the Arab Middle East: The Gulf States*, London: Lloyd's of London Press.

El Alami, D. S. and D. Hinchcliffe (1996) 'The uncodified law', in D. S. El Alami and D. Hinchcliffe, *Islamic Marriage and Divorce Laws of the Arab World*, London and Boston: Kluwer Law International, pp. 1–32.

Mahmood, T. (1995) 'Gulf', in *Statutes of Personal Law in Islamic Countries: History, Texts and Analysis*, 2nd edn, New Delhi: India and Islam Research Council, p. 85.

Price, R. and E. Al-Tamimi (1988), *United Arab Emirates Court of Cassation Judgments: 1989–1997*, The Hague and Boston: Kluwer Law International.

Redden, K. R. (1990) 'UAE', in K. R. Redden (ed.), *Modern Legal Systems Cyclopedia*, Vol. 5, Buffalo, NY: Hein.

YEMEN, Republic of

Legal history Yemen was ruled by the Shi'i Zaydi dynasty of Sa'da, founded by Yahya ibn Husayn ibn Qasim ar-Rassi, from 897 CE until well into the current century, although the region came under nominal Ottoman control from 1517. The first period of Ottoman rule ended in 1636 when the Zaydi rulers reasserted their sovereign rule. The British established the Aden Protectorate in Yemen in 1839, and made a series of treaties with local rulers with the aim of extending British influence to southern Yemen. By 1849, the Turks reasserted control over all of Yemen that was not in British hands. A revolt against the Ottomans led to the granting of autonomy to the Zaydi Imam in 1911, and the Turks retreated from the region altogether within the span of eight years. The British recognized Yemen's independence in 1925. The British succeeded in extending control as far as Hadhramawt by the 1950s, where a 'violet line' separated Turkish Arabia and the South Arabian Protectorate. A military coup in 1962 led by Colonel 'Abdullah al-Sallal established the Yemen Arab Republic in the north, brought an end to centuries of Zaydi rule and ushered in an era of civil war between the Saudi-supported royalists and the Egyptian-backed Republicans. The civil war continued until Egypt's disengagement in 1967 and Saudi Arabia's extension of recognition of the YAR in 1970. By the 1960s, the British presence in southern Yemen was mainly confined to Aden, and guerrilla fighting throughout the decade hastened the British withdrawal from Aden in 1967, leading to the establishment of the People's Republic of South Yemen (later the People's Democratic Republic of Yemen), an Arab Marxist state. Relations between the two Yemens were strained, as evidenced by a series of border conflicts throughout the 1970s, but relations began to improve by the early 1980s, and a Constitution was drafted with the aim of eventually merging to the two states. The proposed reunification did not take place until 1990, however, and not without disagreement over the terms of unification between the north and south resulting in a period of civil war in the summer of 1994.

Following the unification of the two Yemens, Republic Decree Law no. 20 constituting the Yemeni Law of Personal Status was passed in 1992. The legislation followed a Presidential Decree abolishing the 1978 code of personal status of the Yemeni Arab Republic and the 1974 code of personal status of the People's Democratic Republic of Yemen. The post-unification Law of Personal Status closely resembles the former-YAR's legislation. Article 349 provides that the strongest proofs in the Islamic Shari'a are to serve as the residual source of law in absence of specific textual provision. The penal law of the unified Yemen also provides for the application of *hadd* penalties for certain crimes, although such penalties are not often applied in practice.

Schools of *fiqh* The Shafi'i and Zaydi schools are the predominant *madhahib* in Yemen.

Constitutional status of Islam(ic law) The Constitution was adopted on 16 May 1991 and amended 29 September 1994. Article 1 declares Yemen an 'Arab Islamic State'. Article 2 declares Islam the official state religion. Article 3 states that 'Islamic Shari'a shall be the source of all legislation'. Article 23 states that inheritance is regulated by Shari'a. Article 26 states that 'the family is the basis of society and its pillars are religion, custom and love of the homeland'. Article 31 states that women 'have rights and duties, which are guaranteed and assigned by Shari'a and stipulated by law'.

Court system Courts of first instance in each district have jurisdiction over personal status, civil, criminal and commercial cases. Appeals go to the Courts of Appeal in each of the 18 provinces with Civil, Criminal, Matrimonial and Commercial Divisions, each consisting of three-judge benches. The Supreme Court is the highest court of appeal and sits in San'a. The Supreme Court has eight divisions: Constitutional, Appeals' Scrutiny, Criminal, Military, Civil, Family, Commercial, and Administrative.

Notable features The minimum marriage age is 15 years for males and females. Marriage by coercion is invalid. The judge can overrule the guardian if his objection to the marriage of his ward is considered unjust, with the proviso that the wife receive her proper dower from her husband of equal status. The husband and *wali* are responsible for the registration of marriage within one week of the contract, with penal sanctions for non-compliance.

Polygyny is permitted subject to equitable treatment of co-wives, financial means, lawful benefit, and notification of prospective co-wives.

The wife may leave the marital home to work so long as there is no breach of honour or of her marital duties and her husband consents. Arrears of maintenance may be claimed for a period of up to one year prior to the date of the claim, unless the spouses had agreed to other conditions.

Talaq is ineffective if uttered while intoxicated or with intention to coerce. *Talaq* to which a number is attached is only effective as a single revocable repudiation (except the third of three).

Judicial dissolution is available to either spouse on grounds of defect (this right is forfeited if the defect was accepted explicitly or implicitly, except for such defects as insanity, leprosy and other communicable diseases difficult to cure); and inequality of social status. An annulment is to be effected if the husband becomes Muslim and the wife is not *kitabiyya* or if the wife becomes a Muslim and the husband refuses conversion to Islam, or on grounds of either party's apostasy. The wife may request a decree of dissolution (lesser irrevocable) on the following grounds: husband's non-maintenance; husband's absence or disappearance for one year if he left no provision for maintenance or two years if he provided for his wife's maintenance; husband's imprisonment for three years or more after one year of the sentence has passed; husband's breach of maintenance or accommodation obligations towards co-wives; incompatibility (after reconciliation efforts, and if the husband refuses to pronounce *talaq*, in exchange for the wife's return of her dower); husband's proven addiction to alcohol or narcotics. The wife may also obtain a *khul'* in exchange for compensation. The husband is required to pay maintenance during the *'idda*. The judge may award compensation equivalent to up to one year's maintenance to a wife who is arbitrarily divorced without just cause. The divorced mother maintains custody until the age of nine years for boys and twelve for girls, and this period may be extended if it is considered to be in the best interests of the wards. In addition, wards may choose which parent they wish to live with once the period of custody is over.

The YLPS provides for obligatory bequests for orphaned grandchildren by predeceased sons or daughters (to the first generation only), up to the portion their dead parent would have received or up to the bequeathable one-third, depending on the circumstances of the heirs. That is, grandchildren through sons may inherit if they are poor, and grandchildren through daughters if their father is poor. The YLPS allows Qur'anic heirs to share in the residue of an estate in proportion to their shares, but does not allow *radd* to the spouse relict.

Law/case reporting system Law reports or indexes of decisions appeared in several law journals published by the law faculties of the Universities of San'a and Aden, the Jurists' Union, and the Ministries of Justice in San'a and Aden, from the pre-unification period. Laws are now published in *al-Jarida al-Rasmiyya*.

International conventions (with relevant reservations) The Republic of Yemen acceded to the CEDAW in 1984, with a reservation to Article 29(1) relating to arbitration over interpretation or application of the Convention.

Yemen acceded to the ICCPR and ICESCR in 1987, with a general declaration pertaining to non-recognition of the state of Israel. Yemen also acceded to the Convention on Consent to Marriage, Minimum Age for Marriage and Registration of Marriages in 1987.

Yemen signed the CRC in 1990 and ratified it in 1991, without reservations.

Background and sources

Amin, S. H. (1985) *Middle East Legal Systems*, Glasgow: Royston.

El Alami, D. S. and D. Hinchcliffe (1996) *Islamic Marriage and Divorce Laws of the Arab World*, London and Boston: Kluwer Law International.

Lackner, H. (1995) 'Women and development in the Republic of Yemen', in N. F. Khoury and V. Moghadam (eds), *Gender and Development in the Arab World*, London: Zed Books, pp. 71–96.

Mahmood, T. (1995) 'North Yemen', in *Statutes of Personal Law in Islamic Countries: History, Texts and Analysis*, 2nd edn, New Delhi: India and Islam Research Council, pp. 46–8, 182–6.

— (1995) 'South Yemen', in *Statutes of Personal Law in Islamic Countries: History, Texts and Analysis*, 2nd edn, New Delhi: India and Islam Research Council, pp. 48–52, 186–9.

Molyneux, M. (1995) 'Women's rights and political contingency: the case of Yemen, 1990–1994', *Middle East Journal*, 49, 3: 418–31.

Redden, K. R. (1990) 'North Yemen', 'South Yemen', in K. R. Redden (ed.), *Modern Legal Systems Cyclopedia*, Vol. 5, Buffalo, NY: Hein.

Shamiri, N. (1994) 'Yemen', *Yearbook of Islamic and Middle Eastern Law*, 1.

Würth, A. (1995) 'A Sana'a court: the family and the ability to negotiate', *Islamic Law and Society*, 2, 3: 320–40.

Part V
North Africa

1 Social, Cultural and Historical Background

The Region and its History

Islam swept through North Africa very early in its history, spreading west from Egypt starting in the eighth century CE (Martin 1986). Arab conquerors established Egypt's first Muslim seat of government in 658 at Fustat, just south of modern Cairo. As the Arabs pushed out of Egypt and across North Africa, they first brought Islamic civilization to the region's cities. Then, once the nomadic Berbers began to convert to Islam, Islam spread through their contacts all across rural North Africa (Martin 1986). While Arab peoples from the East settled in the cities, the Berbers continued to dominate most rural areas. They absorbed the practice of Islam into their native practices (Nanji 1996).

Around the beginning of the tenth century, religious Islamic regimes began appearing in North Africa. Among the most powerful and influential was that of the Almoravids. This was a Berber regime, largely responsible for the spread of the Maliki school of Islamic jurisprudence in Morocco (Nanji 1996). The Almoravids were followed by another dynasty of Berbers, the Almohads. This regime spread Islam to Spain and much of the rest of North Africa. It was much less successful, however, in its attempt to purge Moroccan Islam of Berber and other non-Islamic influences (Nanji 1996).

When the Arab leader Saladin conquered Egypt in 1171, he opened the way for the installation of Sunni schools of law. Saladin's family, the Ayyudbid house, ruled until 1250, when one of the Mamaluk or slave regiments rebelled, naming one of their own officers as king. The Mamaluks ruled Egypt until the Ottoman conquest in 1517. All three regimes maintained a policy of strong state support for and control of Islam. Though part of the Ottoman Empire, Egypt, 'the Mother of the World', retained its own cultural and political identity.

By the beginning of the seventeenth century, nine out of ten North Africans were Muslim, primarily following Sunni Islam (Martin 1996). In North Africa, the connection between Arab identity and Islamic adherence is almost indistinguishable, unlike in the Middle East, where Arabic speakers include non-Muslims (Burgat and Dowell 1993). Most North African Muslims continue to follow the Maliki school (Sullivan 1986). Meanwhile, the Berbers, and particularly the Tuaregs, a sub-group of Berbers, continue to practise a somewhat syncretic version of Islam, mixing their pre-Islamic traditions with the practice of Islam (Spencer 1978).

All the countries of North Africa experienced colonialism. Aside from a brief period of British control of Egypt, France was the most important colonial power in the region. The French conquered Algeria in 1830, and engaged upon an assimilationist strategy until Algeria's independence in 1962 (Shahin 1997). As a result of this policy, Islamic and Arabic education were both severely restricted. The history of colonial France in Morocco is much shorter. In 1912, the French declared Morocco a protectorate, and were much less eager to assimilate the area than they were in Algeria (Shahin 1997). Further, the French attempted to divide Arab and Berber residents of Morocco by declaring that Berber Moroccans would be subject to French and tribal laws, but excluded from Islamic law (Shahin 1997).

With its huge population and its 7,000-year-old history, Egypt has always been the regional giant. Today nine out of ten of Egypt's 68 million people are Muslim. Since independence, a series of secular governments have ruled Egypt. However, Egypt is also the original home of the most influential Muslim group in the region, the Muslim Brotherhood. Although the Brotherhood has operated under a legal ban for much of the last century, its cells have spread throughout much of North Africa (Burgat and Dowell 1993). The Muslim Brotherhood calls for a return to a strict interpretation of classical Islam exclusively adjudicated through Shari'a.

A single party, the National Liberation Front (FLN), held power in Algeria from independence in 1962 until 1989. Since 1989, Algeria has been technically a multiparty state, but has been in the midst of constant political tension and upheaval (Shahin 1997). In 1992, the army took power after the fundamentalist Islamic Salvation Front (FIS), an Islamist party banned under the FLN, won national elections (Zoubir 1999). Since then Islamist groups have battled the state for control of Algeria's 31 million people.

Libya's five million people have been ruled since 1969 by Colonel Muammar Qaddafi. Colonel Qaddafi advocates a political philosophy based on a mixture of Islam and socialism.

In Morocco, a monarchy holds power over the central government. The kings of Morocco claim descent from the Prophet Mohammed, legitimizing the monarchy's claim to political, religious and legal authority over the country's

29 million people (Shahin 1997). King Hassan II's Constitution was greatly influenced by Charles de Gaulle's Fifth Republic (Shahin 1997). Morocco has established Islamist parties: the al-Tabligh wal-Da'wa Lillah, founded in 1965, is a pro-monarchy association that has called for implementation of Shari'a since its inception (Layachi 1999). Morocco also has the more radical Jam'iyat al-Shabiba al-Islamiyya, which calls for a return to Shari'a by any means necessary (Layachi 1999).

Tunisia is the exception to the regional pattern of governments based on Islam. With a population of ten million, Tunisia has adopted a relatively liberal socialist system, modelled on that of France. Political and legal power is highly concentrated in the secular Democratic Destourian Rally (formerly Socialist Destourian Party) (Shahin 1997).

Economically, North Africa is highly connected to markets in Europe, much more so than to other Islamic countries in the Middle East or to markets in sub-Saharan Africa. This economic connection has influenced the secular nature of the regimes in North Africa (Mortimer 1999). As a region, more than 70 per cent of North Africa's trade is with the countries of the European Union (Mortimer 1999: 185). In fact, Morocco has applied for special trading status within the EU, in effect asking for honorary membership of the EU.

Legal Practices and Institutions

Although a number of North Africa's governments recognize Islam as a state religion, they have markedly different legal systems.

In the years immediately following independence, Egypt's legal system drew heavily on the French and British systems. In 1955, one year before Egypt adopted its first independent constitution, Law 462 eliminated the Shari'a courts and merged them with the secular national courts into unified civil and judicial systems (Talhami 1996). Since the 1980s, however, Egypt has experienced a re-Islamization of its legal code and system of justice.

Algeria's attitude towards Shari'a has oscillated. From the time of independence to 1984, the country witnessed several attempts to modify its Shari'a-based personal laws. Then the 1984 Family Code, most of which is still in effect, restored Maliki Shari'a codes in most personal issues (Women's International Network News 1996a). Morocco's code likewise essentially restates traditional Maliki family law (Charrad 1996).

Libya's Colonel Qaddafi has embarked on several campaigns to reinstitute Shari'a and abrogate laws he considers un-Islamic. However, he has also clashed with the Libyan *ulama* over the interpretation of Islam.

Tunisia, on the other hand, replaced Shari'a courts and French tribunal courts with a unified civil system (Shahin 1997). A new Personal Status Code was introduced, which applied to all Tunisians, regardless of religion. This code radically altered the legal marriage patterns. It prohibited polygyny and denied men the right of divorce by repudiation. Further, it legalized marriages between Muslim women and non-Muslim men, and gave women equal inheritance rights with men (Shahin 1997). Under the code, Tunisian men and women alike gain full adult rights at the age of 20, and Tunisian women who marry foreigners can pass on citizenship to their children just as Tunisian men do (Curtiss 1996).

Seclusion of Women / Purdah

Some North African women are fully covered, while others do not abide by Islamic dress codes at all. Some are strictly secluded, others mix freely with men.

In recent decades, one trend has become clear. Across much of North Africa, women who had not previously chosen to wear a veil have begun to wear the modern headscarf known as *hijab*. *Hijab* has many, often ambiguous, meanings. While it can be seen as an outward sign of holding on to local or national culture, in particular adherence to Islam and a rejection of at least some aspects of Western culture (Musallam 1983), some Islamist women argue that *hijab* allows them to escape the traditional roles of wife and mother to pursue professional lives in public. They say that the veil stops men from using sexual harassment to prevent women from entering public places (Slyomovics 1996).

In Tunisia, the future leader of an independent Tunisia, Bourguiba, at first defended the veil as a symbol of national identity and a form of resistance against the colonial regime (Shahin 1997). Then in the 1970s he banned the veil as well as the *chechia*, a traditional religious hat for men (King 1999).

Algerian girls become aware of the need for modesty quite young, covering their arms and hair even in front of their fathers. They continue to cover themselves throughout their youth, and until they themselves have sons who have married (Rezig 1983). At that point they have more freedom to be out in public, unaccompanied and with less concern about modesty. While it does not appear that Algeria had a period in the twentieth century when women stopped wearing head coverings, and thus the headscarf did not have the same renaissance it did in several other countries, it did become heavily politicized during the struggle for independence (Rezig 1983).

More recently, the nature and degree to which women are secluded has become a key issue in the fight between the government and Islamic groups. Algerian women have traditionally been very secluded from men, staying in the home except for necessary errands (Minces 1978). During the period of FLN rule, the Algerian government encouraged women to join the workforce. Since 1991, Islamist groups have targeted for assassination unveiled women and women who work alongside men. Local governments run by the FIS have banned concerts, cinemas, public dancing, wedding ceremonies in hotels, women on beaches and women in municipal buildings. Meanwhile, vigilante groups with ties to the military government have killed veiled women and called for the reopening of beauty salons and public baths closed by the Islamists (Slyomovics 1996).

In Egypt, many women stopped wearing headscarves, starting in the early 1900s (Musallam 1983). Huda Sha'rawi and Saiza Nabarawi made international headlines and became icons of Egyptian feminists when they publicly took off their veils in 1923 (Zuhur 1992). Sha'rawi followed this act by forming the Egyptian Feminist Union in the same year (Talhami 1996). The movement continued to the political arena in 1951, when activist Doria Shafik and a group of women stormed parliament demanding political rights. Shafik also led a hunger strike in 1954 (Zuhur 1992). Women were finally granted the right to vote in 1956.

Since the 1970s, women, particularly among the educated and professional classes, have started covering themselves again. The return to veiling was often viewed as a sign of protest against the government, and was fuelled by the negotiations of Anwar Sadat with the Israelis following the 1973 war, resulting in the Camp David Accords and Sadat's visit to Jerusalem (Zuhur 1992). As elsewhere in North Africa, following Islamic dress regulations is seen as supporting indigenous culture and, according to one researcher, asserting that choices can be made as to which parts of European culture ought to be adopted (Kader 1987). A study done in 1988 revealed that 62 per cent of a sample of women interviewed in Cairo wore a more modern type of head covering, 14 per cent wore a more complete veil, and only 38 per cent wore no form of veil (Zuhur 1992: 59). The highest percentage of veiled women were under the age of 27.

Regardless of dress, Egyptian women are legally restricted from complete freedom of movement. Unmarried women under age 21 must have permission from their fathers to obtain passports and travel outside Egypt; married women require the same permission from their husbands. Although genital mutilation is banned officially, most Egyptian girls undergo a form in which the clitoris is removed (US Government 1999).

Egypt is the scene of many contrasts and contradictions when it comes to the seclusion of women. The women whose families have lived in working-class neighbourhoods of Cairo for generations, for example, cover themselves, but with black outer dresses left somewhat open to show the colourful dresses underneath. The outer dresses are tight at the waist to flatter the woman's figure, and often allow a woman's arms to be seen (El-Messiri 1978). These women interact regularly with men in public. On the other hand, women who are relatively new to Cairo are much more careful about covering themselves. The newcomers to Cairo accept less interaction between men and women. The upper middle classes allow much greater interaction among men and women, even to the point that some young people have started dating.

In small towns and rural areas of Libya, few women cover themselves. In such places, it is unusual for a woman to run into an unfamiliar man, and when she does, she simply covers her face with her hands or turns her head away while speaking with the man (Attir 1985).

In Morocco, for the educated and professional classes wearing a head covering or not is a woman's choice, apparently with fewer of the political implications seen in Egypt, Tunisia and Algeria (Musallam 1983). Among the more traditional, wealthy sectors of urban society, women are kept secluded and well-covered when they do go out. In the countryside and in small towns, women are generally somewhat freer to go out in public, although this depends largely on the economic position of the family. Young married women in such areas are often free to go out with other young married women, without being accompanied by a male.

Among the different Berber groups, there are distinct variations. In one Berber town, the segregation of the sexes is quite strict. There are different sleeping quarters for males and females, and girls are largely kept home from the time they reach puberty (Rosen 1978). In terms of dress, Jbala women only cover their heads with large straw hats (Spencer 1978). The Tuaregs do not seem to follow common Islamic prescription for dress at all: men keep their heads covered with large scarves, whereas head coverings are less important for women.

Family in the Region

Most North Africans trace descent patrilineally, as is usually the case in Muslim countries. Among almost all the sedentary ethnic groups in Algeria and Morocco, for example, descent is traced though the father (Rezig 1983) and local communities often envision themselves as relatives descended from a single male ancestor. Kin groupings are so strong that the scholar Germaine Tillon has characterized the region as a series of 'republics of cousins' (Tillon 1983). A majority of both men and women perceive women's roles to be primarily in the family. For example, a 1988 study of women in Cairo revealed that only 9 per cent of women interviewed thought it possible to combine a successful career and a family (Zuhur 1992: 65). Among the pastoral and semi-pastoral cultures, however, there is more variation. Although almost all Berbers trace their families patrilineally, one sub-group of Berbers, the Tuaregs, does not have a consistent descent pattern. Some trace their families patrilineally, but some 80,000 Tuaregs trace their families and inherit social standing through the mother (Spencer 1978).

Marriage

Nearly everyone marries in North Africa. Families usually arrange at least the first marriages of their children. There is a general preference for marriage between the children of two brothers. Girls are expected to be virgins at the time of their first marriage. In the traditional Maliki custom widespread across North Africa, the consent of a woman is not required. It is the consent of the woman's guardian, her father or next male kin, that makes the marriage valid (Charrad 1996).

Algerian society, for example, favours marriage to a paternal parallel cousin (father's brother's child) (Rezig 1983). However, a study done in the late 1970s found that this was one of the aspects of family law and tradition that almost two-thirds of the Algierian women surveyed wanted to change (Rezig 1983). The minimum marriage age in Algeria is 18 for women and 21 for men (Women's International Network News 1996a).

In Egypt, a 1997 study found that only one per cent of women aged 45–49 had never been married (Alan Guttmacher Instititute). In the past and probably still in rural areas, a girl's father chose her husband for her, often a cousin, and she had little say in the matter (Morsey 1978). This appears to be changing with higher levels of education for girls and women. One study showed that among women with six years or more of education, women play a role in the choice of their own husbands (Hoodfar 1997). However, these patterns are still predominant. In a 1995 study, 39 per cent of women interviewed were married to a relative and 77 per cent of marriages were arranged (Edwards 1997). In 1980, the average age of marriage for women was 21.3 years; it had increased only slightly to 22.3 years by 1995 (Eltigani 2000). Research also reveals that men and women consider cross-class marriages unfavourable (Zuhur 1992). Minimum ages were originally set in 1923 at 16 for women and 18 for men (Talhami 1996).

Throughout Morocco, marriage to a paternal parallel cousin is common. It appears that this marriage pattern has particularly strong support among the upper classes and in conservative, older cities and towns (Mayer 1978). In 1980, the average age for Moroccan women was the same as in Egypt, 21.3 years. By 1995, this average age had increased to 26.3 years, indicating a significant delay in marriage among Moroccans (Eltigani 2000).

In Libya, marriage to first cousins is acceptable, but it is unclear whether it is particularly preferred over other marriages. Whether to a cousin or not, a girl can be married off by her guardian without having any say in the decision (Khalidi 1989). If her first marriage does not work out, a woman will have more freedom to choose subsequent husbands (Khalidi 1989).

Tunisia is the exception in marriage as in other family law. Tunisia has abolished a father's right to arrange his daughters' marriages. Instead, the consent of both spouses is a condition of marriage (Women's International Network News 1996b). Tunisia first set the legal age of marriage at 15 for women and 18 for men. This was later raised to 17 for women and 20 for men (Women's International Network News 1996b).

Dowry and Brideprice

Traditionally in Algeria, a bride always received a brideprice. Everything the couple owned other than the brideprice belonged to the husband. The brideprice, however, belonged to the wife, and she kept it even in the case of divorce (Minces 1978). This is in direct contrast to the practice in Egypt, where divorced women must return the brideprice.

In Morocco, whether or not a woman receives a brideprice upon her marriage depends in large part on her social class. Women from wealthy families usually receive some brideprice, although some do not. Lower-class women and women in rural areas often receive nothing. However, in one Berber town in Morocco, people say that brideprice is necessary and there are no marriages where the woman does not receive it (Rosen 1978).

Libyan tradition calls for a brideprice that is given all at once at the agreement to marry, rather than one part being given at the agreement, one part at the marriage itself, as is common elsewhere (Khalidi 1989). In Tunisia, the 1956 Personal Status Code stipulated that the dowry remains an obligatory component of a valid marriage. However, the code also states that husbands have no legal claim over any part of the *mahr*, either before or after marriage (Women's International Network News 1996b).

Divorce

Generally, North African men have more rights in initiating a divorce than women – Tunisia being an exception – but women have informal ways of getting out of a marriage.

In Algeria, divorce is quite common. According to the 1984 Family Code, marriages can be dissolved by repudiation of the husband, by mutual consent or by request of the wife due to lack of maintenance (Women's International Network News 1996a). Divorce, to be legal, must be carried out in court (Rezig 1983).

In Egypt, too, divorce is a regular occurrence and there has been an in-crease in the rate of divorce, starting in the 1970s (Kader 1987). Women originally gained the right to sue for divorce in 1921, but only in cases where the husband was found guilty of mistreating his wife (Talhami 1996). In March 2000, a new divorce law amending the Egyptian Personal Status Law came into effect. Under this new law, women can unilaterally apply for *khul'*, which is the right to obtain a divorce without the husband's consent. Under this new law, women are eligible for *khul'* only if they waive any claims to maintenance (Hassan 2000) and return any brideprice paid in the contraction of the mar-riage (Sachs 2000). Apparently, this stipulation has not discouraged women: by mid-March, the Personal Status Court in Cairo alone had received over 3,000 applications (Hassan 2000). Sayed Tantawi, Egypt's Grand Sheikh of Al Azhar, the highest Sunni Muslim authority in the country, has publicly affirmed that the new law is consistent with Islamic law governing divorce (Hassan 2000). A previous liberalization of women's right to divorce from 1979 was overturned in 1985 by the Egyptian Supreme Constitutional Court.

In Tunisia, women gained the right to divorce under the 1956 Personal Status Code. Under this code, both women and men may initiate divorce; in addition, unilateral repudiation by the husband is prohibited (Women's Inter-national Network News 1996b). In 1981, an additional law was passed requiring that husbands who are found at fault in a divorce must pay alimony as a reparation for material and emotional damages (Women's International Net-work News 1996c).

Polygyny

Tunisia is unique in the Arab world in outlawing polygyny. Throughout the rest of North Africa, polygyny is allowed and basically accepted, but seldom practised. However, the practice varies between and within the region. In Algeria, polygyny is practised, but only rarely. A study done in the 1950s showed that only 2 per cent of Muslim men had more than one wife (Baraket 1993). Despite its rarity, it remained an important issue. A study done more than 20 years later in Algiers found that almost two-thirds of the women studied wanted changes in the personal status laws, including the abolition of polygyny (Rezig 1983).

Information about polygyny in Egypt suggests that there are enormous differences in the practices of different socio-economic groups. On the whole, polygyny does not appear to be widely practised. In the early 1950s, 8 per cent of Egyptian Muslim men were married to more than one woman (Baraket 1993). There are sectors of society where polygyny has continued to be common, however, such as the traditional, working-class areas of Cairo (El-Messiri 1978). There is also some indication that polygyny became more common in the 1970s, possibly as a result of economically motivated migration, which both brought in money, making having a second wife more affordable, and kept people moving around (Kader 1987).

In 1979, the Egyptian government passed a package of personal status law reforms, including a limit on polygyny, which granted a woman the right to a divorce if her husband took a second wife without her consent (Sullivan 1986). However, this law was not consistently enforced and the 1979 reforms were declared unconstitutional in 1985. The law eventually passed regarding limits on polygyny allowed a woman to divorce her husband for taking a second wife only if she could prove that she suffered 'moral or material damage' as a result (Sullivan 1986).

In Morocco, polygyny is practised only rarely (Rosen 1978). A more common practice is serial monogamy, practised by both men and women (Rosen 1978).

Polygyny in Libya was thought to be fading away in the 1970s, but continues to be occasionally practised (Khalidi 1989). Polygyny is officially allowed only if the first wife consents, and the husband is both healthy and wealthy enough to be able to support two wives. It is unclear what these legal limitations on polygyny mean in practice.

There is no particular indication that polygyny is practised outside the law in Tunisia. Those violating the prohibition, both men and women, are subject to one year's imprisonment (Women's International Network News 1996c).

Custody of Children

Fertility in North Africa has declined over the last several decades. From the late 1970s to the mid-1990s, fertility declined in Morocco by 44 per cent and in Egypt by 28 per cent (Eltigani 2000). This decline has two main causes. First, the Islamic countries of North Africa are more secular than those in other parts of the world and actively advocate national family planning policies. Second, North Africans are more highly urbanized than their sub-Saharan African counterparts, thus allowing more access to family planning methods (Eltigani 2000). Although abortion on demand is illegal in most of North Africa, a 1973 law in Tunisia allows a woman to abort for any reason and without the consent of her husband (Women's International Network News 1996b). In Egypt, custody of children after a divorce is generally granted to the woman unless her ex-husband can prove she is unfit or if she remarries (Hassan 2000). The 1956 Constitution guaranteed maternity benefits to women, granting one month with pay and up to a three-year leave without pay. Additionally, nursing and pregnant women were also granted one hour of rest per day by the Constitution (Talhami 1996).

In Algeria, mothers are generally awarded custody of minor children, with fathers having legal visitation rights. At the age of ten, sons usually move in with their fathers, while girls remain with their mothers until marriage (Women's International Network News 1996a). In an innovation of traditional Maliki law, Algerian women automatically receive custody of their children if their husband dies (Charrad 1996).

Tunisia's courts work out custody decisions on a case-by-case basis as part of a civil divorce proceedure (Curtiss 1996).

Inheritance / Land Rights

Egyptian practice recognizes that, according to the Qur'an, women are supposed to inherit half as much as male relatives of the same degree of relation to the deceased. However, frequently women inherit nothing from their parents, a practice justified by the woman being able to use the land of her husband (Morsey 1978). When Egyptian women do own land, either through inheritance or by purchasing it, they find ways to protect their ownership of it. A woman may limit her husband's access to her land, either by legally owning it in her name only or by transferring it to one of her brothers (Morsey 1978). Such practices show that women are concerned about retaining control over their land after a divorce or the death of the husband. Law 62, passed in 1971, further guaranteed women's right to inheritance, granting that women have the right to receive their husbands' pensions after the husband's death (Talhami 1996).

Moroccan women who come from upper-class families in towns usually inherit according to the Qur'anic prescriptions. In the countryside, however, women often receive less than their share.

Under Tunisian law, women still inherit half as much as their brothers. However, under certain circumstances, Tunisian women may inherit property at the expense of more distant male kin (Charrad 1996).

Bibliography

Attir, M. O. (1985) 'Ideology, value changes, and women's social position in Libyan society', in E. W. Fernea (ed.), *Women and the Family in the Middle East: New Voices of Change*, Austin: University of Texas Press, pp. 121–33.

Baraket, H. (1993) *The Arab World: Society, Culture and State*, Berkeley: University of California Press.

Burgat, F. and W. Dowell (1993) *The Islamic Movement in North Africa*, Austin: Center for Middle Eastern Studies at the University of Texas.

Charrad, M. (1996) 'State and gender in the Maghrib', in S. Sabbagh (ed.), *Arab Women: Between Defiance and Restraint*, New York: Olive Branch Press, pp. 221–8.

Curtiss, R. H. (1996) 'Women's rights: an affair of state for Tunisia', in S. Sabbagh (ed.), *Arab Women: Between Defiance and Restraint*, New York: Olive Branch Press, pp. 32–7.

Edwards, S. (1997) 'Levels of fertility have declined steadily in Egypt, but unwanted childbearing remains common', *Family Planning Perspectives*, 23, 3, September, Alan Guttmacher Institute. http://www.agi-usa.org/pubs/journals/2313797.html

El-Messiri, S. (1978) 'Self-images of traditional urban women in Cairo', in L. Beck and N. Keddie (eds), *Women in the Muslim World*, Cambridge, MA: Harvard University Press, pp. 522–40.

Eltigani, E. E. (2000) 'Changes in family-building patterns in Egypt and Morocco: a comparative analysis', *International Family Planning Perspectives*, 26: 73.

Hassan, H. (2000) 'Rights–Egypt: new law lets women divorce if they waive support', *Interpress Service* (Global Information Network), 28 March.

Hoodfar, H. (1997) 'The impact of male migration on domestic budgeting: Egyptian women striving for an Islamic budgeting pattern', *Journal of Comparative Family Studies*, 28: 90.

Kader, S. A. (1987) *Egyptian Women in a Changing Society, 1899–1987*, Boulder, CO: Lynne Reinner Publishers.

Khalidi, M. S. (1989) 'Divorce in Libya', *Journal of Comparative Family Studies*, 20: 124.

King, R. J. (1999) 'Regime type, economic reform, and political change in Tunisia', in Y. H. Zoubir (ed.), *North Africa in Transition: State, Society, and Economic Transformation in the 1990s*, Gainesville: University Press of Florida, pp. 61–76.

Layachi, A. (1999) 'Economic reform and elusive political change in Morocco', in Y. H. Zoubir (ed.), *North Africa in Transition: State, Society, and Economic Transformation in the 1990s*, Gainesville: University Press of Florida, pp. 43–60.

'Levels of fertility have declined steadily in Egypt, but unwanted childbearing remains common' (1997), *International Family Planning Perspectives*, 23: 197–8.

Martin, B. G. (1986) 'The spread of Islam', in P. M. Martin and P. O'Meara (eds), *Africa*, Bloomington: Indiana University Press, pp. 87–103.

Mayer, V. (1978) 'Women and social change in Morocco', in L. Beck and N. Keddie (eds), *Women in the Muslim World*, Cambridge, MA: Harvard University Press, pp. 100–23.

Minces, J. (1978) 'Women in Algeria', in L. Beck and N. Keddie (eds), *Women in the Muslim World*, Cambridge, MA: Harvard University Press, pp. 159–70.

Morsey, S. (1978) 'Sex differences and folk illness in an Egyptian village', in L. Beck and N. Keddie (eds), *Women in the Muslim World*, Cambridge, MA: Harvard University Press, pp. 599–616.

Mortimer, R. A. (1999) 'The Arab Maghreb Union: myth and reality', in Y. H. Zoubir (ed.), *North Africa in Transition: State, Society, and Economic Transformation in the 1990s*, Gainesville: University Press of Florida, pp. 177–91.

Musallam, B. (1983) *The Arabs: A Living History*, London: Collins/Harvill.

Nanji, A. (1996) *The Muslim Almanac: A Reference Work on the History, Faith, Culture, and Peoples of Islam*, Detroit, MI: Gale Research.

Rezig, I. (1983) 'Women's roles in contemporary Algeria: tradition and modernism', in B. Utas (ed.), *Women in Islamic Societies: Social Attitudes and Historical Perspectives*, London: Curzon Press, pp. 192–210.

Rosen, L. (1978) 'The negotiation of reality: male–female relations in Sefron, Morocco', in L. Beck and N. Keddie (eds), *Women in the Muslim World*, Cambridge, MA: Harvard University Press, pp. 561–84.

Sachs, S. (2000) 'Egypt's women win equal rights to divorce', *New York Times*, 1 March, p. A1.

Shahin, E. E. (1997) *Political Ascent: Contemporary Islamic Movements in North Africa*, Boulder, CO: Westview Press.

Slyomovics, S. (1996) 'Hassiba Ben Bouali, if you could see our Algeria: women and public space in Algeria', in S. Sabbagh (ed.), *Arab Women: Between Defiance and Restraint*, New York: Olive Branch Press, pp. 211–20.

Spencer, W. (1978) 'Berbers', in R. V. Weekes (ed.), *Muslim Peoples: A World Ethnographic Study*, Vol. 1, Westport, CT: Greenwood Press, pp. 146–54.

Sullivan, E. L. (1986) *Women in Egyptian Public Life*, Syracuse, NY: Syracuse University Press.

Talhami, G. H. (1996) *The Mobilization of Muslim Women in Egypt*, Gainesville: University Press of Florida.

Tillon, G. (1983) *The Republic of Cousins: Women's Oppression in Mediterranean Society*, London: Saqi.

United States Government (1999) *U.S. Department of State–Egypt Country Report on Human Rights Practices for 1998*, Washington, DC: United States Government.

Women's International Network News (1996a) 'The status of women in Algeria', *Women's International Network News*, 22: 56–7.

— (1996b) 'The status of women in Tunisia', *Women's International Network News*, 22: 57–8.

— (1996c) 'Tunisia: national report on women', *Women's International Network News*, 22: 59.

Zoubir, Y. H. (1999) 'State and civil society in Algeria', in Y. H. Zoubir (ed.), *North Africa in Transition: State, Society, and Economic Transformation in the 1990s*, Gainesville: University Press of Florida, pp. 29–42.

Zuhur, S. (1992) *Revealing Reveiling: Islamist Gender Ideology in Contemporary Egypt*, Albany: State University Press of New York.

2 Legal Profiles

ALGERIA, Democratic and Popular Republic of

Legal history The Algerian legal system is based on French and Islamic law. Algeria remained under French rule for 132 years, constituting the longest direct European colonization of any region in North Africa. After a brutal eight-year struggle for independence, Algeria became a sovereign state in July 1962.

Under French rule, courts applied Maliki principles in matters relating to personal status and succession (unless the parties were Ibadi). Commentators note that the process of adjudication and interpretation in the Franco-Algerian courts led to distinctive developments in the area of family law. In 1916, a commission headed by the French jurist Marcel Morand was appointed to formulate a draft code of Muslim law. The draft code, *Avant-project de code du droit Musulman Algérien*, based mainly on Maliki principles but incorporating some non-Maliki (mainly Hanafi) provisions, was never formally passed into law, although it did influence the application and administration of family law in Algeria. The government eventually issued a Marriage Ordinance in 1959, enacting some Maliki principles relating to family matters; the Ibadi minority was initially exempted from the Ordinance. The legislation may have been inspired by the codification of family law in Tunisia and Morocco in 1956 and 1958 under newly independent national governments. Although the Marriage Ordinance did not introduce substantial changes to family law, there were some provisions based on Hanafi principles. The Ordinance established rules for solemnization and registration of marriage, raised the minimum marriage ages for both parties, and established certain regulations relating to judicial dissolution and court orders for post-divorce reliefs; its application was specific to those who registered their option for state legislation.

The first Constitution promulgated in 1964 declared Islam the state religion. The new regime also amended the Marriage Ordinance of 1959, repealing or amending certain provisions such as the exemption of Ibadi marital relations from the terms of the Ordinance and the minimum marriage age. The second

Constitution adopted in 1976 reaffirmed Islam as the state religion. Periodic demands for comprehensive codification of personal status and inheritance laws eventually led to a draft code being presented to the National Assembly in 1980. After several years of debate, discussion and protest, the Family Code was enacted in 1984.

Schools of *fiqh* The Maliki school is the predominant *madhhab* in Algeria. There is an Ibadi minority. There are also small Christian and Jewish minorities.

Constitutional status of Islam(ic law) The current Constitution was adopted on 19 November 1976 and has been amended several times, with the last revisions approved by referendum in November and signed into law in December 1996. Article 2 of the Constitution provides that Islam is the religion of the state.

Court system The judiciary in Algeria is organized into three levels. *Daira* tribunals (numbering 183 in the late 1980s) are the courts of first instance for civil and certain criminal matters. The 48 *Wilaya* courts in each province are organized into four chambers (civil, criminal, administrative and accusation) and are constituted by three-judge panels that must hear all cases. In civil suits, these courts have appellate jurisdiction over the decisions of lower courts. The highest level of the judiciary is the Supreme Court (with a Private Law chamber for civil and commercial cases, Social Division for social security and labour cases, a Criminal Court, and an Administrative Division).

Notable features The provisions of the Family Code 1984 are drawn from various schools of law, the Algerian draft code of Muslim law formulated by a commission headed by Marcel Morand in 1916, and parallel legislation from neighbouring countries (particularly Moroccan enactments). Article 222 of the Code specifies the Shari'a as the residuary source of law, thus allowing for selection of appropriate interpretations from any school of law or directly from the original sources of law (Qur'an and *Sunna*) or from secondary sources.

The minimum marriage age is 21 years for men and 18 for women, with scope for judicial discretion if necessity or benefit is established. Compulsion by the marriage guardian, whether the *wali* is the father or anyone else, is expressly forbidden, as is giving a woman into marriage without her consent. Nevertheless, the law does state that the contracting of a woman's marriage is the guardian's duty, whether he be the father or another close male relation (or the judge if there is no *wali*). The marriage guardian may not prevent his ward from contracting a marriage that is to her benefit, but a father may oppose the marriage of his virgin daughter if it is considered to be in her best interests. If the guardian opposes the marriage without valid cause, the judge may authorize it.

The Code of Civil Status governs procedural matters related to obligatory marriage registration. The Family Code does state that, if there is no register entry, a marriage may be validated by judgment of the court 'if the elements which constitute the marriage are fulfilled in accordance with the provisions of the law'. Following such judgment, the marriage shall be entered into the Register of Civil Status. A valid marriage is constituted by consent of the spouses before the *wali* and two witnesses, and the establishment of *mahr*.

Spouses' rights and obligations generally follow classical law. The husband is required to provide maintenance from the time the marriage is consummated so long as the wife remains in the matrimonial home, and is required to treat co-wives equitably. Maintenance is payable from the date that a claim is filed, although a judge may direct the payment of arrears of maintenance (on the production of valid evidence) for a period of not more than one year preceding the filing of the claim. The wife is required to obey and respect her husband and his family and suckle her offspring if she is able to do so.

On polygyny, classical injunctions regarding the equal treatment of co-wives are reiterated, with the additional proviso that the reason for contracting a polygynous marriage must be justified. It is not stated exactly how a 'just reason' is defined. Prior notification of existing and future wives is required by the law. Any wife in a polygynous union may initiate legal action against her husband in case of harm (*darar*), or petition for divorce if her consent was not obtained.

Divorce is established only by a judgment of the court, and must be preceded by reconciliation efforts by the judge. Efforts at reconciliation are not to exceed three months. The wife may petition for divorce on the following grounds: non-payment of maintenance (requiring a court judgment ordering maintenance and upon condition that the wife didn't know of the husband's financial incapacity at the time of marriage); infirmity preventing conjugal relations; the husband's refusal to share his wife's bed for over four months; the husband's imprisonment for more than a year for a crime that brings disgrace to the family; the husband's absence without valid reason or provision of maintenance for over a year; any legally recognized harm (relating to the provision of maintenance or the contracting of a polygamous marriage, for instance); and any grave moral impropriety that is proved. The wife may also obtain a *khul'* with her husband's consent in return for some compensation. In case there is any disagreement over the terms of the *khul'*, the judge may order the wife to pay a particular sum that must not exceed the value of her proper dower. If the husband initiates divorce and the judge concludes the husband has abused his right of *talaq*, the wife is to be awarded damages; the law does not specify the upper limit for compensation to the arbitrarily divorced wife.

If the wife is granted custody of the children, the husband must provide for their accommodation in keeping with his means. A divorcée is entitled to maintenance during her waiting period, a provision adapted from the Hanafi school. The divorcée's custody of her children ceases at 16 years for boys (or ten if she remarries) and until the legal age of marriage (18 years) for girls (so long as the mother does not remarry or marries someone within the prohibited degrees to her daughter), with the proviso that the decision to terminate custody is in the ward's best interests. Full guardianship reverts to the mother upon the father's death unless his will provides otherwise.

On succession, the Family Code introduced the 'obligatory bequest' in favour of orphaned grandchildren by predeceased sons, as well as the Hanafi doctrine of *radd* (return), extended from its classical formulation to allow the spouse relict to share in the residue of the deceased's estate.

In the CEDAW Committee's concluding comments to Algeria's initial report to the 20th CEDAW session in 1999, it is noted that, partly due to Algeria's accession to the Convention in 1993, the Family Code 1984 is being revised. Some of the suggested changes may lead to the withdrawal of certain reservations submitted by Algeria upon accession to the CEDAW.

Law/case reporting system Laws are published in the *Journal Officiel*.

International conventions (with relevant reservations) Algeria signed the ICCPR and the ICESCR in 1968 and ratified them in 1989, with several interpretative declarations. The final declaration relates to Article 23(4) of the ICCPR on rights and responsibilities of spouses in marriage and divorce being interpreted in such a way that it does not impair 'the essential foundations of the Algerian legal system'.

Algeria signed the CRC in 1990 and ratified it in 1993, with the following interpretative declarations: to Article 14(1) and (2) on children's freedom of conscience and religion, as Algerian law stipulates that a child's education is determined by the religion of the father; and to Articles 13, 16 and 17 of the Convention on children's freedom of expression, right to privacy and access to information, relating to particular provisions of the Algerian Penal and Information Codes and the interpretation of the provisions of the CRC in light of possible breaches of public order and decency and incitement of minors. The latter declaration also cites Article 26 of the Information Code, which states that 'national and foreign periodicals and specialized publications … must not contain any illustration, narrative, information or insertion contrary to Islamic morality, national values or human rights or advocate racism, fanaticism and treason'.

Algeria acceded to the CEDAW in 1996, with the following reservations: to Article 2, as Algeria reiterated its willingness to apply the provisions relating to the elimination of all discrimination by legislation and other appropriate means on condition that 'they do not conflict with the provisions of the Algerian Family Code'; to Article 9(2) on equal nationality rights on the basis that the provision is inconsistent with the Algerian Nationality and Family Codes; to Article 15(4) relating to freedom of movement and freedom in choice of residence and domicile, stating that the provision 'should not be interpreted in such a manner as to contradict the provisions of Article 37 of Chapter 4 of the Algerian Family Code'; and to Article 16 on equality of rights in personal status and family law, asserting that the provisions of that Article should not be taken to contradict the Algerian Family Code.

Background and sources

Algeria (1999) *Initial Report to the Committee on the Elimination of Discrimination against Women*, 1 September, CEDAW 20th Session, 19 January to 5 February 1999, New York: United Nations.

Christelow, A. (1985) *Muslim Law Courts and the French Colonial State in Algeria*, Princeton, NJ: Princeton University Press.

El Alami, D. S. and D. Hinchcliffe (1996) *Islamic Marriage and Divorce Laws of the Arab World*, London and Boston: Kluwer Law International.

Knauss, P. R. (1987) *The Persistence of Patriarchy: Class, Gender, and Ideology in Twentieth Century Algeria*, New York: Praeger Publishers.

Lazreg, M. (1994) *The Eloquence of Silence: Algerian Women in Question*, New York: Routledge.

Mahmood, T. (1995) 'Algeria', in *Statutes of Personal Law in Islamic Countries: History, Texts and Analysis*, 2nd edn, New Delhi: India and Islam Research Council, pp. 7–9, 101–6.

Metz, H. C. (1994) (ed.) *Algeria: A Country Study*, 5th edn, Washington, DC: Federal Research Division, Library of Congress.

Mitchell, R. (1997) 'Family law in Algeria before and after the 1404/1984 Family Code', in R. Gleave and E. Kermelli (eds), *Islamic Law: Theory and Practice*, London: I.B.Tauris, pp. 194–204.

Nasir, J. J. (1990) *The Islamic Law of Personal Status*, 2nd edn, London: Graham and Trotman.

Redden, K. R. (1990) 'Algeria', in K. R. Redden (ed.), *Modern Legal Systems Cyclopedia*, Vol. 6, Buffalo, NY: Hein.

EGYPT, Arab Republic of

Legal history   The legal system is based on Islamic law and civil law (particularly French codes). Egypt attained independence from the Ottoman Empire in matters of administration of law and the judiciary in 1874. A reformist movement developed in the late nineteenth century, led by such prominent thinkers and commentators as the Grand Mufti Muhammad 'Abduh, Rashid Rida and Qasim Amin. Changes in the interpretation and application of family law were an important part of the reformists' agenda.

The reform of the judicial administration began in 1875, leading to the establishment of *mukhtalatat* (mixed) and *ahli* (national) courts. As Egypt increasingly came under foreign influence, the legal system began resembling European systems to a greater extent. New legislation relating to penal, commercial and maritime law also reflected the growing influence of Europe, but personal law remained unreformed until 1920. (The renowned jurist Qudri Pasha prepared an unofficial code of personal status law based on the *rajih* [majority, dominant] views of the Hanafi school, a source still referred to in the Shari'a courts of some neighbouring states as a guide to Hanafi law.)

The Shari'a courts were integrated into the National Courts in 1956. There are judges trained in Shari'a presiding over family law cases within the National Courts. Appeals are heard by regular judges in the Court of Appeals and then the Court of Cassation.

From 1920 to the early 1950s, on the basis of recommendations made by several committees, the Egyptian legislature enacted a number of laws effecting important changes in legal principles relating to family law and succession. These included the Law of Maintenance and Personal Status (Law no. 25/1920), a law regulating minimum marriage age (Law no. 56/1923), a Law of Personal Status (Law no. 25/1929) on the dissolution of marriage and family disputes, the Civil Code of 1931, the Law of Inheritance (Law no. 77/1943) and the Law of Bequest (Law no. 71/1946). In 1976, a new law established rules for the enforcement of court orders for payment of maintenance to wives, ex-wives, children and parents.

Through the 1960s and 1970s, despite various reports and proposals relating to legal reform, political events time and again preempted the enactment of new laws in this area. Finally, in 1979, after failing to achieve any consensus on matters of family law, Sadat unilaterally issued an emergency decree passing one of the proposals into law in 1979. Law no. 44/1979 was popularly referred to as 'Jihan's Law' or 'Jiji's Law'. This controversial amendment introduced extensive changes to the two Egyptian Laws of Personal Status of

1920 and 1929, drawing from the interpretations of scholars of all four Sunni schools of law.

In May 1985, the 1979 law was struck down by the High Constitutional Court of Egypt on technical grounds and declared *ultra vires* the Egyptian Constitution; the initial emergency decree issued by Sadat had been issued in the absence of a true state of emergency and so was deemed invalid. A few months after the verdict, a Personal Status (Amendment) Law (Law no. 100/ 1985) was enacted to revise the 1920 and 1929 Laws on Personal Status. A number of the changes made by the 1979 law were reintroduced as well as some new provisions added. One element that was conspicuous by its absence in the 1985 legislation was the wife's automatic right to a divorce from her husband if he married polygynously. As a concession to religious conservatives, the presumption of injury occasioned by a polygynous marriage was removed, requiring the wife to establish that she has suffered harm from her husband's polygynous union if she wishes to divorce. Thus the ground for divorce was no longer automatic but was left up to the discretion of the courts, as being the wife of a polygynous husband was no longer automatically equated with 'harm' (constituting a return to the classical position).

The second compromise related to the requirement that the divorced wife in custody of minor children had exclusive rights to the rented marital home for as long as she retained custody (unless her former husband provided another dwelling). While the requirement to provide accommodation for the custodial mother was retained in the 1985 legislation, the former husband was given exclusive rights over his unrented dwelling. The Law of Personal Status was again amended in January 2000, giving women more options for divorce.

Schools of *fiqh*   The Hanafi school is the predominant school of *fiqh*. Earlier on, Egypt was the home of the Shafi'i school and under the Fatimids, the ruling classes were Isma'ili. There is also a significant Coptic Christian minority in Egypt.

Constitutional status of Islam(ic law)   The Constitution was adopted on 11 September 1971 and amended by referendum in May 1980. The amendment made Islamic law 'the principal source of legislation' in Egypt. Article 2 of the Constitution reads in full: 'Islam is the religion of the State and Arabic its official language. Islamic jurisprudence is the principal source of legislation.'

Court system   Shari'a courts were integrated into the national court system in 1956. Family law is administered within the National Courts by judges trained in Shari'a (with separate judges for and legislation applicable to cases involving Copts and Muslims). Appeals are heard by regular judges in the Courts of Appeal and, ultimately, the Court of Cassation.

Notable features   There are a number of enactments relating to personal status, although the core of family law is formed by Laws no. 25/1920 and no. 25/1929 as amended by Law no. 100/1985. The Civil Code (no. 131/1948), drafted by Professor 'Abd al-Razzaq al-Sanhuri, the renowned Egyptian jurist who played a role in the drafting of legislation in a number of Arab states during the 1940s and 1950s, does not cover family law or succession, but does govern majority and civil status; Article 280 of the Civil Code directs that recourse should be had to the most appropriate opinion from the Hanafi school in the absence of any textual provision in the legislation.

The minimum marriage age is 18 for males and 16 for females (lunar calendar). Registration is compulsory but does not determine the validity of marriage. Courts may not hear cases where the parties have not attained the minimum marriage age, or where claim of marriage is disputed and there is no official documentation.

Guardianship is governed by the Civil Code but does not extend to the power of compulsion in marriage; a *wali* cannot prevent his ward from marrying for reasons relating to social status or the amount of dower, for example, as judges may authorize marriages if *walis* refuse.

Maintenance is due from the date of a valid marriage contract and valid retirement unless the wife apostasizes, denies her husband conjugal rights without justification, or leaves the matrimonial home without his permission (except for circumstances permitted by rules of the Shari'a). However, leaving the home for lawful work does not constitute disobedience so long as the wife does not abuse this right, it is not contrary to the interests of her family, and her husband has not explicitly asked her to refrain from working. Maintenance is deemed to be a debt against the husband from the date that he fails to maintain until the debt is paid or excused, and claims for arrears of maintenance may not be heard for a period exceeding one year from the date of the claim.

Polygyny is permissible, with notification of the existing and intended wives. The existing wife may obtain a judicial dissolution on grounds of material or moral harm up to one year from the date of her knowledge of her husband's polygynous union if such harm makes cohabitation as husband and wife impossible.

Talaq expressed indirectly, while intoxicated or under coercion, or con-
ditionally with the intent of forcing the taking of some action, has no effect.
A *talaq* to which a number is added verbally or by gesture is effective only as
a single and revocable *talaq*, except for the third of three, *talaq* before consummation or in consideration of payment. A written and notarized certification
of *talaq* must be produced within 30 days of repudiation and the notary must
forward a copy of the certificate to the wife. Certain financial effects of *talaq*
are suspended on the wife's knowledge of the repudiation if the husband is
found to have concealed it.

The wife may obtain an irrevocable judicial divorce on the following
grounds: serious or incurable defect of the husband (unless the woman married
in full knowledge of the defect or it occurred after the contract and she
implicitly or explicitly accepted it); harm making cohabitation as husband
and wife impossible (if the harm is proved and reconciliation efforts fail);
material or moral harm if the husband marries polygynously (subject to the
aforementioned conditions); non-payment of maintenance; the husband's
imprisonment for three years or more (after one year of the sentence has
passed); and discord, if reconciliation efforts fail, with a financial settlement
proportionate to the allocation of blame as determined by the arbitrators. A
woman can also seek a divorce on the grounds of incompatibility, but in such
case she forfeits all financial claims against her husband.

A divorcée repudiated by her husband without cause or consent on her
part is entitled to maintenance during her *'idda* and compensation (*mut'a al-
talaq*) of at least two years' maintenance (with consideration for the husband's
means, the circumstances of the divorce, and the length of the marriage); no
upper limit for compensation is stipulated. Maintenance claims for the *'idda*
period can be heard up to one year from the date of the divorce. A divorcing
husband must provide independent accommodation for his former wife who
has custody of their minor children.

The divorced mother is entitled to custody of boys until the age of ten and
girls until the age of twelve. Custody may be extended till the age of 15 for
boys and till marriage for girls if the judge deems such an extension to be in
the best interests of the ward.

On succession, notable reforms introduced by legislation in 1946 legalized
bequests to heirs, and also established 'obligatory bequests' to benefit descendants of predeceased sons and daughters. The doctrine of *radd* was also
extended to allow the spouse relict to share in the residue of the deceased
spouse's estate.

Notable cases Case no. 29 of 1980 in the Badari Court of Summary Justice for Guardianship of the Person (*Mahkama Juz'iyya li'l-Wilaya 'ala'l-Nafs*) precipitated the 4 May 1985 judgment of the High Constitutional Court (*al-Mahkama al-Dusturiyya al-'Ulya*) that the implementing resolution of Law no. 44/1979 ('Jihan's Law') was unconstitutional on technical grounds as the initial emergency decree by which Sadat implemented the legislation was issued in the absence of a true state of emergency.

A 1993 *hisba* suit before the Giza Court of First Instance called for divorcing Professor Nasr Abu Zayd from his wife on grounds of his alleged apostasy. The Giza Court dismissed the suit and the petitioners appealed to the Cairo Court of Appeal (Department of Personal Status). The Appeals Court ruled in favour of the petitioners, and the case was brought before the Supreme Court in 1995. The Supreme Court ruled for divorcing Professor Abu Zayd from his wife. The case led to the passage of Law no. 3/1996 preventing claims by private individuals on the basis of *hisba*.

Law/case reporting system Laws are published in *al-Jarida al-Rasmiyya*. Case reports of civil and criminal judgments of the Court of Cassation are published six times annually. Judges' and practitioners' indexes and summaries of the same are compiled less frequently. Practitioners' collections of principles in court rulings on Shari'a and personal status matters are also compiled.

International conventions (with relevant reservations) Egypt signed the ICCPR and ICESCR in 1967 and ratified them in 1982. Egypt submitted a general declaration relating to the provisions of the Shari'a not conflicting with the text annexed to the instrument(s). Egypt signed the CEDAW in 1980 and ratified it in 1981. One of the reservations submitted by Egypt relates to Article 9(2) on gender equality in nationality rights. 'It is clear that the child's acquisition of his father's nationality is the procedure most suitable for the child and that this does not infringe upon the principle of equality between men and women, since it is customary for a woman to agree, upon marrying an alien, that her children shall be of the father's nationality.' The next reservation is to Article 16 relating to gender equality in family relations. The reservation relates to the status of the Shari'a; Article 16 is accepted in so far as it does not prejudice *shar'i* provisions whereby women are granted rights 'equivalent' to men's rights in order to 'ensure a just balance between them'. The reservation is made 'out of respect for the sacrosanct nature of the firm religious beliefs which govern marital relations in Egypt and which may not be called in question and in view of the fact that one of the most important bases of these relations is an equivalency of rights and duties so as to ensure complementarity which guarantees true equality between the spouses'. The reservation to Article 2 states that, although 'Egypt is willing to comply with the content of this article', it is with the proviso that 'such compliance does not run counter to the Islamic Shari'a'.

Egypt signed and ratified the CRC in 1990. Egypt submitted a general reservation concerning areas of conflict between the Shari'a (as one of the fundamental sources of Egyptian positive legislation) and the CRC, particularly in relation to provisions on adoption in Articles 20 and 21.

Background and sources

Brown, N. J. (1997) *The Rule of Law in the Arab World: Courts in Egypt and the Gulf*, Cambridge: Cambridge University Press.

El Alami, D. S. (1992) *The Marriage Contract and Islamic Law in the Shari'ah and Personal Status Laws of Egypt and Morocco*, London: Graham and Trotman.

— (1994) 'Law no. 100 of 1985 amending certain provisions of Egypt's Personal Status Laws', *Islamic Law and Society*, 1, 1: 116–36.

El Alami, D. S. and D. Hinchcliffe (1996) *Islamic Marriage and Divorce Laws of the Arab World*, London and Boston: Kluwer Law International.

Hill, E. (1979) *Mahkama! Studies in the Egyptian Legal System: Courts and Crimes, Law and Society*, London: Ithaca Press.

Mahmood, T. (1995) 'Egypt', in *Statutes of Personal Law in Islamic Countries: History, Texts and Analysis*, 2nd edn, New Delhi: India and Islam Research Council, pp. 10–15, 106–16.

Najjar, F. (1988) 'Egypt's Laws of Personal Status', *Arab Studies Quarterly* 10, 3: 319–45.

Nasir, J. J. (1990) *The Islamic Law of Personal Status*, 2nd edn, London: Graham and Trotman.

Pearl, D. (1987) *A Textbook on Muslim Law*, 2nd edn, London: Croom Helm.

Redden, K. R. (1990) 'Egypt', in K. R. Redden (ed.), *Modern Legal Systems Cyclopedia*, Vol. 5, Buffalo, NY: Hein.

Sfeir, G. N. (1998) 'Basic freedoms in a fractured legal culture: Egypt and the case of Nasr Hamid Abu Zayd', *Middle East Journal*, 52, 3: 402–14.

(LIBYA) Socialist People's Libyan Arab Jamahiriya

Legal history The legal system includes elements of French, Islamic and Italian law. Libya became a part of the Ottoman Empire in 1551. Following the Italo-Turkish War (1911–12), Italy annexed Libya in 1934 after exiling the most resistant elements of Libyan society, led by the Sanusiyya. Libya remained an Italian colony until World War II, when the Allied forces and Libyan returnee fighters ousted German and Italian forces, following which the British and French shared control over the region. Libya gained independence in

1951, under its first king, Syed Idris al-Sanusi. A military coup in 1969 brought an end to the monarchy, and a republic was established under Colonel Muammar al-Qaddafi. The Revolutionary Command Council established a Committee for the Codification of Personal Law in the early years following the revolution.

While the Committee was still in deliberation, the RCC issued a decree identifying the Shari'a as the principal source of all legislation and establishing a High Commission to examine all existing legislation in order to make it consistent with *shar'i* principles. Legal provisions for the purpose of bringing legislation into accord with the Shari'a were to be based on *takhayyur*, *maslaha*, and custom and usage where the Maliki is the predominant school. Some of the recommendations of the Personal Law Codification Committee led to the passage of the Law on Women's Rights in Marriage and Divorce in 1972, introducing innovative provisions on *khul'*. The Penal Code 1953 was also amended by several laws passed in the early 1970s, making Libya the first country to introduce *hadd* punishments by state legislation. Penalties for various crimes, such as theft, *zina*, *qadhf* and artificial insemination, were introduced by the amendments, although commentators note that the punishments have rarely been applied in practice.

A new Family Law enacted in 1984 raised the marriage age, restricted polygyny and divorce, and to a lesser extent evened the spouses' mutual rights and obligations. Article 72 of the Family Law directs recourse to the sources of the Shari'a as a residual source of law in the absence of specific provisions in the legislation.

Schools of *fiqh* The Maliki school is the predominant *madhhab* in Libya. Libya also has a small Christian minority.

Constitutional status of Islam(ic law) A Constitutional Proclamation was issued on 11 December 1969 and amended on 2 March 1977. Article 2 declares Islam the official state religion. The state also protects religious freedoms 'in accordance with established customs'. Article 37 of the Proclamation stated that a permanent constitution is to be drafted, but it has yet to be produced. Article 2 of the Declaration on the Establishment of the Authority of the People issued in March 1977 provides that '[t]he Holy Qur'an is the Constitution of the Socialist People's Libyan Arab Jamahiriya'. Colonel Qaddafi also elucidates his own political and social theories in the Green Book, based on a speech delivered in April 1975.

Court system After the revolution, Qaddafi abolished the dual system, and civil and Shari'a courts were merged in 1973. There are four levels of courts: Summary Courts, Courts of First Instance, Appeal Courts and the Supreme Court. Courts of First Instance have numerous divisions, including a Personal Status Division. The Courts of Appeal (numbering three in 1987, at Tripoli, Benghazi and Sabha) and the Courts of First Instance are both constituted by three-judge panels with judgments confirmed by majority decisions. The Shari'a judges who once would have constituted the personnel of the Shari'a Court of Appeals now sit in the regular Courts of Appeal, specializing in Shari'a appellate cases. The Supreme Court has five chambers: civil and commercial, criminal, administrative, constitutional and Shari'a.

Notable features The minimum marriage age is 20 years for men and women. There is scope for judicial discretion on grounds of benefit or necessity and with the *wali*'s consent, though no minimum age is specified. The marriage guardian may not force a ward of either sex into marriage or prevent his ward from marrying; if the guardian withholds consent, the ward may take the matter to court to obtain permission. Marriage registration is obligatory.

Polygyny is permitted with prior judicial permission, and on grounds of the husband's financial and physical ability. Amendments to the law on polygyny also permit the husband to marry polygynously with the written agreement of the first wife, or with judicial permission granted for serious reasons.

Maintenance is the husband's duty, within the limits of his ability, unless he is in hardship and his wife is wealthy. Either spouse may obtain a maintenance order, or be awarded interim maintenance during a suit if the plaintiff appears to be eligible according to a provision which clearly diverges from classical rules of Islamic law. No maximum time limit is specified for claiming arrears of maintenance.

With reference to divorce, Article 28 of the Code states that '[i]n all cases, divorce shall not be established except by a decree by the relevant court'. *Talaq* uttered by a minor, insane, demented or coerced husband or without deliberate intent is invalid, as is *talaq* that is suspended or conditional. Any *talaq* to which a number is attached is considered singly revocable (except the third of three). Judicial divorce is available on the following grounds: husband's failure to maintain without cause; husband's inability to maintain (of which the wife was ignorant at the time of the marriage, and after an appropriate grace period); husband's absence without justification; grounds of defect preventing fulfilment of the aims of marriage or other grave defect (whether such defect developed before or after the contract) and was not known to other party; and *hajr*, defined as the husband's sexual abstinence for four months or more without justification, after an appropriate grace period. Most of the above grounds for judicial divorce are available to men as well as women. Judicial divorce may be obtained if the parties do not agree to *talaq* by mutual consent and arbitration and reconciliation efforts fail and harm is established. If the 'harm' is deemed to be the wife's fault, her deferred dower is forfeit, maintenance is frozen and compensation is required; if it is deemed to be the husband's fault, he must pay the deferred dower and compensation. The wife may also obtain a *khul'* for appropriate compensation, which may include the forfeiture of maintenance rights, her deferred dower or custody over her children and courts are empowered to rule for *khul'* if the husband retracts his offer of *khul'* 'due to obstinacy'. Payment of compensation to the husband may be deferred if the wife establishes hardship. Annulment is effected due to difference of religion in cases of conversion where the wife becomes Muslim and the husband does not or if the husband becomes Muslim and his non-*kitabiyya* wife does not.

The divorcing husband must pay his wife maintenance for the *'idda*, and for children in her custody. Compensation to the wife can be awarded by the court if the husband is considered to bear the responsibility for the causes of a *talaq*. The divorced mother's custody ends at the age of marriage for girls and puberty for boys.

The Law on Women's Right to Inheritance 1959 reiterates the application of classical law and introduces penal sanctions of imprisonment for anyone withholding from a woman her lawful share (until the payment of her share).

Law/case reporting system Law reports are published in the official journal, *al-Jarida al-Rasmiya*. Supreme Court decisions are published in *Majallat al-Mahkama al-'Ulya*.

International conventions (with relevant reservations) Libya acceded to the ICCPR and ICESCR in 1970, with a general declaration to the effect that its accession shall in no way signify recognition of Israel or entry into dealings with Israel under the terms of the Covenants. Libya acceded to the CEDAW in 1989, with reservations relating to the following: Article 2 being implemented 'with due regard for the peremptory norms of the Islamic Shari'a relating to determination of the inheritance portions of the estate of a deceased person'; and to Articles 16(c) and (d) being implemented 'without prejudice to any of the rights guaranteed to women by the Islamic Shari'a'. Libya acceded to the CRC in 1993, without reservations.

Background and sources

El Alami, D. S. and D. Hinchcliffe (1996) *Islamic Marriage and Divorce Laws of the Arab World*, London and Boston: Kluwer Law International.

Layish, A. (1991) *Divorce in the Libyan Family*, Jerusalem: Magnes Press, Hebrew University.

'Libya' (1994) *Yearbook of Islamic and Middle Eastern Law*, 1: 225–36.

Mahmood, T. (1995) 'Libya', in *Statutes of Personal Law in Islamic Countries: History, Texts and Analysis*, 2nd edn, New Delhi: India and Islam Research Council, pp. 29–33, 151–5.

— (1996) 'Legal system of modern Libya: enforcement of Islamic penal laws', in T. Mahmood et al., *Criminal Law in Islam and the Muslim World: A Comparative Perspective*, 1st edn, New Delhi: Institute of Objective Studies.

Mayer, A. E. (1977) *Islamic Law in Libya: Analyses of Selected Laws Enacted since the 1969 Revolution*, London.

— (1990) 'Reinstating Islamic criminal law in Libya', in D. H. Dwyer (ed.), *Law and Islam in the Middle East*, New York: Bergin and Garvey.

— (1996) 'Libyan legislation in defense of Arabo-Islamic sexual mores', in T. Mahmood et al., *Criminal Law in Islam and the Muslim World: A Comparative Perspective*, 1st edn, New Delhi: Institute of Objective Studies.

Metz, H. C (ed.) (1989) *Libya: A Country Study*, Washington, DC: Federal Research Division, Library of Congress.

Redden, K. R. (1990) 'Libya', in K. R. Redden (ed.), *Modern Legal Systems Cyclopedia*, Vol. 5, Buffalo, NY: Hein.

MOROCCO, Kingdom of (and Western Sahara)

Legal history Spanish and Portuguese power in Morocco and the Western Sahara was in its ascendancy in the fifteenth century, with several coastal areas being the subject of rival claims. By the early twentieth century, the British acknowledged Morocco as part of the French sphere of influence, with Morocco being divided between Spain and France in 1904. A French protectorate was established in 1912. Spanish Morocco faced fierce resistance and a revolt in 1920 nearly succeeded in driving the Spanish out, when a French and Spanish alliance re-established Spanish authority in 1926. Morocco gained independence from France in 1956 and Spain relinquished authority over most of its Moroccan holdings during the same period. The status of the Western Sahara remains unresolved, with contesting claims on the part of the Moroccan state and the Polisario Front (Popular Front for the Liberation of the Saquia el-Hamra and Rio de Oro) which proclaimed a government in exile of the Sahrawi Arab Democratic Republic (SADR) in February 1976. The region was divided between Morocco and Mauritania in April of that year, with Morocco taking over the remaining one-third of the territory soon after Mauritania succumbed to pressure from Polisario in 1979 and abandoned its claims. Preparations for a long-delayed UN-sponsored referendum on the future of the territory continue.

Under French and Spanish rule, the colonial legal systems influenced local developments outside of the sphere of family law. Shari'a courts continued to apply Maliki *fiqh* during the first half of the century (in addition to local tribunals applying customary law). Following independence in 1956, a Law Reform Commission was established in order to draft a Code of Personal Status. A Code was passed into law within the next year, based on dominant Maliki doctrines as well as *takhayyur, maslaha,* and legislation from other Muslim countries (perhaps most importantly the Tunisian Code of Personal Status 1956). Article 82 of the Code directs that '[w]ith regard to anything not covered by this law, reference shall be made to the most appropriate or accepted opinion or prevailing practice of the school of Imam Malik'. Major amendments to the Code's provisions relating to marriage guardianship, polygyny, *talaq* and *mut'a al-talaq* were made in 1993.

Schools of *fiqh* The Maliki school is the predominant *madhhab* in Morocco. There are also Jewish and Christian minorities.

Constitutional status of Islam(ic law) The Constitution was adopted on 10 March 1972, and underwent major revisions in 1992 and 1996. Article 6 declares Islam the official state religion and guarantees freedom of worship for all citizens.

Court system There are four levels of courts: 27 *Sadad* courts, 30 Regional Courts, 9 Courts of Appeal and the Supreme Court in Rabat [figures as of late 1980s]. The *Sadad* and Regional Courts are divided into four sections: Shari'a; rabbinical; civil, commercial and administrative; and penal. *Sadad* courts are courts of first instance for Muslim and Jewish personal law. Shari'a sections of Regional Courts also hear all matters of Islamic law affecting Moroccan Muslims.

Notable features The minimum marriage age is 18 years for males and 15 for females. There is scope for judicial discretion for males under 18 if there is fear of immorality. Marriage of a minor below the age of majority (*rushd*) requires the guardian's consent, and if the guardian refuses, the parties may take the matter to court.

Compatibility of age in marriage is the sole right of the wife. The marriage guardian is not to contract the marriage of his ward unless she authorizes it.

The *wali*'s right of coercion (*ijbar*) under certain circumstances was revoked under the 1993 amendments to the Code. The ward may take the matter to court if her guardian refuses consent for her marriage, and if a ward of the age of majority has no father, she may choose either to appoint a *wali* of her choice or contract her own marriage.

The provisions relating to registration include the requirement of a notarized contract before two witnesses. Preliminaries include the filing of documents attesting to the identity, age, domicile, guardian's name, husband's personal status, and proof of dissolution for previously married women, as well as specification of the dower.

Polygyny is not permitted for fear of unequal treatment. There is a requirement of notification for the second wife, and the 1993 amendments to the Code also require notification of the existing wife. A woman who did not insert a stipulation restricting her husband's right to marry polygynously in the marriage contract and whose husband does so may request a judicial divorce on grounds of harm. The Code specifies maintenance as one of the rights of the wife, and obedience as one of the rights of the husband.

Talaq must be registered in the presence of two male witnesses and, under the 1993 amendments, in the wife's presence (unless she fails to appear at the summons), within the jurisdiction of the marital residence. If *talaq* is found to have been exercised while the wife is menstruating, the judge shall oblige the husband to revoke it. *Talaq* uttered while intoxicated, under coercion, enraged, upon condition, by oath or with intention to coerce is ineffective. *Talaq* to which a number is attached is effective as a single revocable repudiation (except the third of three). The wife may seek a judicial divorce on the following grounds: husband's non-maintenance; husband's grave and incurable or long-term defect, although such right is forfeit if the wife married in full knowledge of the defect or if it occurred after the contract and she implicitly or explicitly accepted it; such harm caused by the husband as makes cohabitation impossible (after reconciliation efforts); husband's absence for over one year without valid reason; and husband's oath of abstinence if he does not comply with a judicial decision allowing four months' grace period. All judicial divorces are irrevocable except divorce granted because of the husband's oath of abstinence or inability to maintain. Regulations relating to *khul'* are based on classical law. The divorcing husband is obliged to pay compensation if the *talaq* was on his part. The 1993 amendments to the Code add to this that the *qadi* shall assess the injury sustained by the arbitrarily divorced wife in awarding compensation, with no upper or lower limits set to compensation awards. The divorced mother has right of custody until puberty for sons and until marriage for daughters.

Matters of testate and intestate succession are covered in Books V and VI of the Code of Personal Status, respectively. Obligatory bequests were introduced in favour of orphaned grandchildren by predeceased sons.

Law/case reporting system Law reports are published in the *Bulletin Officiel*.

International conventions (with relevant reservations) Morocco signed the ICCPR and ICESCR in 1977 and ratified both in 1979 without submitting any reservations. Morocco signed the CRC in 1990 and ratified it in 1993, with a reservation to Article 14 according children freedom of religion, 'in view of the fact that Islam is the State religion'. Morocco acceded to the CEDAW in 1993. It submitted the following declarations: it confirmed its willingness to apply the provisions of Article 2 on the elimination of discrimination provided that they do not 'prejudice the constitutional requirement that regulates the rules of succession to the throne ... (and) do not conflict with the provisions of the Islamic Shari'a'; it also stated that, with respect to Article 15(4), 'Morocco declares that it can only be bound by the provisions of this paragraph, in particular those relating to the right of women to choose their residence and domicile, to the extent that they are not incompatible with Articles 34 and 36 of the Moroccan Code of Personal Status'. Morocco also submitted the following reservations: its reservation relating to Article 15(4) states that 'the Law of Moroccan Nationality permits a child to bear the nationality of its mother only in the cases where it is born to an unknown ... or to a stateless father, when born in Morocco'; Morocco also expressed reservations regarding Article 16 stating that equality in family law 'is considered incompatible with the Islamic Shari'a, which guarantees to each of the spouses rights and responsibilities within a framework of equilibrium and complementarity in order to preserve the sacred bond of matrimony'.

Background and sources

Blanc, F. P. and R. Zeidguy (compilers) (1996) *Moudawana: Code de Statut Personnel et des Successions* (édition Synoptique Franco-Arabe) Sochepress-Université.

El Alami, D. S. and D. Hinchcliffe (1996) *Islamic Marriage and Divorce Laws of the Arab World*, London and Boston: Kluwer Law International.

Mahmood, T. (1995) 'Morocco', in *Statutes of Personal Law in Islamic Countries: History, Texts and Analysis*, 2nd edn, New Delhi: India and Islam Research Council, pp. 33–5, 155–62.

Mir-Hosseini, Z. (1993) *Marriage on Trial: A Study of Islamic Family Law, Iran and Morocco Compared*, London: I.B.Tauris.

Nasir, J. J. (1990) *The Islamic Law of Personal Status*, 2nd edn, London: Graham and Trotman.

Pearl, D. (1987) *A Textbook on Muslim Law*, 2nd edn, London: Croom Helm.

Redden, K. R. (1990) 'Morocco', in K. R. Redden (ed.), *Modern Legal Systems Cyclopedia*, Vol. 6, Buffalo, NY: Hein.

Welchman, L. (1996) '*Islamic Marriage and Divorce Laws of the Arab World* by El Alami and Hinchcliffe' (book review), *Yearbook of Islamic and Middle Eastern Law*, 3: 547–50.

TUNISIA, Republic of

Legal history The legal system is based on the French civil law system and Islamic law. As Tunisia was an autonomous province of the Ottoman Empire from 1574, Hanafi *fiqh* was influential, but never displaced the position of the Maliki school. Tunisia became a French Protectorate in 1881 and attained full independence in March 1956. The Law of Personal Status, inspired by un-official draft codes of Maliki and Hanafi family law, was passed soon after independence. The TLPS was extended to apply to all Tunisian citizens in 1957, thus ending the application of rabbinical law to Jewish personal status matters and the French Civil Code to personal status cases relating to non-Muslim Tunisians. Among the most controversial provisions of the TLPS were those banning polygyny and extra-judicial divorce.

Schools of *fiqh* The Maliki school is the predominant *madhhab* in Tunisia.

Constitutional status of Islam(ic law) The Constitution was adopted 1 June 1959. Article 1 declares Islam the state religion, and Article 38 provides that the president of the Republic must be a Muslim.

Court system Shari'a courts were abolished in 1956. There are four levels of courts in the judiciary. Cantonal courts have limited criminal jurisdiction. Courts of first instance have civil, commercial, correctional, social and per-sonal status chambers. Three courts of appeal (in Tunis, Sousse and Sfax) have civil, correctional, criminal and accusation chambers (the final one being similar to a grand jury). The Court of Cassation in Tunis is the highest court of appeal, with three civil and commercial chambers and a criminal chamber.

Notable features The minimum age of marriage is 20 for males and 17 for females. Marriage below these ages requires special permission from the courts, which may be given only for 'pressing reasons' and on the basis of a 'clear interest' or benefit to be realized by both spouses by the marriage. Marriage below the age of legal majority requires the consent of the guardian and (since 1993) of the mother; recourse may be had to the judge in the event of their refusal. The age of legal majority is 20 for both males and females, but marriage gives rise to legal majority for matters of personal status, civil and commercial transactions provided the party concerned is over the age of 17 (see Article 153). Marriage can be proven only by official document as prescribed by law. Polygyny is prohibited, and offenders are liable to a prison sentence of one year and/or a fine.

During marriage, spouses are to treat each other well, to fulfil their marital duties 'as required by custom and usage' and to cooperate in running family affairs, including the upbringing of children. As 'head of the family' the husband is responsible for the maintenance of his wife and children, while the wife is to contribute to family maintenance if she has the means to do so.

Divorce is a strictly judicial matter; extra-judicial *talaq* has no validity. The occurrence of three divorces between a couple creates a permanent prohibition on their future remarriage. The court may grant divorce based on: 1) agreement of the spouses; 2) a petition from one spouse by reason of injury caused by the other; or 3) the will of the husband or the petition of the wife. No divorce may be decreed until after the family judge appointed by the court has tried and failed to reconcile the couple. Where divorce is not by mutual agreement (i.e. in either of the last two cases) the court may award compensation for that injury. If the injured spouse is the wife, this may take the form of a lump sum or of regular alimony payments until she no longer has need of them – that is, she dies or remarries or otherwise her social circumstances change.

If the marriage ends by the death of one of the spouses, custody goes to the surviving spouse; if it ends by divorce, the judge is required to take the best interest of the ward into account in assigning custody either to one of the parents or to a third party. If the mother is awarded custody, she is authorized to exercise the prerogatives of the guardian in matters related to the ward's travel, education and financial affairs; she may be granted full powers of guardianship if the guardian is unable or unfit to exercise them.

In succession, the obligatory bequest has been legislated for orphaned grandchildren through a predeceased father or mother, entitling them to the proportion of the dead parent's share to a maximum of one-third of the estate. The spouse relict share in the *radd* of the estate; daughters as well as brothers may exclude collaterals and other more remote male relatives of the deceased from inheritance.

Law/case reporting system Law reporting is through the *Journal Officiel*.

International conventions (with relevant reservations)   Tunisia signed the ICCPR and ICESCR in 1968 and ratified them in 1969. Tunisia signed the CEDAW in 1980 and ratified it in 1985, with a number of declarations and reservations. The general declaration states that Tunisia 'declares that it shall not take any organisational or legislative decision in conformity with the requirements of this Convention where such a decision would conflict with the provisions of chapter I of the Tunisian Constitution' relating to general provisions as well as to fundamental rights and duties. Tunisia submitted the following reservations: the reservation to Article 9(2) states that the provision must not conflict with the provisions of chapter VI of the Tunisian Nationality Code; Tunisia also does not consider itself bound by Article 16(c), (d), (f), (g) and (h) and that paragraphs (g) and (h) of that Article 'must not conflict with the provisions of the Personal Status Code concerning the granting of family names to children and the acquisition of property through inheritance'. Tunisia also submitted a declaration concerning Article 15(4), stating that requirements relating to women's right to choice of residence and domicile 'must not be interpreted in a manner which conflicts with the (relevant) provisions of the Personal Status Code ... as set forth in chapters 23 and 61 of the Code'.

Tunisia signed the CRC in 1990 and ratified it in 1992, with a number of declarations and reservations. The first general declaration submitted by Tunisia states that it shall not adopt any legislation in conflict with the Tunisian Constitution in the implementation of the Convention. A further declaration states that implementation of the provisions of the CRC shall be limited by the means at Tunisia's disposal. The final declaration states that the Preamble to and provisions of the Convention (particularly Article 6) 'shall not be interpreted in such a way as to impede the application of Tunisian legislation concerning voluntary termination of pregnancy'. Tunisia also submitted the following reservations: Article 2 of the CRC 'may not impede the implementation of the provisions of its national legislation concerning personal status, particularly in relation to marriage and inheritance rights'; Article 40(2)(b)(v) on the review of judgments applying penal sanctions to minors is to be regarded as a general principle to which exceptions may be made by national legislation; and Article 7 of the CRC 'cannot be interpreted as prohibiting the implementation of the provisions of national legislation relating to nationality and, in particular, to cases in which it is forfeited'.

Background and sources
Brand, L. A. (1988) *Women, the State, and Political Liberalization: Middle Eastern and North African Experiences*, New York: Columbia University Press.

El Alami, D. S. and D. Hinchcliffe (1996) *Islamic Marriage and Divorce Laws of the Arab World*, London and Boston: Kluwer Law International.

Mahmood, T. (1972) 'Tunisia', in *Statutes of Personal Law in Islamic Countries: History, Texts and Analysis*, 2nd edn, New Delhi: India and Islam Research Council, pp. 42–5, 173–81.

Nasir, J. J. (1990) *The Islamic Law of Personal Status*, 2nd edn, London: Graham and Trotman.

Nelson, H. D. (ed.) (1988) *Tunisia: A Country Study*, 3rd edn, Washington, DC, Library of Congress, Federal Research Division.

Pearl, D. (1987) *A Textbook on Muslim Law*, 2nd edn, London: Croom Helm.

Tunisia, *Combined Initial and Second Reports to CEDAW*, 12 April 1994, New York: United Nations.

Website: *www.jurisitetunisie.com*

Part VI
Southern Africa

1 Social, Cultural and Historical Background

The Region and its History

Although most of the people who live in southern Africa do not follow Islam, the region is home to several long-established and influential Muslim communities. The country of Mozambique has the largest Muslim population. Over four million of Mozambique's nineteen million people follow Islam. The Muslims are concentrated in the northern and coastal regions. Islam came to Mozambique through traders and religious clergy from the Swahili coast. The pre-colonial port of Sofala, located near the modern port city of Beira, was an important Muslim trading centre until the Portuguese subjugated the Sofala Sultanate in 1525. Muslims in Mozambique today constitute a significant political and social minority. They often unify across party lines to support Muslim causes (Morier-Genoud 2000). Their numbers are growing. In 1997, Muslims in Mozambique represented approximately 18 per cent of the total population, increasing from only 13 per cent in 1975 (Morier-Genoud 2000).

The Muslim Yao of Malawi originated in Mozambique, then known as Portuguese East Africa. Prior to European exploration and eventual colonization, the Yao were heavily involved in the Arab coastal trade, especially the slave trade. Although the Yao historically were matriarchal, most of them converted to Islam as a result of this contact with the coastal Arab trade. During the eighteenth century, the Yao began to fracture into several sections. Although the causes of these fissures are debated, the results are generally not. The Yao began to move southwest into present-day Malawi, conquering or displacing the original inhabitants – predominantly Nyanja. They remained highly involved in the Arab coastal slave trade and predominantly Muslim. Today the Yao constitute the largest majority south and east of Lake Malawi in the Southern Region of Malawi. The current president of Malawi is a Yao Muslim, and his government has been strengthening ties with Islamic countries in the Middle East and North Africa. In addition, the president was publicly married to two wives during the majority of his first term in office.

Muslims in Malawi have lagged behind their Christian counterparts in terms of education and income. Colonial education practices seem to be the main cause. Although the British colonial government established exclusively 'Muslim' schools for the country's Muslim population, the Education Ordinance of 1927 also required mandatory Christian religious education in all schools. As a result, most Muslims kept their children out of schools, resulting in an education gap that still affects Muslims in Malawi today (Matiki 1999).

The first wave of Muslim immigration to South Africa began in the mid-1600s. The Dutch East India Company imported slaves into the Cape area, with the first registered Muslims arriving in 1658 (Tayob 1995). These slaves were brought from India, Ceylon (Sri Lanka), Mauritius, Malaya, Madagascar and Mozambique (Ersack 1997). In the Cape, this group of slaves and exiles formed the basis of the community that later came to be known as 'coloured' in the South African racial system. Then, over the next several decades, the Dutch East India Company imported thousands of Muslim slaves and political exiles from the Bengal coast and the Malay islands of Indonesia. This group of Muslims became known as 'Malays' (Tayob 1995). The Cape Muslims were organized around dynamic exiles who served as religious leaders, and were adherents to Sufism. When the Dutch rulers of the Cape restricted religious practice to the Dutch Reformed Church, Cape Muslims developed an underground religious community. With the declaration of religious freedom in 1804, the community began to thrive (Tayob 1995). Muslim schools were open to local Africans, spurring many Africans to convert in the early nineteenth century (Tayob 1995).

A second wave of Muslim immigration occurred after Britian colonized the Natal region in 1860. The British brought indentured workers from India on five-year contracts (Tayoub 1995). If they completed two of these five-year contracts, they were offered a piece of land in Natal. Between 7 and 10 per cent of these Indian indentured workers were Muslim, mainly from Gujarat and Bombay. A second influx of Indian Muslims arrived in the 1970s. These Indians were called 'passenger' Indians, because they paid their own fares to South Africa, with the intention of becoming traders. Almost 80 per cent of these Indians were Muslims (Tayob 1995).

The Cape and Indian Muslims have retained distinct ethnic identities that make it difficult for them to form a unified Islamic community. The two groups adhere to different schools of Islam: the Cape Muslims are primarily Sunni Shafi Muslims, while Indian Muslims are split between Hanafi and Deobandi Muslims. The preceeding Cape Muslims have often viewed the Indian Muslims as potential threats to their social and economic status, a view revealed in the term for an Indian trader in Malay – *babi*, which means 'pig' (Tayob 1995).

Islam in South Africa has undergone periods of revival thoughout its history. The most important of these movements is intricately tied to the anti-apartheid movement in South Africa. The leaders of the Muslim communities in South Africa denounced apartheid as being against Islamic principles, and promoted Islam as a potential solution to a divided South Africa (Tayob 1995). Muslims were encouraged to increase their own adherence to Islamic principles and to serve as role models for the rest of South Africa. In 1976, the Islamic Council of South Africa was formed as an umbrella group for Muslims in South Africa. However, conservative Muslim groups such as the Deobandi Jamiatul Ulama Transvaal and the Mujlisul-Ulama have refused to join the council (Tayob 1995). Today, Muslims in South Africa represent approximately one per cent of the total population of 43 million. About half are Malay or Cape Muslims, while the other half are Indian Muslims, with a small number of African or other Muslims (Vahed 2000).

Zimbabwe and Zambia each host Muslim populations of between 150,000 and 200,000. Most of these people are descendants of Indian Muslims who are concentrated in the cities and large trading centres of the countries. However, research shows that Islam has been in the area since the ninth century, when Arab traders migrated into the area, although this trading did not lead to as many conversions at it did along the Mozambican coast and in Malawi (Tichagwa 1998).

Legal Practices and Institutions

South Africa's apartheid system reinforced the division between its Muslim communities. Like other South Africans, Muslims were classified under the law according to race.

Indian Muslims were generally classified as 'Asian' and Cape Muslims as 'Coloured'. No distinctions were made between Hindu or Muslim Indians under this system (Vahed 2000). Muslim converts from indigenous African populations were assigned to the most oppressive restrictions. During the period from African National Congress leader Nelson Mandela's release from Robben Island through the elections of 1994, the Muslim community debated among itself and the larger South African political arena about the status of Muslim law in a post-apartheid South Africa. Although Mandela tentatively promised to cooperate with Muslims to establish some regulation and application of Islamic law in a democratic South Africa, this promise was not fulfilled (Ersack 1997). Muslim personal law is allowable and legally recognized, but it may not infringe upon rights outlined in the Constitution and the Bill of Rights (Flood et al. 1997). The final draft of the South African Constitution, adopted in 1996, firmly entrenched one system of law, with one of the most progressive and expansive protections of equality and civil liberties found anywhere in the world (Ersack 1997). Under the Constitution, South Africans, regardless of religion, are subject to the same civil and criminal codes.

Botswana, Zimbabwe, Lesotho and Zambia all recognize systems of customary and civil law. In family law, customary law is assumed to be the applicable system, unless the parties explicitly request civil law or unless customary law has no mechanism or tradition to deal with the matter (Molokomme 1990). In Botswana, both civil and customary courts have the option to apply either system in cases before the court, leaving the application decision up to respective judges (Molokomme 1990). Similarly, Malawi recognizes both customary African and civil law, in addition to separate family law systems for Asians and expatriates (Mvula and Kakhongwa 1997).

In contrast, Mozambique, with the largest Muslim population in Southern Africa, recognizes only one legal system. During the period of Portuguese colonization, separate systems of civil and customary law were applied; however, upon independence, Mozambique designed and implemented a unified civil code (Casimiro et al. 1990). However, there is little enforcement of the civil code in family matters.

Seclusion of Women / Purdah

The role of Muslim women within the religious community has been a point of debate in South Africa. Among the Muslims in Natal, the more progressive Muslim Youth Movement, which is dominated by Hanafi Muslims, supports the participation of women in services at the mosques and even the participation of women as leaders of services (Tayob 1995). However, the more conservative Deobandi Muslims reject women's participation in public religious events, instead urging women to pray and worship individually in their own houses. In general, South Africans of all religions are visible in the public sphere. In South Africa, 25 per cent of parliament members are women, making it one of the top seven countries in the world for female representation in political office (Flood et. al. 1997).

Veiling is becoming more common in South Africa, especially among upper-class Muslims (Vahed 2000). The conservative Jamiat, composed primarily of Deobandi Muslims, has ruled that women should veil, although the Sunni Ulema Council, which serves more working-class Muslims, has in fact ruled the opposite (Vahed 2000). The Jamiat has also obtained permission from the Department of Home Affairs in South Africa for women to cover their heads when taking pictures for passports or identification cards (Vahed 2000).

Family in the Region

The majority of family structures in South Africa, Mozambique and Zimbabwe are patrilineal, with authority and decision-making resting with the men in the families. However, Southern Africa also includes what is known as the 'matrilineal belt' in Africa, comprising large populations of matrilineal groups in Malawi and Zambia, and a few groups in Mozambique and Zimbabwe (Davison 1997). In Zimbabwe, approximately 5 per cent of the population is matrilineal (Tichagwa 1998). In Malawi particularly, the Yao have combined matrilineality with Islam, creating a unique family and social structure.

Marriage

Under the apartheid system in South Africa, Muslim and other non-Christian marriages were not recognized unless they were officially registered, as either civil or customary marriages. As a result, wives married in traditional Muslim ceremonies but not registered officially had no civil recourse for maintenance during marriage or in cases of divorce (Ersack 1997).

In 2000, South Africa unveiled a new Customary Marriages Act, which recognizes customary as well as civil unions, including polygynous marriages. The law recognizes unregistered marriages contracted in the past, but it requires all future marriages to be registered, a point that some say is likely to undermine its effectiveness. South African Law Commission representative Thandabantu Nhlapo has pointed that despite a similar law, nearby Swaziland has failed to persuade most couples to register their marriages with the state. The new law also raises the marriage age for men and women to 18; younger people may enter marriage only with permission from the home affairs minister (Ngqiyaza 2000). The law also repeals a section of the apartheid code that considered African women as legal minors. Under the new South African Constitution, women are granted full legal rights as both single and married women (Flood et al. 1997).

Early Muslim marriages in South Africa were often influenced by Christian marriage practices, as a result of the prohibition on any other religion than Christianity. For example, many Muslim brides during the nineteenth century wore wedding veils, similar to their Christian counterparts (Dangor 1997).

Among Indian Muslims, the Hindu and Muslim marriage traditions are also blurred. As one local *moulana* in South Africa argues, 'Here in South Africa, you cannot distinguish between a Hindu and a Muslim wedding. The customs are the same in our marriages and feasts' (Vahed 2000).

In Botswana, Lesotho, Zimbabwe and Zambia, couples choose between civil or customary marriages. In the majority of cases, traditional Muslim marriages are contracted under customary systems (Molokomme 1990). In Zambia, under customary law, women are considered minors, even in cases of marriage choice. A woman married under customary law must obtain the consent of her relatives, regardless of her age (Himonga et al. 1990). In Zimbabwe, the Customary Marriage Act stipulates that only Africans are allowed to marry under customary marriage systems. As a result, Indian Muslims are forced to marry under Zimbabwe's civil marriage codes for marriages to be legally recognized. Further, this stipulation effectively eliminates the option of poly-gynous marriages, or at least recognized polygynous marriages, among Indian Muslims in Zimbabwe (Tichagwa 1998). In Mozambique, which has a unified family code, minimum marriage ages are set at 14 for girls and 16 for boys. These age limits apply to all Mozambicans, regardless of religion or ethnicity (Casimiro et al. 1990). In Zimbabwe, the minimum marriage age for civil marriages is 16 for girls and 18 for boys (Steward et al. 1990). There is no minimum age for customary marriages, although the pledging of girls below age twelve is forbidden (Steward et al. 1990).

The combination of Islam and matrilineality in Malawi has created interest-ing marriage patterns. Among the Yao, couples reside with the wife's family; at the same time, polygyny is also widely practised. As a result, men often have wives (both officially and unofficially) living in different villages and rotate their time between the various houses (Davison 1997).

Malawi recognizes four types of marriage systems: civil marriage, customary marriage, Asiatic marriage and foreign customary marriage (Mvula and Kakhongwa 1997). African Muslims generally marry under customary law; these marriages are assumed to be potentially polygynous and are under the administration of local customary authorities. Asiatic marriage codes apply to non-Christian Asians (primarily Indians) who wish to marry under customary traditions; Muslim Indians in Malawi generally marry under Asiatic marriage codes (Mvula and Kakhongwa 1997). In addition, most African groups in Malawi recognize some form of 'temporary marriage', which may in fact last for only days or for entire lifetimes, but are not administered under official marriage codes. The legal minimum age for marriage for girls under any mar-riage code in Malawi is 15 (Mvula and Kakhongwa 1997).

Dowry and Brideprice

Under the South African Bill of Rights, both the Islamic tradition of *mahr* and the local African practice of *lobola* were prohibited. However, enforcement of this law is rare, and both practices continue virtually undisturbed (Flood et al. 1997).

Among matrilineal groups in Southern Africa, traditions of dowry and brideprice are not as common as they are among patrilineal groups (Mvula and Kakhongwa 1997). Rather, the exchange of gifts in matrilineal marriages is more of a symbolic or token gesture, as opposed to the more formal and required practice of *lobola* that is common among patrilineal groups in Southern Africa.

Divorce

Women have the same legal rights to divorce as men in South Africa. South Africa's Customary Marriages Act allows women to petition the court for maintenance and alimony. Courts have wide discretion in the division of family assets after divorce. Most black and Muslim South Africans, however, are accustomed to handling divorce and other family matters outside of court (Ngqiyaza 2000).

Women married under customary law in Botswana are limited to grounds for divorce. Men can petition for divorce on the grounds of infidelity, barrenness, repeated adultery, sorcery or refusal to perform household duties. In contrast, women married under customary law cannot petition for divorce based on either infidelity or cruelty (Molokomme 1990).

In Zimbabwe, a 1981 law called the Customary Law and Primary Courts Act gave local community courts power to enforce maintenance claims for women in unregistered marriages and in divorce cases. This act applies to all women married under customary traditions, including women in polygynous unions, regardless of whether or not the marriages were officially registered (Tichagwa 1998).

Polygyny

South Africa first recognized polgynous marriages in its Customary Marriages Acts of 2000. The authors of the act said that a ban on polygyny would be impossible to enforce and that the practice was waning (Ngqiyaza 2000). Polygyny is legal in Botswana only in cases where couples choose to be married under customary law, which includes Muslim law. Marriages contracted under civil marriage codes in Botswana, Zimbabwe and Zambia are by law monogamous, while all marriages under customary law are presumed to be potentially polygynous (Molokomme 1990; Himonga et al. 1990). However, in Zimbabwe, only Africans can contract customary marriages, leaving Indian Muslims (the majority of the Muslim population in Zimbabwe) in an ambiguous position regarding polygyny (Steward et al. 1990). Lesotho also presumes customary marriages to be potentially polygynous, with no restrictions on the number of wives a man may have (Seeiso et al. 1990). In Malawi, polygyny remains common. As of 1997, over 20 per cent of all men over the age of 40 had more than one wife (Mvula and Kakhongwa 1997). Polygyny is legal in Malawi for couples married under customary or Asiatic marriage codes.

Custody of Children

In Botswana, children born of customary unions, which include Islamic marriages, are generally given to the care of the fathers in cases of divorce. The major exception occurs when the father's family failed to pay the dowry or brideprice, in which case mothers are generally awarded custody (Molokomme 1990). In contrast, in Lesotho, women are the preferred guardians of children born of both civil and customary marriages, except in specific cases of poverty or mental illness of the mother (Seeiso et al. 1990). Among both Islamic and non-Islamic matrilineal groups in Malawi, Zambia and Mozambique, children are included in the mothers' lineages. Fathers have little authority or decision-making powers concerning their children; instead the eldest maternal uncle is generally the primary authority in a child's life (Mvula and Kakhongwa 1997). South Africa's courts have authority to grant custody to either the mother or the father 'in the best interests of the child'.

Inheritance / Land Rights

Mozambique's Civil Code provides that a woman receives half of the matrimonial property on the death of her husband, regardless of other potential civil or customary heirs (Casimiro 1990). Even if a man completely excludes his wife from a written will, the wife is still entitled to half of his property. But women must petition the court for the provision to be enforced.

In Zimbabwe, women married under either civil or customary law are protected by the 1997 Administration of Estates Amendment Act 6 (Tichagwa 1998). Under this act, a widow or widower is legally entitled to ownership and occupation of the matrimonial residence and a share in the assets, which varies depending on whether the marriage was monogamous or polygynous. Unfortunately, despite this legal protection, many women either do not know or do not have the resources to claim their legal entitlement (Tichagwa 1998).

Bibliography

Casimiro, I., I. Chicalia and A. Pessoa (1990) 'The legal situation of women in Mozambique', in J. Stewart and A. Armstrong (eds), *The Legal Situation of Women in Southern Africa*, Harare: University of Zimbabwe Publications, pp. 75–96.

Dangor, S. (1997) 'The expression of Islam in South Africa', *Journal of Muslim Minority Affairs*, 17: 141–52.

Davison, J. (1997) *Gender, Lineage, and Ethnicity in Southern Africa*, Boulder, CO: Westview Press.

Ersack, F. (1997) *Qur'an, Liberation and Pluralism: An Islamic Perspective of Interreligious Solidarity Against Oppression*, Oxford: Oneworld Publications.

Flood, T., M. Hoosain and N. Primo (1997) *Beyond Inequalities: Women in South Africa*, Harare: Southern African Research and Documentation Centre.

Himonga, C. N., K. A. Turner and C. S. Beyani (1990) 'An outline of the legal status of women in Zambia', in J. Stewart and A. Armstrong (eds), *The Legal Situation of Women in Southern Africa*, Harare: University of Zimbabwe Publications, pp. 139–64.

Matiki, A. J. (1999) 'The social and educational marginalization of Muslim youth in Malawi', *Journal of Muslim Minority Affairs*, 19: 249–60.

Mitchell, J. C. (1956) *The Yao Village: A Study in the Social Structure of a Malawian People*, Manchester: University of Manchester Press.

Molokomme, A. (1990) 'Women's law in Botswana: laws and research needs', in J. Stewart and A. Armstrong (eds), *The Legal Situation of Women in Southern Africa*, Harare: University of Zimbabwe Publications, pp. 7–46.

Morier-Genoud, E. (2000) 'The 1996 "Muslim holidays" affair: religious competition and state mediation in contemporary Mozambique', *Journal of Southern African Studies*, 26: 409–28.

Mvula, P. M. and P. Kakhongwa (1997) *Beyond Inequalities: Women in Malawi*, Harare: Southern African Research and Documentation Centre.

Ngqiyaza, B. (2000) 'South Africa gets divorce from apartheid marriage law', *Business Day* (South Africa), 16 November, p. 2.

Nkrumah, G. G. (1991) 'Islam in Southern Africa' *Review of African Political Economy*, 19, 52: 94–7.

Seeiso, S. M., L. M. Kanono, M. N. Tsotsi and T. E. Monaphathi (1990) 'The legal situation of women in Lesotho', in J. Stewart and A. Armstrong (eds), *The Legal Situation of Women in Southern Africa*, Harare: University of Zimbabwe Publications, pp. 47–74.

Steward, J., W. Ncube, M. Maboreke and A. Armstrong (1990) 'The legal situation of women in Zimbabwe', in J. Stewart and A. Armstrong (eds), *The Legal Situation of Women in Southern Africa*, Harare: University of Zimbabwe Publications, pp. 165–222.

Tayob, A. (1995) *Islamic Resurgence in South Africa: The Muslim Youth Movement*, Cape Town: University of Cape Town Press.

Tichagwa, W. (1998) *Beyond Inequalities: Women in Zimbabwe*, Harare: Southern African Research and Documentation Centre.

Vahed, G. (2000) 'Changing Islamic traditions and emerging identities in South Africa', *Journal of Muslim Minority Affairs*, 20: 43–74.

Part VII
South Asia

1 Social, Cultural and Historical Background

The Region and its History

Islam is the newest of South Asia's major religions and a highly visible presence in all the countries of the region. It is the faith of nearly all the people of Pakistan and Bangladesh, as well as the national religion of the tiny island of Maldives. Muslims also make up important minorities in India, Nepal and Sri Lanka.

South Asia has a complicated history of interaction between Hindus and Muslims, as well as a long history of British rule. As Schimmel states, 'the historian who tries to give a survey of the history and situation of Islam in Indo-Pakistan is faced with constant contradictions ... Popular religion, often tinged by or almost blended with customs from Hindu neighbours, stands side by side with lofty reformist movements of theologians who fought for the purity of Islamic monotheism' (Schimmel 1980: 1–2).

The history of Islam in the subcontinent dates from the time of the demise of the Abbasid empire in the middle of the tenth century. Although there was an earlier period of Muslim rule in the region, as a result of Arab invasions in 711–13, in Sind, the 'definitive Muslim conquest came from the post-Abbasid military regimes in Afghanistan' (Lapidus 1988: 438). When the Turkish ruler Mahmud of Ghazni, 'champion of Sunni Islam' (Schimmel 1980: 6), defeated the Hindu Rajputs in 1192 CE, he inaugurated a 500-year period of Muslim power in Central Asia. With Mahmud of Ghazni began the Islamization of larger parts of northwestern India (Schimmel 1980: 7). Within only eight years, Muslim conquerors had founded the Delhi Sultanate, annexed Bihar in the east and captured Gwalior to the south. Within 30 years, Bengal had been added to the Turkish Empire.

The Ghaznavids ruled till the late twelfth century, when they were replaced by the Ghurid dynasty, which embarked upon a systematic conquest of India. In 1206, Qutb al-Din Aybeg, a Ghurid general who had conquered Delhi, inaugurated a succession of dynasties that are collectively termed Delhi

Sultanates (1206–1526). As Lapidus states, the Sultanates 'represent a single period in Muslim-Indian history because of the continuity of the ruling elite, composed of Afghan or Turkish Inner Asian military lords and their clients' (Lapidus 1988: 138).

When the Mongols crushed the Arab caliphate in the middle of the thirteenth century, the Delhi Sultans were left on their own to exercise Islamic authority. Muslim scholars, scribes, Sufis and intellectuals flocked to India in search of patronage. The Delhi Sultanates developed their own cultural and political identity, built upon Persian and Indic languages, literature and arts, brought together in a new Indian-Islamic civilization.

During the historical era of the Sultanates, the short 37-year Sayyid period in the fifteenth century, commencing in 1414 with the rule of Sayyid Khizr Khan, formed a 'kind of watershed in Indo-Muslim history' (Schimmel 1980: 36). In addition to the till-now predominant Sunni form, various branches of Shi'ism were also practised. Also noteworthy of the spread of Islam in this period of the Sultanates is the vital role played by Sufism in shaping a Muslim community in India. Khwaja Hsan Moinuddin Chishti was the first missionary to reach the subcontinent, where he established the Chishtiyya Sufi tradition. The Suhrawadiya and Shattariya were other influential Sufi orders. Apart from the Qur'an and *hadith*, 'the most important religious influence on Indian Islam was the teaching of Ibn al-Arabi and the doctrine of *wahdat al-wujud*, the unity of being' (Lapidus 1988: 449), which was spread by both the Chistis and Shattaris.

During the golden age of Muslim rule, the aristocracy or the *ashraf* was composed mainly of families who traced their descent from the migrants from Afghanistan, Persia and inner Asia. Meanwhile, the caste system, Brahamic Hinduism and Buddhism defined the Indian society over which they ruled; no more than a quarter of the populace of the subcontinent converted to Islam. Most of the converts clustered in the Indus valley, Bengal and the northwest part of the subcontinent. They usually were drawn from the lower castes, attracted to Islam's egalitarian message. Still, these non-*ashraf* Muslim communities, or *atrap*, remained organized in caste-like social groups similar to those of their Hindu neighbours. The Sufis played an important role in these conversions, and the Islam followed by the masses tended to be far more devotional and pietistic than the legalistic interpretation the *ashraf* followed.

The largest Muslim conversions occurred in the area of Bengal, now divided between India, Pakistan and Bangladesh. Bengal still contains the largest concentration of Muslims in South Asia (Ahmed 1988). Sufi missionaries and saints brought Islam to Bengal in the thirteenth and fourteenth centuries. In Bengal, Islam and Hinduism have often merged in practice (Prindle 1988). Roy contributes this blending to a distinction between social and religious conversion; he claims that the experience of Muslims in Bengal 'scarcely involved an immediate spiritual experience and transformation and meant more a change of fellowship' (Roy 1996: 18).

The state of Gujarat was the home of several Isma'ili communities, where the first conversions were carried out by missionaries, *da'is*, from the Fatimid court of Egypt. A faction of the Fatimid followers are known in India as Bohoras. The Bohoras 'accepted the presence of the *da'I mutlaq* in Yemen' (Schimmel 1980: 71). They profess a strong faith in the *da'I*, who is called *Mulla ji Sahib* or *Sayyidina*, and they generally follow Fatimid tenets. A large-scale conversion to the Bohora faith took place in the city of Cambay, but in the mid-fifteenth century, following a divide in the community, an independent community of Sunni Bohoras was formed. There are several other groups of Bohoras, such as the Da'udi Bohoras, Sulaimani Bohoras and Mahdi-baghwala Bohoras (Schimmel 1980: 72–4).

Developments in the Nizari line of the Isma'ilis also had a significant impact on Indian Islam. In the twelfth century Hasan 'ala dhikrihi's-salam announced the *qiyamat*, which means a spiritualization of the Shari'a. Pir Sadr, a Nizari missionary who lived in the early part of the fifteenth century, carried out the conversion of the Sindhi Lohanas to Islam. The new converts were given the title of *khwaja*, hence the sect is known as *khoja*. There are several branches of Khojas, all of which are significantly Hinduized in their customs. The Nizari Khojas do not follow the Fatimid code of law; instead they have a customary law that includes many Hindu elements (Schimmel 1980: 72–4).

The Mughal Empire was a continuation of the Delhi Sultanate expanded by Babur and Akbar, his grandson (1556 to 1605), who continued and further expanded it. Akbar added Kabul, Kashmir, Sind and Baluchistan to his dominions. At the end of the seventeenth century, the Mughals took possession of Bijapur, Golconda and other formerly independent provinces in the south. During the Mughal era, Islam in India manifested itself in a range of diverse, and even conflicting, practices, mirroring the diversity of Muslim social and religious groups in the region. These groups were divided by 'allegiance of schools of law, Sufi orders and the teaching of individual shakykhs, scholars and saints. Some were Sunnis and some Shi'a ... Sunnis were themselves divided between those commited to scriptural Islam ... and those devoted to popular Sufism' (Lapidus 1988: 458).

In the eighteenth century, the Mughal Empire fell into a long period of decline. India dissolved into many smaller states. The British, who had been trading in India since 1600 CE, took the opportunity to extend their influence. In a long series of wars with their French rivals, the East India Company established themselves as the effective rulers of Bengal. The India Act of 1784 required that company officials be responsible to parliament. In Bengal, the British created a new system of taxation and judicial administration. British power was soon extended to other parts of India, and by 1818, most of the subcontinent's rulers acknowledged Britain as the paramount power.

Initially, some Muslims viewed the British as a potential ally against the Hindus. However, this potential diminished as British colonialism expanded and Muslim separatism grew (Roy 1996). Muslim scholars and clergy began to blame British colonialism for the perceived straying from Shari'a. This perception lead to revivalist movements in the late nineteenth and twentieth centuries in South Asia, particularly in Bengal (Ewing 1988). This revivalist movement often equated 'Bengali' identity with 'Hindu'; Muslim Bengalis were known simply as 'Musalman' (Roy 1996). In Punjab, today part of Pakistan, this blending also involved patterns and traditions of tribalism (Gilmartin 1988).

When India gained its independence in 1947, the Muslim minority demanded a state of its own. The state of Pakistan came into being on 14 August, one day before India became an independent state. Pakistan itself split into two after a civil war, with east Pakistan becoming the independent state of Bangladesh in 1971. In the years since independence, Pakistan has struggled over the role of Islam in public life. Bangladesh, on the other hand, has sought to ground itself in a national rather than an Islamic identity. Meanwhile, the hundred million Muslims who still live in India tend to see themselves as an embattled minority, fearing intercommunal violence and the interference of a non-Muslim state.

Legal Practices and Institutions

The vast majority of Muslims in South Asia are Sunni, holding to the Hanafi school of law, although followers of the Shaf'i, Maliki and Hanbali groups may also be found, as well as small pockets of Shi'a believers. Yet another small group of Muslims in the region are the Ismailis, who regard their leader, the Aga Khan, as their spiritual leader (Roy 1996).

Prior to 1937, the enforcement of Islamic personal law in India varied by region and community. Pressure from conservative Muslim groups led the British Raj to implement a compulsory Islamic system with the 1937 passage of Muslim Personal Law Shari'at Application Act. Under this Act, the state accepted Islamic law for Muslims in all personal and family matters (Hassan 1999).

In British-ruled Punjab, personal status laws had been linked to customary tribal law, often excluding and ignoring Islamic personal law. The push to establish Islamic personal law helped foster both Islamic revivalism and Punjabi nationalism, which eventually led to the creation of the Muslim state of Pakistan (Gilmartin 1988). Muslim identity in the twentieth century in Punjab was closely tied to anti-colonial opposition and nationalism, as well as in opposition to Hindu identity.

With the creation of an independent Pakistan in 1948, Shari'a was adopted as the official state legal system of personal and family law (Gilmartin 1988). In 1949, the first prime minister of Pakistan declared, 'Pakistan was founded because the Muslims of the sub-continent wanted to build up their lives in accordance with the teachings and traditions of Islam' (Roy 1996: 161). However, in 1964, President 'Ayub Khan banned the Islamist party Jama'at-i Islami and declared them a 'danger to the public peace' (Roy 1996: 151). In 1961, Pakistan passed the Muslim Family Laws Ordinance, outlining codes for marriage, divorce and family law (Roy 1996). The ordinance was based on the recommendation of a commission that polygyny be discouraged, divorce restrictions be tightened, and women's right to divorce be acknowledged. Further, the ordinance stipulated that all marriages and divorces should be registered, adequate maintenance be enforced and the marriage age raised to 16 for girls (Roy 1996). In 1963, the Fundamental Rights Bill, the first amendment to the Constitution, specified that the Muslim Family Laws Ordinance was not open to judicial review (Roy 1996).

Since the 1960s, Pakistanis have continued to wrangle over what sort of government and institutions will allow its people to cultivate a Muslim style of life. The country has had several constitutions and a number of civilian and military regimes. Islamist groups such as the Jama'at-i-Islami have gained increasing influence. In 1979, President Zia ul-Haq passed the so-called 'Hudood Ordinances' as part of a larger programme to make Pakistan's legal code and system of government more Islamic. The ordinances made *zina*, or sex outside marriage, a crime. Under the ordinances, women who bring charges of rape often find themselves charged with adultery. The ordinances also decreed that two women's testimony was equal to that of one man and that in compensation cases, the value of a woman's life was to be half that of a man's. In 1991, President Nawaz Sharif passed a law giving religious courts the right to overrule existing laws.

Although Bangladesh has the second largest Muslim population in the world, it has not seen as much public controversy as Pakistan over the role of Islam in public life. Bangladesh's Constitution is avowedly secular and its civil code is based on laws inherited from the British. The government of Bangladesh has implemented specific legal protections for women, including the 1980 Anti-dowry Prohibition Act and the 1983 Cruelty to Women Law (US Government 1996). Bangladesh has also passed laws protecting women from arbitrary divorce and from husbands taking additional wives without the consent of the first wife. But these protections apply only to registered marriages and, in rural areas where most Bangladeshis live, few marriages are registered.

The traditional arbitration courts, which are the main judicial bodies in Bangladeshi villages, usually base their decisions on local custom rather than statutory law. Women are almost always represented before such courts by their male kin (Chowdury 1993). Some local communities have started turning to Islamist mullahs to rule on their disputes according to Shari'a. In such areas, the populace has more respect for the mullahs than for the state police or judiciary.

Indian law draws on a number of sources. The new Constitution of the independent India gave equal rights to women under Indian civic law. At the same time, Muslims and Hindus were guaranteed the right to adhere to personal law in marriage, divorce and other family matters. Since independence, the Indian state has aimed at abolishing the various Hindu personal laws in favour of a uniform civil code. For example, the Special Marriage Act of 1954 provided the right for a couple to marry, irrespective of community, in a civil ceremony. Subsequent efforts to institute a uniform legal code have faltered.

Muslim women in rural India seldom bring cases to court. In Uttar Pradesh, for instance, it would be perceived as a shame to the community if women were obliged to come and settle their disputes in a public space. If a woman has a complaint, the chief of the village or one of his colleagues on the village council will endeavour to persuade her to obtain some sort of settlement outside the village council (Bhatty 1980; Sinha 1991).

The kingdom of Nepal is an explicitly Hindu state, although about 5 per cent of its citizens are Muslim. Hinduism is the state religion, and all Nepalese are subject to Hindu law founded on *dharma-shastra* (Gaborieau 1995). The Nepalese state does not restrict the practice of other religions, however, and Muslims are free to follow any religious practice that does not directly violate Hindu law, such as eating beef. Nepalese law does make some exceptions to Hindu law for Muslims, particularly in the area of marriage. For example, Muslims are allowed to marry their cousins, although Hindus do not generally accept such marriages.

Seclusion of Women / Purdah

In South Asia, the practice of secluding and veiling women is known as purdah. Hindus as well as Muslims have traditions of purdah. Particularly in India, seclusion is intricately linked to the caste system, and is routinely practised regardless of religion (Papanek 1982). For middle- and upper-class families, seclusion usually includes separate women's quarters called the *zenana*, with separate entrances and extensive window coverings.

But purdah is conceived and implemented to serve different purposes among Muslims and Hindus. Muslim women are secluded from men whom they might potentially marry from the time of puberty, if not earlier. In contrast, Hindu women are secluded from the senior male and female relatives of their husband's family. Hindu purdah is thus only a post-marital practice (Sinha 1991).

Despite its prevalence, the practices of purdah differ widely among various classes, ethnic groups and historical periods. For example, during the process of partition in 1947, many Muslim women stopped veiling so they could not be recognized as Muslims, which caused harassment and violence in some areas (Papanek 1982). The traditions of Muslims and Hindus with regard to veiling have also blurred. In some Muslim communities, women have adopted the Hindu codes of veiling in front of in-laws, a practice not common among Muslims in other parts of the world (Vatuk 1982).

Upper-class women participate in political life more vigorously in South Asia than in many other parts of the world. In Sri Lanka, studies show women have voted in equal proportion to men since gaining the vote in 1931. Since Sri Lanka made history in 1960 by becoming the first state in the world to elect a female head of state, women have also been elected heads of state in India, Bangladesh and Pakistan. India has attempted to increase women's participation in public politics. The 1988 Draft National Perspective Plan for Women proposed reserving 30 per cent of all seats in local government for women and temporary quotas at the state level (Bardhan 1991). In Bangladesh, the government instituted a policy in 1982 called the New Industrial Policy (NIP). This policy established export enclaves, which greatly increased the participation of women in the public labour force, a policy that directly countered conservative Islamic seclusion codes (Feldman 1993).

Nevertheless, purdah is strictly enforced in the rural areas where the overwhelming majority of South Asian women live. In India, Pakistan and Bangladesh, purdah makes it difficult for rural women to engage in public, political or economic processes that involve unrelated men. The public nature of institutions such as courts mean few women may take advantage of them.

Family in the Region

Most South Asian families are patrilineal. Several groups from the Maldives are an exception. They trace their descent through the mother and divide property among the mother's children (Dube 1997). Women leave their parental homes when they marry to take up residence in the joint or extended family of their husband's kin. Typically younger people are expected to defer to their older relatives. Young brides, in particular, come under the authority of their husband's mother.

The division in South Asian Muslim society between the *ashraf*, who claim Arab and Persian origins, and the *atrap*, who descend from Indian converts, is accentuated by the differing roles women play in their families. The *ashraf* ideal is for women to confine themselves exclusively to the work of being a wife and mother. As Joseph Minattur argues, 'A girl, right from birth, is molded for marriage and motherhood' (Minattur 1980: 201). *Atrap* women, on the other hand, are expected to contribute to the income of the family and therefore cannot conform to the strict purdah of *ashraf* women. Further, although *atrap* women are expected to be virtuous, the requirements are not as strict as those for *ashraf* women, nor are infractions punished as severely (Minattur 1980).

South Asians often discriminate between sons and daughters at meal times, with male children receiving more food than females. Female infanticide is common, even among Muslims, despite the explicit Qur'anic injunction against it.

Marriage

Muslim, Hindu or Buddhist, most South Asian marriages are arranged. South Asian Muslims prefer cross-cousin marriage. Among Hindus, cross-cousin marriage is prohibited; instead Hindus prefer exogamous marriages (Papanek 1982). Muslim and Hindu marriage patterns also differ with regard to rules regarding proximity of marriage partners. Generally speaking, Muslims marry someone within their own village, while Hindus marry outside their natal villages. In Pakistan, one study found that nine out of ten marriages are arranged and six out of ten are arranged with close relatives, especially cousins (Women's International Network 1995: 66). But this pattern is not consistent along religious lines. For example, Indian Muslims in Bijnor oppose within-village marriages just as Hindus do (Jeffrey and Jeffrey 1993).

In urban areas, a woman's employment status and potential income have become negotiating factors in marriage contracts with the increased participation of women in the labour force. Women's incomes are considered when arranging marriage partners and dowries. Further, women's increased presence in public employment has led to a decrease in arranged marriages and an accompanying increase in marriages where spouses are self-selected (Feldman 1993).

Hindus and Muslims alike prize virginity at the time of a girl's first marriage. Historically South Asian girls were married as early as possible. India, Pakistan and Bangladesh all have laws specifying the age at which girls may be married, but families often ignore the laws. In 1929 the Child Marriage Restraint Act was passed in India, making it a criminal offence to marry a girl under the age of 15. This law was modified in 1978, and raised the marriage age to 18 years for girls and 21 years for boys. Under this act, parents of the under-age spouses and the marriage officials performing the ceremonies are also subject to criminal prosecution (Minattur 1980). In Pakistan and Bangladesh, families sometimes kill girls who violate the purdah code or try to escape arranged marriages. Such honour killings are seldom prosecuted (Cohn 1999).

The subcontinental custom of the bride's family paying dowry to the groom's family cuts across religious lines, despite Shari'a's stipulation that it is the groom who should pay *mahr* to the bride. A Dowry Prohibition Act was passed in India in 1961, declaring both the giving and receiving of dowry prohibited. However, this code is rarely followed, and infractions against it are almost never prosecuted (Minattur 1980). Women in India, Pakistan and Bangladesh often face violence and torture in the event of a disagreement over dowry payments. Florence McCarthy argues that the economic difficulties in Bangladesh have affected dowry patterns. Families of prospective grooms have started asking for exorbitant dowries and young wives are being killed more frequently in dowry disputes (McCarthy 1993).

Divorce

Divorced women are stigmatized and face a difficult time socially and economically in Pakistan. In India, Muslim women have the right to seek divorce under certain circumstances. If a girl is married before the age of 15, she has the right to repudiate her marriage before she turns 18, even if the marriage has been consummated. The Dissolution of Muslim Marriages Act of 1939 also gives Muslim women the right of divorce if a husband fails to provide maintenance for two years. Women can also petition the court for divorce in cases of desertion, insanity of the husband, leprosy and cruelty (Shankarjha and Pujari 1996).

In Bangladesh, women are able to seek divorce only when a husband marries for a second time without the permission of the first wife and the local Union council (Islam 2000).

Polygyny

Polygyny is illegal for all Indians who are not Muslim, and fieldwork conducted from the 1970s to the present shows that it is rare even among Muslims. According to official census reports, only 5 to 7 per cent of Indian Muslims are engaged in polygynous marriages. In the province of Kerala, fewer than one per cent are engaged in such unions. Surveys show that Muslim women generally are opposed to polygyny (Shankarijha and Pujari 1996). Among non-Muslims, polygyny is a criminal offence subject to fines and imprisonment.

Bangladesh's Muslim Family Law Ordinance, passed in 1962, requires a husband to consult his wife before taking another wife. However, husbands sometimes force wives to accept a second wife by threatening them with divorce. The country's 1991 census recorded 1.4 million polygynous marriages, but demographers believe there are probably many more such marriages (Islam 2000).

Custody of Children

In India, Muslim women are less likely than Hindu women to retain custody of their children. The 1956 Hindu Minority and Guardianship Act gives custody rights to mothers in the event of divorce or death of a spouse. This Act provides that mothers are the natural guardians of their children, even if the father announces a different guardian (Minattur 1980). In the same year, the Hindu Adoption and Maintenance Act also gave women the right to adopt a child, a right not previously allowed (Minattur 1980). However, Muslim women are not covered by these Acts, but fall under the terms of Muslim personal status law.

In Bangladesh, a widow or divorcée who remarries must give custody of her children to her previous husband's family (Dube 1997).

Inheritance/Land Rights

Several scholars have recorded instances of women renouncing their inheritance as prescribed by the Qur'an. This practice is particularly common among the middle and upper classes. Women renounce their shares as a way to maintain strong relationships with their brothers, and to secure their brothers' protection and support if they should be divorced or widowed (Papanek 1982).

Customary tribal inheritance patterns in Punjab excluded women from inheritance. As women traditionally married exogamously, they were universally denied inheritance rights to land and property. Although Islamic law among Punjabi Muslims would dictate otherwise, the customary inheritance patterns were codified under British rule (Gilmartin 1988). Under colonial rule, male heirs, no matter how distant the relation, were always assumed to be the rightful heirs ahead of women, unless positive proof could be provided otherwise. The 1956 Hindu Succession Act, which applies to Hindus, Buddhists and Sikhs, stipulates that heirs be decided without regard to or discrimination based on sex. The Act also provides that women retain full ownership of inherited property, regardless of later marital status (Minattur 1980). Muslim women's inheritance rights are not subject to this Act.

In Bangladesh, a woman's right to inherit half a brother's share of patrimonial property is more formal than real. In practice, Bengali Muslim inheritance patterns seem to resemble Hindu ones. Seclusion and a widespread preference for village exogamy do not allow women to retain control over their shares of the family land. Many women waive their right to ancestral property in favour of their brothers, in a kind of bargain in which they retain the right to visit the natal home, where they can relax, and from which they seek support and protection in times of crisis (Dube 1997).

Bibliography

Ahmed, R. (1988) 'Conflict and contradictions in Bengali Islam: problems of change and adjustment', in K. P. Ewing (ed.), *Shari'at and Ambiguity in South Asian Islam*, Berkeley: University of California Press, pp. 114–42.

Alavi, H. (1995) 'The two biraderies: kinship in rural West Punjab', in T. N. Madan (ed.), *Muslim Communities of South Asia: Culture, Society, and Power*, New Delhi: Manohar Publishers, pp. 1–62.

Associated Press (1995) 'Women feel sting of Shari'a Bangladeshi "courts" targeting feminists', *St Louis Press Dispatch*, 1 January.

Bardhan, K. (1991) 'Women and feminism in a stratified society: developments in South Asia', in S. J. M. Sutherland (ed.), *Bridging Worlds: Studies on Women in South Asia*, Berkeley, CA: Centers for South and Southeast Asian Studies, pp. 163–202.

Basu, A. (1999) 'Women's activism and the vicissitudes of Hindu nationalism', *Journal of Women's History*, 10: 110.

Begum, R. (1998) 'Incidence of polygyny among Muslims in India', in H. Hashia (ed.), *Muslim Women in India Since Independence (Feminine Perspectives)*, New Delhi: Institute of Objective Studies, pp. 129–39.

Bhatty, Z. (1980) 'Muslim women in Uttar Pradesh: social mobility and directions of change', in A. de Souza (ed.), *Women in Contemporary India and South Asia*, New Delhi: Manohar Publications.

Chowdhury, T. A. (1993) 'Segregation of women in Islamic societies of South Asia and its reflection in rural housing', MA thesis, McGill University, Montreal. http://ww2.mcgill. ca.mchg/mchg/tas/tasnl.htm

Cohn, M. R. (1999) 'They kill their own in the name of honor', *The Toronto Star,* 1 August.

Dube, L. (1997) *Women and Kinship: Comparative Perspectives on Gender in South and Southeast Asia*, Tokyo and New York: UN University Publications.

Ewing, K. P. (1988) 'Introduction: ambiguity and Shari'at – a perspective on the problem of moral principles in tension', in K. P. Ewing (ed.), *Shari'at and Ambiguity in South Asian Islam*, Berkeley: University of California Press, pp. 1–32.

Feldman, J. L. R. (1991) 'Mentioning the unmentionable: sexually frustrated wives in the stories of Rajender Singh Bedi', in S. J. M. Sutherland (ed.), *Bridging Worlds: Studies on Women in South Asia*, Berkeley, CA: Centers for South and Southeast Asian Studies, pp. 119–36.

Feldman, S. (1993) 'Contradictions of gender inequality: urban class formation in contemporary Bangladesh', in A. W. Clark (ed.), *Gender and Political Economy: Explorations of South Asian Systems*, Oxford: Oxford University Press, pp. 215–45.

Gaborieau, M. (1995) 'Muslims in the Hindu kingdom of Nepal', in T. N. Madan (ed.), *Muslim Communities of South Asia: Culture, Society, and Power*, New Delhi: Manohar Publishers, pp. 211–40.

Gilmartin, D. (1988) 'Customary law and Shari'at in British Punjab', in K. P. Ewing (ed.), *Shari'at and Ambiguity in South Asian Islam*, Berkeley: University of California Press, pp. 43–62.

Hassan Z. (1999) 'Muslim women and the debate on legal reforms', in B. Ray and A. Basu (eds), *From Independence Towards Freedom: Indian Women Since 1947*, New Delhi: Oxford University Press, pp. 120–34.

Hussain, R., F. F. Fikree and H. W. Berendes (2000) 'The role of son preference in reproductive behaviour in Pakistan', *Bulletin of the World Health Organization,* 78: 379.

Islam, T. (2000) 'Bangladesh: family laws need to include women', 21 May (IPS), <http:/ /www.oneworld.org/news/by_country/index.html.>

Jeffrey, R. and P. M. Jeffrey (1993) 'A woman belongs to her husband: female autonomy, women's work and childbearing in Bijnor', in A. W. Clark (ed.); *Gender and Political Economy: Explorations of South Asian Systems*, Oxford: Oxford University Press, pp. 66–114.

Kurin, R. (1988) 'The culture of ethnicity in Pakistan', in K. P. Ewing (ed.), *Shari'at and Ambiguity in South Asian Islam*, Berkeley: University of California Press, pp. 220–47.

Lapidus, I. M. (1988) *A History of Islamic Societies*, Cambridge: Cambridge University Press.

McCarthy, F. (1993) 'Development from within: forms of resistance to development processes among rural Bangladeshi women', in A. W. Clark. (ed.), *Gender and Political Economy: Explorations of South Asian Systems*, Oxford: Oxford University Press, pp. 322–53.

Minattur, J. (1980). 'Women and the law: constitutional rights and continuing inequalities', in A. de Souza (ed.), *Women in Contemporary India and South Asia*, New Delhi: Manohar Publications, pp. 165–78.

Mohanty, B. (1999) 'Panchayat Raj institutions and women', in B. Ray and A. Basu (eds), *From Independence Towards Freedom: Indian Women Since 1947*, New Delhi: Oxford University Press, pp. 19–33.

Mustikhan, A. (1997) 'Pakistan women: fight goes on for gender justice', *Interpress Service,* 17 August.

Nilsson, U. (1991) 'Women in contemporary Indian literature: revised scripts and changed roles', in S. J. M. Sutherland (ed.), *Bridging Worlds: Studies on Women in South Asia*, Berkeley, CA: Centers for South and Southeast Asian Studies, pp. 99–118.

Papanek, H. (1982) 'Purdah: separate worlds and symbolic shelter', in H. Papanek and G. Minault (eds), *Separate Worlds: Studies of Purdah in South Asia*, Delhi: Chanakya Publications, pp. 3–53.

Prindle, C. (1988) 'Occupation and orthopraxy in Bengali Muslim rank', in K. P. Ewing (ed.), *Shari'at and Ambiguity in South Asian Islam*, Berkeley: University of California Press, pp. 269–87.

Pugh, J. F. (1988) 'Divination and ideology in the Banaras Muslim community', in K. P. Ewing (ed.), *Shari'at and Ambiguity in South Asian Islam*, Berkeley: University of California Press, pp. 288–306.

Rafat, Z. (1998) 'Muslim women's marriage and divorce in a town of Uttar Pradesh', in H. Hashia (ed.), *Muslim Women in India Since Independence (Feminine Perspectives)*, New Delhi: Institute of Objective Studies, pp. 109–28.

Roy, A. (1996) *Islam in South Asia: A Regional Perspective*, New Delhi: South Asian Publishers.

Schimmel, A. (1980) *Islam in the Indian Subcontinent*, Leiden and Cologne: E.J. Brill.

Shankarjha, U. and P. Pujari (1996) *Indian Women Today: Tradition, Modernity and Challenge*, New Delhi: Kanishka Publishers.

Shastri, A. (1993) 'Women in development and politics: the changing situation in Sri Lanka', in A. W. Clark (ed.), *Gender and Political Economy: Explorations of South Asian Systems*, Oxford: Oxford University Press, pp. 246–72.

Sinha, A. (1991) 'Women's local space: home and neighborhood', in S. J. M. Sutherland (ed.), *Bridging Worlds: Studies on Women in South Asia*, Berkeley, CA: Centers for South and Southeast Asian Studies, pp. 203–24.

US Government (1996) *Country Reports on Human Rights Practices for 1995*, Washington, DC: US Government.

Vatuk, S. (1982) 'Purdah revisited: a comparison of Hindu and Muslim interpretations of the cultural meaning of purdah in South Asia', in H. Papanek and G. Minault (eds), *Separate Worlds: Studies of Purdah in South Asia*, Delhi: Chanakya Publications, pp. 54–78.

Women's International Network (1995) 'Arranged Marriages in Pakistan' (1995) *Women's International Network News*, 21, 3: 33.

2 Legal Profiles

BANGLADESH, People's Republic of

Legal history [see also: Legal history, Republic of India and Legal history, Islamic Republic of Pakistan]

Bangladesh seceded from Pakistan in December of 1971. Following independence, the British-era legislation that had continued to be applied in Pakistan, as well as the post-1947 legislation enacted by Pakistan, remained the basis of Bangladeshi personal status laws. Pearl and Menski (1998) state that legal developments in Bangladesh and Pakistan since 1972 have been quite distinct. The prospect of a Uniform Family Code has been a subject attracting much lobbying by women's groups in Bangladesh, but there is no equivalent to India's constitutional directive regarding a Uniform Civil Code.

Schools of *fiqh* The Hanafi school is the predominant *madhhab* in Bangladesh. There are also Hindu and Christian minorities.

Constitutional status of Islam(ic law) The Constitution was adopted on 4 November 1972. An amendment to the Constitution under President Ziaur Rahman in 1977 removed the principle of secularism that had been enshrined in Part II: Fundamental State Policy, replacing it with 'absolute trust and faith in Almighty Allah'. The Eighth Amendment of 1988 inserted Article 2A, affirming that '[t]he state religion of the Republic is Islam, but other religions may be practised in peace and harmony in the republic'. Some women's groups challenged this move on the grounds that it risked exposing women to discriminatory laws.

At the same time, state law in South Asia has always afforded recognition to, and left a sphere for, the application of the family laws of different religious communities. Constitutional protection of women's rights and the assertion of gender equality comes under the Fundamental Principles of State Policy and is enshrined in Article 10 on the participation of women in national life, as well as in Articles 26 to 29 of the section on fundamental rights affirming equality of all citizens before the law. This is balanced against the constitutional protection of minority rights provided for in Article 41 on freedom of religion and the freedom of every religious community or denomination to establish, manage and maintain its religious institutions (subject to law, public order and morality). This affects the significant Hindu minority in Bangladesh (roughly equivalent in proportion to India's Muslim minority), in addition to Christian and Buddhist minorities.

Court system The judiciary is organized at two levels, with subordinate courts and a Supreme Court with Appellate and High Court Divisions. The Family Courts Ordinance 1985 governs the application of the personal laws of all Bangladeshis through the state judiciary by the creation of Family Courts. The Family Courts have jurisdiction over personal status cases of all communities, although religious minorities are governed by their own personal laws. The Family Courts are convened in Assistant Judges' Courts and have special procedures and reduced formalities. The Family Courts may hear suits *in camera* at the request of both parties, and the court fees are nominal, but lawyers' and notaries' fees considerably increase the costs associated with going to court. Under the terms of the Ordinance, Family Courts have exclusive jurisdiction to try and dispose of suits relating to the dissolution of marriage, the restitution of conjugal rights, dower, maintenance, and guardianship and custody.

The jurisdiction of the Family Courts is restricted so that if any criminal offence arises in the context of a civil case, it comes under the jurisdiction of Criminal or Magistrates' Courts. This has created some inconsistencies within the legal system, with magistrates still hearing maintenance claims under section 488 of the Criminal Procedure Code, while Family Courts are supposed to retain exclusive jurisdiction to try and determine maintenance cases. The Bangladeshi legislation relating to Family Courts is quite similar to the legislation applicable in Pakistan. However, the Pakistani Family Courts have broader jurisdiction extending beyond civil suits.

Notable features [see also: Notable features, Republic of India and Notable features, Islamic Republic of Pakistan]

As elsewhere in South Asia, much of the Muslim personal law is unlegislated, the basis for the law being classical Hanafi *fiqh* except where this has been amended by legislation. The Muslim Personal Law (Shari'at) Application Act 1937 continues to govern the application of Muslim family law in Bangladesh. (The pre-independence legislation that replaced this Act in 1962 applied only to West Pakistan.) According to the Act, Bangladeshis are subject to local custom and usage in matters relating to wills, legacies or adoption, unless a person declares his or her express preference for being governed by Islamic law. Thus estates may validly devolve in proportions favouring women under customary law.

The Child Marriage Restraint Act 1929 was amended by ordinance in 1984 so that the minimum ages of marriage are 21 for men and 18 for women. The legislation provides penal sanctions for those who knowingly participate in the contracting of an under-age marriage, but does not invalidate such marriages.

The Muslim Marriages and Divorces (Registration) Act 1974 enacted to strengthen the inducements for civil registration states that 'every marriage solemnised under Muslim law shall be registered in accordance with the provisions of this Act' and establishes the licensing of *nikah* registrars. The punishment for not registering a marriage is a prison sentence and/or a fine. Failure to register does not invalidate the marriage. It should also be noted that, although there is no legislation to this effect, there is a customary trend in Bangladesh towards encouraging the insertion of stipulations relating to delegated divorce in the marriage contract.

The issues of maintenance and obedience within marriage continue to be governed by classical law for the most part. Much legal development has occurred through case law. In *Nelly Zaman* v. *Giasuddin Khan* (34 DLR [1982] 221), the Court ruled that, with the passage of time, the husband's suing for forcible restitution of conjugal rights against an unwilling wife is both out-moded and untenable if considered with relation to the principle of equality of men and women enshrined in Articles 27 and 31 of the Constitution.

In the husband's unilateral plea for forcible restitution of conjugal rights as against a wife unwilling to live with her husband, there is no mutuality and reciprocity between the respective rights of the husband and the wife, since such a plea for restitution of conjugal rights is not available to a wife as against her husband apart from claiming maintenance and alimony. A reference to Article 28(2) of the Constitution of Bangladesh guaranteeing equal rights of women and men in all spheres of the state and public life would clearly indicate that any unilateral plea of a husband for forcible restitution of conjugal rights as against a wife unwilling to live with her husband is 'violative of the accepted State and Public Principle and Policy' (34 DLR [1982] 221, at p. 222).

With respect to arrears of maintenance, in *Rustom Ali* v. *Jamila Khatun* (43 DLR [1991] 301), the Court ruled (in accordance with classical Hanafi law) that a wife is not entitled to arrears of maintenance. Maintenance will be allowed only from the date the suit is brought before the Family Court until three months from the decree of dissolution of marriage. The former wife or the child may not claim past maintenance unless the parties have a previously established agreement. In *Muhammad Hefzur Rahman* v. *Shamsun Nahar Begum* (15 BLD [1995] 34) relating to the maintenance of divorcées, the Court ruled that a Muslim husband's responsibility to maintain his divorced wife does not cease with the expiry of the *'idda*. The Court stated that the former husband is bound to provide his divorced wife with maintenance on a reasonable scale for an indefinite period, until her status as a divorcée changes, that is, if she remarries. The ruling was based on an interpretation of a Qur'anic verse relating to provisions for divorced wives (2: 241). The Supreme Court overturned the High Court's judgment on 3 December 1998, leaving the classical Hanafi interpretation intact for the moment.

The Bangladeshi Muslim Family Laws Ordinance, based on the Pakistani MFLO of 1961, has incorporated some amendments to the original legislation. There are administrative differences in terms of the governmental bodies that apply the provisions of the MFLO at the local level. Applications, appeals and conciliation procedures go to the Union Parishad, Pourashava or Municipal Corporation. This includes the application process for contracting polygynous marriages, the application process itself remaining the same (i.e., requiring the reasons for wanting to contract a polygynous marriage and certification attesting to the existing wife's or wives' consent). Legislation introduced in 1974 to encourage and facilitate the registration of marriages has also been used to amend the MFLO and use registration as a method of controlling polygyny. The MFLO also establishes penalties for contracting polygynous marriages in contravention of the law. Polygynous marriages contracted without the permission of the relevant authorities are not rendered invalid, nor is there a penalty for failing to obtain the existing wife's consent (as long as the council has permitted the polygynous marriage). In *Jesmin Sultana* v. *Mohammad Elias* (1997 [17] BLD 4), the Court ruled that Section 6 of the MFLO prohibiting the contracting of a polygynous marriage without the prior permission of the Arbitration Council is against the principles of Islamic law. The Court stated that Muslim jurists and scholars are nearly unanimous in the view that it is practically impossible to deal with co-wives justly, and so the Qur'anic injunction that a second wife may be taken under specific conditions is virtually a prohibition. The Court also noted that Tunisia has given legislative effect to this interpretation. Thus the Court recommended that section 6 of the MFLO should be repealed and replaced by a section prohibiting polygyny altogether. The Court also directed that a copy of the judgment be sent to the Ministry of Law for consideration. No action is known to have been taken on it.

The Dissolution of Muslim Marriages Act 1939 also remains in force in Bangladesh, with the amendments initiated in Pakistan by the Muslim Family Laws Ordinance 1961; that is, a polygynous marriage by the husband in contravention of the provisions of the MFLO is included as sufficient grounds for the first wife to obtain a decree of dissolution. A post-independence amendment to the provision relates to the exercise of the option of puberty, entitling a girl contracted into marriage by her father or other guardian before the age of 18 to repudiate the marriage (provided it has not been consummated) before attaining the age of 19. In addition, judicial *khul'* granted by the courts without the husband's consent allows for women to obtain divorce by waiving their financial rights. In *Hasina Ahmed* v. *Syed Abul Fazal* (32 DLR [1980] 294), the Court ruled that a woman may be granted a *khul'* by a judicial decision without the husband's consent.

Custody continues to be governed by the Guardians and Wards Act 1890 in Bangladesh. The Act stipulates that the courts are to be guided by the personal law to which the minor is subject. Courts are also directed to consider the age, gender and religion of the minor and the character and capacity of the proposed guardian, as well as considering the minor's own opinion if s/he is old enough to form an intelligent preference. For Muslims, the general rule is that the divorced mother is entitled to custody of male children until the age of seven (classical Hanafi position) and of female children until puberty. Under the legislation, if the minor is very young or is a female, the courts are directed to give preference to the mother. In all cases, the interests of the ward are paramount. This has been confirmed by a number of judgments, such as *Muhammad Abu Baker Siddique* v. *S.M.A. Bakar & others* (38 DLR [AD] 1986). The court's ruling contradicted the classical dictates of Hanafi law according to which the mother's custody over a boy ends at seven. The court stated that '[i]ndeed, the principle of Islamic Law (in the instant case, the rule of *hizanat* or guardianship of a minor child as stated in the Hanafi school) has to be regarded, but deviation therefrom would seem permissible as the paramount consideration should be the child's welfare'. The court also pointed out that the rationale for the departure from classical positions is justified as there is no clear and distinct statement of the Qur'an or *Sunna* to rely upon, and also because the jurists themselves never reached any consensus. The *Zohra Begum* v. *Latif Ahmed Munawar* (1965 [17] DLR [WP] and PLD 1965 [Lah] 695) case, and other rulings deviating from classical law, are also cited.

As there are detailed rules for the division of estates according to classical law, there is little legislation in this area. In general, property devolves upon the heirs according to Hanafi or Ja'fari rules of succession. The Muslim Family

Laws Ordinance 1961 also introduced obligatory bequests in favour of orphaned grandchildren, allowing them to inherit from their maternal or paternal grandparents in place of their deceased mothers or fathers.

The Repression against Women and Children Act of January 2000 recognizes offences of sexual assault and sexual harassment. It also authorizes a tribunal to decide to keep a woman in protective custody against her will for her safety.

Law/case reporting system *Bangladesh Legal Decisions, Dhaka Law Cases, Dhaka Law Reports.*

International conventions (with relevant reservations) Bangladesh acceded to the CEDAW in 1984 with a reservation relating to Article 2 regarding the elimination of discrimination against women and the Article 16(1)(c) regarding equality of rights in marriage and upon its dissolution; Bangladesh does not consider these provisions binding as they 'conflict with the Shari'a law based on (the) Holy Qur'an and *Sunna*'.

Bangladesh signed the CRC in 1990 and ratified the same year, with reservations to Articles 14(1) on children's freedom of religion and 21 relating to adoption. The reservation to the latter states that the provision will apply subject to the existing laws and practices in Bangladesh.

Bangladesh acceded to the ICESCR in 1998, with a number of declarations. The interpretative declaration relating to Articles 2 and 3 of the Covenant states that equality of rights between men and women is to be implemented in so far as they agree with the Constitution of Bangladesh and, more specifically, subject to Bangladeshi state inheritance law. Bangladesh acceded to the Convention on Consent to Marriage, Minimum Age for Marriage and Registration of Marriages in 1998, with reservations to Articles 1 and 2, stating that the treaty would be applied 'in accordance with the Personal Laws of different religious communities of the country', and allowing for a 'dispensation as to age, for serious reasons, in the interest of the intending spouses'.

Background and sources

Hossain, S. (1994) 'Equality in the home: women's rights and personal laws in South Asia', in R. J. Cook (ed.), *Human Rights of Women: National and International Perspectives*, Philadelphia: University of Pennsylvania Press, pp. 466–94.

Mahmood, T. (1995) 'Bangladesh', in *Statutes of Personal Law in Islamic Countries: History, Texts and Analysis*, 2nd edn, New Delhi: India and Islam Research Council, pp. 54–8, 205–13.

Monsoor, T. 'From patriarchy to gender equity: family law and its impact on women in Bangladesh', unpublished Ph.D. dissertation, SOAS, University of London.

Pearl, D. and W. Menski (1998) *Muslim Family Law*, 3rd edn, London: Sweet and Maxwell.

Redden, K. R. (1990) 'Bangladesh', in K. R. Redden (ed.), *Modern Legal Systems Cyclopedia*, Vol. 9, Buffalo, NY: Hein.

Robinson, F. (ed.) (1989) *The Cambridge Encyclopaedia of India, Pakistan, Bangladesh, Sri Lanka, Nepal, Bhutan and the Maldives*, Cambridge: Cambridge University Press.

INDIA, Republic of

Legal history The Indian legal system is based in part on the English common law system. With respect to Muslim personal law as applied in India, the sources of law are Hanafi *fiqh* along with some resort to other schools, legislation, precedent, certain juridical texts (both classical and modern) that are considered authoritative, and custom.

Under the British Raj, the colonial courts were directed to apply 'indigenous legal norms' in matters relating to family law and religion, with 'native law officers' advising the courts on the determination of those norms. A number of Hanafi sources (notably *al-Hidaya* and the *Fatawa Alamgiri*) were translated into English. The advisory positions of legal experts on Hindu and Muslim law were abolished in 1864. Legal commentators on the development of the indigenous system of 'Anglo-Muhammadan' law (now more commonly referred to as Indo-Muslim law) attach varying degrees of significance to the subsequently authoritative position of these works (and the quality of the translations), the absence of judicial expertise in Muslim law, the introduction of principles of English law and procedure through judges trained in the English legal tradition and through interpretation of the residual formula of 'justice and right' or 'justice, equity and good conscience' to imply mainly English law, and to the position taken on customary law.

The status of the personal laws of minority communities, and the plurality of religious laws in general, is much debated in India. Article 44 of the Constitution legislates a commitment to the gradual establishment of legal uniformity in India, the aim being that the state 'shall endeavour to secure for the citizens a uniform civil code throughout the territory of India'. This directive is considered a threat by elements of religious minority communities, who continue to be governed by their own personal laws in family matters, as applied within the superstructure of the Indian legal system.

Schools of *fiqh* The predominant *madhhab* is the Hanafi, with sizeable

Shafi'i, Ja'fari and Isma'ili minorities. India's minority religious communities also include Sikhs, Jains, Buddhists, Christians and Jews.

Constitutional status of Islam(ic law) The Indian Constitution was adopted on 26 November 1949 and has been amended many times. The preamble of the Constitution affirms that India is a 'sovereign socialist secular democratic republic'. India's secularity is framed in terms of neither favouring nor officially adopting any particular religion, and Article 26 guarantees the freedom to manage religious affairs (subject to constraints imposed by the requirements of public order, morality and health) for every recognized religious denomination or sect. The aforementioned Article 44 of the Constitution contains the Directive Provision stating that Indian legislators shall aim to establish a uniform civil code throughout India. For the time being, religious communities continue to be governed by their own personal laws (apart from Muslims, this applies to Christians, Zoroastrians, Jews and Hindus, as well as to Buddhists and Sikhs who, for legal purposes, are classified as Hindus). Although the option of civil marriage exists, it is not often the only regime under which Indians marry. The difficulty of reconciling the secularity of the republic and the objective of establishing legal uniformity with the protection of minority rights (also enshrined in the Constitution) has meant that, over fifty years since the adoption of the Constitution, the goal of the directive principle in Article 44 is still far from being realized.

Court system Muslim personal law is applied by the regular court system. As the majority of Muslims are Hanafi, courts presume that litigants are Hanafi unless the contrary is established. There are four levels of courts in the judiciary. The first are civil courts with jurisdiction over arbitration, marriage and divorce, guardianship, probate, and so on. The next level of courts is established in the subdivisions of each state, at the district level. Each district comes under the jurisdiction of a principal district civil court presided over by a district judge. There are State High Courts in each of the 28 states of the federation. The Supreme Court is constituted by one Chief Justice and not more than 17 judges.

The courts of first instance for personal status are generally the Family Courts, organized under the Family Courts Act of 1984. The Family Courts are deemed to be the equivalent of any district or subordinate civil court. Their jurisdiction is enumerated in the Act and covers suits for decrees of nullity, restitution of conjugal rights, judicial separation or dissolution, validity of marriage, matrimonial property, orders or injunctions arising out of the circumstances of marriage, legitimacy, maintenance, guardianship, custody, and access to minors. These courts have some criminal jurisdiction in terms of maintenance orders. Suits in these courts may be held *in camera* if the Family Court so desires or at the request of the parties to the case.

Notable features With the exception of some enactments, most of the personal law applicable to Indian Muslims is uncodified and administered by state courts on the basis of Indo-Muslim judicial precedents. With one exception, the legislation regulating Islamic family law dates from the period of British colonial rule.

The Muslim Personal Law (Shari'at) Application Act 1937 directs the application of Muslim Personal Law to Muslims in a number of different areas mainly related to family law. The Act also directs the application of Muslim personal law in matters relating to intestate succession among Muslims. On the matter of Islamic inheritance law, as the Qur'an provides a systematic scheme for intestate succession, there has been no particular legislation in that area. The courts generally apply the classical rules relating to intestate succession.

The Child Marriage Restraint Act 1929 introduced under the British provided penal sanctions for contracting marriages below the specified minimum age, originally established at 18 and 15 years. As the Act currently stands in India (amended by Act 2 of 1978), the minimum marriage age is 21 for men and 18 for women. However, as registration is not compulsory in India, and as the Act does not instruct the dissolution of under-age marriages, such unions are not rendered invalid.

The Registration of Mohammedan Marriages and Divorces Act 1876 is still in operation in Bihar and West Bengal. Other states of the federation have similar Acts, and there are facilities for voluntary registration. However, registration is not a requirement in India. The option of registering a marriage under the Special Marriage Act 1954 (under which all inter-religious marriages must be registered) also exists, in which case a different set of secular marriage and divorce laws would apply; it does not, however, appear to be very common to do so in practice. Registration may prove useful if recourse is had to the courts, but because it is not compulsory, other evidence may be used to prove the existence of an unregistered marriage. Upon signature to the CEDAW, India submitted a declaration affirming the government's commitment to the principle of obligatory registration of marriage, but stating that, for the present, the diversity and size of India's population make strict adherence to this principle impractical.

With regard to polygyny, the Criminal Procedure Code establishes that a woman who refuses to live with her husband on just grounds will still be entitled to maintenance and those just grounds, as defined in the Code, include the contracting of a polygynous marriage by the husband, even if the personal law applicable to the parties permits polygyny. This proviso only actually applies to Muslims as polygyny has been abolished for all other communities. In *Itwari* v. *Asghari* (AIR 1960 All 684), a suit for the restitution of conjugal rights by a Muslim husband against his first wife, the Allahabad Court stated that the onus was on the husband to prove that his second marriage did not constitute any insult or cruelty to the first wife. Although the Muslim husband has the right to contract a polygynous marriage, the Court held that it does not necessarily follow that the first wife should be forced to live with him under threat of severe penalties after the husband has taken a second wife. Even in the absence of proof of cruelty, the Court would not pass a decree for restitution of conjugal rights if it appeared that it would be unjust and inequitable to compel her to return to her husband under the circumstances of the case.

The Dissolution of Muslim Marriages Act 1939 introduced changes to the extremely restricted Hanafi rules on judicial divorce at the petition of the wife by the adoption and adaptation of certain Maliki principles. The nine grounds upon which a woman is entitled to obtain a decree of dissolution of her marriage under the Act are as follows: if the husband's whereabouts have not been known for four years; if the husband neglects to maintain the wife for two years; if the husband has been sentenced to seven or more years' imprisonment; if the husband has failed to perform his marital obligations for three years; if the husband was impotent at the time of marriage and continues to be so; if the husband has been insane for a period of two years or suffers from a serious illness harmful to the wife; if the wife was contracted into marriage by her father or other guardian before the age of 15 and repudiates the marriage before she becomes 18 (provided the marriage has not been consummated); if the husband treats her with cruelty (including physical or other ill-treatment or unequal treatment of co-wives); and any other ground which is recognized as valid for the dissolution of marriage under Muslim law. On the other hand, apostasy by the Muslim wife, including conversion to another religion, does not in and of itself dissolve her marriage. The Act expressly extends the option of puberty to women who were contracted into marriage as minors by their fathers or paternal grandfathers, broadening the classical Hanafi rules. There has, however, been no substantial reform of the classical law relating to *talaq*. The Muslim husband retains the right to repudiate his wife extra-judicially, and from the available sources it appears that the most common form of divorce is the triple *talaq*. The stance of the pre- and post-independence courts has generally been to accept extra-judicial repudiation as 'good in law, bad in theology'. A major issue of concern is the determination of the time from which maintenance becomes due in cases where the *talaq* has not been communicated to the wife, but the validity of such repudiations has not been called into serious question. Pearl and Menski also note that the scarcity of case law reflects the fact that, in actual practice, the exercise of *talaq* doesn't often involve the courts.

With regard to maintenance upon divorce, classical Hanafi law has been modified in India by the Muslim Women (Protection of Rights on Divorce) Act 1986, passed following fierce protest by sectors of the Muslim community that viewed the Supreme Court's ruling in the Shah Bano case as a gross interference in matters of Muslim personal status. In *Mohammad Ahmed Khan v. Shah Bano Begum* (AIR 1985 SC 945), the Supreme Court ruled that there was no conflict between classical Hanafi law, which specifies only the obligation to maintain a wife during her *'idda* period, and the requirement to support a former wife unable to maintain herself established by state legislation. During the aftermath of the controversial judgment, the Congress government passed the Muslim Women (Protection of Rights on Divorce) Act. The Act entitles the divorced Muslim woman to 'a reasonable and fair provision and maintenance to be made and paid to her within the *'idda* period by her former husband'. Although the Act itself provoked differing reactions as to what its effect would be, court practice allows the Muslim divorcée to appeal to the courts if her former husband has not provided her with a reasonable sum for maintenance during her *'idda* period. As in classical law, the *'idda* period is defined as three menstrual cycles after the divorce; three lunar months if the wife is not subject to menstruation; or until delivery of the child or termination of pregnancy if the woman is pregnant. The Act also stipulates that the divorced wife is entitled to any outstanding dower, any property given her before or during marriage, and maintenance for children in her custody born before or after the finalization of the divorce. There appears to be some modification to classical Hanafi law in the definition of a divorcée entitled to claim such support, as the Act specifies that its application pertains to marriages conducted according to Muslim law where a Muslim woman has obtained a divorce from or has been divorced by her husband in accordance with Muslim law. The Act directs that if neither the former wife or husband has the means to provide for her support, the responsibility of maintenance of the divorcée falls on her relations, that is, those relatives who would stand to inherit from her. If she has no close relations or they are unable to support her, liability falls to the State *Waqf* Board. Section 5 of the Act also allows for a divorced Muslim woman and her former husband to declare to the Court their willingness to be governed by the provisions of sections 125 to 128 of the Code of Criminal Procedure relating to the maintenance of dependants unable to support themselves. In the first reported case relating to the Act (*Ali* v. *Sufaira* 1988 [2] KLT), the Kerala High Court rejected a narrow interpretation of the legislation as only requiring Muslim men to support their divorced wives during the *'idda* period. Rather, the Court stated that the appropriate interpretation of section 3(1)(a), 'a divorced woman shall be entitled to a reasonable and fair provision and maintenance to be made and paid to her within the *'idda* period by her former husband', was that maintenance during the waiting period and reasonable and fair provision were two separate issues. Thus the Court ruled that the Muslim divorcée is entitled not only to maintenance for her waiting period, but also to a reasonable and fair provision to provide 'for her future livelihood, from her former husband'. This has since been confirmed by a large number of judgments.

Custody is governed by the Guardians and Wards Act (1890) applicable to all religious communities in India. The Act stipulates that courts are to be guided by the personal law to which the minor is subject. The courts are also directed to consider the age, gender and religion of the minor and the character and capacity of the proposed guardian, and the minor's own opinion if s/he is old enough to form an intelligent preference. If the minor is very young or is female, the courts are directed to give preference to the mother. In all cases, the interests of the ward are paramount. In custody cases involving Muslims, courts tend to follow the general rule that the divorced mother is entitled to custody until the age of seven for boys (classical Hanafi position) and puberty for girls.

Law/case reporting system Law reports are published in *Supreme Court Reports* (SCR), *All India Reporter* (AIR), *Indian Law Reports* (ILR) and a large number of state law reports.

International conventions (with relevant reservations) India acceded to the ICESCR and the ICCPR in 1979, with a number of declarations, including one to the effect that 'the right of self-determination' mentioned in common Article 1 is interpreted by India as applying only to peoples under foreign domination and not to sovereign independent states or a section of a people or nation.

India became a signatory to the CEDAW in 1980 and ratified it in 1993. India submitted a declaration regarding Articles 5(a) and 16(1) that reiterates its commitment to abiding by the provisions 'in conformity with its policy of non-interference in the personal affairs of any Community without its initiative and consent'. India also registered a declaration regarding Article 16(2) on minimum marriage ages and compulsory registration; although it fully supports the principle, 'it is not practical in a vast country like India with its variety of customs, religions and level of literacy'.

India acceded to the CRC in 1992, with a declaration regarding the progressive implementation of Article 32 thereof on child labour, particularly with reference to paragraph 2(a) on the provision of a minimum employment age.

Background and sources

Anderson, M. (1990) 'Islamic law and the colonial encounter in British India', in C. Mallat and J. Connors (eds), *Islamic Family Law*, London: Graham and Trotman, pp. 205–24.

Baxi, U. (1986) 'People's law in India', in M. Chiba (ed.), *Asian Indigenous Law in Interaction with Received Law*, New York: KPI, pp. 216–66.

Diwan, P. and P. Diwan (1995), *Women and Legal Protection*, New Delhi: Deep.

Engineer, A. A. (1987) *The Shah Bano Controversy*, Delhi: Orient Longman.

Mahmood, T. (1995) 'India', in *Statutes of Personal Law in Islamic Countries: History, Texts and Analysis*, 2nd edn, New Delhi: India and Islam Research Council, pp. 87–8, 219–24.

Menski, W. (1990) 'The reform of family law and a Uniform Civil Code for India', in C. Mallat and J. Connors (eds), *Islamic Family Law*, London: Graham and Trotman, pp. 253–94.

Pearl, D. and W. Menski (1998) *Muslim Family Law*, 3rd edn, London: Sweet and Maxwell.

Redden, K. R. (1990) 'India', in K. R. Redden (ed.), *Modern Legal Systems Cyclopedia*, Vol. 9, Buffalo, NY: Hein.

Robinson, F. (ed.) (1989) *The Cambridge Encyclopaedia of India, Pakistan, Bangladesh, Sri Lanka, Nepal, Bhutan and the Maldives*, Cambridge: Cambridge University Press.

MALDIVES, Republic of

Legal history The Republic of the Maldives was never under direct British rule. As the British came to control virtually all of the area of the Indian Ocean by the late nineteenth century, the Maldivian Sultan established an agreement with the governor of Ceylon in 1887. This agreement allowed the Maldives to enjoy the status of a protected state without actually becoming a protectorate. Thus, the British only controlled external affairs and had no jurisdiction to involve themselves in the internal matters of the islands (although it is said that attempts at interference in internal affairs were made at times). The Maldives obtained full independence from their protected status under the United Kingdom in July 1965.

The legal system is based on an admixture of Islamic law and English common law, with the latter being more influential in some areas, such as commercial law. With relation to personal status, the basis for the law is the Shari'a, as adapted to the modern Maldivian judicial system. Much of what is known about the legal history of the Maldives is of an anecdotal nature and is drawn from the works of travellers who had visited the islands at different times. There are indications that Persians had visited the islands by the sixth century, and there are also numerous accounts of European travellers, such as the Frenchman François Pyrard, who was shipwrecked in the Maldives in 1602. One of the most well-known travelogues including the Maldives is that of Ibn Battuta, who served as the Chief *Qadi* of the islands for over a year. From his own account, he attempted to enforce certain *hadd* penalties, e.g., for theft (although it is not clear whether he actually introduced or reinstated them); some of these punishments were unknown to the Maldivians and later fell into disuse. Article 7 of the Maldivian Constitution prohibits the infliction of physical injury.

Schools of *fiqh* Maldivians are mainly Shafi'i with a Ja'fari minority, although the Maliki school predominated until the sixteenth century. The only non-Muslim Maldivian residents are expatriates as Maldivian citizenship is granted only to Muslims.

Constitutional status of Islam(ic law) Before conversion to Islam, Arabic and Persian sources indicate that women often served as rulers of the Maldives. Historical records indicate that there has long been some form of democracy in the Maldives, with the Sultan's role being similar to that of a constitutional monarch. The Sultan was aided by a number of councils, of which he (or she) was an equal member. There is evidence of Sultans being deposed for deviating from normal procedures and precedents against the advice of their counsellors. There have been at least three Sultanas in the Maldives. The accounts of women rulers date back to the fourteenth century. There have also been a number of cases where men have served in the office of Sultan in the name of the legitimate female successors. Ibn Battuta said of this that '[i]t is a strange thing about these islands that their ruler is a woman, Khadija … When (her father) was deposed … none of the royal house remained but Khadija and her two younger sisters, so they raised Khadija to the throne.'

The first written Constitution of the Maldives was adopted in 1932 and

was based on customs and conventions and the traditional modes of administration. The Maldives were established as a republic in 1953 but the Sultanate
was restored the following year. After a referendum on the issue in April of
1968, the Sultanate was abolished and the Maldives again established as a
republic.

The current Constitution came into effect on 1 January 1998. Article 1
identifies the Maldives as a 'democratic republic based on the principles of
Islam'. Article 7 states that Islam is the state religion. Article 16 allows for
criminal defence 'in accordance with Shari'a'. Article 23 protects property
rights, except 'as provided by law or Shari'a'. Article 25 allows for limits on
free expression for the purpose of 'protecting the basic tenets of Islam'; Article
38 states that the president is the 'supreme authority to propagate the tenets
of Islam'; Article 156 states that 'law includes the norms and provisions of
Shari'a'.

Court system The Republic of the Maldives has a highly decentralized
system of administration; a result of geographic exigencies as the country is
made up of approximately 200 inhabited and almost 1,000 uninhabited islands.
The administrative units are organized into 19 atolls, with each atoll governed
by an atoll chief (*atholhuvarin*) appointed by the president. There is also a
magistrate or *ghazi* on each inhabited island who deals with legal and criminal
matters. Serious cases are referred to the courts in Male, the capital and
twentieth administrative unit. The High Court sits in Male and, in addition
to being the ultimate court of appeal, also handles any politically sensitive
cases; there are also eight lower courts in Male dealing with theft, debt or
property cases. There are no jury trials. Judges are appointed by the president
and removable by him, and they must be Muslims. Shari'a is incorporated into
the legal system.

Notable features According to custom, the minimum age for marriage is
15; the Law on the Protection of the Rights of the Child discourages marriage
before the age of 16.

In the case of divorce, children under seven years will, primarily, remain
with their mother; if this is not deemed appropriate (if, for example, the
mother is to remarry and have other children), custody will be offered to the
maternal grandmother, the paternal grandmother or the father, in descending
order of priority. Children over the age of seven years can choose in whose
custody they wish to remain.

Law/case reporting system   *Government Gazette.*

International conventions (with relevant reservations)   The Maldives signed the CRC in 1990 and ratified it in 1991. Reservations made upon signature relate to the Islamic Shari'a being one of the fundamental sources of Maldivian law and not recognizing the system of adoption, as well as to the provision relating to children's freedom of religion because 'the Constitution and the Laws of the Republic of Maldives stipulate that all Maldivians should be Muslims'. The reservations to Articles 14 and 21 were reiterated upon ratification.

The Maldives acceded to the CEDAW in 1993, with general reservations regarding any provisions contradictory to the Shari'a or Maldivian tradition and legal and constitutional autonomy.

Background and sources

Bell, H. C. P (1921) *The Maldives Islands: Report on a Visit to Male, January 20 to February 21, 1920,* Colombo: Government Record Office.

Ellis, R. and G. Amarasinghe (1995) *Guide to Maldives,* Old Saybrook, CT: Globe Pequot Press.

Ibn Battuta (1983) *Travels in Asia and Africa 1325–1354,* trans. H. A. R. Gibb, London: Routledge.

Maldives, *Initial Reports of States Parties Due in 1993: Maldives* 05/08/96. CRC/C/8/Add.33.

Maloney, C. (1980) *People of the Maldive Islands,* London: Longman.

Redden, K. R. (1990) 'Bangladesh', in K. R. Redden (ed.), *Modern Legal Systems Cyclopedia,* Vol. 9, Buffalo, NY: Hein.

Robinson, F. (ed.) (1989) *The Cambridge Encyclopaedia of India, Pakistan, Bangladesh, Sri Lanka, Nepal, Bhutan and the Maldives,* Cambridge: Cambridge University Press.

PAKISTAN, Islamic Republic of

Legal history [see also: Legal history, Republic of India]   The legal system is based on English common law with provisions to accommodate Pakistan's status as an 'Islamic state', most notably in the area of personal status, but also to some extent in the areas of criminal law and commercial law.

After the partition of India in 1947, the legislation relating to Muslim family law introduced in British India continued to govern personal status. A seven-member Commission on Marriage and Family Laws was established in 1955 with a remit to consider the personal status laws applicable in the new state and determine the areas needing reform. The Commission submitted its report in 1956, suggesting a number of reforms, including, for example, the consideration of all triple *talaqs* (except for the third of three) as single, revocable repudiations. The report led to much debate, with many leading *ulama* (including Maulana Abu'l 'Ala Maududi, leader of the *Jama'at-i-Islami*) opposing its recommendations. The Muslim Family Laws Ordinance 1961 adopted some of the provisions of the Report of the Marriage and Family Laws Commission, aiming to reform divorce law and inheritance law relating to orphaned grandchildren, introduce compulsory marriage registration, place restrictions on the practice of polygyny, and reform the law relating to dower and maintenance in marriage and divorce, as well as to amend existing legislation with relation to marriage age. Again, various sectors of the *ulama* regarded this as unjustified interference or tampering with the classical law. When the first Constitution of Pakistan was finally promulgated in 1956, it included a provision that came to be referred to as the 'repugnancy clause'. This clause stated that no law repugnant to Islamic injunctions would be enacted and that all existing laws would be considered in light of this provision, in order to institute appropriate amendments. This 'repugnancy' provision has been retained and actually strengthened in the succeeding constitutions.

After a military takeover in 1999, the Constitution was again suspended. During 2000, discussions continued about possible amendments to the Constitution.

Schools of *fiqh* The predominant *madhhab* is the Hanafi, and there are sizeable Ja'fari and Isma'ili minorities. The legal status of the Ahmadis is somewhat unclear. They self-identify as Sunni Muslims, but were declared 'non-Muslims' by the state. In 1974, the then Prime Minister Zulfiqar Ali Bhutto finally conceded to a long-standing campaign waged by conservative religious elements agitating for the official designation of Ahmadis as non-Muslims. There have been Ahmadi initiatives to adopt a modified version of the Muslim Family Laws Ordinance 1961 to be applied to Ahmadi personal status cases. There are also Christian, Zoroastrian, Hindu, Sikh and Jewish minorities in Pakistan.

Constitutional status of Islam(ic law) The third Constitution was adopted on 10 April 1973, suspended in 1977, and reinstituted in 1985; it has undergone numerous amendments over time. It was suspended again in 1999 and remained suspended at the time of writing.

Article 1 of the Constitution declares that Pakistan shall be known as 'the Islamic Republic of Pakistan' and Article 2 declares Islam the state religion.

In 1985, the Objectives Resolution contained in the Preamble of the Constitution was made a substantive provision by the insertion of Article 2A, thereby requiring all laws to be brought into consonance with the Qur'an and Sunna. Chapter 3A establishes the Federal Shari'at Court and stipulates that the Court shall take up the examination of any law or provision of law that may be repugnant to the '[i]njunctions of Islam, as laid down in the Holy Qur'an and the *Sunna*'. If a law or provision is determined to be 'repugnant', the Court is to provide notice to the federal or provincial government specifying the reasons for the decision. The Court may also examine any decisions relating to the application of the *hudud* penalties that have been decided by any criminal court, and may suspend the sentence if there is any question as to the correctness, legality or propriety of any finding, sentence or order or the regularity of the proceedings. The Supreme Court also has a Shari'at Appellate Bench empowered to review the decisions of the Federal Shari'at Court and consisting of three Muslim Supreme Court judges and up to two *ulama*. Part IX of the Constitution is entitled 'Islamic Provisions' and provides for the Islamization of all existing laws, reiterating that no laws shall be enacted that are 'repugnant' to the injunctions of Islam. An explanation appended to Part IX clarifies that, with respect to personal law, the expression 'Qur'an and *Sunna*' means the laws of any sect as interpreted by that sect.

The Islamic provisions also provide for the creation of an Islamic Ideology Council of eight to 20 members appointed by the president. They must have 'knowledge of the principles and philosophy of Islam as enunciated in the Holy Qur'an and Sunna, or understanding of the economic, political, legal or administrative problems of Pakistan'. The Islamic Council is meant to represent various schools of thought as far as that may be practical, and at least one woman should be appointed. Its function is to make recommendations to the *Majlis-e-Shoora* (parliament) and the Provincial Assemblies 'as to the ways and means of enabling and encouraging the Muslims of Pakistan to order their lives individually and collectively in all respects in accordance with the principles and concepts of Islam as enunciated in the Holy Qur'an and *Sunna*'. The Council also determines for the federal and provincial governments whether or not proposed laws are 'repugnant', and compiles for them in suitable form 'such Injunctions of Islam as can be given legislative effect'.

Court system The judiciary is composed of three levels of federal courts, three divisions of lower courts and a Supreme Judicial Council. There are district courts in every district of each province, having both civil and criminal jurisdiction though they deal mainly with civil matters. The High Court of each province has jurisdiction over civil and criminal appeals from lower courts within the provinces. The Supreme Court sits in Islamabad and has exclusive jurisdiction over disputes between or among federal and provincial governments, and appellate jurisdiction over High Court decisions. There is also a Federal Shari'at Court established by Presidential Order on 26 May 1980. This Court has exclusive jurisdiction to determine, upon petition by any citizen or the federal or provincial governments or on its own motion, whether or not a law conforms to the injunctions of Islam. An Islamic advisory council of *ulama* assists the Federal Shari'at Court in this capacity.

The West Pakistan Family Courts Act 1964 continues to govern the jurisdiction and functioning of the Pakistani Family Courts; the Act was never applied to East Pakistan before Bangladeshi independence. Appeals from the Family Courts lie with the High Court only. The Family Courts have exclusive jurisdiction over matters pertaining to the dissolution of marriage, dower, maintenance, the restitution of conjugal rights, the custody of children, and guardianship.

Notable features The West Pakistan Muslim Personal Law (Shari'at) Application Act 1962 repealed the 1937 Muslim Personal Law (Shari'at) Application Act as well as provincial legislation on the application of Muslim personal law. The new Act directs the application of Muslim personal law, notwithstanding any custom or usage, to all questions of personal status and succession where the parties are Muslims. One particular provision of the new legislation states that, '[t]he limited estates in respect of immovable property held by Muslim females under the customary law are hereby terminated'; this constitutes the opposite stance to customary land law to the 1937 enactment, and so the new Act provides that it will not apply retrospectively.

The Child Marriage Restraint Act 1929 introduced penal sanctions for contracting child marriages. The minimum marriage age as the Act currently stands is 18 for males and 16 for females. Despite the provision of penalties for contracting under-age marriages, such unions are not rendered invalid. The issue of marriage guardianship is governed by classical law; according to the Hanafi school, an adult woman may contract her marriage without a *wali*, but the influence of custom is strong, as shown by the events surrounding the Saima Waheed case. In *Abdul Waheed* v. *Asma Jehangir* (PLD 1997 Lah 331), the question put before the Court was whether or not an adult Hanafi Muslim woman may contract herself in marriage without the consent of her *wali*. In this particular case, the woman was an adult Hanafi Muslim of 22 years of age who contracted a marriage with a college lecturer without the knowledge of her parents. Her father disapproved of her choice and attempted to file a suit under the *Zina* Ordinance 1979. The majority judgment of the Lahore High Court held that the basic essential requirement for the validity of the contract was the woman's consent to the marriage, and not that of the *wali*. However, the tone of the discussion, including the recognition of the customary role of the *wali*, the endorsement of purdah, the focus on moral decline, the setting of the judgment (largely in terms of Shari'a law, with little reference to the Constitution) and the call for legislation on the matter all indicate that the classical Hanafi position and customary dictates are not in full accordance. In addition, the decisions of the Federal Shari'a Court on matters relative to family law were held to be binding on the High Courts, while the Constitution had expressly barred the Federal Shari'a Court from interfering with Muslim personal law. Some commentators predict this may lead to a 'gradual erosion of the protective features of the MFLO 1961'.

The Muslim Family Laws Ordinance 1961 introduced reforms to various aspects of the classical law. The reforms concern the registration of marriage and divorce, inheritance rights of orphaned grandchildren, restrictions on polygyny, consideration of every *talaq* (except the third of three) as single and revocable, formalization of reconciliation procedures in disputes relating to maintenance or dissolution of marriage, and recovery of *mahr*, along with specified penalties for non-compliance.

The MFLO introduced marriage registration and provides for penalties of fines or imprisonment for failure to register. However, a Muslim marriage is still legal if it is contracted only according to the religious requisites. The MFLO also instituted some limited reforms in the law relating to polygyny, with the introduction of the requirement that the husband must submit an application and pay a fee to the local Union Council in order to obtain prior written permission for contracting a polygynous marriage. The application must state the reasons for the proposed marriage and indicate whether the applicant has obtained the consent of the existing wife or wives. The chairman of the Union Council forms an Arbitration Council with representatives of the existing wife or wives and the applicant in order to determine the necessity of the proposed marriage. The penalty for contracting a polygynous marriage without prior permission is that the husband must immediately pay the entire dower to the existing wife or wives as well as being subject to a fine and/or imprisonment; any polygynous marriage contracted without the Union Council's approval cannot be registered under the MFLO. Nevertheless, if a man does not seek the permission of his existing wife or the Union Council, his subsequent marriage remains valid. Furthermore, the difficulty in enforcing resort to the application process to the Union Council, and the judiciary's reluctance to apply the penalties contained in the MFLO (as indicated by the case law), tend to restrict the efficacy of the reform provisions. This has led some observers to describe the provisions requiring the permission of the Arbitration Council as a mere 'formality'.

Efforts were also made to reform the classical law as it relates to the exercise of *talaq*. The MFLO requires that the divorcing husband shall, as soon as possible after a *talaq* pronounced 'in any form whatsoever', give the chairman of the Union Council notice in writing. The chairman is to supply a copy of the notice to the wife. Non-compliance is punishable by imprisonment and/ or a fine. Within 30 days of receipt of the notice of repudiation, the chairman must constitute an Arbitration Council in order to take steps to bring about a reconciliation. Should that fail, a *talaq* that is not revoked, either expressly or implicitly, takes effect after the expiry of 90 days from the day on which the notice of repudiation was delivered to the chairman. If the wife is pregnant at the time of the pronouncement of *talaq*, the *talaq* does not take effect until 90 days have elapsed or the end of the pregnancy, whichever is later. The classical law regarding the requirement of an intervening marriage in order to remarry a former husband who has repudiated the same woman three times is retained. Failure to notify invalidated the *talaq* until the late 1970s and early 1980s, but the introduction of the *Zina* Ordinance allowed scope for abuse as repudiated wives were left open to charges of *zina* if their husbands had not followed the MFLO's notification procedure. Thus, judicial practice has, since the early 1980s, recognized as valid repudiations in contravention of the notification procedure. The rules regarding notification and arbitration apply, *mutatis mutandis* and so far as applicable, to delegated divorce (*talaq al-tafwid*), or to marriage dissolved other than by *talaq*. The chairman of the Union Council will also constitute an Arbitration Council to determine the matter in cases where a husband fails to maintain his wife or wives, or fails to maintain co-wives equitably (at the application of one or more wife or wives, and in addition to their seeking any other legal remedy). Any outstanding dower or maintenance not paid in due time is recoverable as arrears of land revenue. Also, where no details regarding the mode of payment of *mahr* are recorded in the marriage contract, the entire sum of the dower stipulated therein is presumed to be payable as prompt dower.

The MFLO also introduced a significant reform to the classical law of inheritance by allowing for orphaned grandchildren by predeceased sons or daughters to inherit from their maternal or paternal grandparents.

The Dissolution of Muslim Marriages Act 1939 continues to govern divorce in Pakistan. The Act has been amended by the Muslim Family Laws Ordinance 1961 to include the contracting of a polygynous marriage in contravention of the MFLO in the grounds entitling a woman to a decree for the dissolution of her marriage. Another amendment raises the age at which a woman has to have been married by her father or other guardian to exercise her option of puberty from 15 to 16; thus the option of puberty may be exercised if the girl was married before the age of 16 if she repudiates the marriage before the age of 18 so long as the marriage was not consummated. The 'judicial *khul''* is a significant feature of divorce law in Pakistan. It is welcomed by some as giving women the 'right' to divorce regardless of grounds, provided that she is pre-pared to forgo her financial rights (i.e., repaying her dower). It is criticized by others who point out that judges may rule for a judicial *khul'* in cases where women are clearly entitled to a judicial divorce under the terms of the DMMA without losing their financial rights. In *Khurshid Bibi* v. *Mohd. Amin* (PLD 1967 SC 97), the question for the Supreme Court to determine was stated as follows: '[Is] a wife, under the Muslim law, – entitled, as of right, to claim *khul'*, despite the unwillingness of the husband to release her from the matrimonial tie, if she satisfies the Court that there is no possibility of their living together consistently with their conjugal duties and obligations?' The Supreme Court stated that the Muslim wife is indeed entitled to *khul'* as of right, if she satisfies the Court that she would be forced into a 'hateful union' if the option of *khul'* was denied her by her husband.

In terms of maintenance during and after marriage, the classical law is applied. The post-independence changes to the Indian Criminal Procedure Code that allow a divorced wife who is unable to support herself to claim maintenance from her former husband have not been reflected in the Criminal Procedure Code of Pakistan. While the Indian Criminal Procedure Code was extended so as to apply to divorcées, no such reforms have been made to section 488 of the Criminal Procedure Codes of either Pakistan or Bang-ladesh.

Child custody continues to be governed by the Guardians and Wards Act 1890. The Act stipulates that the courts are to be guided by the personal law to which the minor is subject. The general rule for Muslims is that the divorcée is entitled to custody until seven years for males (classical Hanafi position) and puberty for females. The courts are also directed to consider the age, sex and religion of the minor and the character and capacity of the proposed guardian, as well as considering the minor's own opinion if s/he is old enough to form an intelligent preference. If the minor is very young or is a female, the courts are directed to give preference to the mother. In all cases, the interests of the ward are paramount.

The *Qanun-e-Shahadat* (law of evidence) Order 1984 replaced the Evidence Act 1872, although it essentially restates the original legislation, but as it was intended to bring the law of evidence closer to Islamic injunctions, there were changes that specifically impacted upon women. The Order introduced changes to the law as it relates to the presumption of legitimacy. The original Evidence Act did not provide for a minimum period of gestation, and the maximum was 280 days. Now, the minimum gestation period is set at six months and the maximum at two years, bringing the provision into accordance with the majority position in classical Hanafi *fiqh*. With regard to the changes introduced relating to women's testimony, practice since the Order's issuance has been for instruments pertaining to financial or future obligations to be attested by two men, or one man and two women while courts may accept or act on the testimony of one man or one woman in all other cases.

The Offence of *Zina* (Enforcement of *Hudood*) Ordinance 1979 introduced the concepts of fornication and adultery into criminal law. The Pakistani Penal Code had not afforded any recognition to fornication as a crime, and adultery was defined as an offence under section 497 only if a man had intercourse with the wife of another man without his permission; the woman involved bore no criminal liability. The *Zina* Ordinance provides for severe penalties for committing adultery or fornication, and reiterates the classical distinction between married and unmarried parties in determining punishments. Thus, the *hadd* punishment for a married person convicted of *zina* is *rajm*, stoning to death, a penalty that has not been carried out by the state, and the *hadd* for an unmarried person found guilty of *zina* is one hundred lashes in a public place. The Ordinance also makes a distinction between *ta'zir* and *hadd* punishments for *zina*, as *hadd* punishments are generally more severe and require a more rigorous standard of proof. If the accused confesses to the crime, or if there are four pious adult Muslim male eye-witnesses to the actual act of penetration, the *hadd* penalty may be applied. Often the higher standard of evidentiary requirements is not met, and if there are other complications as well (appeals, retractions of confessions, and so on), the usual course has been to apply *ta'zir* punishments, defined as imprisonment for up to ten years, 30 lashes and a fine.

The Enforcement of Shari'a Act 1991 affirms the supremacy of the Shari'a (defined in the Act as the injunctions of Islam as laid down in the Holy Qur'an and Sunna) as the supreme law of Pakistan. The Act states that all statute law is to be interpreted in the light of the Shari'a and that all Muslim citizens of

Pakistan shall observe the Shari'a and act accordingly. Section 20 of the Act states that '[n]otwithstanding anything contained in this Act, the rights of women as guaranteed by the Constitution shall not be affected'.

Law/case reporting system The decisions of Pakistani courts are published in *Pakistan Legal Decisions* (PLD), *Civil Law Cases* (CLC), *Monthly Legal Digest* (MLD) and a number of other law reports.

International conventions (with relevant reservations) Pakistan signed the CRC in 1990, and ratified the Convention the same year. The reservation made upon signature regarding the CRC being interpreted in the light of Islamic legal principles and values was withdrawn in 1997. Pakistan acceded to the CEDAW in 1996, with a general declaration to the effect that Pakistan's accession to the Convention is subject to the provisions of the national Constitution.

Background and sources

Ali, S. S. (1996) 'Is an adult Muslim woman *sui juris*? Some reflections on the concept of "consent in marriage" without a *wali* (with particular reference to the Saima Waheed case)', *Yearbook of Islamic and Middle Eastern Law*, London and Boston: Kluwer Law International, pp. 156–74.

Carroll, L. (1996) 'Qur'an 2:229: "A charter granted to the wife"? Judicial *khul'* in Pakistan', *Islamic Law and Society*, 3: 1.

Lau, M. (1996) 'Case note on the Saima Waheed Case', *Yearbook of Islamic and Middle Eastern Law*, London and Boston: Kluwer Law International, p. 518–31.

Mahmood, T. (1995) 'Pakistan', in *Statutes of Personal Law in Islamic Countries*, 2nd edn, New Delhi, pp. 74–8, 205–13.

Mehdi R. (1994) *The Islamization of the Law in Pakistan*, Richmond, Surrey: Curzon Press.

Pearl, D. (1990) 'Three decades of executive, legislative and judicial amendments to Islamic family law in Pakistan', in C. Mallat and J. Connors (eds), *Islamic Family Law*, London: Graham and Trotman, pp. 321–38.

Pearl, D. and W. Menski (1998) *Muslim Family Law*, 3rd edn, London: Sweet and Maxwell.

Redden, K. R. (1990) 'Pakistan', in K. R. Redden (ed.), *Modern Legal Systems Cyclopedia*, Vol. 9, Buffalo, NY: Hein.

Robinson, F. (ed.) (1989) *The Cambridge Encyclopaedia of India, Pakistan, Bangladesh, Sri Lanka, Nepal, Bhutan and the Maldives*, Cambridge: Cambridge University Press.

SRI LANKA, Democratic Socialist Republic of

Legal history   Sri Lanka has been subject to centuries of Portuguese, Dutch and British domination. From the time of independence in 1948, the legal system of Sri Lanka has developed into a complex mixture of English common law and Roman-Dutch, Sinhalese, Muslim, and customary law.

Under Dutch rule in the late eighteenth century, the colonial administrators codified the rules of inheritance, marriage and divorce law in order to facilitate the application of Muslim family law. Preference was given to customary usage and the provisions of the 'Mohammedan Code' over classical legal treatises. These special laws were preserved and adapted after the British defeat of the Dutch in 1799. The Code was initially applied only to the Muslims of the Province of Colombo, but its application was extended to the rest of the island by the late nineteenth century. Another piece of legislation, the Registration of Muslim Marriages Ordinance 1896, was enacted under the British, repealing parts of the earlier Code. The Muslim Marriage and Divorce Registration Ordinance 1929 replaced the 1896 legislation and further amended the Anglo-Dutch 'Mohammedan Code'. The next item of legislation, the Muslim Intestate Succession Ordinance 1931, continues to be in force in Sri Lanka today, and the 1929 Ordinance was finally replaced by the post-independence Muslim Marriage and Divorce Act in 1951. The essential principle reinforced by the 1951 Act is that, in matters of personal status, the rights and duties of the parties involved are to be governed by the school of law to which the parties belong.

Schools of *fiqh*   Sri Lankan Muslims mainly follow the Shafi'i or Hanafi schools. There are also Hindu and Christian minorities in Sri Lanka.

Constitutional status of Islam(ic law)   The current Constitution was adopted on 16 August 1978. Article 9 falls short of establishing Buddhism as the state religion; rather, the provision gives Buddhism the 'foremost place', making it the duty of the state to 'protect and foster the Buddha Sasana', while assuring to all religions the rights enshrined in Articles 10 and 14(1)(e) of the Constitution. Those articles guarantee every person freedom of thought, conscience and religion, including the freedom to profess or adopt a religion or belief of his/her choice, and guarantee all citizens the freedom to manifest their religious beliefs in worship, observance, practice and teaching. These are the only provisions expressly relating to religion and implicitly to minority rights. No change to these provisions is put forward in the draft Constitution tabled in 1997. The draft has been the subject of heated debate but is unlikely to be passed into law in the near future due to the current composition of the parliament.

Court system The Muslim Marriage and Divorce Act 1951 constitutes the main body of legislation relating to the application of Muslim family law, and also regulates the functions, qualifications and powers of the *Qadis'* Courts applying that law. *Qadis'* Courts are staffed by judges (*qadis*) appointed by the Judicial Services Commission. Male Muslims of good character and position and suitable attainments are eligible for appointment as *qadis*. Appeals from the *Qadis'* Courts lie with the Board of *Qadis'*, then with the Court of Appeal and ultimately with the Supreme Court. A board of three judges is required to hear appeals to the Board of *Qadis'*. The Board's other function is to furnish the registrar-general or any *qadis* that request such advice with a written opinion on any question of Muslim law that may arise in relation to the administration of the MMDA. The MMDA also delineates the limits of jurisdiction between the civil judicial system and the *Qadis'* Courts, as well as the powers of the *qadi*. The *qadi* has exclusive jurisdiction over the adjudication of *mahr* or maintenance claims, mediation between spouses upon application, adjudication of decrees of nullity, and a number of other administrative and judicial matters relating to Muslim personal law.

Notable features There is very limited legislation relating to Muslim personal status in Sri Lanka, following the characteristics of the application of Muslim personal law elsewhere in South Asia in that much of Muslim personal law remains uncodified. The legislation that does apply is largely of an administrative nature, and does not necessarily alter or reinterpret many of the substantive classical provisions of Islamic family law.

The Muslim Marriage and Divorce Act 1951 regulates matrimonial law for Muslims. The Act repealed the Muslim Marriage and Divorce Registration Ordinance 1929 and has been revised a number of times since its passage.

In 1995, the minimum age of marriage was raised to 18. However, the marriage age for Muslims is governed by the Muslim Marriage and Divorce Act, allowing for a girl to marry as young as twelve without the permission of a *qadi*, and younger with the *qadi*'s permission after any such inquiry as he may deem necessary. With respect to capacity, the Act states that for any Shafi'i woman, no contract of marriage is valid under the law applicable to that sect unless her rightful *wali* is present at the time and place at which the contract is entered into and he communicates her consent to as well as his own approval of the contract. No person may knowingly act as a *wali* unless he is entitled to do so under the law governing the sect to which the bride belongs, and no marriage for which a person acts as a *wali* in contravention of that provision can be registered. The *qadi* may inquire into any complaint by a woman against a *wali* who unreasonably withholds his consent to her marriage, and authorize the marriage and dispense with the necessity for his presence or consent if he rules in favour of the woman. He may authorize marriage in cases where a woman has no *wali* as well. The MMDA makes registration upon conclusion of the *nikah* mandatory and shares the responsibility of registration between the bridegroom, the *wali* of the bride (if a *wali* is required by the law governing the sect to which the bride belongs) and the person conducting the *nikah* ceremony. Nothing in the act renders an unregistered marriage or divorce invalid, so long as the marriage or divorce is valid according to the sect to which the parties belong. Every person responsible for registering a marriage or divorce who fails to do so is liable to a fine upon the first offence, and a fine or imprisonment or both for additional convictions.

The MMDA also requires notification in the event of a Muslim male wishing to enter into a polygynous marriage. He must give notice of his intention to the *qadis* of the area where he resides and the area where his wife (or wives) resides, as well as to the *qadi* of the area where the intended bride resides, at least 30 days before contracting the subsequent marriage. The notice provided to the *qadis*, in a prescribed form, must contain the full names and address of the husband and all prospective co-wives. It is the duty of each of the *qadis* to whom notice is given to post such notices at the *Jumma* (Friday) mosques within his area and in a 'conspicuous place' at each address within his area that is specified in that notice. No polygynous marriage can be registered under the Act if the husband fails to go through this process before contracting the second or subsequent marriage.

The MMDA provides detailed rules regarding the registration of divorce by the husband and the wife. A husband who 'intends to pronounce the *talaq* on his wife' shall give notice to the *qadi* of the area where she is resident, and the *qadi*'s duty is to attempt to effect a reconciliation, with the help of the relatives of both parties, as well as elders and influential Muslims of the area. If within 30 days no reconciliation is effected, the husband shall pronounce the *talaq* in the presence of the *qadi* and two witnesses and the *qadi* shall record the pronouncement and cause notice of it to be served to the wife if she is not present; the 'alleged reasons' for which the husband seeks to divorce his wife are *not* to be recorded by the *qadi*. It is the *qadi*'s duty, where conciliation proceedings have failed, to recover any unpaid *mahr* from the husband, whether or not the wife has claimed her outstanding dower debt. The remaining dower due to her is deposited with the court in the name of the wife and the wife is served notice that such money is deposited in her name. If the husband does not appear on the dates he was called before the *qadi* for the reconciliation process, the *qadi* may, at any time after the expiry of three months from the date of the pronouncement of *talaq*, and upon the oath or affirmation of the wife, register the divorce.

The Act also outlines the procedure the Muslim wife must follow to effect a divorce from her husband, without his consent, on grounds of ill-treatment or on account of any act or omission on his part which amounts to a 'fault' under the Muslim law governing the sect to which the parties belong. In such cases, the Muslim wife must apply for divorce to the *qadi* of the area in which she is resident. The *qadi* convenes a panel of three Muslim assessors to hear the application, and they must endeavour to effect an amicable settlement and remove the cause of the conflict between the husband and wife. If reconciliation efforts fail, the *qadi* and the assessors proceed to hear the case for divorce and a decision is made according to the sect of the parties. (There is no provision relating to cases where the parties belong to different sects.) After the appealable time elapses, if there has been no appeal of the order of the *qadii* allowing the divorce, or if the Board of *Qadis'* or the Court of Appeal has decided to allow a divorce upon appeal, the *qadi* shall register the divorce.

The MMDA contains provisions relating to maintenance, *mahr* and *kaikuli*. The time for the prescription of a suit or action for a woman's *mahr* (in whole or part) shall not begin until the dissolution of the marriage by death or divorce, and such suit or action must be commenced within three years from the date of such dissolution. The Act does not specify regulations for a woman claiming maintenance from her husband during the subsistence of their marriage, though there is explicit mention of the *qadi*'s powers to examine and decide upon claims by wives or divorced wives for *kaikuli* or lying-in expenses. The court may specify that maintenance arrears may be awarded from the date of the claim.

The Muslim Intestate Succession Act 1931 directs that the estate of any Muslim who dies intestate and who resided in Sri Lanka or owned any immovable property there at the time of his or her death shall devolve according to the Muslim law of the sect to which the deceased belonged. The same is the case for any donations (not involving usufructs and trusts) made by Muslims domiciled in Sri Lanka or owning immovable property there.

Law/case reporting system   Supreme Court and Court of Appeal decisions are published in *Sri Lanka Law Reports*.

International conventions (with relevant reservations) Sri Lanka signed the CEDAW in 1980 and ratified it in 1981. Sri Lanka acceded to the ICCPR and ICESCR in 1980. Sri Lanka signed the CRC in 1990 and ratified it in 1991. Sri Lanka did not submit any reservations or declarations upon signature, ratification or accession to any of the above instruments.

Background and sources

Goonesekere (1979) 'Sri Lanka', in R. Watson and J. E. Sihombing (eds), *Lawasia Family Law Series*, Singapore: Singapore University Press.

Mahmood, T. (1995) 'Sri Lanka', in *Statutes of Personal Law in Islamic Countries: History, Texts and Analysis*, 2nd edn, New Delhi: India and Islam Research Council, pp. 91, 234–40.

Tambiah and Markhani (eds) (1996) *Muslim Law in Sri Lanka*, Colombo.

Redden, K. R. (1990) 'Sri Lanka', in K. R. Redden (ed.), *Modern Legal Systems Cyclopedia*, Vol. 9, Buffalo, NY: Hein.

Robinson, F. (ed.) (1989) *The Cambridge Encyclopaedia of India, Pakistan, Bangladesh, Sri Lanka, Nepal, Bhutan and the Maldives*, Cambridge: Cambridge University Press.

Part VIII
Southeast Asia

1 Social, Cultural and Historical Background

The Region and its History

Southeast Asia encompasses the huge peninsula of Indochina and the extensive archipelago once known as the East Indies. Within this region lie the states of Burma, Brunei Darussalam, Thailand, Laos, Cambodia, Vietnam, Malaysia, Singapore, Indonesia and the Philippines. Islam is the religion of two-fifths of the region's people, most of them living in the Malay Peninsula and the Malay Archipelago, and on the Philippine island of Mindanao. Indonesia is the single largest Muslim country in the world, with a population of 212 million. Two-thirds of Malaysia's 23 million people are Muslim.

The Muslim traders who landed in Indonesia in the seventh century found a Hindu–Buddhist civilization that was already centuries old. There have been well-organized and developed societies in the Indonesian archipelago since the seventh century BCE. Southeast Asia has always had close economic and social ties with the Indian subcontinent. The oldest Hindu works of art in Indonesia date back to the third century CE. During the ninth century, both Hinduism and Buddhism were practised as court religions. The blending of the two religions continued until the rise of Islam in the fourteenth century. Reflecting all the religious changes of the court level, the common people adopted part of each new religion as an additional layer over their basic indigenous beliefs.

Islam has perhaps bound its adherents together more strongly than have the other religions found in Southeast Asia. It has profoundly affected cultural, social, political and economic matters in areas where it is practised. From the thirteenth through to the seventeenth century Sunnite Islam spread widely, coming from the Middle East via India. In the fifteenth, sixteenth and seventeenth centuries, insular Southeast Asia attracted Islamic merchants and missionaries from India and farther west (later the Portuguese and the Dutch.) If economic interest drove Islam's introduction, the new religion also offered an egalitarian message that challenged the power of traditional elites and a complex theology that held great appeal for peasants and merchants in the coastal regions.

The first converts to Islam were local rulers who hoped to attract Muslim traffic. Muslim traders and teachers were probably associated with court administration from the beginning and introduced the religious institutions that made foreign Muslims feel at home. After the consolidation of Islam on the Indian subcontinent, Muslim merchants and Sufi missionaries also began to proselytize extensively (Lapidus 1990). The city-state of Pasai and the other early Muslim beachheads in Indonesia were to a considerable extent genuine Muslim creations that commanded the loyalty of the local population.

There were similar new harbour kingdoms on the northern coast of Java. The rulers of Malacca, though of prestigious Palembang origin, accepted Islam precisely in order to attract Muslim and Javanese traders to their port. Islam's asssertion of the equality of all believers and its very profitable communications with the Muslim world throughout Asia gave formerly peripheral regions the opportunity to begin to influence the course of events in Indonesia.

But Indonesian history is that of many distinct and often vastly separated regions. The history of early Indonesian Islam is no exception. What happened in the fifteenth and sixteenth centuries cannot be explained simply in terms of the influence of new ideas. The political ambitions of many regional princes intervened, and there was no uniform pattern of early Muslim life in the archipelago.

Ache (or Acheh), which succeeded Pasai in the sixteenth century as the leading harbour kingdom in northern Sumatra, eventually became a self-consciously Muslim state; however, a persuasive case has been made for the persistence as late as the seventeenth century of 'Hindu' notions of divine kingship familiar in Java. Ache had contacts with Muslim India and its own heterodox school of Muslim mysticism. The single and most notable gain for Islam in Sumatra was in the Minangkabau country, where Shaivite-Mahayana Tantric cults had flourished in the fourteenth century. Islam's penetration of Minangkabau by way of the Achinese west coast of Sumatra was far advanced by the beginning of the seventeenth century. Minangkabau was later to exercise a significant influence in the affairs of the archipelago.

Ships from the Netherlands began arriving in Java at the end of the sixteenth century. Spain claimed the Philippines around the same time. During the nineteenth century most of Indonesia fell under Dutch rule, while the British took control of Malaysia and the USA ousted Spain from the Philippines. All three countries gained independence after World War II.

The mostly Islamicized people of the Malacca area were the first to call

themselves 'Malays' (a likely reference to earlier Shrivijayan origins). Thereafter, the term Malay applied to those who practised Islam and spoke a version
of the Malay language. Identity and behaviour, rather than descent, became
the criteria for being Malay, so that previously animist and Hindu–Buddhist
peoples of various origins could identify themselves (and even merge) with the
Malays. Over time a loose cultural designation became a coherent ethnic
group distributed throughout Malaya, northern and western Borneo, eastern
Sumatra and the smaller islands in between – a region that can be termed the
'Malay world'.

The Malays originated in different parts of the peninsula and archipelagic
Southeast Asia. They constitute about two-thirds of the population and are
politically the most important group in the area. They share with each other
a common culture, speak a common Austronesian language – Malay (officially
called Bahasa Malaysia), which is the national language – and are overwhelmingly Muslim. Adherence to Islam is regarded as one of the most
important factors distinguishing a Malay from a non-Malay.

For most of the post-war period, secular political parties dominated the
governments of Indonesia and Malaysia. Then, in the 1980s, Dr Mahatir
Mohamed came to power on a platform of bringing 'official Islam' to Malaysia.
The same period saw a flowering of Islamist think-tanks and research centres
in Indonesia. When an economic and political crisis struck both countries in
1997, the Islamist opposition was able to portray its struggle against the ruling
elite of the two countries in religious terms. Islamist political parties scored
large gains in 1999 elections held in Malaysia and Indonesia (Noor 1999).

Legal Practices and Institutions

In general, Muslim communities in Southeast Asia are mainly Sunni Muslims
of the Shafi'i school with vestiges of Sufi influence in religious ceremonies,
and with a strong adherence to mystical tradition. Research shows that Islam
in Southeast Asia is contextual or blended with pre-Islamic traditions and
beliefs, and with degrees of Hindu–Buddhist influence. Communities differ in
the way they balance and apply Shari'a and the customary legal code or *Adat*,
conditioned by the social structure of the community, its historical processes,
kinships system and economics.

Before the colonial impact, Southeast Asia had no hierarchical organization
of *ulama* or of any other Muslim religious leaders and therefore no state control
of religious affairs as was the case in the Middle East and in India. Instead,
Islam was organized on a local scale around individual teachers and holy

men. While these teachers adhered to the Shari'a code of law, the local schools were independent of each other.

When the Dutch first arrived in Indonesia, they assumed that Indonesian Muslims observed the whole corpus of Islamic law. More careful study revealed that the only parts of Islamic law incorporated into all types of *Adat* law were those on marriage, divorce, and polygyny, which apply to all Indonesian Muslims. *Adat* law prevails over Qur'anic principles in many places. The Dutch upheld only those parts of Islamic law that had become part of local custom. The current government has followed the same policy (Lapidus 1990).

The judicial system in Indonesia is based on Romano-Dutch law. It consists of a Supreme Court (Mahkamah Agung) in Jakarta, which is the final court of appeal, and High Courts located in principal cities on Java, Sumatra, Celebes, Kalimantan, Bali, the Moluccas, and Irian Jaya, which deal with the appeals from more than 250 district courts. There are four judicial spheres (general, religious, military and administrative), each with its own courts.

The religious, military and administrative courts deal with special cases or particular groups of people, while the general courts deal with normal cases, both civil and criminal. There is one codified criminal law for all of Indonesia; the Dutch codified civil code is applied to foreigners. For Indonesians the civil law is the uncodified *humuk Adat* or local customary law, which varies from one district or ethnic group to another.

The field of law in Malaysia is as complex as most of its other cultural and social heritage, with several intertwining traditions. Those concerning the Malay population are Islamic law, *Adat* or customary law, and a British colonial influence. Since 1963 Malaysia has maintained a quasi-democratic parliamentary political system that includes regular elections and moderate political diversity, but also some restrictions on civil liberties, including a ban on public discussion of 'sensitive' issues. In Malaysia the legal system is based on English common law. The constitution of Malaysia, which is the supreme law of the country, provides that the judicial power of the federation shall be vested in two High Courts, one in Peninsular Malaysia and the other in East Malaysia, and also in subordinate courts. Above the High Courts is the Supreme Court (Mahkamah Agung), with jurisdiction to hear and determine appeals of decisions by any High Court. The supreme head of the judiciary is the Lord President of the Supreme Court.

Each High Court consists of a chief justice and a number of other judges – up to 33 in Peninsular Malaysia and up to eight in East Malaysia. The High Court has unlimited criminal and civil jurisdiction and may pass any sentence allowed by the law. Below the High Court are the subordinate courts, which

consist of the Sessions Courts and the Magistrates' Courts. Both of these lower courts have criminal and civil jurisdiction – criminal cases coming before one or the other court depending on the seriousness of the offence and civil cases depending on the sum involved. In' addition, there are religious courts in those Malay states that are established under Islamic law. These courts are governed by state, not federal legislation.

Within both Indonesia and Malaysia, the unwritten, traditional code called *Adat* governs most aspects of personal conduct from birth to death. Two kinds of Malay *Adat* law developed prior to the fifteenth century: *Adat Perpateh* developed in a matrilineal kinship structure in areas occupied by the Minangkabau people in Sumatra and Negeri Sembilan; *Adat Temenggong* originated in bilaterally based territorial social units. Both *Adat* forms were markedly transformed by Islamic and later European legal systems. *Adat Perpateh* emphasized law based on group responsibility. Criminal and civil offences were not differentiated. Enforced by community pressure, punishment stressed compensation rather than retribution. A crime was absolved by payment in kind, or by a reconciliation feast given to the aggrieved person. Mutilation and death penalties were rarely invoked, and acceptance of circumstantial evidence was a prominent feature of *Adat Perpateh*.

Prior to Islamic influence *Adat Temenggong* consisted of a mixture of Hindu law and native custom. It encompassed civil, criminal, constitutional and maritime law and included torture, amputation or death as punishment for offences. Both *Adat* systems continued into the twentieth century, until formalized European jurisprudence largely displaced them. Suwarni Salyo (1985) argues that *Adat* applied currently, especially in regulation of the family law, but states that there is no single body of *Adat*. *Adat* and its application varies from community to community and from region to region. There are at least nineteen *Adat* communities in Indonesia alone.

Indonesia has some 100 women sitting as Shari'a (*syariah*) court judges, but in Malaysia the general view is that women are not qualified to become judges. Women have complained that Malaysia's Shari'a court system is prejudiced against them (Othman 1996). The wife of Indonesia's president, Abdurrahman Wahid, is currently engaged in revising the country's standard guidebook of religious edicts to make sure that the book stresses the rights of women as much as their obligations under Islamic law (Asmarani 2000).

Shari'a courts also operate in Brunei and in the Muslim minority communities of Thailand, the Philippines, and Singapore.

Seclusion of Women / Purdah

Southeast Asia's Muslims traditionally have not been as concerned about the management of female sexuality as some other Muslim communities, although rules differ from one ethnic group to the next. The researcher Leela Dube sees the definitive factors that contribute to this development being the absence of a caste system, the system of descent, inheritance and group membership, as well as residence and the nature of conjugal relations (Dube 1997: 57–9). For example, in general, Southeast Asian women are not driven out of their homes for sexual offences. The notion of the protection of women and control over them seems not to be a part of the bilateral kinship system and not a part of the ethos of the region. In the matrilineal communities in Southeast Asia, the men who are looked upon as the custodians of women's sexuality, such as brothers and uncles, are not the users of women's sexuality.

Generally, Southeast Asian Muslim women, in addition to their roles as wives and mothers, are also engaged in earning an income. They seem to have a significant share of economic power and autonomy, particularly Malaysian Peninsular, Javanese and Filipina women. Typically, women are integral to the peasant economy, entirely responsible for the commercial production of vegetables and for the care of domestic animals. In general they retain legal control over what they produce and earn, and it appears that, besides rules of inheritance, the institutionalization of marital property in this region also encourages women's control over resources. Yet women's active economic roles are also conditioned by the classes to which women belong. In poor families, for example, economic activity gives women positions of considerable importance, and in the wealthier families it gives a material basis for acquiring increased social power. Although not many women 'reach the top' a lot of them are found on the middle levels of various professions (Dube 1997: 46–8).

As a rule, unmarried Indonesian women are subject to more social restrictions than are married women. In Indonesia, the matrilineal Muslims of the Lakshadweep Islands, such as the Minangkabau and Sasak believe that Islam requires a first-time bride to be a virgin. They therefore place restrictions upon young women with the onset of puberty. In Java also, unmarried girls are expected to be modest and cautious in their behaviour.

After marriage, restrictions on women's movement are negligible. Very often married women migrate to towns, leaving their husbands at home to look after the children and the land (Dube 1997: 57–9). *Adat* has a strong influence on women's role and position in the society. Indonesia's Muslim communities view female education and business as fully in line with Shari'a. This fact

reinforces the independence allowed to women within the traditional parental and matrilineal systems to own and administer property and to conduct business. It also mitigates the restriction imposed on women belonging to the patrilineal communities. But in tradition and culture, even women who have jobs or careers are regarded primarily as home-makers.

In Malaysia both sexes are subject to more or less the same codes of sexual behaviour (Dube 1997: 57–9). Although the young girl is expected to remain chaste and virtuous until she is ready for marriage and the term used for a young woman, meaning 'unopened flower', indicates greater emphasis on the virginity of women than that of men, male youths too are bound by strong rules of social decorum and propriety; sexual promiscuity in men is greatly condemned and a demure male is much preferred as a husband or son-in-law to one who is known to have had sexual experiences with other women (Dube 1997: 57–9). After marriage women are more freely able to participate in economic and productive activities, and are not seen as being under the control of men.

The Kelantan of Malaysia are an exception. Kelantan women are segregated but not secluded. While sexual segregation is not unique to Islam, this feature of social life is codified, and the Kelantan see it as a feature of Islam (Rudie 1983: 134). Kelantan women usually move around in groupings, and at social occasions both sexes are present but segregated to the highest degree practically possible (Rudie 1983: 130–1). Although Islam in Kelantan circumscribes sex-role behaviour quite strictly, particularly for women, it has no direct rule against women's economic autonomy.

Women in other parts of Malaysia who follow bilateral patterns of kinship enjoy freedom of movement, absence of seclusion and independent involvement in economic activities. They attend educational institutions without chaperoning and protection. A relatively recent social movement demanding conformity with Islamic injunctions has brought in a special cloak that covers women's hair, neck and arms, and also covers the bust with a double thickness of fabric. A similar cloak is being adopted by some women in Southeast Asia only for special public occasions. Sometimes men who complete the hadj insist on veiling their wives, but the latter remain largely unconvinced. Older women in particular argue against it: 'This is not our custom. We have never done it. Have we not been good Muslims?' (personal interview cited in Dube 1997: 60–9).

However, the pressure for women to cover their heads and use the cloak continues to grow. In Kedah, reports Dube, there is media agitation for the usage of the cloak through television and radio broadcasts (Dube 1997: 60–9). As a response to such demands, a compromise evolved in the form of a scarf that covers the hair, but even this is used by many women only when they go out with their husbands or other male relatives who insist on the observance of a certain degree of purdah for the sake of Islam. Some women in Kuala Lumpur wear the cloak out of a conviction of its appropriateness to Islamic injunctions. While theoretically virginity and chastity before marriage is valued in the Philippines, in practice there are no concrete rules or customs in place to 'regulate' women's sexual behaviour once they are courting or engaged. Among the Yakan of the Philippines, women are not secluded. Males and females are able to congregate in the same rooms or areas.

In general, the assumptions and reasons that underlie the seclusion of women in other Muslim communities are not apparent in the Indonesian, Malaysian or Philippine contexts. Dube suggests that the final analysis on the differences that exist among the followers of Islam is in the principles and ideologies of kinship (Dube 1997: 64). Based on this thesis, the total or relative lack of female seclusion in Southeast Asia needs to be viewed as a function of the bilateral and matrilineal forms of kinship organization found there. Nevertheless, Muslims are the only Southeast Asians to circumcise girls. Traditional midwives make a small incision in the clitoris of female infants shortly after birth. It is commonly believed that the operation prevents girls from becoming hypersexual (Hosken 1982).

Family in the Region

In Muslim communities of Southeast Asia, residence patterns vary, with three kinship systems prevailing: patrilineal, matrilineal and parental (bilateral). Of these parental is the most prevalent. Suwarni Salyo argues that the status of women depends on to which system they belong. Among the Minangkabau, who number about a million, for example, residence patterns are not in keeping with Islamic injunctions. Women have exclusive rights over the longhouses (a long communal dwelling), and most remain there throughout their lives. They also own rice paddies, orchards and all other major property, although each clan's administrator must be a man (Dube 1997: 88–9). So far as worship is concerned, the Minangkabau are devout Muslims, but they tend to follow *Adat* where property and residence are concerned. This is also seen in the fact that the Islamic procedure of unilateral divorce, in the Lakshadweep Islands, and easy remarriage can be made to function in the interests of women as often as men, because women have a privileged position in the economic and trade activities compared to other Muslim communities in the Middle East or South Asia.

Among the Malays and Javanese, households usually consist of one nuclear family, although one may also see uxorilocal extended families (usually extended, nuclear, joint and laterally joint families). Among the matrilineal Minangkabau, males tend to assume a partial 'father role' towards their sisters' children, while partially relinquishing paternal care of their own children to their wives' brothers.

Like the families found throughout most of Muslim Indonesia, the Philippine Yakan families consist of primarily nuclear families, composed of a husband, wife, and unmarried or newly married children.

Marriage

In Southeast Asia, marriage has a different texture and character in terms of relationships between spouses, rights over children, and choice of residence than is the case in many other Islamic societies. Marriage is a relatively egalitarian relationship promoted by kinship organization, the active participation of women in economic production, and access to rights over strategic resources. The difference stems from traditional customs, which are characteristic of the pre-Islamic lifestyle of the Southeast Asian communities. Although the institutions of marriage and divorce are primarily Islamic today, they still tend to incorporate pre-Islamic traditions. These societies offer institutionalized choices in such matters as entering and leaving marriages, marital residence, and the nurturing of children. These choices have been aided by the general absence of purdah (Dube, 1997: 65).

Although Muslim communities in Southeast Asia are rooted in different kinship systems, all essentially base marriage on Shari'a, following and fulfilling the basic requirements of the law. However, in practice the way these requirements are applied in different Muslim communities is radically different from that visualized and emphasized by Islam. In the mainstream interpretation of Islam, Islam assumes patrilineal structure to be the natural form of social organization. In Southeast Asia there are specific Islamic courts, but people are often guided by *Adat*, which has also influenced them together with modern demands.

In rural areas, early marriage is common. It may be decided by parents, or by partners with the consent of their parents. Marriage releases some of the constraints put on young women's mobility. There is no stigma attached to divorce and remarriage is common. *Mahr* is usually small, and payment can be deferred (Dube 1997: 121–31); it does not act as a deterrent to divorce and does not establish a husband's authority over his wife, in keeping with Qur'anic injunctions. In some communities, such as the Lakshadweep group of Kalpeni Island, *mahr* is only a formal compliance with the religious prescription and does not dictate women's behaviour towards men. Generally, the ideal marriage is one arranged by parents to a first or second cousin, but not necessarily. In Malaysia, a woman needs a guardian or *wali* to give her away in marriage. In Indonesia, the husband is the head of the family who decides the place of the conjugal home. Indonesian men are allowed to marry up to four wives without the consent of the previous wife or wives. Indonesia's 1974 Marriage Act outlines the procedure of divorce through the court; allows for a polygynous marriage with the court's approval; states that both parties have a right to conduct legal actions; demands consent of the aspirant bride and groom; and provides a provision that overrules the right of a family member to force any side into marriage. Muslim groups have mounted a campaign to overturn a 1973 rule that civil servants cannot enter polygynous marriages, arguing that the regulation gave rise to extramarital affairs and unregistered marriages performed only by Muslim clerics (Asmarani 2000).

Among the Minangkabau, the woman's family usually proposes marriage and negotiates the terms with the family of a prospective groom. The husband provides a bed, chairs and other furnishings for the room he will share with his wife in her family's house (Dorgan 1998). Among the Malays, marriages are traditionally arranged by the parents according to Islamic law. However, while most marriages are probably no longer parentally arranged among the Javanese, parental approval remains an important factor. Young men often send intermediaries to gain the approval of a girl's guardian, who, following Islamic law, is usually her father or brother. Marriage is a protracted process of betrothal (negotiation, gift exchanges, formal announcement), setting the wedding date, holding the ceremony, paying the brideprice, and possibly carrying out post-wedding familial exchanges. Women are usually 15 to 18 and men between 17 and 20 when they marry, especially in rural areas, and a newly married couple is usually not expected to be economically or residentially independent. Newly wed Javanese couples frequently reside for several years with the bride's parents.

Unlike most patrilineally based Muslims, who may include payment of a brideprice as part of marital arrangements, the Minangkabau have a practice of giving a male dowry or groomprice before marriage. This divergence results from the fact that the Minangkabau have largely retained their pre-Muslim matrilineal customs, despite their general conversion to Islam. Among the Sasak, marriage is governed by *Adat*. Marriages between first, second or third cousins is preferred.

Within the Philippines, the Maguindanao customs of marriage are also Islamic. Marriages between persons of varying rank are common, with children assigned a rank intermediate between those of their parents. This lead to an integrated spectrum of rank rather than sharply defined social classes. Social rank is important for the determination of the amount of bridewealth to be exchanged at marriage. Marriage to one's second cousin is preferred. Depending on the social status, a man might have multiple wives, but polygyny is rarely practised among the lower-ranked people. Among the Tausug communities, marriages are ideally arranged by parents, in line with Islamic law. First and second cousins are favoured spouses since their parents are kinsmen and the problems of inheritance are simplified. The bridewealth must be given to the bride's family before the wedding is held, and the newly married couple first lives with the bride's family. Among the Yakan, marriage is usually initiated by the groom. He not only pays a brideprice, but must also pay all expenses connected with the wedding ceremony. The newly married couple initially live with either of their parents, then later build their own home on either the wife's or husband's land.

Divorce

Talaq is the most common form of divorce among Southeast Asia's Muslims. There are two other forms of divorce: *khula*, the purchase by the wife of her freedom; and *fasaq*, pronounced by the *qadi* or judge on grounds such as lunacy, impotence or disease. However, these two forms are rarely applied (Dube 1997: 121–31). Although the initiative in *talaq* formally lies with the husband, a woman may indicate to her husband that she does not want him to visit her any more and thus create a situation in which he has no options but to pronounce *talaq*. Divorces of this type are common on the islands and in Southeast Asia in general (Dube 1997: 121–31).

Historically it was difficult for an Indonesian wife to get a dissolution of marriage. However, the Marriage Act of 1974 does provide provisions under which a wife may seek judicial divorce, including conditions such as the other spouse's adultery or cruelty. While divorce is common, and usually based on incompatibility of the partners, adultery, or non-payment of a brideprice, its application varies within communities, with divorce being equally accessible for males and females in some communities, but still difficult for females in others.

In cases of divorce among the Malays and Javanese of Indonesia, each spouse retains personal property. Women whose husbands divorce them receive the whole amount of their dowry or 'marriage gold', usually in the form of jewellery. One researcher notes: 'It is common to see village women performing their household tasks adored with 22-carat gold earrings, bracelets, necklaces and rings set with gems. Women must be prepared to fend for themselves, due to the ease of a husband's obtaining a divorce' (Laderman 1996: 67). Communal property, which includes all that was acquired by the couple during their marriage, is divided equally between the husband and wife on a ratio of 2:1. This ratio is identified with Islamic law, whereas the principle of equal division is associated with the Malayan and Javanese tradition. Generally, divorce and remarriage do not carry a social stigma for women. Additionally, Malay cultural values discredit a man who holds his wife against her will (Dube 1997: 121–31). Some provisions are usually put into a marriage contract, the contravention of which automatically frees the woman from the marriage.

Within the Philippines, divorce among the Maguindanao occurs among those of all ranks, especially in cases of incompatibility, adultery, or non-payment of promised amounts of bridewealth. Divorce is also practised among the Tausug, with causes including divorce, barrenness, gambling, mistreatment of the children and non-support. Since, among the Yakan, a couple's home may be located on either the husband's or wife's land, in cases of divorce – which are not uncommon – the one on whose land the couple live will keep the house and the other spouse leaves. The right to initiate a divorce is equally available between Yakan men and women. Additionally, any property the wife brought into her marriage, as well as what she may have acquired during the marriage, remains her property upon divorce.

In matrilineal societies of Southeast Asia, women retain their right to the ownership of the house in cases of divorce or separation. In general, both sides keep ownership of the property that they brought to the marriage and share equally the common property.

Polygyny

Generally, polygyny is allowed but rarely practised in Southeast Asia, partly owing to the widespread requirement of obtaining a current wife's consent, and partly because few men have sufficient income to support two or more wives.

Polygyny was a custom in Indonesia before the arrival of Islam (as with other Southeast Asian communities), and may still occur with legal permission. Specifically, while polygyny is rare among Indonesia's Malayans, Javanese, and Minangkabau, it is common among the orthodox Muslims of the Sasak – although the Marriage Act had led to some decline in polygynous marriages within this community.

Within the Philippines, polygyny is most commonly practised among the Tausug. Among the Yakan, polygyny is also practised, but most men have only one wife. As under Indonesia's Marriage Law, Yakan men cannot marry a second or subsequent time without the consent of the first wife.

Children

Families that have no children or grandparents are often given children to raise by relatives who have an abundance of children. In the central Javanese principalities and in the Begelen region it is customary for a young couple to leave their firstborn child with its grandparents when they move away from the parental house. Childless couples commonly adopt a child, most usually a nephew or a niece from either side (Dube 1997: 104–5). Often little girls are preferred, because in the long run they are seen as more useful to the household than boys.

Among Javanese there is a small ceremonial act in which the foster parents make the biological parents a specific payment to avoid complications induced by supernatural agencies. There is no legality to such adoptions, and it should be noted that Islam forbids adoption. Although considered one's own, an adopted child is not entitled to inherit the *pusaka*, or ancestral family property (Dube 1997: 104–5).

Custody of Children

In Southeast Asia the mother–child relationship is given priority, often at the expense of the father's religious or legal rights. Children always remain close to their mothers, and in the event of divorce or separation children usually remain with their mothers. In matrilineal communities, marriage does not establish a man's rights over his children. For example, among bilateral Javanese and Malays, despite what the law says, children either follow their mother or, if they are old enough, decide for themselves where they wish to live. Fathers are generally seen as peripheral, a significant point of incongruity between actual practice and the injunctions of Islamic law.

Inheritance / Land Rights

In most parts of the region, *Adat* seems to take precedence over classical Shari'a in governing inheritance, with inheritance rights determined by a community's status as patrilineal, matrilineal or bilateral. In matrilineal and parental kinship systems women inherit either equally with men or receive a 2:1 share (according to the Qur'anic regulations or *Adat*), but in patrilineal systems women may not inherit at all or at least not in equal share. Suwarni Salyo (1985) highlights that the 1985 draft bill on inheritance rights outlines provisions for the equal division of inheritance among men and women. In Malaysia, *Adat* law requires an equal division of property between male and female children.

In Indonesia more often than not the house in the family goes to the child (usually the younger daughter) who will look after the parents, and a share of various kinds of property are given to both female and male children. The flexibility of the residence patterns (a newly-wed couple often move in with or near the bride's parents, and children often have a right to choose relatives that they would want to live with) does not produce static set ideas about rights to resources. The notion of common marital property is more widespread than the idea that one spouse has exclusive ownership (Dube 1997: 83–7).

Indonesian *Adat* tends to be more advantageous to women than Shari'a on the matter of inheritance. Its most important rule is inheritance of ancestral land from a mother to her daughters. In Kelantanese practice, the majority of the land transfers tended towards equal shares to men and women. In the Kelantan Plain the essential rules to be stated here are that land rights belong to individuals and that children inherit from their mother and father separately. The understanding of local *Adat* is to the effect that brothers and sisters should get equal shares (Utas 1983: 132–3).

Malay women have a variable, though always sizeable, share in land rights. The variation spans from the matrilineal option of Negri Sembilan, to families who follow the letter of Islamic law. The core rule of double inheritance for men is only given a theological explanation: 'The Lord has ordered it to be so.' The divine commandment does not contain any statements that men are stronger or more important persons. Frequent resort to *Adat* inheritance practices creates an expectation on the wife in most marriages to provide roughly half of the new family's land resources and usually also an equal contribution as far as work is concerned: 'It is because women have fewer possibilities for earning money than men have' (Utas 1983: 134).

Negri Sembilan communities are also known for their particularly complex political history, in which Minangkabau traditions are intertwined with the Muslim and colonial structures. It should be noted that the matrilineal traditions are supported by a codified customary law (Utas 1983: 130). Although Islam is the accepted faith in Malaysia, among the people of Negri Sembilan and Malacca – who follow *Adat perpateh* (which essentially applies to matrilineal communities) rather than *Adat Temenggong* (which essentially applies to bilateral communities) – local custom rather than Muslim law is effective in inheritance, the custody of children, and the division of property following divorce.

In other regions Islam has considerable influence, but *Adat* moderates its strict interpretation. For example, a woman who has worked land is entitled to half of it whereas one who has not worked is entitled only to one-third (Dube 1997: 154).

Among the Batak of Indonesia, emphasis is on patrilineal clans and patrilineal inheritance coincides with the patrilineal stress of Islamic family law. In Minangkabau, by contrast, tradition was based on matrilineal clans and on passing property from a man to his sister's son. Among the Malay, in *Adat* or customary law, brothers and sisters have equal shares in inheritance.

In contrast, however, the Minangkabau combine their matrilineal customs with the patrilineal-based Islam, resulting in inheritance structures in which the right to use ancestral property, such as wet rice land or a longhouse, is inherited through females, while individual property, such as a vehicle, may be inherited through males in accordance with Qur'anic rules of inheritance. In his wife's home a man holds no property, and at best exercises only supervisory control over the affairs of his wife's property. In his own natal home, a husband inherits property through his mother. Males do not directly inherit rights to ancestral property and cannot pass to heirs that which they do not possess. However, what they possess through individual effort can be passed to heirs according to the Islamic rules of inheritance. Despite their matrilineal orientation, however, Minangkabau royal ties are inherited through males. Similar to the Minangkabau, the Cham (located in the Malay Peninsula, Indonesia, the Philippines and elsewhere) are primarily matrilineal, with property inherited through women.

Despite Islamic and national law, Sasak *Adat* prohibits women from owning or inheriting land. But, within their orthodox Muslim communities, inheritance rights are governed and practised according to Islamic law, while some villages allow females to inherit one out of every three shares of land. Within the Philippines, the Maguindanao are characterized by a bilateral kinship system, therefore in a majority of cases males and females inherit equally. This is also the custom among the Yakan, with sons and daughters inheriting equally from both parents.

References

Asmarani, D. (2000) 'Aisyah ponders new gender awareness in Islam', *Jakarta Post*, 23 April.
Dorgan, M. (1998) 'Sumatran women hold land, wield power', *Knight-Ridder Newspapers*, 15 February.

Dube, L. (1997) *Women and Kinship: Comparative Perspectives on Gender in South and Southeast Asia*, Tokyo and New York: UN University Publications.

Fawzi El-Solh, C. and J. Mabro (eds) (1994) *Muslim Women's Choices: Religious Belief and Social Reality*, Providence, RI: Berg.

Hefner, R. M. and P. Horvatich (eds) (1997) *Islam in an Era of Nation States*, Honolulu, Hawaii: University of Hawai'i Press.

Hosken, F. P. (1982) *The Hosken Report: Genital and Sexual Mutilation of Females*, 3rd rev. edn, Lexington, MA: Women's International Network News.

Jawad, H. (1998) *The Rights of Women in Islam: An Authentic Approach*, New York: St Martin's Press.

Laderman, C. C. (1996) 'Putting Malay women in their place', in P. van Esterik (ed.), *Women of Southeast Asia*, Monograph Series on Southeast Asia, Occasional Paper No. 17, Northern Illinois University, Center for Southeast Asian Studies, pp. 62–77.

Lapidus, I. M. (1990) *A History of Islamic Societies*, Cambridge: Cambridge University Press.

Mallat, C. and J. Connors (eds) (1990) *Islamic Family Law*, London: Graham and Trotman.

Noor, F. A. (1999) 'Islam vs. secularism? The new political terrain in Malaysia and Indonesia', *ISIM Newsletter*, 4, December.

Othman, M. (1996) 'Syariah court comes under fire', *New Straits Times*, 16 December.

Roy, A. (1996) *Islam in South Asia: A Regional Perspective*, New Delhi: South Asian Publishers.

Rudie, I. (1983) 'Women in Malaysia: economic autonomy, ritual segregation and some future possibilities', in B. Utas (ed.), *Women in Islamic Societies: Social Attitudes and Historical Perspectives*, Atlantic Highlands, NJ: Humanities Press, pp. 128–43.

Suwarni Salyo (1985) *Mizan Journal*, 5, 2: 15–21.

Utas, B. (ed.) (1983) *Women in Islamic Societies: Social Attitudes and Historical Perspectives*, Atlantic Highlands, NJ: Humanities Press.

2 Legal Profiles

BRUNEI (Negara Brunei Darussalam)

Legal history For Muslim Bruneians, Islamic law is particularly influential in the area of family law. Sources of law are legislation (imperial statutes, common law, equity, and so on), Islamic law (Shafi'i views, or opinions of other three Sunni schools with the Sultan's approval), ancient custom and Malay custom.

During the fifteenth and sixteenth centuries, the Brunei Sultanate controlled the northwestern coast of Borneo and parts of Kalimantan and the Philippines. European expansion from the sixteenth century led to the loss of Brunei's possessions to the Spanish and Dutch. In the nineteenth century, the Sultan of Brunei sought British aid in defending his coasts from piracy. The British explorer James Brooke was made Rajah of Sarawak in 1839 and the British annexed the island of Labuan in 1846. The Sultan accepted protectorate status under Britain by the late nineteenth century, formalized in 1906 by a treaty providing that the Sultan would seek the advice of the British Resident on all matters outside of local custom and religion. The Constitution was adopted in 1959 allowing for internal self-rule and establishing a Legislative Council, with the powers of the British Resident transferred to the Sultan and his appointed officials. A 1971 agreement ended Brunei's protectorate status, with Britain retaining control over defence and foreign relations. Brunei gained full independence in 1984.

The Mohammedan Laws Enactment 1912 promulgated under British rule was based on both custom and Islamic law. The Enactment covered limited aspects of family and criminal law and delineated the jurisdiction of *Qadis'* Courts. It was followed by the Mohammedan Marriage and Divorce Enactment 1913 providing for registration through *qadis*. Both Acts were repealed by the 1955 Religious Councils, *Qadis'* Courts and State Customs Act. Section VI of the Act contains provisions on marriage and divorce applicable to marriages where both parties are Muslim and that were solemnized according to Muslim law. The Act also regulates the judicial application of Islamic family law, provides penalties for breach of its terms, and so on.

Schools of *fiqh* The majority of the population are Shafi'i Muslims. There are also Buddhist and Christian minorities, as well as segments of the population adhering to indigenous religions.

Constitutional status of Islam(ic law) The Constitution was promulgated on 29 September 1959 (with some provisions suspended under the State of Emergency since December 1962 and others since independence on 1 January 1984). Article 3 declares Islam the state religion, 'according to the Shafi'i sect'. Article 3 also provides that 'the Head of the religion of Brunei Darussalam shall be His Majesty the Sultan and *Yang Di-Pertuan* (Head of State)'.

Court system Brunei maintains separate Shari'a and regular court systems, with the former having jurisdiction over Muslim personal status. Shari'a courts decide personal status cases or cases relating to religious offences following Shafi'i opinion, then legislation by the Religious Council (*Majlis*) under the terms of the 1955 Religious Council, State Customs and *Qadis'* Courts Enactment. The Council may have recourse to non-*rajih* Shafi'i interpretations or positions from other schools of *fiqh* if required by *maslaha* and approved by the Sultan.

Notable features The minimum marriage age is not specified, but the legislation does provide that validity of marriage requires meeting all the conditions of validity according to the sect to which the parties belong. The *wali*'s consent is also a requirement for validity of marriage. A marriage is void if both parties have not given consent. Marriage registration is obligatory, through *qadis* authorized as registrars, or solemnized by a *qadi* in the presence of a registrar. Polygyny is governed by classical law. Obedience and maintenance are governed by classical law, and a wife deemed to be *nashiza* is also liable to penal sanctions. In case of the husband's failure to maintain, the wife may apply to a *qadi* for a maintenance order, but sums and the time period for which the wife may claim arrears are not specified.

The legislation specifies that the husband may divorce his wife with one, two or three *talaqs* in accordance with Muslim law. The divorcing husband must report the divorce to the registrar within seven days. A woman may obtain a judicial dissolution according to Muslim law by applying to the *qadi*, who will summon the husband. If the husband consents, the divorce is registered. If the husband refuses, the *qadi* may propose *cherai tebus talak* (*khul'*), with the court assessing the sum payable by the wife to the husband according to the status and means of the parties. If the husband does not agree to granting a *khul'* the *qadi* will appoint two arbitrators who may be given the authority to decree a divorce if parties agree to such a settlement. The wife may also be issued a certificate of presumption of death if her husband is believed to have died or has not been heard from for an extended period of time. A woman divorced by her husband may apply to the *qadi* for *mattah* (*muta' al-talaq/* consolatory gift) or maintenance (of a sum and for such period as the court sees fit). Child custody and guardianship is governed by classical law.

Succession is governed by classical law.

Law/case reporting system Case reporting is through the *Law Reports of Brunei*, continued in *Judgments of the Courts of Brunei Darussalam* from 1986.

International conventions (with relevant reservations) Brunei acceded to the CRC in 1995, submitting that Brunei 'expresses its reservations on the provisions ... which may be contrary to (Brunei's) Constitution and to the beliefs and principles of Islam, the State religion, and without prejudice to the generality of the said reservations, in particular expresses its reservations on Articles 14, 20 and 21'. (Article 14 relates to the child's freedom of religion and conscience and Articles 20 and 21 relate to adoption.)

Background and sources
Hooker, M. B. (1984) *Islamic Law in South-East Asia*, Singapore: Oxford University Press.
Ibrahim, A. (1965) *The Status of Muslim Women in Family Law in Malaysia, Singapore and Brunei*, Singapore: Malayan Law Journal.
Mahmood, T. (1995) 'Brunei', in *Statutes of Personal Law in Islamic Countries: History, Texts and Analysis*, 2nd edn, New Delhi: India and Islam Research Council, pp. 58–61.
Redden, K. R. (1990) 'Brunei', in K. R. Redden (ed.), *Modern Legal Systems Cyclopedia*, Vol. 9, Buffalo, NY: Hein.

INDONESIA, Republic of

Legal history The Indonesian legal system is based on Roman-Dutch law, modified by custom and Islamic law. Sources of law are Islamic law, statutory legislation, presidential instructions and official compilations of Islamic law.

European explorers arrived in the region in the sixteenth century, and the Dutch East India Company was founded in 1602. The Dutch established a trading post on the north coast of Java, later named Jakarta. The Dutch gradually asserted political and military control beyond Java from the eighteenth century until most of the archipelago was under Dutch rule by the start of the twentieth century.

Under Dutch rule, the Netherlands Indies' population was divided into Europeans, Natives and Foreign Orientals. The Dutch established separate tribunals for Europeans and 'Natives'. Indonesians were subject to *Adat* law, with the Netherlands East Indies divided into several jurisdictions based on cultural and linguistic criteria. Dutch scholars identified and classified nineteen different systems of customary law in the region. In areas under direct rule, there were European courts, native courts and general courts for all of the population. In areas under indirect rule, there were native courts applying *Adat* with very limited criminal jurisdiction and no jurisdiction over Europeans or foreigners. The basic principle was dominance of the received civil law system, and application of *Adat* for 'Natives' as far as it was not replaced by statute. The first legislation relating to the application of Islamic law was an 1882 Royal Decree establishing a 'Priest Court' for Java and Madura, although the decree acknowledged that most Indonesians were also subject to *Adat* law administered by native courts. The 'Priest Court' had jurisdiction over Muslim family and inheritance law where all parties were Muslim and *awqaf*, and had concurrent jurisdiction with the native courts of Java and Madura. The Priest Court was composed of a president selected from the native courts' officers and three to eight *qadis*, all appointed by the governor-general. Subsequent legislation by Dutch authorities was also of a largely regulatory and administrative nature. Independence was declared two days after Japanese occupying forces withdrew in 1945. Calls for the reform of marriage laws led to various proposals from members of government, women's groups and the National Institute for Law Reform from 1945 to 1973, but conflicting interests prevented any consensus being reached. The only statutory reform of Muslim personal status in that period was the enactment of the Muslim Marriage and Divorce Registration Law 1946 requiring registration. A new Marriage Law, the first that was applicable to all Indonesians, was eventually passed in 1974 amid much controversy, particularly with regard to such issues as permission for divorce and polygyny. Some compromises made by the government included increasing the jurisdiction of Shari'a courts and eliminating registration as a requirement for validity of marriage. The Marriage Law is applied by the regular court system for religious minorities and by Shari'a courts for Muslim Indonesians.

Following the controversy over the Marriage Law, since the mid-1980s Compilations of Islamic Law in Indonesia (*Kompilasi Hukum Islam di Indonesia*) authored by officials from the Ministry of Religion and Supreme Court judges have been used to clarify points on personal law and inheritance for application by Shari'a courts. They are based on arguments from various schools, comparisons of application of Islamic law in different countries, decisions from religious courts, and so on. The Compilations are presented as Presidential Instructions (*Inpres*), which have lower status than statutes in the Indonesian legal system. A 1991 Compilation of Islamic Law directed the restriction of *hiba* (gifts) to a maximum of one-third of the donor's estate. While this represents a reassertion of classical interpretations, the Compilations also draw from eclectic sources, and Supreme Court judgments on appeal from the religious appellate courts diverge from classical law in many matters.

Schools of *fiqh* The majority of the population is Shafi'i Muslim. There are also Ahmadi minorities. The other recognized religious minorities are Roman Catholic, Protestant, Hindu and Buddhist. There are also significant minorities following tribal religions, but they are not afforded any official recognition.

Constitutional status of Islam(ic law) The Constitution was promulgated in August 1945. It does not adopt any official religion, but Article 29(1) provides that 'the State is based upon the belief in the One, Supreme God', also embodied in the Pancasila. Article 29(2) guarantees freedom of religion.

Court system There are four judicial branches outlined in the Basic Law on Judicial Power 1970: general, religious, military and administrative courts. General courts include District Courts of First Instance, High Courts of Appeal, and the Supreme Court (*Mahkamah Agung*). Religious courts (*Pengadilan Agama*) are established side by side with District Courts. Religious courts are organized at two levels: courts of first instance in each district and appellate courts in all provinces (approximately 300 and 25, respectively; figures as of the mid-1990s) and have jurisdiction over civil cases between Muslim spouses on matters concerning marriage, divorce, reconciliation and alimony. Appeals from the religious appeals court (*Mahkamah Islam Tinggi*) go to the Supreme Court, although the supervisory jurisdiction of regular courts over religious courts ended with the passing of the Law on Religious Courts 1989. Religious courts have limited or special jurisdiction and secular courts have general jurisdiction. The competence of religious courts is not exclusive, and parties can apply to District Courts for adjudication on the basis of Dutch-derived civil law or local *Adat*.

Notable features The minimum marriage age is 19 for males and 16 for females, with provision for marriage below the minimum age, subject to judicial discretion and parental consent. The free consent of marrying parties is a requirement for the validity of a marriage, unless the religious law governing the parties directs otherwise. The Marriage Law 1974 defines as legal a marriage 'solemnized according to the laws of the respective religions and beliefs of each of the parties'. Parties under 21 years require parental permission to marry; this refers to the consent of both parents, the surviving parent or the guardian. Marriage registration is obligatory; the Marriage Registrar Office of the Department of Religious Affairs is responsible for the registration of Muslim marriages and the Civil Marriage Registrar Office of the Department of Internal Affairs for all other marriages. The basis of marriage is considered monogamy, but the Marriage Law does not prohibit polygyny for those religions that allow it (Islam, Hinduism, Buddhism). Polygyny is permissible with the consent of the existing wife or wives and with judicial permission, by fulfilling conditions specified by law: proof of financial capacity, safeguards that husband will treat wives and children equally; and a court inquiry into the validity of the reasons for wishing to contract a polygynous marriage (for instance, the existing wife's physical disfigurement, infertility, incurable disease). The law specifies that both spouses are equal and both are responsible for maintaining the home and caring for children. The permanent domicile is to be decided by both parties. The husband, as the head of the family, is required to protect the wife and provide for her according to his means and the wife's duty is to manage the household.

The Marriage Law provides that divorce shall be carried out only before a court of law, after the court has endeavoured to reconcile the parties. A husband married under Islamic law may submit a letter notifying the religious court of his intention to divorce and giving his reasons. If the husband's reasons accord with any of the six grounds for judicial divorce outlined in the Marriage Law and the court determines that reconciliation is not possible, the court will grant a session in order to witness the divorce. Either spouse may seek a judicial divorce (preceded by reconciliation efforts by the judge) on the following grounds: the other spouse's adultery; alcoholism, addiction to narcotics, gambling or 'any other vice that is difficult to cure'; abandonment for two years without valid reason; cruelty or mistreatment endangering life; physical disfigurement or malady preventing performance of marital duties; constant disputes without hope of resolution; and sentencing to a prison term of five years or more. Property acquired during marriage is considered joint property, although the Marriage Law directs only that division is according to the law applicable to the parties. The court may order alimony for children or maintenance for the former wife. In terms of custody, the Marriage Law simply provides that in case of dispute over custody, the court shall render its judgment; the father shall have responsibility for maintenance expenses, unless he is unable to bear such responsibility, in which case the court may order the mother to share such expenses.

Succession is governed by classical law. Some commentators have also noted that the Indonesian Supreme Court has often sought to equalize the rights of male and female inheritors.

Law/case reporting system   There is no regular system of case reporting in Indonesia.

International conventions (with relevant reservations)   Indonesia signed the CEDAW in 1980 and ratified it in 1984, with a declaration regarding Article 29(1). Indonesia signed and ratified the CRC in 1990, submitting a general reservation to the effect that Articles 1, 14, 16, 17, 21, 22 and 29 are to be applied in conformity with the Constitution of Indonesia. (The articles indicated relate to majority, children's freedom of religion and conscience, right to privacy, and right to access to information, adoption, and the direction of children's education.)

Background and sources

Bowen, J. R. (1998) '"You may not give it away": how social norms shape Islamic law in contemporary Indonesian jurisprudence', *Islamic Law and Society*, 5, 3: 382–408.

Hooker, M. B. (1978) *A Concise Legal History of South-East Asia*, Oxford: Clarendon Press.

— (1984) *Islamic Law in South-East Asia*, Singapore: Oxford University Press.

Indonesia (1997) *2nd & 3rd Period Report to CEDAW*, 12 February.

Katz, J. S. and R. S. Katz (1975) 'The new Indonesian marriage law: a mirror of Indonesia's political, cultural and legal systems', *American Journal of Comparative Law*, 23: 653–81.

— (1978) 'Legislating social change in a developing country: the new Indonesian marriage law revisited', *American Journal of Comparative Law*, 26: 309–20.

Mahmood, T. (1995) 'Indonesia', in *Statutes of Personal Law in Islamic Countries: History, Texts and Analysis*, 2nd edn, New Delhi: India and Islam Research Council, pp. 61–5, 189–93.

Pompe, S. (1998) 'Islamic law in Indonesia', *Yearbook of Islamic and Middle Eastern Law*, Vol. 4, pp. 180–200.

Redden, K. R. (1990) 'Indonesia', in K. R. Redden (ed.), *Modern Legal Systems Cyclopedia*, Vol. 2, Buffalo, NY: Hein.

Supriadi, W. C. (1995) 'Indonesian marriage law', in A. Bainham (ed.), *The International Survey of Family Law*, pp. 279–85.

MALAYSIA

Legal history The legal system is based on English common law, with both Islamic law and *Adat* constituting significant sources of law, particularly in matters of personal status.

Parts of present-day Malaysia were under Portuguese and Dutch control, and starting from Penang in the late eighteenth century, the region eventually came under British rule, formalized by the Anglo-Dutch Treaty 1824. Malaysia and Singapore were the eventual successor states to the Straits Settlements (Penang, Singapore, Malacca), Federated Malay States (Selangor, Perak, Pahang and Negri Sembilan) and Unfederated Malay States (Perlis, Kedah, Kelantan, Trengganu and Johor). Sabah and Sarawak, formerly constituents of British Borneo, later joined Malaysia.

Under British rule, the first legislation regulating Islamic marriage in the Straits Settlements was the Mohammedan Marriage Ordinance 1880, mainly procedural in content. The Ordinance was amended in 1908 to make registration of marriage and divorce compulsory, non-compliance being punishable by fine or imprisonment. A 1923 amendment directed the application of Islamic law to intestate succession of Muslims in so far as local custom would permit, and without disinheriting non-Muslim kin. The Ordinance continued to be applied in Penang and Malacca until State Acts were passed in 1959. The first codification of Malay customary law (a mixture of *Adat* and Islamic law) came in 1915 with the enactment of the Laws of the Malay Courts 1915 in Sarawak.

The region was occupied by Japanese forces from 1942 to 1945, with control reverting to the British after World War II. A legislative assembly was established in 1955 and independence achieved in 1957. From 1948, the states were granted jurisdiction over the application and legislation of Shari'a, and from 1952 to 1978, new laws were promulgated in the eleven Muslim-majority states of Malaysia and Sabah, generally entitled Administration of Islamic/Muslim Law Enactments and covering the official determination of Islamic law, explanation of substantive law, and jurisdiction of *Syariah* courts. New laws relating to personal law were enacted in most states between 1983 and 1987.

Efforts by Kelantan State to pass a *Syariah* Criminal Code Enactment 1993 relating to the application of *hadd* penalties resulted in a stand-off between the federal and state governments. It was passed by the state legislature but never brought into force. It was a matter of much controversy as criminal matters are within federal and not state legislatures' jurisdiction.

Schools of *fiqh* The majority of Muslims are Shafi'i, with Hanafi minorities. There are also significant Buddhist, Hindu and Christian minorities and a high proportion of followers of indigenous religions, particularly in Sabah and Sarawak (both states are Muslim-minority).

Constitutional status of Islam(ic law) The Constitution was adopted on 31 August 1957 and has been amended several times. Article 3(1) declares Islam the official state religion and guarantees religious freedom. Articles 3(3) and (5) provide that the ruler of each state is the head of the religion of Islam by the constitution of that state. In the absence of a Muslim ruler (in the states of Malacca, Penang, Sabah and Sarawak) or in the Federal Territories (Kuala Lumpur and Labuan), *Yang di-Pertuan Agong* (head of state) is declared the head of the religion of Islam.

The Ninth Schedule of the Constitution outlines the legislative lists. Malaysia is a federation of 13 states with both state- and federal-level executive and legislative powers; civil law (and family law as a subset of civil law) come under the federal legislature's jurisdiction, but persons of the Malay race are defined as Muslims under the Constitution and the states are empowered to make personal laws governing Muslims and laws relating to religious offences, and to establish and regulate *Syariah* courts for the application of Islamic law. Personal status law relating to non-Muslims is within the federal legislature's jurisdiction – governed by the Malaysian Law Reform (Marriage and Divorce) Act 1976 that repealed all previous statutes on marriage and divorce governing non-Muslims. Clarification of points of Islamic law comes under the jurisdiction of each state's *Majlis* (Council of Religion and Malay Custom). The *Majlis* generally issue *fatawa* that are in keeping with Shafi'i tenets except where such may conflict with public interest. In such instances, the Councils (with the approval of state authorities) may follow minority Shafi'i views or interpretations from other three major Sunni *madhahib*.

Court system There are three levels of *Syariah* courts in a system parallel to and independent of the civil courts: *Syariah* Subordinate Courts, *Syariah* High Court and *Syariah* Appeal Court.

Syariah Subordinate Courts have jurisdiction as indicated by state legislation over criminal suits liable to punishment up to 2,000 ringgit and/or imprisonment up to two years and civil suits in which the value of the subject in dispute is up to 100,000 ringgit or not estimable in cash.

The *Syariah* High Court has appellate jurisdiction over Subordinate Court decisions in civil suits of 500 ringgit or more and criminal suits. The *Syariah*

High Court has original jurisdiction as indicated by state legislation in criminal suits and civil jurisdiction over betrothal and marriage, divorce, nullification or separation, marital property claims, maintenance of dependants, legitimacy, guardianship and custody, testate and intestate succession, gifts *inter vivos* and *awqaf*, in cases where all the parties are Muslims.

The *Syariah* Appeal Court has appellate jurisdiction over decisions arising out of the *Syariah* High Court's original jurisdiction; all appeals are heard by the Chief *Syarie* Judge and two other members and decisions are by majority opinion.

In September 2000, the government announced that it would establish a separate family court.

Notable features The minimum marriage age is 18 for males and 16 for females, with provision for judicial permission for under-age marriages. A valid marriage requires both parties' consent as well as the consent of the *wali* or *Syariah* judge if no *wali* is available; compulsion of wards or unreasonable objection to their valid marriage is punishable by fine and/or imprisonment.

Marriage registration is obligatory; both parties must apply to the registrar for permission to marry at least seven days before the wedding. Marriage is not to be solemnized except in the *kariah masjid* of the woman's normal residence or by special permission to marry elsewhere. The registrar is required to record the value and contents of items of dower given and promised at the solemnization of marriage. There is a provision for the appointment of registrars in public offices as well as in *kariah masjid*. Non-registration is punishable by fine and/or imprisonment, although it does not determine the validity of marriage.

Polygyny is allowed with judicial permission, contingent upon application to the court and a hearing with existing wife or wives. The court requires proof of necessity (for instance, first wife's sterility, physical infirmity, wilful avoidance of restitution order); proof of financial capacity; guarantee of equitable treatment of co-wives; and proof that the proposed marriage will not lower the standard of life of the existing wife or wives and other dependants. Contravention of the application procedure and permission requirements is punishable by requiring immediate payment of any outstanding dower to the existing wife or wives and by fine and/or imprisonment.

The wife's right to maintenance is subject to classical definitions of obedience. The wife may obtain a maintenance order from the court in cases where her husband fails to provide maintenance; the levels and period for which the wife might sue for arrears are not specified. The wife's disobedience can result in a restitution order or punishment or fine.

Extra-judicial repudiation is punishable by fine and/or imprisonment. A husband wishing to pronounce *talaq* is required to apply for judicial permission, outlining his reasons as well as the amounts of payments of *nafkah edah* ('*idda* period maintenance), *mutaah* (consolatory gift) and *maskahwin* (dower) he intends to make and provisions for the division of *harta sepencarian* (matrimonial property). If a court hearing determines the consent of the other party and the irretrievability of the breakdown, the court advises the husband's pronouncement of a single *talaq* and registers the divorce. If the other party disagrees or the court is not convinced of irretrievable breakdown, the court begins reconciliation efforts. The conciliation committee has up to six months to effect a reconciliation; if the committee fails to do so, it issues a certificate of its failure, including any recommendations regarding custody, maintenance, division of property, and so on. (The Act only provides penalties for extra-judicial repudiations and does not refer to their validity; courts tend to adjudicate on the validity of a *talaq* pronounced outside of court on the basis of classical law.)

The wife may apply for judicial dissolution on the following grounds: the husband's disappearance for over one year; failure to maintain for three months; sentencing to three years or more in prison; failure to perform marital obligations for one year; continued impotence, if the wife was unaware of it upon marriage; mental illness lasting two years, leprosy or communicable venereal disease; the wife's repudiation of a marriage concluded by her father or grandfather before she attained 16, if she is below 18 years and the marriage was not consummated; cruel treatment; husband's refusal to consummate for four months; invalidity of her consent (obtained under duress, mistaken, and so on); and any other grounds for dissolution or nullification recognized in *hukm shar'*. A wife divorced without just cause may apply for maintenance during her *'idda* and *mut'a*, levels of which are to be set by the court.

The court also divides assets acquired by joint effort during marriage, and may also order the division of assets acquired by sole efforts, with consideration of the contribution made by the other party in terms of housework and caring for the family, although the other party will in all cases receive the smaller portion. The divorced wife is also entitled to reside in the marital home during the *'idda* or until the expiry of her custody or her remarriage, if the former husband cannot provide other suitable accommodation.

The divorced mother is entitled to custody over boys until seven years and girls until nine years, subject to classical conditions. The court may extend custody to nine and eleven years respectively upon the *hadinah*'s application. After the expiry of the *hadinah*'s custody, the father becomes custodian, with the proviso that wards having reached the age of discernment may choose with which parent to live, unless the court directs otherwise.

Succession is governed by classical law as modified by Malay custom. This is particularly important in rural areas and with reference to the inheritance of land, as all Malay *Adat* have specific rules on inheritance of land and such rules are often inconsistent with Islamic law. For example, inheritance in Malaccan *Adat* is matrilineal.

Law/case reporting system Case reporting of Federal Court and High Court decisions is through the *Malayan Law Journal*. Law reporting is through the Federal and State *Official Gazettes*. Some *Syariah* Court judgments are included in some issues of the *Syariah Law Journal* of the International Islamic University of Malaysia.

International conventions (with relevant reservations) Malaysia acceded to the CEDAW in 1995 with a number of reservations relating to discriminatory aspects of customary and personal status laws and discrimination to appointments in public office (particularly relating to the offices of *mufti* or *qadi*). These reservations were withdrawn in 1998. The reservation to Article 11 on the elimination of discrimination against women in employment still stands, stating that 'Malaysia interprets the provisions of this article as a reference to the prohibition of discrimination on the basis of equality between men and women only'.

Malaysia acceded to the CRC in 1995, with a general reservation to Articles 1, 2, 7, 13, 14, 15, 22, 28, 37, 40(3) and (4), 44 and 45, declaring that 'said provisions shall be applicable only if they are in conformity with the Constitution, national laws and national policies of the Government of Malaysia'. (The articles mentioned relate to majority, measures to eliminate discrimination against children, birth registration and nationality rights, children's freedom of expression, religion, and association, adoption, right to education, children's rights and liberties in criminal law, the system of reporting to the CRC and cooperation with UNICEF.)

Background and sources
Hooker, M. B. (1984) *Islamic Law in South-East Asia*, Singapore: Oxford University Press.

Ibrahim, A. (1978) *Family Law in Malaysia and Singapore*, Singapore: Malayan Law Journal.

Kamali, M. H. (1998) 'Islamic law in Malaysia: issues and developments', *Yearbook of Islamic and Middle Eastern Law*, vol. 4, pp. 158–79.

Mahmood, T. (1995) 'Malaysia', in *Statutes of Personal Law in Islamic Countries: History, Texts and Analysis*, 2nd edn, New Delhi: India and Islam Research Council, pp. 69–73, 194–204.

Redden, K. R. (1990) 'Malaysia' in K. R. Redden (ed.), *Modern Legal Systems Cyclopedia*, Vol. 9, Buffalo, NY: Hein.

Selangor (1992) *Selangor Administration of Islamic Law Enactment 1989 and Islamic Family Law Enactment 1984 (as at 15th September 1991)*, comp. Legal Research Board, Kuala Lumpur.

Siraj, M. (1994) 'Women and the law: significant developments in Malaysia', *Law and Society Review*, 28, 3: 561–81.

PHILIPPINES, Republic of the

Legal history The term 'Moros' (Filipino Muslims) is a label given by the Spanish in the sixteenth century to 13 ethno-linguistic groups, mainly concentrated in the southwestern Philippines. Under Spanish rule, colonial authority was not extended to the Moro areas due to considerable resistance on the part of the local population. Spain lost the Philippines to the USA, which ruled the area from 1899 to 1946. The US military rulers initially obtained the acknowledgement of the Sultan of Sulu in the Bates Agreement, preserving the Sultan's jurisdiction over Moros.

US policy eventually changed, limiting the powers of traditional authorities and encouraging Christian Filipino settlement in Muslim areas. The 1914 Organic Act for the Department of Mindanao and Sulu extended state laws to the area, within certain limits, and redrew existing boundaries to establish provinces and municipalities. The Philippine Commission Act 1915 allowed for assessors such as *kalis*, *panditas*, or Muslims well-versed in local laws and customs, to sit with Moroland Courts, and permitted the modification of US law in cases where the parties were Muslims. The principle of exemption continued, but over time came to be limited to the area of family law.

After independence, a separatist movement emerged among students and intellectuals in the late 1960s, gaining popular support after the eruption of communal violence in Cotabato in 1970. The movement developed into an armed struggle for secession after President Ferdinand Marcos declared martial law in 1972. The conflict continued into the mid-1970s, with a ceasefire declared and Libyan-brokered peace talks held in 1976. The settlement offered to the separatists included a Muslim Autonomous Region in 13 provinces, but negotiations broke down. Marcos began implementing parts of the 'Tripoli Agreement' unilaterally, including passing a Code of Muslim Personal Laws in 1977.

A new round of talks began under President Corazon Aquino in 1986. After much debate, an Organic Act was passed in 1989 allowing for the

creation of an autonomous region in Muslim Mindanao, followed by a pleb-
iscite in which four provinces (Lanao del Sur, Maguindanao, Sulu and Tawi-
Tawi) opted for inclusion in the Autonomous Region for Muslim Mindanao
(ARMM). A final Peace Accord was signed between the government and the
Moro National Liberation Front in September 1996.

Schools of *fiqh* Muslims of the Philippines are almost all Shafi'i. The
majority of the population is Roman Catholic, and there are Protestant and
Buddhist minorities.

Constitutional status of Islam(ic law) The current Constitution was
adopted on 15 October 1986. Article II, section 6 states that 'the separation of
Church and State shall be inviolable'. Article III, section 5 guarantees the
free exercise of religion and states that there shall be no religious test for
exercising civil and political rights. Article X relates to local government and
section 1 thereof states that 'there shall be autonomous regions in Muslim
Mindanao and the Cordilleras as hereinafter provided', to which sections 15
to 21 relate. Under section 20, personal, family and property relations are
subject to the legislative power of each autonomous region.

Court System Shari'a courts are organized at two levels. The Shari'a Circuit
Courts in five Shari'a judicial districts have exclusive original jurisdiction over:
cases relating to offences defined in the (Muslim) Family Code and civil actions
between Muslims married under the terms of Family Code (relating to marriage, divorce, betrothal, dower, division of property upon divorce, maintenance
and consolatory gifts, restitution of marital rights and disputes over communal
property).

The five Shari'a District Courts, each presided over by one judge, have
exclusive original jurisdiction over: custody, guardianship, legitimacy, paternity
and filiation cases arising under the Family Code; the disposition, distribution
and settlement of estates or wills of Muslims and the appointment of ex-
ecutors; petitions for declaration of death or absence or correction of entries
in Muslim civil status registers; and actions arising from customary contracts
between Muslims. The District Courts also have appellate jurisdiction over
Shari'a Circuit Court decisions. Decisions of Shari'a District Courts are final.

An Office of Jurisconsult in Islamic Law is constituted under the supervision
of the Supreme Court. The Jurisconsult's Office shall, upon the written request
of any party on any question concerning Muslim Law, issue legal opinions
based on recognized authorities, and shall compile and publish all legal opinions
issued.

Notable features The minimum marriage age is 15 years for males and puberty for females (a female is presumed to have attained puberty at 15 years). The Shari'a District Court may authorize the marriage of a female between twelve and 15 years if she has attained puberty, upon petition of her *wali*. The marriage of minors is defined as betrothal and may be annulled by either party within four years of attaining puberty if the marriage was not voluntarily consummated and neither the father nor paternal grandfather served as *wali*. There is a penalty of imprisonment or fines or both for illegal solemnization of marriage. Validity of marriage requires the free consent of marrying parties and the presence and consent of the *wali*.

Marriage registration is obligatory, backed up by penal sanctions of fines for failure to register any change in civil status. The Family Code states that no Muslim man may take more than one wife 'unless he can deal with them with equal companionship and just treatment as enjoined by Islamic law and only in exceptional cases'. The grounds for determination of exceptional cases are not specified.

The husband's rights and obligations in marriage relate to fixing the residence of the family (subject to classical conditions) and providing maintenance. The wife may not work without her husband's consent, but may take the matter to an arbitration council in case her husband withholds his consent.

Divorce may be effected by *talaq, ila, zihar, li'an, khuli', tafwid* or *faskh*, according to the Family Code. Divorce by *talaq* must be effected by the husband in a single repudiation during the wife's *tuhr*. Any *talaq* to which a number is attached counts only as a single revocable repudiation until the expiry of the *'idda*. A woman may seek a judicial divorce on the following grounds: in cases of the husband's oath of abstinence (*ila*), *zihar* (likening of his wife to his relations within the prohibited degrees), *li'an* (imprecation of adultery); or a decree of *faskh* on the following grounds: husband's failure to maintain her for six months; husband's conviction to one year's imprisonment; husband's impotence or abstention from conjugal relations for six months; husband's insanity or affliction with an incurable disease injurious to his family; husband's cruelty; and any other cause valid under Muslim law. Until the passage of the Family Code, Muslims were the only Filipinos with a possibility for legally ending a marriage.

The divorced wife is entitled to maintenance only during *'idda*, in addition to maintenance for the duration of nursing if the divorced mother continues to nurse her child for two years. The divorced mother has the right to custody over sons and daughters until seven years, after which age the ward may choose to reside with either parent. The custody of an unmarried female ward who has reached puberty reverts to the father, and the son in the same circumstances resides with the mother. Succession is governed by classical law, as defined in the Family Code.

Law/case reporting system Law reporting is through the *Official Gazette*.

International conventions (with relevant reservations) The Philippines signed the ICESCR and ICCPR in 1966, ratifying the former in 1974 and the latter in 1986 without reservations. The Philippines signed the CEDAW in 1980 and ratified it in 1981, without reservations. The Philippines signed and ratified the CRC in 1990, without reservations. The Philippines signed the Convention on Consent to Marriage, Minimum Age for Marriage and Registration of Marriages in 1963 and ratified it in 1965, without reservations.

Background and sources

Hooker, M. B. (1984) *Islamic Law in South-East Asia*, Singapore: Oxford University Press.

McKenna, T. (1998) *Muslim Rulers and Rebels*, Berkeley: University of California Press.

Mahmood, T. (1995) 'Philippines', in *Statutes of Personal Law in Islamic Countries: History, Texts and Analysis*, 2nd edn, New Delhi: India and Islam Research Council, pp. 89–90, 224–33.

Mercado, E. R. (1999) *Southern Philippines Question: The Challenge of Peace and Development*, Cotabato City, Philippines: Notre Dame Press.

Philippines (1996) *Fourth Periodic Report to CEDAW*, 25 July 1996, New York: United Nations.

Philippine Shari'ah Institute (1983) *Code of Muslim Personal Laws of the Philippines*, Manila: Philippine Shari'ah Institute.

Redden, K. R. (1990) 'Philippines', in K. R. Redden (ed.), *Modern Legal Systems Cyclopedia*, Vol. 9, Buffalo, NY: Hein.

SINGAPORE, Republic of

Legal history [see also: Legal system, Malaysia] The legal system is based on English common law. The Port of Singapore was founded in 1819 on the advice of Sir Stamford Raffles, Lieutenant-Governor of Java and employee of the British East India Company. It became part of the British Straits Settlement (of Malacca and Penang) in 1826. Singapore had a small population of Malay fishermen; Chinese and Indian settlement began after British rule. The Straits Settlements Act 1866 established the Straits as a colony separate from British India, to be administered directly from London. In 1946, Singapore became a separate Crown Colony and Penang and Malacca joined the Malayan Union, which achieved independence as the Federation of Malaya in 1957. Singapore gained independence in 1959, and joined Malaysia (with Malaya, Sarawak and North Borneo) in 1963, but it withdrew from the federation after two years and became an independent city-state.

Singaporean Muslim personal status is governed by the Muslims Ordinance 1957 covering registration, Shari'a courts and property matters, and repealing the previous applicable Ordinance. It contained very limited substantive provisions, but the Ordinance did transfer jurisdiction over Muslim personal status to Shari'a courts from the regular judiciary. It was replaced by the Administration of Muslim Law Act 1966, providing more detailed regulations. The 1966 Act established the *Majlis Ugama Islam Singapore* (Singapore Islamic Council) to administer endowments and execute wills. The Council also has a Legal Committee consisting of the *Mufti* of Singapore, two other member of the *Majlis* and two non-members; the function of the Legal Committee is to issue *fatawa* on any point of Muslim law. The 1966 legislation also contains more substantive provisions than its predecessor. The Women's Charter, passed in 1961, superseded non-Muslim family law systems applied in Singapore. It imposed a monogamous marriage regime on all Singaporeans except Muslims, although Muslim men married to non-Muslims under the terms of the Women's Charter are prohibited from marrying polygynously. Muslims are expressly exempted from certain provisions of the Women's Charter, for example, those relating to solemnization, nullity, divorce, and so on. The regular court system has jurisdiction over adoption, succession and custody even for those married under Muslim law, and the Muslim wife may choose to go to the regular or the Shari'a judicial system to obtain a maintenance order.

Schools of *fiqh*　The majority of Muslims are Shafi'i. The majority of the population is Buddhist. The other religions represented are Christianity, Hinduism, Sikhism, Taoism, Confucianism, Zoroastrianism and Judaism.

Constitutional status of Islam(ic law)　The Constitution was adopted on 3 June 1959 and amended in 1965 when the Malaysian State of Singapore left Malaysia. The Constitution contains a number of provisions enshrining freedom of religion and prohibiting discrimination on grounds of religion. Article 153 under General Provisions states that 'the Legislature shall by law make provision for regulating Muslim religious affairs and for constituting a Council to advise the President in matters relating to the Muslim religion'.

Court system　There is one Shari'a Court in Singapore; it may hear and determine actions in which all parties are Muslims or in which the parties involved were married under Muslim law (i.e., the husband is Muslim). The Shari'a Court has jurisdiction over cases related to marriage, divorce, betrothal, nullity of marriage, judicial separation, division of property on divorce, payment of dowry, maintenance and *mut'a*. Appeals from Shari'a Court decisions or decisions of *qadis* lie with an Appeal Board, comprising three Muslims chosen by the registrar of the Supreme Court from a panel of seven nominated by the president annually. Appeal Board decisions are final.

Notable features The minimum marriage age is 16 years for both parties. The *qadi* may permit the marriage of a girl under 16 years who has attained puberty under certain circumstances. The *wali* of the bride may solemnize her marriage according to Muslim law or may request the *qadi* to do so. The *qadi* may serve as *wali* where a woman has no *wali* or where he rules that the *wali*'s opposition to her marriage is unreasonable. Whether or not the *wali*'s agreement is required for validity of marriage is governed according to the classical position of the school of law applicable to the parties. In all cases, the *qadi* is directed to make an inquiry to determine that there are no lawful obstacles to a proposed marriage under either Muslim law or Administration of Muslim Law Act.

Marriage registration is obligatory. All Muslim marriages must be registered with a *qadi* or *naib qadi*. The president of Singapore appoints a registrar of Muslim Marriages and all *qadis* and *naib qadis* are deputy registrars. Non-registration of marriage or divorce does not determine validity.

Polygyny is permitted, but marriage by a man who is already married must be solemnized by a *qadi* or with the *qadi*'s written permission. Also, as with any Muslim marriage, the *qadi* is directed to make such inquiry as is necessary to determine that there are no lawful obstacles to the proposed marriage. The wife may apply to the court for a maintenance order; the sums and time period for which arrears may be claimed is not specified.

The registration of divorce and revocation of divorce is compulsory, and non-compliance is punishable by a fine. A *qadi* may not register a divorce without an inquiry establishing both parties' consent. A *qadi* may not register any divorce by triple *talaq* and the case must be referred to the Shari'a Court. The wife may be granted a judicial dissolution with her husband's consent. If the husband agrees to a *khul'*, the Court will assess the amount of compensation to be paid by the wife according to the means and status of both parties. The wife may also apply for *faskh* on the following grounds: the husband's failure to maintain for three months; his imprisonment for three years or more; failure to perform marital obligations for one year; continued impotence since marriage; insanity or serious illness making cohabitation injurious to his wife; and cruel treatment (defined as habitual physical abuse or cruelty of conduct, associating with women of ill repute, obstruction of wife's religious observance, unequal treatment of co-wives, cohabiting with another woman, or trying to force the wife to lead immoral life). Before granting a decree of divorce or nullification, the Court may appoint arbitrators to attempt a reconciliation.

The divorced wife may apply to the Court to order maintenance for her *'idda*. If the former wife is not entitled to maintenance under classical law, the Court may award her maintenance in consideration of the particular circumstances of the case. Child custody is governed by the Guardians of Infants Act 1961. The Courts are directed to consider the religious and customary practices of the community to which the parties belong, but the best interests of the ward are of paramount consideration. The regular court system has jurisdiction over all custody cases.

The property of a Muslim dying intestate is to be divided according to Islamic law 'as modified by Malay custom', although this appears to be a relic from pre-independence legislation, as commentators note that there have been no cases of such modification in the city-state of Singapore. Muslims may dispose of property by will only in accordance with the particular school of law to which they are subject.

Law/case reporting system Case reporting is through the *Singapore Law Journal* (formerly case reports were through the *Malayan Law Journal*). Law reporting is through the *Official Gazette*.

International conventions (with relevant reservations) Singapore acceded to the CEDAW in 1995, with a number of reservations. The reservation to Articles 2 and 6 states that due to the multi-racial and multi-religious composition of the population and the respect for freedom of religion, 'Singapore reserves the right not to apply the provisions of (said) Articles where compliance with these provisions would be contrary to (minority communities') religious or personal laws.'

Singapore acceded to the CRC in 1995, with declarations regarding the interpretation of Articles 12, 17, 19, 28(1a) 32 and 37. The declaration relating to Articles 12 and 17 states that the exercise of children's rights must be balanced against the authority of parents, schools, and so on, and with regard for the customs and values of the multi-racial and multi-religious society of Singapore.

Background and sources

Hooker, M. B. (1984) *Islamic Law in South-East Asia*, Singapore: Oxford University Press.

Kum, L. W. (1990), *Family Law in Singapore: Cases and Commentary on the Women's Charter and Family Law*, Singapore: Malayan Law Journal.

Mahmood, T. (1995) 'Singapore', in *Statutes of Personal Law in Islamic Countries: History, Texts and Analysis*, 2nd edn, New Delhi: India and Islam Research Council, p. 90.

Redden, K. R. (1990) 'Singapore', in K. R. Redden (ed.), *Modern Legal Systems Cyclopedia*, Vol. 9, Buffalo, NY: Hein.

Seng, K. W. K. (1976), *Family Law*, Singapore Law Series No. 2, Singapore: Malaya Law Review, Faculty of Law, University of Singapore.

Part IX
West Africa

1 Social, Cultural and Historical Background

The Region and its History

Islam first reached West Africa by way of traders from North Africa and the Middle East who settled in the area in the late tenth and early eleventh centuries. Over the next five hundred years, assorted West African rulers and local merchants who wanted to do business with the Muslim traders adapted themselves to Islam and its customs. But the practice of the religion did not spread far outside of towns and the commercial elite until the Muslim *jihad*s of the eighteenth and nineteenth centuries. These wars were led by Muslim scholars and teachers who were determined to turn the region's small Islamic colonies into Muslim states. They arose in dispersed places all the way from modern-day Chad to Benin, but gradually they influenced each other and culminated in the region-wide struggle to conquer pagan populations, convert them to Islam and rule them according to Islamic law (Lapidus 1990).

Usman dan Fodio led what became the most important *jihad*, starting in 1804. Usman began his career as an itinerant *mallam* or religious scholar who condemned the petty Muslim rulers of the Hausa for unjust and illegal taxes, for confiscation of property, for the enslavement of Muslims, for allowing the free socializing of men and women, and for permitting other customs he saw as contrary to Islamic law. He found his principal constituency among the Fulani, a pastoral people scattered across West Africa. The wars that followed his declaration of *jihad* engulfed most of what is now northern Nigeria and the northern Cameroons. At the height of his influence, the Muslim regime Usman founded, called the Caliphate of Sokoto, ruled all of Hausaland and extended into parts of Yorubaland in what is now southern Nigeria.

Some fifty years after Usman's *jihad*, Al-Haji 'Umar, a cleric from Senegal, began another. 'Umar had been initiated into the Tijani religious order on a pilgrimage to Mecca in 1826. He returned as the order's *khalifa*. His *jihad* began in 1852 and established a state that lasted until 1893. Spreading east from Senegal, its power eventually extended as far as Timbuktu in northern

Mali. Then, at the very moment when masses of West Africans were being converted to Islam, Europe checked the Muslim expansion. The French took possession of the state founded by 'Umar in 1893. In 1903 the British defeated the Sokoto Caliphate. Until the 1950s, the region remained under colonial rule.

Islam is not a uniform culture across West Africa, but has a plethora of local variations. However, almost all of the region's approximately 215 million Muslims are Sunni, most of whom follow the Maliki school of jurisprudence. Africa's two largest Muslim ethnic groups, the Hausa and the Fulani, are located in the region. About 50 million Hausa live in northern Nigeria and southern Niger, most of them according to a demanding interpretation of Shari'a family law (Callaway and Creevey 1994). The Fulani are divided into numerous subgroups spread from Cameroon to Chad and all the way to Senegal. Some Fulani, such as the Mbororo, are pastoralists and only nominally Muslim. Few Mbororo have had any Qur'anic schooling and they know little about orthodox Islam. Mbororo women are engaged in the milk trade, and are free to move about in public. Another Fulani group, the Foulbe, are much stricter in their practice of the religion, priding themselves on their orthodoxy (Burnham 1991).

Legal Practices and Institutions

Most West African countries maintain legal systems that are to some degree conflations of customary, colonial and Islamic law. The degree to which one type of law predominates differs not only between countries but also among regions and ethnic groups. Even in countries with large Muslim populations, the degree to which communities adhere to Shari'a varies. In essence, while the national law of a country may follow colonial or Western legal patterns – for example, giving equal rights of inheritance to men and women – most disputes involving family law are resolved outside the formal court system at the village or local administrative level. In settling such causes, local communities may give precedence to customary law, Shari'a or some combination of the two.

For example, Nigeria, Africa's most populous country, has traditionally given priority to customary law, instructing courts in the case of a conflict to apply 'the law prevailing in the area of the jurisdiction of the court, or any law binding between the two parties' (Akande 1979.). In the northern and predominantly Muslim part of Nigeria, a combination of *al'ada* (Hausa customary law) and Shari'a has historically governed family law. More recently, several northern states have adopted a stricter form of Shari'a law as the basis of their legal systems. In these areas, women are disqualified from voting and only men may be elected to high political office.

Many West African peoples rarely make use of state legal systems. Instead they rely on their community chiefs to govern according to customary law, using Shari'a as a basis only for divorce.

Mauritania declared Islam its state religion and made Shari'a the law of the land in 1985. However, in practice Islamic courts exist alongside secular courts, and conflicts between customary laws and differing practices in communities has led to an uneven implementation of Islamic rules.

In Niger, family law remains one of the few areas of the legal code that has not been the object of any regulation. The now-suspended 1960 Nigerien Constitution expressly declared that 'the family is part of the reserved domain of the law', and subsequent governments have hesitated to intervene (Dunbar 1983).

Across the region, women find it difficult to protect what rights they may have under law. Only women from the most wealthy and educated spheres of society have the means to engage a lawyer.

Seclusion of Women / Purdah

In many West African communities, there is no separation between the sexes and women dress as they did before their people converted to Islam. Other communities, such as the Hausa, value a form of strict purdah, although in practice only wealthy families and the families of religious leaders usually carry it out. In these families, women seldom go outside the house, and then only when fully covered.

The separation of Hausa boys and girls and the emphasis on modesty for girls begins quite early. By the time a girl is six years old, she begins dressing according to the codes of dress applied to women, covering all but her face, hands and feet. Small girls continue to move about in public, though, running errands and doing marketing for grown women in their homes. Boys are kept out of women's quarters in their homes from the time they are about ten years old to when they being to sleep in the men's areas of the house (Callaway and Creevey 1994).

Generally Hausa men decide if and when their wives may work. Educated Hausa women sometimes speak of practising 'seclusion of the heart', by which they mean that they shield themselves from men by means of a mental or spiritual barrier rather than by physically separating themselves. Among the poor, few men have the luxury of keeping their wives at home. The popular Tijani Sufi brotherhood places little emphasis on this aspect of Shari'a. In recent years, reformist movements such as Yan Izala have sought to maximize Muslim voting power by encouraging women to vote (Loimeier 1997).

Certain Hausa subgroups, however, take a different view. The Kanuri, a group of some four million Nigerian Muslims, practise a very strict form of purdah. In the cities, some Kanuri women basically never leave their homes. Others leave only with male chaperons. Meanwhile, Yoruba Muslim women do not dress any differently from Yoruba Christian women.

Since the imposition of strict Islamic law in the Nigerian states of Kano, Zamfara and Kaduna, women have been barred from many jobs and sex outside marriage has become a crime. The government has promised to segregate men and women on public transport and in schools (McGreal 2000). Authorities in the town of Kano have ordered women to remain indoors between the hours of 6 p.m. and 6 a.m.

In Senegal and Gambia, most women are not secluded. Wolof women go out in public without men from their families, but they are expected to dress and act appropriately. For women of the upper classes, propriety requires more modest clothing than it does for working-class women (Weekes 1984).

In Mali, only the wives of wealthy merchants are secluded. Most women are free to go outside and many women work. There is little concern about contact between the sexes. For example, women from all levels of society participated in popular demonstrations against the government in 1990.

In Nigeria, Niger and many other parts of the region, the custom of women marrying at a far younger age than men often means that girls are less likely to attend school than boys. Men are therefore better equipped than women to take advantage of whatever legal system exists.

Female circumcision is widespread among West Africans of all faiths, who often see it as a method of protecting the chastity and modesty of women. Muslim religious leaders in the region often justify the practice on religious grounds, although Islamic scholars in other parts of the world argue that it is not a religious requirement. All of Nigeria's major ethnic groups excise the clitoris. In Côte d'Ivoire, older women excise young Dyula girls of the clitoris and labia minora. In Senegal, the Muslim Wolof and Serer people do not circumcise girls, but the Tukulor practise infibulation, the most radical form of female circumcision. In Mali, Mande women are infibulated, while Tuareg and Moor women are not (Hosken 1982).

Family in the Region

Most West African peoples follow patrilineal patterns of descent. Some ethnic groups, such as the Malinke, trace their heritage back to a single male ancestor. Others have a less complex system, tracing their lineages through the father's line without concern for the clan's connection to a distant ancestor or ancestors. However, there are numerous exceptions, Muslim and non-Muslim, to the rule of patrilineal descent. The Kanuri, for example, trace their family lines bilaterally, or through both parents. The Serer of Senegal, a mostly Muslim group of almost one million, are solidly matrilineal. At the same time, the Tukulor, a group of about 750,000 who have been Islamic for some nine centuries, trace their families patrilineally. But they believe that on Judgment Day, they will be recognized by a maternal uncle, rather than someone from their father's family. Islam has helped move some peoples towards a patrilineal system. For example, the Wolof, a predominantly Muslim population of about 2.3 million in Senegal and Gambia, now trace their descent from their fathers. In the past, many Wolof were matrilineal, and they preserve some matrilineal customs, depending on maternal relatives for emotional support, while expecting training and discipline from paternal relatives (Weekes 1984).

Marriage

West Africans generally perceive marriage as an alliance between two kinship groups and only secondarily a union of individuals (Akande 1979; Dunabar 1983). Some Muslim ethnic groups, such as the Serer in Senegal, or the Songhay in Mali, Niger and Nigeria, are exogamous, preferring to marry outside their lineages. In Nigeria, Islamic law prohibits marriage between Muslim men and animist women, though Muslim men may marry Christian women. Muslim Nigerian women may only marry other Muslim men. In Senegal, Tukulor men adhere to the Qur'anic injunction against marrying pagan women. Dyula men do marry pagan women, but Dyula women do not marry pagan men.

Other groups have very specific rules against marrying outside the ethnic group, rather than outside the Islamic religion. Among the Malinke, a group of some four million Muslims in several coastal countries, men can marry women who are not Malinke, but women may marry only Malinke men. Similarly, the Jahanka allow their men to marry non-Jahanka women, but women may marry only Jahanka men (Weekes 1984).

The age of first marriage and betrothal customs vary widely in West Africa. Traditionally, most West African peoples regarded girls as marriageable at the time of puberty. In Senegal and Mauritania, the average age of a woman at her first marriage is 23. Women in Mali and Niger marry earlier, at an average age of 16. Hausa girls are generally married between the ages of ten and twelve. The girl's family arranges her first marriage. If she has not yet reached puberty, she will stay in the home of her parents until her first menstruation and then go immediately to her husband's home. The girl's consent is not required, but she may repudiate the marriage after puberty. Men, on the other hand, do not marry until they are capable of supporting a wife, which means that many Hausa men are 30 before they wed.

The payment of bridewealth is an essential part of marriage in most West African communities, Islamic or not. The payment usually follows indigenous rules rather than the classical Islamic tradition of *mahr*. In Niger, for example, the negotiations leading to marriage are marked by a series of gifts. In practice, the bride's family often spends as much as the groom's on these exchanges. Nevertheless, the marriage is not valid until the payment of bridewealth and the announcement of the amount. Among most West Africans, the bride's family receives the payment rather than the bride herself.

The government of Niger encourages people to register marriages, but registration is not required for a marriage to be valid. A Nigerien husband is obliged to provide his wife with food, clothes, lodging and pocket-money. A wife has the right to acquire and administer property, as well as the right to respect, good treatment and conjugal relations. She is obliged to obey her husband, including seeking his permission to leave the house, whether for visits or for work. If she does not, he has the right to send her from his bed or administer a light beating (Dunbar 1983).

Malian husbands are legally required to support their wives and children. In practice, however, women have difficulty enforcing the law (Hosken 1982).

In Nigeria, married Muslim women have certain rights to property that other Nigerian women do not. Under statutory Nigerian law, a married man controls his wife's property and she may not enter contracts that would jeopardize his right to such property. She cannot enter into loan or hiring agreements without her husband's consent, nor can she obtain a passport without it. However, under Shari'a law a married woman's property is her own (Akande 1979).

Marriage practices among the Mbororo of Cameroon downplay the relations between husband and wife. Once a woman becomes pregnant the first time, she returns to her parents' household and stays there until the child is weaned, about three years after she gives birth. During that time she has no contact with her husband.

Divorce

Divorce is extremely common in West Africa. Among the Hausa, divorce occurs almost as frequently as marriage. All forms of divorce sanctioned by Shari'a are allowed, but repudiation is the most common. In Niger and Senegal, however, divorce is not valid until registered with a court. In the rest of West Africa, repudiation is sufficient, meaning that many women do not actually know their marital status. Women who initiate divorce must return the bride-wealth their husband paid at the time of the marriage. If a Muslim couple divorces, the woman is expected to observe 'idda, the 40-day waiting period prescribed in the Qur'an. During this period, the ex-husband is supposed to support her, although women have no way of enforcing this (Akande 1979).

Once a woman is divorced and her 'idda period has passed, she will generally remarry within a few months, as most West African Muslims consider it socially unacceptable for a woman of childbearing age to remain single. Divorced women do not suffer any social stigma in Mauritania, unless their family or the family of their ex-husband blame them for the failure of the marriage. However, a few groups, such as the Daza in Chad and the Nupe in central Nigeria, allow divorced women to remain single and to serve as the head of their household.

Among the Fulani, divorce is relatively easy for either partner to obtain, although men are more likely to initiate it. Prior to the final divorce, the spouses must observe a period of conjugal separation in which the wife returns to her father or guardian. The wife's 'idda period begins after this separation. The Woodaabe also recognize a process of divorce in which the wife leaves her husband and establishes an informal remarriage prior to or without proper dissolution of the first marriage (Weekes 1984). Among some West African groups, women keep their houses after divorce. Others expect women to return to their natal home.

Polygyny

Polygyny pre-dates Islam in West Africa and is practised by most ethnic groups, regardless of religion. A man's wealth is determined by the number of wives and children he has (Akande 1979). Many West African Muslims see polygyny as part of being devout, as well as a status symbol for men. Affluence, rather than any other factor, usually determines whether or not a man has more than one wife. In mostly Muslim Senegal, approximately one-quarter of urban marriages and one-third of rural marriages are polygynous. Although the law requires first marriages to be declared polygynous or monogamous at the time of the wedding, in practice this is rarely done and there are no sanctions against men who change their minds. Frequently even men who start out wanting to be monogamous change their minds as they grow older. As they become more prosperous, they are better able to afford having multiple wives. Senegalese men who are literate, whether they have studied only through primary education, or all the way through university, are more likely to have several wives than are men with no education. On the other hand, Senegalese women who have higher education are less likely than others to be in polygynous marriages (Antoine and Nantilelamio 1996).

Hausa men see polygyny as an obligation, if they can afford it. Some Hausa subgroups, such as the Kanuri, also allow men to keep concubines. When a Hausa man has more than one wife, the co-wives live in separate rooms within the same house, not in separate homes.

In Mali, many men, particularly of the merchant class, perceive having more than one wife as part of being a serious person (Warms 1994). Similarly for the Sosa of Guinea and Sierre Leone, a predominantly Muslim people of about a million, having multiple wives, sometimes more than four, conveys prestige. One exception to the general rule is Mauritania. There the Maures, who are the elite of the country, are basically monogamous, while the rest of the population is frequently polygynous. At the time of the wedding, a woman can stipulate that the marriage is dissolved if the husband takes a second wife. Maure women use this provision regularly.

In Niger, the first wife divides the goods and supplies from the husband among the other wives. Stress and strain between wives lead to frequent flights from the urban marriage home. Some rural women, however, welcome other wives as additional workers (Dunbar 1983).

In both Guinea and Côte d'Ivoire, polygyny is illegal but widely practised among the Muslim Dyula and the Jahanka. In Sierre Leone, Muslim Limba men sometimes have more than four wives.

Children

Throughout West Africa, procreation is considered an obligation as well as a right. Men and women place a huge importance on having children; a childless marriage is regarded as a curse. Boys are traditionally prized more than girls. It would be unthinkable for a Nigerian woman to use a contraceptive device without the consent of her husband (Akande 1979).

Custody of Children

Hausa custom differs from Maliki law with regard to child custody. Though Maliki law stipulates that the wife retains custody of a male until puberty and a female until puberty or marriage, Hausa children remain with their mother only until the age of seven (Akande 1979).

A Songhay father or his family get custody of the children after divorce, as they are considered part of his lineage. In Equatorial Guinea, Muslim men, like others, get custody of any children born during a marriage. Among the Fulani, when a marriage dissolves, the husband decides who will take the children.

Inheritance

On the whole, Muslim women fare better in the area of inheritance and land rights than their Christian or pagan counterparts in West Africa. Nevertheless, even the region's Muslim populations tend to follow customary inheritance practices, leaving women with little or nothing, rather than the Qur'anic division.

Although under Maliki law Hausa women should inherit half as much as their brothers, they seldom do. By local custom, only the sons of the deceased are entitled to divide up his land. When a landowner leaves only female offspring, his brothers occupy the land in their own right. But female children are entitled to the proceeds of farmland.

Unlike Yoruba women, Hausa widows have the right to inherit whether or not they have children. The family of a Hausa widow's husband has no claim on her after his death. Yoruba widows, by contrast, are handed on to one of their husband's male heirs as part of the estate of the dead man (Akande 1979).

In Mali, by law, women are supposed to receive the same share of an inheritance as a man of the same relation to the deceased. However, few women are aware of this law and custom does not allow women to inherit.

In countries with small Muslim populations, local traditions tend to overpower Shari'a in questions of inheritance. In Liberia, for example, women may not inherit. The Central African Republic, Ghana and the Republic of Congo also follow customary law in inheritance.

Among the Fulani, women may not inherit cattle, the main property. The Limba have a system of land rights passing from the oldest brother down through his youngest brothers until it reaches the youngest man, then passing to the oldest son of the oldest brother, without ever falling into the hands of a woman. In Gabon, which is 40 per cent Muslim, a widow may inherit only if her husband's family agrees to it (US Department of State 1994).

Bibliography

Akande, J. O. D. (1979) 'Law and the status of women in Nigeria', report prepared for the African Training and Research Centre for Women, Addis Ababa.

Antoine, P. and J. Nanitelamio (1996) 'Can polygamy be avoided in Dakar?', in K. Sheldon (ed.), *Courtyards, Markets, City Streets: Urban Women in Africa*, Boulder, CO: Westview Press.

Burnham, P. (1991) 'L'ethnie, la religion et l'état: Le role des Peuls dans la vie politique et social du Nord-Cameroun', *Journal des Africanistes*, 61.

Callaway, B. and L. Creevey (1994) *The Heritage of Islam: Women, Religion, and Politics in West Africa*, Boulder, CO: Lynne Rienner.

Dunbar, R. A. (1983) 'Islamized law and the status of women in Niger', paper prepared for the Southeastern Regional Seminar in African Studies, 15 October, 1983, Charlottesville, VA.

Hosken, F. P. (1982) *The Hosken Report: Genital and Sexual Mutilation of Females*, 3rd rev. edn, Lexington, MA: Women's International Network News.

Lapidus, I. M. (1990) *A History of Islamic Societies*, Cambridge: Cambridge University Press.

Lesthaeghe, R. (1989) *Reproduction and Social Organization in Sub-Saharan Africa*, Berkeley: University of California Press.

Loimeier, R. (1997) 'Islamic reform and political change: the example of Abubakar Gumi and the Yan Izala Movment in northern Nigeria', in D. Westerlund and E. E. Rosander (eds), *African Islam and Islam in Africa: Encounters Between Sufis and Islamists*, Athens: Ohio University Press, pp. 286–307.

McGreal, C. (2000), 'Islamic law advances in Nigeria', *Guardian*, 28 November.

Thomas-Emeagwali, G. (1994) 'Islam and gender: the Nigerian case', in C. F. El-Sohl and J. Mabro (eds), *Muslim Women's Choices: Religious and Social Reality*, Providence, RI: Berg Publishers.

US Department of State (1994) *Country Reports on Human Rights Practices*, Washington, DC: US Department of State.

Warms, R. L. (1994) 'Commerce and continuity: paths to success for Malian merchants', *African Studies Review*, 37: 2.

Weekes, R. V. (ed.) (1984) *Muslim Peoples: A World Ethnographic Survey*, 2nd edn, Westport, CT: Greenwood Press.

2 Legal Profiles

GAMBIA, Republic of the

Legal history The legal system is based on an amalgam of English common law, Islamic law and customary law. The Portuguese sent expeditions to Gambia in the mid-fifteenth century, and British trade in the region and exploration of the Gambia River began in the late sixteenth century. Gambia was incorporated into the British colony of Senegambia in 1765, but in response to growing French influence in Senegal, the British seized the Gambia River in 1888. In 1892, Banjul (then Bathurst) was established as the capital. Gambia gained independence in 1965. A republican Constitution was adopted in 1970.

Marriage is governed by several regimes: customary, Islamic, Christian under the Christian Marriage Act 1862, and statutory under the Civil Marriage Act 1938. Colonial-era legislation, relating to Muslim personal law, the Mohammedan Marriage and Divorce Ordinance 1941, was retained after independence. The legislation is mainly of a regulatory nature.

The Law Reform Commission and the Women's Bureau of Gambia made proposals for the codification of Muslim personal status laws in the mid- to late 1980s, but the suggestions were not adopted into law. Some of the provisions put forward in a proposed draft published in 1987 relate to establishing a minimum marriage age of 18 for males and 15 for females, broader grounds for divorce available to both parties (including irreparable breakdown) and limiting extra-judicial repudiation.

Schools of *fiqh* The majority of Gambians are Maliki Muslim. There are significant Christian minority communities, as well as followers of indigenous beliefs.

Constitutional status of Islam(ic law) The current Constitution was adopted in 1970, suspended in July 1994, revised and adopted by national referendum in August 1996 and reinstated January 1997.

The Constitution adopts no official religion. Article 7 identifies the following sources of law in addition to the Constitution: legislation; common law and principles of equity; customary law so far as it concerns members of the communities to which it applies; and Shari'a as regards matters of personal status and inheritance among members of communities to which it applies. Article 33(1) proclaims the equality of all persons before the law; Article 33(5c) exempts from the rest of Article 33 those laws relating to adoption, marriage, divorce, burial, devolution of property on death or other matters of personal law.

Court system The regular court system consists of the Supreme Court, High Court, Court of Appeal, and subordinate courts. Part 3 of the Constitution establishes *Qadis'* Courts in such places as the Chief Justice determines. *Qadis'* Courts are to be composed of a panel of one *qadi* and two other scholars of Shari'a for hearings at first instance. For hearings on review, the panel is to consist of the *qadi* and four *ulama*. The decision is made by the majority view of the panel. The jurisdiction of *Qadis'* Courts applies to matters of marriage, divorce and inheritance where the parties or other persons interested are Muslims. Appeals of *Qadis'* Courts' decisions at first instance may be made within three months of the decision by applying to the same court. There are two *Qadis'* Courts (in Banjul and Kanifing).

Notable features The *Qadis'* Courts apply classical Maliki *fiqh* to matters of personal status. The Mohammedan Marriage and Divorce Ordinance 1941 makes registration of both obligatory within one month, but registration does not determine validity.

Law/case reporting system Law reporting is through the *Official Gazette*. A loose-leaf collection of the Laws of Gambia was issued in 1990.

International conventions (with relevant reservations) Gambia signed the ICCPR in 1979, with a reservation to Article 14(3)(d). Gambia signed the ICESCR in 1978 without reservations. Gambia signed the CEDAW in 1980 and ratified it in 1993, without reservations. Gambia signed and ratified the CRC in 1990, without reservations.

Background and sources
Annual Survey of African Law, Vol. 1 (1967) and Vol. 4 (1970), London: Frank Cass.
Gambia Law Reform Commission and Gambia Women's Bureau (1987) *Law Reform Project No. 7: Muslim Marriages: Formation and Dissolution*, Banjul: Gambia Law Reform Commission and Gambia Women's Bureau.

Gambia Women's Bureau (1987) *First and Second Workshops on the Legal Status of Women, with Emphasis on the Matrimonial Bill on Formation and Dissolution of Muslim Marriages,* 7–8 October 1987 and 11–12 November 1987, Banjul, Gambia: Gambia Women's Bureau.

Redden, K. R. (1990) 'Gambia', in K. R. Redden (ed.), *Modern Legal Systems Cyclopedia,* Vol. 6, Buffalo, NY: Hein.

GHANA, Republic of

Legal history   The legal system is based on English common law and customary law. Over one hundred distinct ethno-linguistic groups are represented in Ghana. The gold and later the slave trade attracted European explorers to the region; first the Portuguese in the late fifteenth century, followed by Dutch, Danish, English and Swedish explorers. By the early nineteenth century, the British came to dominate the 'Gold Coast', extending their control further inland. By 1902 most of modern-day Ghana was a British crown colony, with Volta joining Ghana in 1956. The British policy of indirect rule utilized local chiefs in government and administration, thus traditional authorities retained their jurisdiction over the internal affairs of their communities. Following World War II, pressure for self-rule increased, and independence was gained in 1957.

Ghana became a republic under the 1960 Constitution and the first prime minister, Kwame Nkrumah, was elected president. By 1964, Nkrumah had centralized power and limited opposition, had himself declared president for life and established a single-party state. A military coup in 1966 brought an end to Nkrumah's rule. Military rule continued until 1993, with brief periods of democratic civilian rule (1969–72, 1979–81). The fourth republican Constitution came into effect in 1993, and in 1996, the first elected government to complete its first term was elected to a second term, under the former military ruler Jerry Rawlings.

British-era legislation relating to family law provided for civil registration under a monogamous regime under the Marriage Ordinance 1951. Until now, no single body of law regulated personal status matters. The colonial legislation applicable to Muslims, the Marriage of Mohammedans Ordinance 1907, is limited to administrative or procedural matters such as providing for registration of marriage and divorce. Muslim marriages are also affected by some other laws of universal application. Although the Ordinance has been retained, few Muslim marriages are registered under it and more commonly come under customary legal regimes.

The Ghana Law Reform Commission established in 1968 was given the task of reviewing statutory and customary laws and suggesting reforms. Its first programme identified inheritance and marriage law as among the main areas requiring attention. Among the successes of the Commission are counted the Maintenance of Children Decree 1977 and Intestate Succession Law 1985. The Maintenance of Children Decree establishes Family Tribunals to hear complaints about maintenance of children during the subsistence of marriage and after divorce. The Intestate Succession Law provides protection for children in communities where they are not entitled to shares of their deceased parents' estates. The unification of family laws was identified in its 1996 report as a goal of the Commission. To that end, the Commission outlined a plan to assess the application and efficacy of existing legislation through questionnaires to be drafted in coordination with women's groups and NGOs.

Schools of *fiqh* The majority of Muslims are Maliki. The other major religions represented are Christianity and indigenous religions.

Constitutional status of Islam(ic law) The current Constitution was approved on 28 April 1992, and adopts no official religion. Article 11 identifies the sources of Ghanaian law as: the Constitution; legislation; existing law; and common law. Existing law is defined as the written and unwritten laws of Ghana pre-dating the current Constitution, as adapted to conform to the Constitution. Article 270(1) provides for the recognition of the institution of chieftaincy, together with its traditional councils under customary law. Article 272 states that the National House of Chiefs shall undertake a progressive study and codification of customary law to establish unified rules and evaluate such laws with the aim of 'eliminating those customs and usages that are outmoded and socially harmful'.

Court system The higher courts are the Supreme Court (the highest court of appeal in civil and criminal matters), the Court of Appeal, the High Court, and ten Regional Tribunals. The lower courts are circuit courts and tribunals, community tribunals, juvenile and family tribunals, and traditional courts. Traditional courts include the National House of Chiefs, the Regional House of Chiefs, and the Traditional Councils. Islamic law is applied by customary or traditional courts under the broader category of customary law.

Notable features The minimum marriage age is governed by classical or customary law. The Marriage of Mohammedans Ordinance specifies that marriage is solemnized in the presence of the bridegroom, the bride's *wali*, and two witnesses. The Criminal Code identifies causing someone to marry under duress as a misdemeanour. The Marriage of Mohammedans Ordinance provides for the registration of marriage and divorce among Muslims. Marriage must be registered within one week of solemnization.

Polygyny is governed by classical or customary law. All customary marriages are defined as potentially polygynous under Ghanaian law.

The Criminal Code imposes on the husband the duty of maintenance of the wife and children.

Talaq is governed by classical or customary law. It is possible to terminate a customary law marriage by application to the court under the Matrimonial Causes Act, in which case grounds for divorce include those recognized in the personal law of the parties in addition to those enumerated in the Act. Under the Act, divorce may be granted only if the court concludes irreparable breakdown. Courts hearing suits for divorce among Muslims are directed to apply the Matrimonial Causes Act directing guidance by justice, equity and good conscience in determination of post-divorce reliefs and custody. The courts are empowered under the Matrimonial Causes Act to grant maintenance in addition to the reliefs recognized under the personal law of the parties. The Matrimonial Causes Act provides that courts may grant custody according to the ward's best interests, and order provision for his/her education and maintenance out of the assets or income of either or both parents. Courts adjudicating Muslim divorces are required to apply the terms of the Matrimonial Causes Act.

Upon the death of a Muslim whose marriage was registered under the Marriage of Mohammedans Ordinance, property devolves according to Islamic law. The Wills Act 1971 provides for complete freedom of testacy, subject, however, to the customary law applicable to testator. Although Article 22 of the Constitution provides that the government shall endeavour to regulate the property rights of spouses to ensure equal access to jointly acquired property and equal division of such property on divorce, there has been no legislative implementation of the directive as of yet.

Law/case reporting system Law reporting is through the *Official Gazette*. Decisions of the Supreme Court, Court of Appeal and High Court are published in *The Ghana Law Reports Digest*.

International conventions (with relevant reservations) Ghana signed the CEDAW in 1980 and ratified it in 1986, without reservations. Ghana signed the CRC in 1990 and ratified it in 1990, without reservations.

Background and sources

Berry, L. (ed.) (1995) *Ghana: A Country Study*, 3rd edn, Washington, DC: Library of Congress, Federal Research Division.

Center for Reproductive Law and Policy and International Federation of Women Lawyers (1997) 'Ghana', in *Women of the World: Laws and Policies Affecting their Reproductive Lives – Anglophone Africa*, New York: Center for Reproductive Law and Policy and International Federation of Women Lawyers (Kenya Chapter).

Ghana (1991) *Initial, Second and Third Periodic Report to CEDAW*, 5 July, New York: United Nations.

Ghana Law Reform Commission (1971, 1979–82, 1996) *Annual Reports*, Accra.

Mensa-Bonsu, H. J. A. N. (1996) 'Family law policy and research agenda', in E. Ardayfio-Schandorf (ed.), *The Changing Family in Ghana*, Accra: Ghana University Press, pp. 221–41.

Redden, K. R. (1990) 'Algeria', in K. R. Redden (ed.), *Modern Legal Systems Cyclopedia*, Vol. 6, Buffalo, NY: Hein.

Rubin, N. N. and E. Cotran (eds) (1971) *Annual Survey of African Law*, Vol. 5, London: Frank Cass.

NIGERIA, Federal Republic of

Legal history   The legal system is based on English common law, Islamic law, and customary law. Lagos was annexed by Britain in 1861. The Oil Rivers Protectorate was established by treaties with Yoruba rulers. By 1900 the British controlled all of present-day Nigeria. Due to the system of indirect rule, traditional authorities retained powers over their communities. The British introduced a statutory monogamous marriage regime with the 1914 Marriage Act.

Nigeria gained independence from Britain in 1960. A military coup in 1966 marked the beginning of a long period of military rule punctuated by brief periods of civilian rule (1979–83, 1999). The Muslim Fulani Usman dan Fodio led a *jihad* (Fulani *Jihad* or Sokoto *Jihad*) against the Hausa aristocracy in the Kingdom of Gobir in northern Nigeria in the early nineteenth century, establishing a new empire with its capital at Sokoto under which an elaborate Shari'a court structure developed. The British adapted Emirs' Judicial Councils from the existing judicial structures in northern Nigeria; these continued to serve as appellate courts in the emirates until the establishment of the Shari'a Court of Appeal in 1959. Judicial reforms initiated in the late 1960s created grades of *alkalis' (Qadis')* courts; initially there were four grades and as of reforms in the late 1970s, three grades. The first instance courts established were Area Courts Grades 2 and 1, then the Upper Area Court and the Upper Area Court of Appeal, with the highest state level appellate jurisdiction lying with the Shari'a Court of Appeal in each state.

Schools of *fiqh* About half the population is Muslim, about 40 per cent Christian, and about 10 per cent practise traditional indigenous religions or no religion.

Constitutional status of Islam(ic law) The current Constitution was adopted in 1999. Six new states were established in 1996, bringing the total number of states to 36, in addition to the Federal Territory of Abuja. Part 2.10 of the Constitution states that: 'The Government of the Federation or of a State shall not adopt any religion as State Religion.'

Court system The Supreme Court is the highest federal court, with appellate jurisdiction over the lower federal courts and the highest state courts. Each state has its own judicial system, including Magistrates' or District Courts (first instance in civil and criminal matters) and a High Court (original and appellate jurisdiction). The Constitution also provides that states may establish lower and appellate customary courts having limited civil jurisdiction. The northern states have separate Shari'a courts to administer Islamic personal law.

The Constitution provides for establishment of higher Shari'a courts. Article 236(1) establishing the Court of Appeal provides that of at least fifteen judges, no fewer than three shall be well-versed in Islamic law and no fewer than three in customary law; the Court of Appeal hears appeals from the Federal High Court, State High Courts, Shari'a Courts of Appeal, and Customary Courts of Appeal. Article 259(1) provides for Shari'a Courts of Appeal for any states requiring them. Shari'a Courts of Appeal consist of a Grand *Qadi* and as many *qadis* as the State Assembly prescribes, with at least two *qadis* hearing appeals. The 1999 Constitution also provides that the federal government is to establish a Federal Shari'a Court of Appeal and Final Court of Appeal; however, the government has not yet established such courts.

Notable features In terms of child custody, the Matrimonial Causes Act 1970 is applicable to custody suits arising out of the dissolution of civil, customary and Islamic marriages; in all custody matters, the Act directs that the interests of the child shall be paramount. Shari'a courts apply classical Maliki *fiqh* to matters of personal status and succession.

Law/case reporting system Decisions of higher Shari'a courts are published in *Shari'a Law Reports* (Zaria, Nigeria) and *Islamic Law Reports* (Katsina, Katsina State); both are published irregularly. Higher court decisions are reported in *All Nigeria Law Reports* and *Supreme Court Digest*. Law reporting is through the *Official Gazette of the Federal Republic of Nigeria,* and state *Official Gazettes.*

International conventions (with relevant reservations) Nigeria acceded to the ICCPR and ICESCR in 1993, without reservations. Nigeria signed the CEDAW in 1984 and ratified it in 1985, without reservations. Nigeria signed the CRC in 1990 and ratified it in 1991, without reservations.

Background and sources

Center for Reproductive Law and Policy and International Federation of Women Lawyers (1997) 'Nigeria', in *Women of the World: Laws and Policies Affecting their Reproductive Lives – Anglophone Africa,* New York: Center for Reproductive Law and Policy and International Federation of Women Lawyers (Kenya Chapter).

Cooper, B. (1998) 'Gender and religion in Hausaland: variations in Islamic practice in Niger and Nigeria', in H. L. Bodman and N. Tohidi (eds), *Women in Muslim Societies: Unity within Diversity,* Boulder, CO: Lynne Rienner Publishers, pp. 21–38.

Doi, A. I. (1984) *Islam in Nigeria,* Zaria, Nigeria: Gaskiya Corp.

Metz, H. C. (ed.) (1992) *Nigeria: A Country Study,* Washington, DC: Library of Congress, Federal Research Division.

Redden, K. R. (1990) 'Nigeria', in K. R. Redden (ed.), *Modern Legal Systems Cyclopedia,* Vol. 6, Buffalo, NY: Hein.

Rubin, N. N. and E. Cotran (eds) (1970, 1971) *Annual Survey of African Law,* Vol. 4 and Vol. 5, London: Frank Cass.

Yusuf, A. B. (1982) *Nigerian Legal System: Pluralism and Conflict of Laws in the Northern States,* New Delhi, National Publishing House.

Yusufari, M. A. L. (1997–8) 'The application of Islamic law in Nigeria', *YIMEL,* 4: 201–9.

SENEGAL, Republic of

Legal history The legal system is based on the French civil law system. Senegal gained independence from France in 1960. Prior to the enactment of the Family Code in 1972, family relations were governed by Christian, Islamic and customary laws, or under the civil code. Work on codification of a uniform personal status law began in 1961 with a comprehensive listing of customary laws applied in Senegal, and the publication of 68 officially recognized customary regimes. A commission for codification was established in 1961 and began by issuing a questionnaire investigating customary practices. A 27-member committee was given the task of drafting a single code for all Senegalese that would minimize any aspects not uniformly applicable, would be appropriate to modern social conditions, would compromise on matters likely to cause conflict between traditional laws and modern statutes, and would observe prescriptions related to family law in the Qur'an.

The Family Code that was drafted passed into law and came into force on 1 January 1973. The Code regulates marriage, divorce, succession and custody, with a separate section for Muslim succession law. As of 1993, the government established a working group to adapt national legislation to conform with the international instruments ratified by Senegal.

Schools of *fiqh* The majority of the population is Maliki Muslim. A minority of the population follows indigenous religions or is Christian (mainly Roman Catholic).

Constitutional status of Islam(ic law) The Constitution was adopted on 3 March 1963 and has been revised numerous times. Article 1 declares that Senegal is a secular state.

Court system Senegal took steps to abolish separate customary courts and establish a unified judicial system after independence in 1960. Tribunals of first instance and assize courts' decisions are appealable to courts of appeal. The Supreme Court or Court of Cassation is the highest appellate court.

Notable features The minimum marriage age is 20 years for males and 16 for females, with provision for judicial discretion for permitting under-age marriages for serious reasons. Each party must give free consent, even minors, and parties under 20 years require parental consent. Lack of free consent or parental consent is grounds for nullification of marriage.

Marriage registration is obligatory. If a marriage is to be contracted under one of the customary regimes recognized in Senegalese law, the parties must inform the officer of civil status one month prior to the marriage. Non-registration is punishable by a fine but does not determine the validity of a marriage.

Polygyny is permitted, but the groom must register his option for a mono-gamous, limited polygynous or polygynous (up to four wives) regime upon the registration of his first marriage, and the option is for life. It may be altered only to lower the number of wives further. Wives are entitled to equal treatment in polygynous unions.

The husband is identified as the head of the family. The choice of residence lies with the husband, and the wife is required to live with him, unless she is authorized by a judge to reside elsewhere. Although maintenance is defined as an obligation of both spouses during the subsistence of marriage, the obligation is principally that of the husband, and his failure to maintain is provided as a ground for the wife to seek dissolution. Since the 1989 reforms of the Family Code, the husband has not been permitted to forbid his wife from working.

Extra-judicial divorce is not permitted. Either party may seek a judicial dissolution on the following grounds (preceded by reconciliation efforts by the judge): the other party's declared absence; adultery; sentencing for a crime bringing dishonour to the family; failure to fulfil a legal condition stipulated upon marriage; abandonment of the family or conjugal home; maltreatment rendering continuation of marital life impossible; medically established sterility; grave and incurable illness discovered since marriage; incompatibility making continuation of conjugal life intolerable; and for the wife, the husband's failure to maintain her. In case the husband sought the divorce on grounds of in-compatibility or incurable illness of the wife, the obligation to maintain is transformed to obligation to pay alimony. In case the divorce is judged to be the exclusive fault of one party, the judge may grant the other party appropriate compensation.

Custody is determined by judgment of the court and may be granted to either party or to a third party according to the best interests of the ward. Whichever parent has custody, the father is the guardian, unless he is unable to fulfil this role.

Succession is governed by classical law as outlined in Section III on Muslim succession in Book VII of the Family Code. The laws applicable to Muslim intestate succession include a provision for only granddaughters through pre-deceased sons not standing to inherit as residuary heirs from anyone else to receive one-sixth of the grandparent's estate.

Law/case reporting system   Law reporting is through the *Journal Officiel*.

International conventions (with relevant reservations)   Senegal signed the ICCPR and ICESCR in 1970 and ratified them in 1978, without reserva-tions. Senegal signed the CEDAW in 1980 and ratified it in 1985, without reservations. Senegal signed the CRC and ratified it in 1990, without res-ervations.

Background and sources

CEDAW (1995) *Concluding Observations: Senegal's Second Periodic Report to CEDAW*, January, New York: United Nations.

Human Rights Committee (1996) *Fourth Periodic Reports of States Parties Due in 1995: Senegal*, November 1996.

Ndiaye, Y. (1979) *Le Divorce et la Séparation de Corps*, Dakar: Nouvelles Editions Africaines.

Ndoye, D. (1992) *La Cour de Cassation au Sénégal: Les Textes Annotés et Commentés*, Dakar: Editions Juridiques Africaines.

— (1996) *Code de la Famille Annoté*, Dakar: Editions Juridiques Africaines.

Redden, K. R. (1990) 'Senegal', in K. R. Redden (ed.), *Modern Legal Systems Cyclopedia*, Vol. 6, Buffalo, NY: Hein.

Glossary

abbaya (Kuwait)	women's dress – a long black cloak
Adat	custom (Malay/Indonesian)
Adat Perpateh (Malay/Indonesian)	one kind of Malay *Adat* that developed prior to the fifteenth century; *Adat Perpateh* developed in a matrilineal kinship structure in areas occupied by the Minangkabau people in Sumatra and Negeri Sembilan
Adat Temenggong	one kind of Malay *Adat* that developed prior to the (Malay/Indonesian) fifteenth century; *Adat Temenggong* originated in bilaterally based territorial social units
ahli (Egypt)	national courts
Alkalis' courts (Nigeria)	*Qadis'* courts
al-wasiya al-wajiba (Jordan)	obligatory bequest
Amarah (Saudi Arabia)	type of court where the Amir attempts to guide the parties in a dispute to a compromise
Amir	leader
ashraf	people who trace their lineage to the prophet; in India the Mughal classes
atholhuvarin (Maldives)	atoll chief
Atrap (India)	non-*ashraf* Muslim communities, usually drawn from the lower castes
Awqaf	gifts, succession or wills (and *waqf*; in Shari'a, *waqf* refers to the retention of any property that can be benefited from while the property itself still remains, by suspending disposal of it; with the financial proceeds of it going to some permissible expenditure. Thus if a person makes something *waqf* it ceases to be his property, and neither he nor anybody else can either give it or sell it to any person. Also, no one can inherit anything out of it. However, a person may *waqf* this property such that a particular group, such as his descendants, benefit from it. Lexically, *waqf* means setting aside or confining the use of)

Awraja courts (Ethiopia)	courts convened in each of the 102 administrative subdivisions in Ethiopia
baslik (Turkey)	brideprice (paid by the father of the groom to the father of the bride). Has been declared illegal in Turkey, but the practice remains common in rural areas
beit din (Israel)	religious courts; includes the Muslim courts
Bohoras	a Muslim community in India, mainly Isma'ilis. Most are merchants but many are Sunnis and peasants
boshiya (Kuwait)	black cloth veil worn by women
burga (Afghanistan)	a form of dress for women
chechia (Tunisia)	a traditional religious hat for men, banned by Bourguiba in the 1970s
cherai tebus talak (Brunei)	*khul'*
da'i	'summoner'; missionary for Shi'i movements; usually the lowest-ranking figure in a Shi'i hierarchy
Daira tribunals (Algeria)	Courts of first instance for civil and certain criminal matters
darar	cruelty or harm
fasaq (Southeast Asia)	a form of divorce among Southeast Asia's Muslims; specifically, divorce pronounced by the *qadi* or judge on grounds such as lunacy, impotence, or disease
faskh	annulment of marriage, divorce by the court on prescribed grounds
fatwa (plural *fatawa*)	a legal ruling
fiqh	Islamic jurisprudence
ghazi (Maldives)	magistrate
hadd (*hadood*)	Qur'anic penalty(ies), limit
hadinah	mother of a child
Hadith	the collected sayings of the Prophet
hajib	chamberlain, chief of palace administration and sometimes head of the government.
haq	right
harta sepencarian (Malaysia)	matrimonial property
hiba	gift
hisba	standards of religious morality
hizanat	guardianship of a minor child as stated in the Hanafi school
hudood	the strict punishments the Qur'an and/or Sunna provide for certain specified offences, such as *Sariqa* (certain forms of theft) and *zina* (extra-marital sexual relations)

hukum shari	ruling or judgment Shari'a provides for an issue. Could also mean the application of Shari'a in general
humuk Adat (Indonesia)	the civil law for Indonesians; the uncodified or local customary law, which varies from one district or ethnic group to another
'idda	wife's period of waiting after divorce/husband's death
ijbar	means 'to coerce or force' someone to do something. In this context, it means the power of the guardian (*wali*) to force his ward (young woman legally entrusted to his guardianship) into marriage. Some schools grant the *wali* this power, while others do not
ijtihad	personal reasoning
ila'	husband's oath of abstinence; ground on which a woman may seek a divorce
imam	leader
Ismai'lis	a branch of the Shi'a who look to the leadership of Ism'ail, a son of Ja'far and his descendants; this branch includes the Fatimids; later divided into several branches including the Nizariyas, who spread from Syria and Iran into India; subcommunities include the Khojas, Bohoras and others
jahaz	a form of payment at marriage, in the Middle East, specifically, gifts given to a bride by her father
jihad	struggle, religious war
kaikuli (Sri Lanka)	lying-in expenses
kalis (Philippines)	assessors who sat in Moroland courts, as per Philippine Commission Act 1915
kalym (Kazakhstan)	brideprice
kariah masjid (Malaysia)	portion of the woman's residence where marriage may be solemnized
khul'	dissolution of a marriage at the wife's request
khula	separation by mutual agreement, also known as *mubaraat*. A method of divorce or dissolution of marriage; one of three methods of divorce recognized by Islamic family law in East Africa. See also *talaq* and *tafriq*; also, a form of divorce among Southeast Asia's Muslims; specifically, the purchase by the wife of her freedom
kifa'a	equality or parity in social and economic status, and generally refers to the compatibility of a man and woman in social and economic terms for them to be appropriate marriage partners. While the Hanafi

	school does not require the consent of a *wali* (guardian) to a marriage, they require '*kifa'a*' of the two, and gives the *wali* the right to object to a marriage contracted without his consent if he can show lack of '*kifa'a*' on certain specific grounds.
kitabi	man of a revealed religion
kitabbiya	woman of a revealed religion
kuma (Turkey)	term for second wife; the *kuma* has no legal rights under Turkish civil law
li'an	imprecation of adultery; ground on which a woman may seek a divorce
Liwalis, Courts of (Kenya)	courts applying Muslim personal law
lobola (South Africa)	practice of brideprice; prohibited under the South African Bill of Rights
madhhab (plural *madhabib*)	Muslim school of law; the four principal schools are the Hanafi Maliki, Shafi'i and Hanbali
madhush (Iran)	enraged. *Talaq* by a man who is *madhush* is ineffective
madrassas (Pakistan)	Islamic schools
mahr	dower; in Muslim law the gift the bridegroom gives the bride, which becomes her personal property
Mahkamah Agung (Indonesia)	Supreme Court
Mahkamah Islam Tinggi (Indonesia)	religious appeals court
mahram	a man to whom a woman cannot be legally married, like a brother or uncle. A woman is allowed to travel with or be unveiled in the presence of a *mahram*, but not with a man she can legally marry
Majlis	gathering, assembly or council
Majlis al-Istishari (Oman)	Consultative Council
Majlis al-Shura (Saudi Arabia)	Consultative Council
Majlis-e-Shoora (Pakistan)	Parliament
mallam	religious scholar
manshurat	judicial circulars
maskahwin (Malaysia)	dower
mattah (Brunei)	*muta' al-talaq*
miri property	government property
mubaraat	separation by mutual agreement, also known as *khula*. A method of divorce or dissolution of marriage; one of three methods of divorce recognized by Islamic family law in East Africa. See also *talaq* and *tafriq*
Mudirs, Courts of (Kenya)	courts applying Muslim personal law.
mujtahid	jurist who exercises *ijtihad* and is qualified to give authoritative opinions on Islamic law

mukhtalatat (Egypt)	mixed courts
mulk	property held in full ownership (buildings, orchards, vineyards and moveable property) inherited under Islamic codes of succession
muta	temporary marriages
mutaah (Malaysia)	consolatory gift
muta' al-talaq	consolatory gift
nabuusha (Somalia)	term for women who have their marriages annulled against the wishes of their husbands
nafkah edah (Malaysia)	*'idda* period maintenance
Naiba councils (Ethiopia)	Shari'a courts of first instance in Ethiopia
nashiza	disobedient woman
nikah	marriage
nizamiyya (Jordan)	civil or regular courts
panditas (Philippines)	assessors who sat in Moroland courts, as per Philippine Commission Act 1915
Pengadilan Agama (Indonesia)	religious courts
purdah	veiling of women
qadhf	false accusation of unchastity
qadi	judge
Qanun-e-Shahadat Order (Pakistan)	Law of Evidence Order
qiyamat	a spiritualization of the Shari'a, announced in the twelfth century by Hasan 'ala dhikrihi's-salam
radd	return. The distribution of the remainder of an estate to the Qur'anic heirs in proportion to their interest. The surviving spouse benefits only in the absence of other heirs
rajih	dominant or majority view within a school or among the schools/scholars
raji'i	revocable divorce
ruhi courts (Syria)	courts for Christians and Jews
rushd	marriage of a minor below the age of majority
Sadad Courts (Morocco)	courts of first instance for Muslim and Jewish personal law
Shari'a	the recommended path of Islam: Islamic law
Shari'at (Bangladesh, India, Pakistan)	Muslim personal law
Shi'a	the group of Muslims who regard 'Ali and his heirs as the only legitimate successors to the Prophet, divided into sects according to allegiance to different lines of 'Alid descent
shirbaha	a form of payment at marriage, in the Middle East,

	specifically cash provided by the groom to the bride's father to purchase the *jahaz*
Sunna	'the trodden path', custom, the practice of the Prophet and the early community that becomes for all Muslims an authoritative example of the correct way to live a Muslim life
Sunnis	those who accept the Sunna and the historic succession of Caliphs, as opposed to the 'Alids; the majority of the Muslim community
Syariah Courts (Malaysia)	Shari'a courts
tafriq	judicial order of separation. A method of divorce or dissolution of marriage; one of three methods of divorce recognized by Islamic family law in East Africa. *See also talaq* and *khula* (same as *mubaraat*)
tafwid	literally means delegation of a legal power one person has to another person so that s/he can act as the agent of the person who has the power. In the family law context, it usually refers to the husband 'delegating' to his wife the power to 'divorce herself'. Since the power of unilateral divorce belongs to the husband, he can delegate that power (according to the Hanafi school) to his wife through the marriage contract, so that she can divorce herself from him without his consent at any subsequent stage – one of the safeguards the Hanafi school allows to women
takhayyur	eclecticism
talaq	repudiation (divorce)
talaq al-tafwid (Pakistan)	delegated divorce
Tanzimat	reorganization; the name for the Ottoman reforms of the nineteenth century
tawakkul	trust in God
tuhur	ritualistic cleanings, but in family law context it usually referrs to the period between menstrual cycles when a woman is 'religiously clean', thereby being available for sexual relations with her husband. A valid divorce is supposed to occur during this period, and can be revoked by the husband through having sexual relations with his divorcée unless the divorce has become final after three menstrual periods, which requires a new marriage contract
ulama	theologians, the collective term for the scholars or learned men of Islam
umma	community

wahdat al-wujud (South Asia)	Sufi doctrine of unity of being; an important religious influence on Indian Islam
wali	a benefactor, companion, protector, governor; the legal guardian of a minor, woman or incapacitated person
Wilaya courts (Algeria)	courts at the levels of provinces; organized into four chambers (civil, criminal, administrative and accusation)
Woreda courts (Ethiopia)	courts established in each of the 556 districts in Ethiopia
Yang Di-Pertuan (Brunei)	head of state
Yang di-Pertuan Agong (Malaysia)	the head of state, who, in the absence of a Muslim ruler, is declared the head of the religion of Islam
zihar	husband's likening of his wife to his relations within the prohibited degrees; ground on which a woman may seek divorce
zina	illicit sexual relations

Index of Countries

General Index

WHITMAN COLLEGE LIBRARY